ELIZABETHAN RHETORIC

Peter Mack examines the impact of humanist training in rhetoric and argument on a range of Elizabethan prose texts, including political orations, histories, romances, conduct manuals, privy council debates and personal letters. *Elizabethan Rhetoric* reconstructs the knowledge, skills and approaches which an Elizabethan would have acquired at grammar school and university in order to participate in the political and religious debates of the time: approaches to an audience, analysis and replication of textual structures, organisation of arguments and tactics for disputation. Study of the rhetorical codes and conventions in terms of which the debates of the period were conducted is currently a major area of historical and literary enquiry, and Mack provides a wealth of new information about what was taught and how these conventions were exploited in personal memoranda, preparations for meetings, court depositions, sermons and political and religious pamphlets. This important book will be invaluable for all those interested in Elizabethan culture, literature and political history.

PETER MACK is Professor of English at the University of Warwick. He currently edits the journal *Rhetorica*, and is the author of *Renaissance Argument: Valla and Agricola in the Traditions of Rhetoric and Dialectic* (1993), and the editor of *Renaissance Rhetoric* (1994).

T0381640

IDEAS IN CONTEXT

Edited by Quentin Skinner (*General Editor*), Lorraine Daston,
Dorothy Ross and James Tully

The books in this series will discuss the emergence of intellectual traditions and of related new disciplines. The procedures, aims and vocabularies that were generated will be set in the context of the alternatives available within the contemporary frameworks of ideas and institutions. Through detailed studies of the evolution of such traditions, and their modification by different audiences, it is hoped that a new picture will form of the development of ideas in their concrete contexts. By this means, artificial distinctions between the history of philosophy, of the various sciences, of society and politics, and of literature may be seen to dissolve.

The series is published with the support of the Exxon Foundation.

A list of books in the series will be found at the end of the volume.

ELIZABETHAN RHETORIC

Theory and Practice

PETER MACK

University of Warwick

CAMBRIDGE
UNIVERSITY PRESS

CAMBRIDGE UNIVERSITY PRESS
Cambridge, New York, Melbourne, Madrid, Cape Town, Singapore, São Paulo

Cambridge University Press
The Edinburgh Building, Cambridge CB2 2RU, UK

Published in the United States of America by Cambridge University Press, New York

www.cambridge.org
Information on this title: www.cambridge.org/9780521812924

First published 2002
Reprinted 2004
This digitally printed first paperback version 2005

A catalogue record for this publication is available from the British Library

ISBN-13 978-0-521-81292-4 hardback
ISBN-10 0-521-81292-5 hardback

ISBN-13 978-0-521-02099-2 paperback
ISBN-10 0-521-02099-9 paperback

For Johanna, William, Emily and Rosemary

Contents

Acknowledgements

This book shows how the humanist reorientation of rhetoric and dialectic, described in my earlier book, *Renaissance Argument: Valla and Agricola in the Traditions of Rhetoric and Dialectic* (Leiden, 1993), was embedded in the teaching of Elizabethan grammar schools and universities and how that training established the conventions of Elizabethan reading and writing. Correspondence with Ian Michael about a fictionalised history of the teaching of reading contributed to my approach, as, I fear, did the attempts of the National Curriculum and the Quality Assurance Agency to redefine the goals of British education in the 1990s. Some sections of this book originated in my thesis (*Permeations of Renaissance Dialectic into English Discourse, c.1580–c.1620*, 1978) for the MPhil degree of the Warburg Institute, University of London. I am grateful to my supervisor, Michael Baxandall, for his inspiration. A somewhat different version of chapter seven has been published as 'Elizabethan Parliamentary Oratory' in *Huntington Library Quarterly* 63 (2000). I am grateful to the editor, Susan Green, for her advice and for permission to reprint.

The first draft of this book was written in a year's study leave in 1998/9 from the English Department, University of Warwick. I was able to use this time more profitably thanks to a personal grant for photocopying and microfilms from our then Vice-Chancellor, Sir Brian Follett, and to books and facilities provided by librarians and friends, especially Lucia Calboli Montefusco, Christine Fyfe, John Henshall, Peter Larkin, John Perkins, Jim Shaw and Christine Woodland. I am grateful to the Bodleian Library, the British Library and the Public Record Office for allowing me to consult manuscripts in their care. For the sake of readers without immediate access to their rich collections I have cited sixteenth-century documents from printed sources wherever possible. Except when transcribing manuscripts I have generally modernised spellings.

I warmly thank E. J. Ashworth, Linda Bensel-Meyers, Gibson Burrell, Judith Deitch, Steve Hindle, Sophie Holroyd, Lisa Jardine, Jill Kraye,

Elizabeth McGrath, Marc van der Poel, Carol Rutter, Simon Swain, J. B. Trapp, Olga Weijers, Sue Wiseman and Marjorie Woods for contributing materials or reading drafts. I am especially grateful for the generous and detailed advice of Lawrence Green and Kees Meerhoff, who have always regarded the closeness of our research projects as a reason for collaboration. Quentin Skinner's encouragement at a crucial stage was invaluable. Rachel Parkins and Pauline Yates of Warwick University IT Services helped me produce computer copy which Richard Fisher and Rose Bell of Cambridge University Press converted into this book. I am grateful to students, colleagues, and secretaries in the English Department and the Arts Faculty for their support of my research. As always my greatest obligations are to my extended family, my wife Vicki Behm and our children, Johanna, William, Emily and Rosemary.

Introduction

In 1576 when Peter Wentworth delivered his most aggressive attack on the Queen's management of parliament he chose to begin with a general defence of liberty of speech, modelled on the chreia, one of the grammar school composition exercises.

Mr Speaker, I find written in a little volume these words in effect, 'Sweet indeed is the name of libertye and the thing it selfe a value beyond all inestimable treasure'; soe much the more it behoveth us to take heed least we, contenting our selves with the sweetness of the name onely, doe not lose and forgoe the value of the thing: and the greatest value that can come unto this noble realme by the inestimable treasure is the use of it in this House, for unto it it is due.[1]

Wentworth's initial quotation is adapted from 'Libertate nihil dulcius' from the grammar school textbook *Sententiae pueriles*, perhaps by association with Cicero's 'O nomen dulce libertatis' (*In Verrem*, v.163) and the English proverb 'Liberty is worth more than gold'.[2] He elaborates the second half of his first sentence from the key words of his text ('sweetness', 'name', 'value', 'thing', 'inestimable treasure'). Wentworth goes on to list the 'commodityes' of free speech before describing the impediments to freedom of speech he has witnessed in the House. After the opening his arguments are generally buttressed by quotations from scripture, similes and maxims, and amplified by figures of repetition and (in the example below) by the topics of contraries and name of a thing.

Soe that to this point I conclude that in this House which is tearmed a place of free speech there is nothing soe necessary for the preservation of the prince and state as free speech, and without it it is a scorne and mockery to call it a parliament house for in truth it is none, but a very schoole of flattery and

[1] T. E. Hartley (ed.), *Proceedings in the Parliaments of Elizabeth I*, 3 vols. (Leicester, 1981–95), I, p. 425.
[2] M. P. Tilley, *A Dictionary of the Proverbs in England in the Sixteenth and Seventeenth Centuries* (Ann Arbor, 1950), L 223.

dissimulacion and soe a fitt place to serve the Devill and his angells in and not to glorifye God and benefitt the comonwealth.[3]

Wentworth secured a hearing for the astonishing accusations he was about to make by minutely observing the expected forms of Elizabethan discourse. He and his audience absorbed some of these forms by listening to examples of particular genres, such as sermons and parliamentary speeches. But the underlying principles and the majority of the materials and skills were inculcated at grammar school and university. From their training in the analysis of classical texts, pupils learned how to read and how they in turn might expect to be read. At the same time they were trained to reuse the moral substance (and even the verbal expression) of their reading in their own compositions: letters, chreias, themes.

This book aims to contribute to the history of reading and writing by showing how techniques learned in the grammar school and at university (largely through the study of classical literary texts) were used in a wide range of examples of different types of Elizabethan writing. I hope that it will provide historians with additional tools for examining documents and a further understanding of the broad communicative context within which people attempted to achieve results by composing speeches and memoranda. I hope that it will give students of literature a broader sense of the range of Elizabethan writing and of the continuities between self-consciously artistic forms of writing and the practical use of language in the period. The people who wrote the school exercises, letters, notebooks (and who heard the sermons and speeches) which I shall discuss were also the audience of the texts we now recognise as canonical.

In analysing grammar school and university textbooks, teaching methods and exercises I attempt for the first time to describe the skills which pupils were expected to acquire. School pupils were trained to extract moral sentences from their reading and use them in their writing, to analyse and compose moral narratives, to collect historical examples illustrating ethical principles, to compose letters and themes, to amplify and to recognise and use various figures of rhetoric. University students were trained to discover arguments, to form syllogisms, to organise sequences of argument, to define words and distinguish shades of meaning, to read dialectically, to declaim and to take part in disputations.

Preachers, letter-writers and civil servants used these techniques and expectations to give messages, settle disputes or secure consent. Knowing

---

[3] Hartley, *Proceedings*, I, p. 426.

the range of compositional and interpretive skills taught at school helps present-day historians understand how individual writers used them for their particular practical purposes. Grammar school and university ways of reading alerted Elizabethans to the way in which letters they received or speeches they heard employed particular techniques, opening up further possibilities for imitation and variation in their own practical writing. This everyday experience of analysis and composition honed the tools of understanding which they brought to their reading of poems and watching of plays.

Communicative expectations create possibilities for individual expression, but they also institute zones of exclusion. People who cannot master the structures of discourse agreed by a particular community or who do not know the arguments it considers persuasive are excluded from direct participation in debate. Their views will only be listened to if they are translated by someone who understands the expectations and who is recognised (by manner of speech as well as personally) as belonging to the group.[4] Those who did not wish to become dependent upon rhetorically educated men had to acquire (for themselves or for their children) an education in rhetoric. The success of the humanist reform of education in the early sixteenth century can be measured by the increasing participation rate in university.[5] Under Elizabeth even members of the military aristocracy had to learn (and had to present themselves as possessing) skills of presenting persuasive arguments if they wished to be attended to in council.[6] By studying the rhetorical training which pupils acquired at school and university we learn the competence in reading and composition which defined the Elizabethan élite.

In this book I first analyse the Latin rhetorical and dialectical skills which pupils acquired at school and at university (chapters one and two) and discuss the dependence of the English-language manuals on these Latin models (chapter three). Then I look at evidence for everyday uses of rhetoric in notebooks, letters and narratives (chapter four) and describe the exploitation of grammar school rhetorical techniques and

---

[4] See L. Verhoeven (ed.), *Functional Literacy: Theoretical Issues and Educational Implications* (Amsterdam, 1994).

[5] In the course of the century, according to Lawrence Stone, the male participation rate in university education reached the highest levels it would attain before the late nineteenth century. See references in chapter two, note 1.

[6] The link between skills and political success may have been enhanced by Elizabeth's gender. As a female ruler, dispensed from personal leadership in war, she did not need to encourage the loyalty of military comrades or hunting companions by listening to their opinions in council. John Guy, *Tudor England* (Oxford, 1988), pp. 309–11.

ethical principles in English-language texts of informal moral instruction: histories, conduct manuals and romances (chapter five). Finally I analyse the use of rhetorical skills in political argument, from diplomatic letters, memoranda, Privy Council speeches and a pamphlet (chapter six), in parliamentary oratory (chapter seven) and in religious controversy and sermons (chapter eight). Thus the book moves from formal education through informal teaching and private uses of rhetoric to public oratory and debate.

In order to understand what pupils learned at the grammar school it is essential to study the course as a whole, exercises and methods of teaching as well as the syllabus of texts. Pupils acquired skill in identifying and reusing moral maxims, in constructing moral narratives and histories, and in writing letters and speeches from historical situations as well as from their own lives. They learned to imitate classical letters, to amplify early drafts, to use the figures of speech, and to observe a range of structures. The content of their reading was as important as the method in determining what they would later regard as establishing the possibility of being convinced. The range of different skills acquired provided pupils with a repertoire of possibilities to choose from for their own purposes. In the later chapters of the book we shall see how writers could play with and extend grammar school ideas of the function of particular techniques.

In discussing Elizabethan education I have necessarily made use of the technical terminology of rhetoric and dialectic. I hope that my *Index of rhetorical and dialectical terms* will assist readers in finding definitions and examples.[7] In the Note on the Systems of Rhetoric and Dialectic at the end of this introduction I have set out the essential subdivisions and given references for further investigation. It would have added greatly to the length of the book to have included a full systematic treatment here.

In analysing grammar school teaching I depend heavily on the materials collected by T. W. Baldwin, though I am sceptical about some of his conclusions.[8] Like Lawrence Green, I think that the statutes were over-optimistic. I aim to follow the close analyses of educational practice by Tony Grafton and Lisa Jardine but I do not share their pessimism about the practical effect of humanist education. Like Mary Thomas Crane and Ann Moss, I describe the practice of collecting and using moral

[7] See p. 318 below. Also Richard A. Lanham, *A Handlist of Rhetorical Terms*, 2nd edn (Berkeley, 1991); Heinrich Lausberg, *Handbuch der literarischen Rhetorik*, 3rd edn, Stuttgart, 1990.
[8] T. W. Baldwin, *Shakspere's Small Latine and Lesse Greeke*, 2 vols. (Urbana, 1944).

sentences, but I want to insist that this was one of a range of techniques practised in the grammar school.[9]

Recent studies of Oxford and Cambridge, notably the work of James McConica and Mordechai Feingold, have transformed our ideas of Elizabethan university education. They have shown that a wide range of undergraduate studies was followed, around a strong basis in Latin literature, rhetoric and dialectic.[10] University booklists and textbooks by Seton, Case and Sanderson, based on their teaching in Cambridge and Oxford, show how strongly the humanist interpretation of logic, with its emphasis on using the resources of logic in everyday Latin, had taken hold. Pupils were taught topical invention, the presentation of arguments in a range of forms, and the principles of logical method, in its Aristotelian, Melanchthonian and Ramist forms. But the crucial justification for logical skills was the exercise of disputation, which remained the chief requirement in the years of study and in order to graduate. We shall observe both the humanist introduction of rhetorical ideas into disputation and the persistence of forms derived from disputation in religious and political debate. The expectation among members of the élite that reasons would be given by the most powerful statesmen, that disagreement could be maintained and that objections would be answered, derived from the university practice of disputation.

By showing that only four of the English-language manuals were at all successful and that all were dependent on the expectations of the grammar school and university syllabus, I attempt to reorient established traditions and recent fashions in the use of these texts.[11] Most of them were adapted from sixteenth-century continental Latin originals. English authors made several different attempts to translate the renaissance Latin style manual to the needs of English. Some classical figures of rhetoric were altered to fit the English language, while at the same time

[9] Lawrence D. Green, 'Grammatica movet', in P. L. Oesterreich and T. O. Sloane (eds.), *Rhetorica Movet: Essays in Honour of Heinrich Plett* (Leiden, 1999), pp. 73–115; Anthony Grafton and Lisa Jardine, *From Humanism to the Humanities* (London, 1986), especially pp. 1–29, 149–60, 164–200; idem, 'Studied for Action: How Gabriel Harvey read his Livy', *Past and Present* 129 (1990), 30–78; Mary T. Crane, *Framing Authority: Sayings, Self and Society in Sixteenth-century England* (Princeton, 1993); Ann Moss, *Printed Commonplace Books and the Structuring of Renaissance Thought* (Oxford, 1996).
[10] J. K. McConica, 'The Rise of the Undergraduate College', and 'Elizabethan Oxford: The Collegiate Society', in J. K. McConica (ed.), *The History of the University of Oxford*, vol. III, *The Collegiate University* (Oxford, 1986), pp. 1–68, 645–732; M. Feingold, 'The Humanities' and 'The Mathematical Sciences and New Philosophies', in N. Tyacke (ed.), *The History of the University of Oxford*, vol. IV, *Seventeenth-Century Oxford* (Oxford, 1997), pp. 211–448.
[11] W. S. Howell, *Logic and Rhetoric in England 1500–1700* (Princeton, 1956); Frank Whigham, *Ambition and Privilege: The Social Tropes of Elizabethan Courtesy Theory* (Berkeley, 1984); W. Rebhorn, *The Emperor of Men's Minds* (Ithaca, 1995).

features of Latin usage were imported to expand the possibilities of expression in English. Whereas formal education was conducted in Latin, the beneficiaries of education, while reading mainly in Latin, would write in either language depending on their purpose and audience.

In searching for evidence of practices of reading, analysis of issues and formulation of arguments I have been drawn to texts which have not previously received the attention of students of rhetoric (or indeed of literary historians of any kind): official and private letters, court depositions, state papers and especially notebooks. We can learn a lot about the reading, reasoning and compositions of students from their miscellaneous manuscripts. Similarly Cecil's successive drafts of arguments about a meeting with Mary, Queen of Scots or about the Alençon marriage, at first intended for his own eyes, later as preparations for meetings and eventually as drafts of speeches can tell us a great deal about how he used rhetorical principles to frame questions and to refine arguments in order to build up the most powerful case for a particular audience. I hope that historians as well as literary scholars will learn of new sources and new approaches to them through these sections of my book.

The topics and techniques of education are reframed in texts intended for post-school moral education. Histories, conduct manuals and romances, among the bestselling forms of vernacular publication, use narratives, maxims, speeches, amplification and debate (all of them staples of grammar school training) to analyse events and to transform them into confirmation of principles of prudence. In the romances the impetus towards unexpected plot development and entertainment opens up the possibility of paradoxical presentation and questioning of this societally privileged instruction. The expectations about text learned in the grammar school provide modern readers with new ways of understanding the shared inheritance, the original transformations and the impact on the audience of these works.

Politics and religion were the two most important arenas for the use of language to affect practical life in the Elizabethan period. In the final three chapters I examine the use of ideas and techniques derived from grammar school and university training in sermons, in Privy Council and parliamentary speeches and in pamphlets. I analyse the way the model of university disputation affects the organisation of debate, the range of styles and personae employed by speakers and the use of proverbs and commonplaces alongside, or in preference to, arguments. I discuss the role of opposition in parliament, the issue of free speech and the role of parliamentary ceremony in creating a political nation. My guides to the parts of this territory which have been mapped out have been historians: Neale, Read, Hartley, Elton, James, and Alford.[12] In religion under the guidance of Blench, Collinson and Lake,[13] I consider the use of rhetoric in biblical interpretation, and of logical argument, disposition and figures of style in sermons by Cranmer, Jewel, Smith, Rainolds, Hooker, and Andrewes. I compare their views and those of Field and Wilcox, Cartwright and Whitgift on preaching, consolatory oratory, poverty and ecclesiastical authority.

This book builds on *Renaissance Argument,* my study of the revolution in dialectical textbooks brought about by Lorenzo Valla (1407–57) and Rudolph Agricola (1444–85).[14] In disciplinary terms it is part of the project of abolishing the distinction between literary and social/political history.[15] I shall not be arguing that this or that poem was written to influence a particular aspect of foreign policy, but rather that politicians, preachers and writers shared forms of expression and ethical assumptions. For estate managers, diplomats and politicians these were arguments to be deployed in order to bring about particular outcomes in the world. More self-conscious writers were in a position to question these shared assumptions and to use rhetorical methods to open up new ways of thinking about politics and social problems. I do think that Elizabethan habits of reading and ethical concerns help our understanding of Shakespeare but I shall feel more strongly confirmed in this belief if readers of this book make these connections for themselves.

It requires an act of imagination to understand how textbooks, readers and composition exercises came together in training an individual to use language. To infer the particular techniques employed in the composition of a letter or sermon is a matter of judgment which may be presented convincingly but can scarcely be proved. In tackling the problems of rhetorical analysis which are at the heart of this book I have been encouraged and assisted by studies of texts and textbooks by Vasoli, Vickers, Cave, Fumaroli, Meerhoff, Monfasani, Rhodes, Skinner and

---

[12] Sir John Neale, *Queen Elizabeth I and her Parliaments,* 2 vols. (London, 1953–7); Conyers Read, *Mr Secretary Cecil and Queen Elizabeth* (London, 1955), *Lord Burghley and Queen Elizabeth* (London, 1960); Hartley (ed.), *Proceedings*; G. R. Elton, *The Parliament of England, 1559–1581* (Cambridge, 1986); Mervyn James, *Society, Politics and Culture: Studies in Early Modern England* (Cambridge, 1986); Stephen Alford, *The Early Elizabethan Polity* (Cambridge, 1998).

[13] J. W. Blench, *Preaching in England in the late Fifteenth and Sixteenth Centuries* (Oxford, 1964); Patrick Collinson, *The Elizabethan Puritan Movement* (London, 1967); Peter Lake, *Anglicans and Puritans? Presbyterianism and English Conformist Thought from Whitgift to Hooker* (London, 1988).

[14] P. Mack, *Renaissance Argument: Valla and Agricola in the Traditions of Rhetoric and Dialectic* (Leiden, 1993).

[15] Among exemplars of this kind of research in the early modern period one might mention David Norbrook, Kevin Sharpe, Quentin Skinner and Greg Walker.

many other fellow-members of the International Society for the History of Rhetoric.[16]

The syllabi of Elizabethan grammar schools and universities were the result of a deliberate humanist reform of education. Royal servants from outside the ranks of the nobility who had risen as a result of education promoted the establishment of grammar schools, which in turn produced university entrants of the 'middling sort' who became secretaries of state, members of parliament and leaders of the clergy. There is a degree of social reproduction in this pattern.[17]

But there were also unexpected consequences. Colet, Wolsey and More could not have anticipated that the promotion of humanist education would become linked with the rise of Protestantism. Thomas Cromwell encouraged classical education because he saw the need for a non-clerical body of royal servants.[18] From their sometimes different points of view, Elizabeth's bishops and the returning Protestant exiles saw university education as the means to produce the learned Protestant clergy which the reformed church required. None of them foresaw the way in which the training in argument provided by the universities would fuel religious controversy within protestantism.

One might equally well ask how much the largely pagan content of grammar school training sponsored a secular approach to government and practical life. Maxims to justify prudent and even deceitful behaviour could easily be found in classical literature and may have smoothed the way to favourable receptions of Machiavelli's penetrating pragmatic observations.[19] There is also some evidence of a turning away from logical argument. Training in dialectic enhanced someone's ability to marshal persuasive arguments in favour of a particular course of action but the ease with which such arguments could be found showed the essential

[16] C. Vasoli, *La dialettica e la retorica dell' umanesimo* (Milan, 1968); B. Vickers, *Classical Rhetoric in English Poetry* (London, 1968), *In Defence of Rhetoric* (Oxford, 1988); Terence Cave, *The Cornucopian Text* (Oxford, 1979); Marc Fumaroli, *L'âge de l'éloquence* (Geneva, 1980); Kees Meerhoff, *Rhétorique et poétique au XVIe siècle en France* (Leiden, 1986); John Monfasani, 'Humanism and Rhetoric', in A. Rabil jr (ed.), *Renaissance Humanism: Foundations, Forms and Legacy*, 3 vols. (Philadelphia, 1988), III, pp. 171–235; Neil Rhodes, *The Power of Eloquence in English Renaissance Literature* (London, 1992); Q. Skinner, *Reason and Rhetoric in the Philosophy of Hobbes* (Cambridge, 1996).
[17] P. Bourdieu and J. C. Passeron, *La réproduction: éléments pour une théorie du système d' enseignement* (Paris, 1970); B. Bernstein, *Class, Codes and Control*, 3 vols. (London, 1971–5).
[18] J. K. McConica, *English Humanists and Reformation Politics* (Oxford, 1965).
[19] F. Raab, *The English Face of Machiavelli* (London, 1964); S. Gardiner, *A Machiavellian Treatise*, ed. P. Donaldson (Cambridge, 1975); Q. Skinner, *The Foundations of Modern Political Thought*, 2 vols. (Cambridge, 1978), I, pp. 248–53; Victoria Kahn, *Machiavellian Rhetoric* (Princeton, 1994), pp. 93–131; Skinner, *Reason and Rhetoric*, pp. 161–80.

malleability of argument. Logical training enabled persuasive arguments to be found to justify positions which had been taken on other grounds.

Even if part of logic's role was presentational, the format of debate meant that decisions still had to be explained. Reasons had to be given and objections answered. The education which provided men like Bacon, Cecil, Egerton, Mildmay and Wilson with the opportunity to rise to positions of influence also determined the way in which they would behave in council. Royal aspirations to absolutism could not easily overrule the culture of debate formed in Elizabethan grammar schools and universities.

NOTE ON THE SYSTEMS OF RHETORIC AND DIALECTIC

Rhetoric is traditionally divided into five skills: Invention, the assembly of the material of the speech; Disposition, placing that material in an appropriate structure; Elocutio or Style, clothing the ideas of the speech in the most effective words; Memory, memorising the speech; and Delivery, the use of voice and gesture. Under invention we find discussed ways to obtain the sympathy and interest of the audience at the start of a speech; lines of argument appropriate to different types of case in the three genres of oratory listed below; topics of invention to assist in discovering arguments about any subject; forms in which to present arguments; and topics for emotional appeals. Under disposition pupils learn the rationale for the four-part oration (exordium or introduction; narration, setting out the circumstances of the case; argument; and conclusion) and considerations for varying the content and order of the speech. The treatise on style sets out the qualities of good Latin; the three levels of style; techniques for amplification; and definitions and examples of the tropes and figures of rhetoric.[20]

Classical rhetoric identifies three types of oratory distinguished by the type of audience and the aim of the speaker. Judicial oratory is concerned with pleading in court before judge or jury, aiming at the condemnation of a criminal or the acquittal of a client. Deliberative oratory belongs to the popular assembly, arguing for the benefits of a particular course of action or proposed law. Demonstrative oratory is concerned with praise or blame, denouncing an enemy or celebrating a marriage or a funeral.

---

[20] The quickest way to understand the rhetoric syllabus is to read [Cicero], *Rhetorica ad Herennium*, Loeb Classical Library (London, 1954) with Harry Caplan's translation and analysis. Also: Roland Barthes, 'L'ancienne rhétorique: aide-mémoire', *Communications* 16 (1970), 172–229, translated in Barthes, *The Semiotic Challenge* (Oxford, 1988), pp. 11–93; George Kennedy, *The Art of Persuasion in Greece* (Princeton, 1963); Vickers, *In Defence of Rhetoric*; Thomas M. Conley, *Rhetoric in the European Tradition* (New York, 1990).

In the post-classical period authors found a broader range of uses of rhetoric (largely for writing rather than speaking) but they preferred, where possible to assimilate them to these three types.

For the purposes of medieval and renaissance education, dialectic is identical with logic, except that it includes probable reasoning alongside the categorical. Manuals of Aristotelian logic, the dominant form of logic in this period, comprised seven sections.[21] The *Isagoge* or introduction defines the metalanguage for understanding categories: genus, species, differentia, property and accident. The *Categories* distinguishes the ten classes into which all things (or, according to competing analyses, all concepts or all words) are divided, primarily substance, quantity, quality and action. *On Interpretation* analyses the different types of basic assertive sentence according to their quality (affirmative or negative) and quantity (universal or particular) and the relations of agreement or contradiction among the four types (the so-called square of contraries). *Prior Analytics* analyses the syllogism, the valid structures of three-part (and three component) argument according to these four types (see further discussion on pp. 68–9). Later authors added descriptions of other forms of argumentation: induction, enthymeme and example. *Posterior Analytics* describes the organisation of sciences as chains of syllogisms moving from universally true axioms to particular phenomena. Thus sections two to five of the handbook move systematically from the individual things through larger linguistic structures to whole sciences.

By contrast the two final treatises are devoted to reasoning outside the sciences, for example in disputations or in Platonic dialogues. *Topica* outlines a range of argumentative strategies in response to types of argument made by an opponent.[22] *Sophistical Refutations* analyses a number of types of deceptive arguments (fallacies), explaining why they are not valid and how to oppose them. In the middle ages the analysis of fallacies led scholars to open up new approaches to semantics.[23] In *Renaissance Argument* and towards the end of chapter two below I describe the way the humanist educational tradition adapted the heritage of Aristotelian dialectic.

---

[21] For example, Peter of Spain, *Tractatus*, ed. L. M. de Rijk (Assen, 1972). See also W. and M. Kneale, *The Development of Logic* (Oxford, 1962).

[22] On the different ways in which the treatise on the topics was developed in the middle ages and the renaissance see N. J. Green-Pedersen, *The Tradition of the Topics in the Middle Ages* (Munich, 1984) and Mack, *Renaissance Argument*, pp. 32, 130–68, 284–5, 288, 294–9, 327–32, 351–3.

[23] N. Kretzmann, et al. (eds.), *The Cambridge History of Later Medieval Philosophy* (Cambridge, 1982); Sten Ebbesen, *Commentators and Commentaries on Aristotle's Sophistici Elenchi*, 3 vols. (Leiden, 1981).

Rhetoric in the grammar school

In order to understand the relationship between the literary culture which was inculcated in the grammar school and the norms of
Elizabethan discourse, it is necessary to begin by analysing grammar
school education as a whole. My aim in this chapter is to show how the
individual parts of what was a pretty uniform national system[1] came
together to encourage a particular type of literacy and to transmit a
shared heritage of cultural knowledge. T. W. Baldwin has shown that the
founders of sixteenth-century grammar schools took their programme
and their selection of classical and renaissance Latin set-books from continental humanists.[2] Across England grammar schools shared the aim
of making their pupils wise, pious and eloquent. In order to describe
the expectations about reading and writing which all pupils acquired
through this training, I shall analyse the shape of the grammar school
programme, the methods of reading classical Latin texts which pupils
were taught, and the forms and methods of composition they practised.
This will enable me to outline at the end of the chapter the skills which
we might expect pupils to have acquired from the whole process.

The grammar school cultivated particular skills in a range of different
ways but it also emphasised a range of skills. Moral sentences formed
the pupils' elementary reading matter in the *Sententiae pueriles*, which they

---

[1] 'Also by the like good Authors, after the same manner, and for the same cause, were instituted
many other houses of learning, Colledges, and free Schooles, as partly we see in this Towne, and
more amply may knowe and see in the Cities, Townes and Villages throughout the Realme',
William Kempe, *The Education of Children in Learning* (London, 1588) facsimile reprint in R. D.
Pepper, *Four Tudor Books On Education* (Gainesville, 1966), sig. D3v; John Brinsley, *Ludus Literarius*
(London, 1612), ed. E. T. Campagnac (Liverpool, 1917), title-page, pp. 2–8.
[2] D. Erasmus, *De ratione studii*, ed. J. C. Margolin in Erasmus, *Opera omnia*, I–2 (Amsterdam, 1971),
pp. 113–14, trans. Brian McGregor, *Collected Works of Erasmus*, (Toronto, 1978), XXIV, pp. 666–7;
Johann Sturm, *De litterarum ludis recte aperiendis* (Strasburg, 1539), sig. B7r, translated in L. W. Spitz
and B. Sher Tinsley, *Johann Sturm on Education* (St Louis, 1995), p. 85; Roger Ascham, *English Works*,
ed. W. A. Wright (Cambridge, 1904), pp. 265–6; Baldwin, *Shakespere's Small Latine*, I, pp. 77–93
and passim.

learned by heart as examples of Latin syntax.[3] These sentences crop up again when pupils are expected to extract them from their reading of classical texts and when they are instructed to quote them as components of particular composition exercises. But moral sentences are only one example among many. Pupils were also taught how to compose, analyse and use moral narratives, how to amplify, how to construct different types of text and several other skills. Mastery of a range of such techniques (from among which they could choose and combine) offered more scope to the products of the grammar school in the letters and memoranda they would compose in their practical lives.

By identifying the skills acquired in the grammar school I hope to provide a contemporary template with which to approach Elizabethan writing. The techniques of reading and writing taught at the grammar school provide readers with tools of analysis and writers with expectations about how they will be read which can be exploited for different purposes. Looking through this set of categories will enable us to see that individual authors and the expectations of particular genres (the letter, the parliamentary speech) privileged certain of these skills or varied them in special ways (for example in the different uses of narrative in political argument and courtroom discourse).

The grammar school inculcated knowledge as well as skills. The poems and histories pupils read, the maxims and stories they learned and re-produced, provided a shared stock of principles through which persuasion could be articulated. Reading the *Sententiae pueriles*, the dialogues of Cordier, *De officiis*, *De copia*, the *Eclogues*, the *Aeneid* and the *Metamorphoses* with the explanations provided by sixteenth-century commentaries was (and remains) an essential pre-requisite for understanding the discourse of the Elizabethan élite.

THE SHAPE OF THE GRAMMAR SCHOOL SYLLABUS

Erasmus, Sturm, Ascham, Brinsley and the founders of the grammar schools agreed that education served to promote religion, moral virtue, wisdom and eloquence, that these qualities were linked and that the training best suited to produce them was a study of classical languages and literature.[4] The following table summarises the texts prescribed in

---

[3] See Crane, *Framing Authority*.

[4] Although Brinsley's work was first published in 1612, his assumptions are so close to those of the humanist educational theorists and his observations add so much practical detail (which may well have been based on his experiences as pupil and teacher within Elizabeth's reign) that to

four grammar school statutes which give detailed instructions for the syllabus.

Wolsey's Statutes for Ipswich (1523)

1. Eight parts of speech, pronunciation
2. Latin grammar, speaking, Cato
3. Aesop, Terence, Lily
4. Virgil
5. Cicero, *Selected Epistles*
6. Sallust, Caesar
7. Horace, *Epistles*, Ovid, *Metamorphoses, Fasti*
8. Donatus, Figures of Rhetoric, Valla, *Elegantiae*

Harrow (1591, reflecting earlier practice)

1. Grammar, Cato, Mimus etc., Cicero, *Selected Epistles*
2. Aesop, Cato, Erasmus, *Colloquia*, Mancini, *On the Four Virtues*
3. Cicero, *Epistolae familiares*, grammar, Terence, Ovid, *Tristia*
4. Cicero, *De officiis, De amicitia, De senectute* or *De finibus*, Virgil, *Eclogues, Georgics*, or Horace, Erasmus, *De copia, De conscribendis epistolis*, Greek grammar
5. Virgil, *Aeneid*, Caesar, Cicero, *De natura deorum*, Livy, Demosthenes, Isocrates, Hesiod, Heliodorus or Dionysius Halicarnassus

Sandwich (1580)

1. Accidence
2. Constructions, Cato
3. Catechism, Castalio, *Dialogues*
4. Terence, Cicero, *Selected Epistles*, Aphthonius, *Progymnasmata*
5. Sallust, Cicero, *De officiis*, rules of verse, Virgil, *Eclogues* or Christian poet
6. Cicero, *Orations*, Virgil, *Aeneid*, Horace, *Epistles, Odes*

Rivington (1576)

1. Grammar
2. Cato
3. Castalio, *Dialogues*, Erasmus, *Colloquies, Apothegms*
4. Terence, Cicero, *Selected Epistles*, Buchanan's *Psalms*, Ovid, *Heroides*, Horace, *Odes*, Erasmus, *De copia, De conscribendis epistolis*
5. Greek grammar, Isocrates, Cicero, *De officiis, De amicitia, De senectute, Tusculan Disputations*
6. Rhetoric, Cicero, *Orations*, Sallust, Virgil.[5]

exclude him would impoverish our understanding of Elizabethan education. None of my general conclusions rests on Brinsley alone. I cite Erasmus, Melanchthon and other pre-Elizabethan continental writers because their texts and ideas continued to be used.

5 Baldwin, *Shakspere's Small Latine*, I, pp. 122–4, 310, 342–4, 345–51. These tables omit references which the full statutes make to the forms of writing to be practised at each stage, to school

In spite of the obvious differences in the range of authors read and, in particular, in the attitude to Greek, three clear elements emerge from these four syllabi. The first years are given over to learning how to read, write and speak Latin. Pupils begin by learning the rules of Latin grammar, which they practise by learning and imitating elementary texts and dialogues. Several of these elementary texts have a strong Christian orientation and all the statutes refer to prayers and church-going as essential parts of the course. The later years are devoted to a fairly consistent course in Latin literature: Terence, Cicero's *Epistles*, Virgil's *Eclogues* and *Aeneid* (and sometimes the *Georgics* as well), Cicero's *De officiis, De amicitia*, and *De senectute*, Caesar or Sallust, Ovid and Horace.[6] Thirdly, the syllabi and the educational theorists suggest a series of genres of writing practised by the students. Composition in these forms of writing is supported by analysis and imitation of the Latin authors and by three handbooks: a letter-writing manual, Aphthonius's *Progymnasmata* and Erasmus's *De copia*.

READING LATIN LITERATURE

Educational theorists agreed on the broad pattern for the teaching of classical texts. The teacher should begin by giving a general introduction to the author, the genre of writing and the work to be studied. Each brief section of the text should be introduced and read in Latin. Its meaning should be explained, either by Latin paraphrase or by translation.[7] The teacher should then discuss some of the following: difficult or unusual words, historical or cultural issues, questions of style, parallels with other texts. In his instructions for reading, which were included in Lily's *Brevissima institutio*, Erasmus suggested that pupils should re-read texts

---

discipline and to religious observance. It should be taken as axiomatic that in these statutes imitative composition is integrated with the study of the authors. On the Tudor curriculum see Skinner, *Reason and Rhetoric*, pp. 19–23.

[6] There may be some over-optimism in this list. Green, '*Grammatica Movet*', pp. 73–115 (esp. 77–8) has pointed to the immense disparity between the number of editions of Lily's grammar and of all other grammar school 'textbooks'. Our accounts of grammar school education need to take proper cognisance of this important observation. I agree with Green that we should not be drawn into the extreme inference that because no other text was printed anything like as often as Lily's grammar, therefore grammar school pupils read nothing else. This argument seems to me refuted by the attainments of those who passed through grammar school. Latin texts were imported and may have been recycled within schools. Dictated texts may have supplemented bought texts.

[7] Brinsley's frequent remarks (e.g. *Ludus*, pp. xxv–vii, 103–21) about the time which the master would save by providing pupils with a printed translation may suggest that translation in class was actually the norm. Kempe (*Education*, sigs. G1r–2v) implies that translating was an important exercise in expression.

four times: at first straight through to record the general meaning more thoroughly; then word by word noticing vocabulary and constructions; thirdly for rhetoric, picking out figures, elegant expressions, sententiae, proverbs, histories, fables and comparisons; and finally ethically, noting exemplary stories and moral teaching.[8] In his 1502 prologue, Fernando de Rojas named the ideal readers of his *Celestina* as those who avoid concentrating exclusively on the structure of the work or the proverbs, drawing from it useful moral teaching and sententiae which can be reused in their own writings.[9]

Cardinal Wolsey outlines the method of teaching a text in his 1529 statutes for Ipswich Grammar School, which he intended as a model for English schools, and which were reprinted in some versions of Colet's *Grammar*.

In reading those works, we particularly recommend to you to endeavour to make yourselves masters of every passage requiring immediate explanation. As, for instance, supposing you are to give the plan of one of Terence's comedies, you are to preface it with a short account of the author's life, his genius and his manner of writing. You are next to explain both the pleasure and profit that attends the reading of comedies. You are next, in clear but succinct manner, to explain the signification and etymology of the word, to give a summary of the fable and an exact description of the nature of the verse. You are then to construe it in its natural order. Lastly, you are carefully to mark out to your pupils every striking elegance of style, every antiquated expression, everything that is new, every grecisised expression, every thing that is obscure, every etymology, derivation or composition that may arise, whatever is harsh or confused in the arrangement of the sentence. You are to mark every orthography, every figure, every graceful ornament of style, every rhetorical flourish, whatever is proverbial, all passages that ought to be imitated and all that ought not.[10]

---

[8] William Lily, *Brevissima institutio*, (London, 1573) STC 15616, sig. H5r–v. Erasmus, letter 56 in P. S. Allen (ed.), *Opus Epistolarum Erasmi*, 12 vols. (Oxford, 1906), I, pp. 171–3; example of epistola monitoria in *De conscribendis epistolis*, ed. J. C. Margolin, *Opera omnia*, I–2 (Amsterdam, 1971), pp. 496–8. This letter had also formed part of *Familiarum colloquiorum formulae*. J. Chomarat, *Grammaire et Rhétorique chez Erasme*, 2 vols. (Paris, 1981), I, pp. 513–16.
[9] Fernando de Rojas et al., *Las Celestinas*, ed. J. M. Valveda, et al. (Barcelona, 1976), p. 16. I owe this reference to Craig Kallendorf.
[10] 'In quibus praelegendis vos admonitos velimus ut ea duntaxat quam explicanda praesenti loco sint idonea conemini dicere, veluti comoediam Terentianam ennarraturi in primis authoris fortunam, ingenium, sermonis elegantiam paucis disseratis. Deinde quantum habeat voluptatis et utilitatis comoediarum lectio. Deinde quid significet ea vox et unde ducta. Deinde delucide et breviter summam argumenti explicetis, carminis genus diligenter indicetis. Postea ordinetis simplicius. Deinde si qua insignis elegantia, si quid prisce dictum, si quid novatum, si quid graecanicum, si quid obscurius, si qua etymologia, si qua derivatio et compositio, si quis ordo durior et perturbatior. Si qua orthographia, si qua figura, si quod egregium orationis decus, si qua exornatio rethorica, si proverbium, si quid imitandum, si quid non imitandum sit, diligenter gregem admoneatis.' T. Wolsey, in J. Colet, *Rudimenta grammatices et docendi methodus . . . per Thomam*

Over ambitious though Wolsey's instructions are, they can be reduced to four elements which correspond with other humanist advice on lecturing, particularly that of Erasmus in *De ratione studii*. In the first place the teacher must provide a preface to every book. This will include the life of the author, the genre of the work, an outline of the story and a description of the verse form.[11] Each separate section of the work will have its own brief introduction. Secondly the teacher must construe the text sentence by sentence, showing how each sentence fits together and providing a Latin paraphrase or a translation. In the third place the teacher must explain points of grammatical interest within the passage, such as the etymologies and derivations of particular words and special cases of word-order. Fourthly the teacher must discuss rhetorical features, that is to say figures of speech, proverbs and passages for imitation.

Let us now examine each of these aspects in more detail, using as a guide the editions of classical texts printed in England for the use of Elizabethan schools under the terms of Bynneman's patent.[12] Although none of these commentated editions was printed very frequently, their texts and supplementary material were chosen from among a range of continental editions as particularly suitable for English grammar schools. Where authoritative biographies of their authors existed (and where space allowed) these editions usually included lives of their authors.[13] Philip Melanchthon's son-in-law George Sabinus opens his commentary

---

cardinalem (London: P. Treveris, 1529) STC 5542.3 (=25944), sig. A4r–v, translated in J. T. Philipps, *A Compendious Way of Teaching Antient and Modern Languages* (London, 1750), pp. 350–1, quoted by T. W. Baldwin in *Shakspere's Five-Act Structure* (Urbana, 1947), p. 169. Wolsey's expressions are almost identical to Erasmus, *De ratione studii*, pp. 137–8.

[11] This form of introduction is related to the medieval type B accessus, itself based on Servius. See R. W. Hunt, 'The Introductions to the *Artes* in the Twelfth Century', now in his *The History of Grammar in the Middle Ages* (Amsterdam, 1980), pp. 117–44; R. B. C. Huygens (ed.), *Accessus ad auctores* (Leiden, 1970); A. J. Minnis and A. B. Scott (eds. and trs.), *Medieval Literary Theory and Criticism*, Revised Edition (Oxford, 1991), pp. 15–36.

[12] Thanks to a letter of recommendation from Archbishop Parker in August 1569, Bynneman received a patent in classical school texts, some of which he published himself while licensing others to other printers. As a result the following authors or works were published in England in editions with commentary in the 1570s and 1580s: Virgil, Terence, Horace, Cicero, *Selected Epistles* (Sturm's selection), *Epistolae ad familiares*, *De amicitia*, *De senectute* and *De officiis*, Ovid, *Metamorphoses*, Sallust and Caesar. Baldwin, *Shakspere's Small Latine*, I, pp. 494–531, *Short Title Catalogue*, III, Appendix D, pp. 200–2. Prior to 1570 the classical texts employed in grammar school teaching were imported. See Margaret Lane Ford, 'Importation of Printed Books into England and Scotland', in L. Hellinga and J. B. Trapp (eds.), *The Cambridge History of the Book in Britain*, III, *1400–1557* (Cambridge, 1999), pp. 179–201.

[13] E.g. Sallust, *De Catilinae coniuratione* (London: Thomas Marsh, 1569) STC 21622.2, sigs. *2r–4v; Terence, *Comoediae* (London: Thomas Marsh, 1583) STC 23886, sigs. A5r–B5r; Virgil, *Opera* (London: Felix Kingston, 1597) STC 24791, sigs. A2v–7v.

on Ovid's *Metamorphoses*, reprinted in Cambridge in 1584,[14] by explaining the usefulness of reading fables ('since poetry is nothing other than philosophy arranged in verses and fables, through which the teachings of honourable arts and precepts about morals illustrated with examples of rulers are contained')[15] and praising Ovid's poem because it includes the most important fables of all the poets. Sabinus advocates a combination of moral and historical interpretation, arguing that myths record both reactions to specific moments and general views about human life.[16] Although the moral teaching which can be drawn from the poem is its most valuable feature,[17] it also provides useful information about astronomy, physics and geography.

Finally it has many other uses, not least that it teaches those who wish to learn eloquence with all the rhetorical doctrine of words and figures of speech, and it teaches how the different things invented should be organised and some subject-matter explained clearly, copiously and pleasingly. For the variety of figures, emotions and meanings in the telling of these fables is astonishing.[18]

Pupils are encouraged to read the *Metamorphoses* because it teaches moral lessons, because it retells the Greek myths most likely to be met in Latin poetry, because it conveys information about science and geography and because it can be used to teach rhetoric.

The most important purpose of reading classical Latin literature in the classroom was to improve pupils' understanding of the Latin language and to provide them with vocabulary and phrases for Latin conversation and composition. The Latin texts to be studied earlier, such as the poems and letters included in Lily's *Grammar*, the *Sententiae pueriles* and the dialogues, were examples of Latin syntax, which pupils could learn by heart and reuse (either in identical form or mechanically varied) in

[14] The introductory material and the annotations for the Cambridge edition of 1584 by George Sabinus were first published in Wittenberg in 1555 and later printed in French editions. Ann Moss, *Ovid in Renaissance France*, Warburg Institute Surveys VII (London, 1982) pp. 48–53. That the English editions of Ovid's *Heroides* and *Tristia* are plain texts may possibly indicate that by the 1570s *Metamorphoses* was the preferred text, though *Tristia* is mentioned more frequently in the statutes.

[15] 'Poetica nihil aliud est nisi philosophia numeris et fabulis concinna, qua honestarum artium doctrina et praecepta de moribus illustrata regnorum exemplis continentur.' Ovid, *Metamorphoses*, with the commentary of Sabinus (Cambridge, 1584) STC 18951, sig. ¶7v.

[16] Ibid., sigs. ¶2r–3v.   [17] Ibid., sigs. ¶7v–8r.

[18] 'Non est igitur nugatorium hoc poema, ac tantum ad delectationem confictum, sed thesaurus eruditionis, cuius quidem lectio conducit primum ad formandos vitae mores . . . Postremo alias quoque utilitates adfert, quarum haec non minima est quod instruit eloquentiae studiosos omni apparatu oratorio verborum et figurarum, ac docet quomodo rerum diversarum inventio distribuenda, res vero perspicue, copiose, iucundeque explicandae sint, mira est enim varietas figurarum, affectuum et sententiarum in narratione harum fabularum.' Ibid., sig. ¶8v.

their own Latin conversation and writing.[19] Pupils would be questioned and drilled on this material in exactly the same way as on the Latin accidence itself.[20] The earlier 'literary' texts, the simpler letters from Cicero's *Ad familiares* and Terence's comedies were used in the same way as the elementary readers: as examples of Latin syntax and as sources of phrases for reuse. Pupils were expected to analyse sentences word by word. With the later texts (Virgil, *De officiis*, Sallust or Caesar, Horace and Ovid) and with abler pupils, grammatical analysis focused on difficult words and phrases whose explanation might advance pupils' understanding of Latin grammar. Many of the notes in the commentaries gloss difficult words and explain constructions.

In his manual for teachers first published in 1612 John Brinsley argued that pupils would be helped to construe more accurately if they understood the shape and purpose of the text they were reading. His grammatical translations provide summaries of the content and organisation of the text which he advises teachers to present to pupils before they begin the exercise of construing.[21] In his chapter on construing extempore, to which he often cross-refers as his model of commentary he draws attention to the importance of understanding the place of particular sentences within their local context.

2 Where they have no help but the bare author and that they must construe wholly of themselves, call upon them oft to labour to understand and keep in fresh memory the argument, matter and drift of the place which they are to construe . . .

3 To consider well of all the circumstances of each place, which are comprehended most of them in this plain verse:

    Quis, quid, cui, causa, locus, quo tempore, prima sequela.

---

[19] Leonhard Culmann, *Sententiae pueriles* (London, 1639) STC 6107; [Cato] *Libellus elegantissimus qui inscribitur Cato* (London, 1572) STC 4846; M. Cordier, *Colloquiorum scholasticorum libri quatuor* (London, 1608) STC 5759.4. The Lily–Colet grammar included such supplementary Latin reading matter as: the Creed, the ten commandments, the Lord's Prayer, Lily's *Carmen de moribus*, two letters by Erasmus on the approach to schooling and the method of reading texts and further Latin prayers and graces: William Lily and John Colet, *A Shorte Introduction of Grammar* (London, 1572) STC 15616, sigs. D5r–6r, *Brevissima institutio*, sigs. H3v–6r. Not all this material appeared in all editions. The two letters by Erasmus appeared together in *De conscribendis epistolis*, pp. 492–8. J. C. Margolin discusses the part which these letters played in the evolution of *De ratione studii* in his introduction, pp. 85–7.

[20] Kempe, *Education*, sigs. F3v–G1r; Brinsley, *Ludus*, pp. 125–30, 142–5; John Stockwood, *A Plaine and Easie Laying Open of the Meaning and Understanding of the Rules of Construction* (London, 1590) STC 23280.

[21] John Brinsley, *Ovid's Metamorphosis Grammatically Translated* (London, 1618) STC 18963, sigs. ¶4r, A2v; Brinsley, *Ludus*, p. 146.

That is, who speaks in that place, what he speakes, to whom he speakes, upon what occasion he speakes, or to what end, where he spake, at what time it was, what went before in the sentences next, what followeth next after . . . [22]

Brinsley believes that the best aid to construing is an awareness of the local and general context of a passage. He urges his pupils to explore local context in terms of speaker, audience, purpose and occasion. He asks not for the technical rhetoric of a labelling of verbal patterns but for an approach to the text as embedded in the relation between speaker, audience, purpose and occasion which is rhetorical in the broader sense.

Many of the commentaries reprinted for use in schools exhibit the structure and local content of the text. Hegendorff provides arguments for each of Cicero's letters to his friends. His marginal notes classify each and label the progress of the argument. Melanchthon's commentary on Terence describes the context of each scene while marginal notes mark the structure of the longer speeches. Commentators on Virgil analyse the argument of each of the eclogues and annotate the topics of some of the longer speeches in the *Aeneid*.[23] To some extent these sectional summaries counteract the tendency to fragmentation implicit in the emphasis on the analysis and recording of individual sentences.

Commentaries assist the reader's comprehension with summaries of the historical situation of particular letters and with notes on political institutions and religious customs.[24] Teachers were expected to provide this type of material to pupils both to enable them to understand what they were reading and to enlarge their general knowledge about Rome. Guarino and Erasmus urged pupils to familiarise themselves with the encyclopaedic works of the ancient world so as to be able to locate such information for themselves.[25]

---

[22] Brinsley, *Ludus*, pp. 123–4. In Brinsley's text, '*quid*' in line seven is omitted, but the following paragraph makes it clear that it is required. Marjorie Woods points out that these seven topics (ultimately derived from status theory) provide the structure for the type A accessus. See bibliography at note 11 above and Rita Copeland, *Rhetoric, Hermeneutics and Translation in the Middle Ages* (Cambridge, 1991), pp. 64–6. In the accessus the circumstantiae are used to introduce the whole text. For Brinsley they are questions that a reader might ask at any point to clarify the meaning of the text.

[23] E.g. Cicero, *Ad familiares*, with the commentary of Hegendorff (London: Thomas Marsh, 1574) STC 5296, sigs. A4r, B4r–C2v; Terence, *Comoediae*, sigs. C1r–4r; Virgil, *Opera* (London: H. Middleton, 1580) STC 24789, sigs. C3r–4v, L2r–4r.

[24] E.g. Cicero, *Ad familiares* (London: Vautrollier, 1575) STC 5297, sigs. *3r–6r, A3v, A6r–v.

[25] Battista Guarini, 'De ordine docendi et discendi', in E. Garin (ed.), *Il pensiero pedagogico dell'Umanesimo* (Florence, 1958), pp. 456–61; Erasmus, *De ratione studii*, pp. 120–5.

Even more valuable than the factual information to be derived from classical texts was their moral teaching. Commentaries on *De officiis* note the key moral *sententiae* and commonplaces.[26] The first English edition of Horace provides arguments to each ode (and to the other poems) which emphasise their moral and prudential teaching.

> II. 3. Exhortatory ode to his friend Q. Delius, in which he advises that both types of fortune must be experienced with moderation. One must not be carried away by things which turn out well nor cast down by disasters but should observe an equable, happy medium. In the meantime, certain of death's coming however long he had lived, he should heap up familiar things wherever they originate and on this account live happily as long as age and declining faculties permit.[27]

This argument strips away all the poem's particularity of landscape and luxury but preserves and generalises its moral message. Where Horace had specified typical possessions or named the fates or the denizens of the underworld, the argument prefers flat abstraction. Sabinus's commentary on the *Metamorphoses* interprets the fables as moral (the story of Pygmalion teaches that men should pray to God to provide a chaste wife)[28] and political lessons (Phaeton as political allegory; Pentheus as the image of the tyrant)[29] but also suggests ways of thinking about Ovid's narratives and classical literature more generally.

> Many things have been cleverly contrived by poets but I do not know whether any of them are more fitting than this imagining: how the Furies are summoned from hell moved by the wrath of God; how they bring with them mourning, fear and madness; how they cause men to rush into crimes because they are bitten by a snake and filled with poison; lastly how they attack criminals with whips and stir them with burning torches. These things have been devised very appropriately and seriously by the wisest of men, who have carefully considered the greatness of divine wrath and the causes of human disasters. For the Furies are nothing other than wicked desires, or impulses of the mind opposed to right reason, by which some are driven to hate, envy, ambition and murder, others

---

[26] 'Proverbium: quae dubitas ne feceris . . . Quod in punienda iniuria officium.' Cicero, *De officiis*, with Erasmus's commentary (London: Orwin, 1590) STC 5266.6, sigs. G1v, G2v.

[27] 'Ode paraenetica ad Q. Delium amicum, qua monet ut utraque fortuna moderate utatur, rebus laetis non efferatur, adversis non deiiciatur, sed mediocritatem et aequabilitatem quandam servet: interim certus de morte utcunque vixerit, rem familiarem extruxerit undecunque natus sit atque ob id hilaris vivat dum per aetatem et facultates licet.' Horace, *Poemata omnia doctissimis scholiis illustrata* (London: Norton, 1574) STC 13784, ad II. 3, sig. D3r.

[28] Ovid, *Metamorphoses* (1584), sig. Bb7v, repr. in Philipp Melanchthon, *Opera omnia*, ed. C. Bretschneider, *Corpus Reformatorum*, 28 vols. (Brunswick, 1834–60), XIX, col. 605.

[29] Ovid, *Metamorphoses* (1584), sigs. D8r–E2r, H5v–6r, repr. in Melanchthon, *Opera omnia*, XIX, cols. 519–23, 534–5.

to debauchery, adultery and incest; and others are incited by the devil to other brutal and criminal offences.[30]

In his often reprinted preface to Virgil's works of 1533,[31] Melanchthon rejects moral readings of the *Aeneid* which simply extract pithy phrases from the poem. Explicitly linking the poem to the aims of humanist education, he insists that its large narrative moments also be registered as lessons.

Knowledge of things feeds prudence; words nourish eloquence. So Virgil when he describes Aeneas creates a certain picture of a wise man, who among so many dangers overcomes everything that opposes him through reason and planning. But to this he also adds the Gods, rulers of favourable occurences. For the poets saw that great things are achieved through reason, subject to the control and favour of the Fates. In the same way they conceive undeserved destinies in which someone dies in spite of the merit of their valour. For example Pallas here in Virgil. But there are others who are made excessively bold by fortune and favourable events, as Euryalus and Nisus were. In places like these the poets lament the misery of human kind. There are also places where bad things happen to those who deserve ill, for example those who abuse their fortune, as happens to the tyrant Mezentius. In the same way there are those who become insolent through good fortune, as in

The human mind is ignorant of the fates etc. [10, 501]

These things belong to justice. For the poets see that the final ends of robbers and tyrants are always cruel. But because Aeneas is imagined to be a ruler, so it should be seen that the poet gives him the arts of ruling a republic, the knowledge of war and justice. Thus he said

I struggle to say whether your justice or feats in war are greater. [11, 126]

The same with clemency.

Also I should like to make peace with the living. [11, 111]

And the authority to suppress rebellions.

Such a man of duty etc. [1, 151]

Throughout, descriptions of emotions are added to the actions being carried out. In the same way there are descriptions of places and times, of diseases, of wounds and cures, all of which belong to natural science. There are also fables in the

[30] 'Multa quidem scite excogitata sunt a poetis, sed haud scio, an quicquam hoc figmento aptius, nemper quomodo Furiae commota ira Dei evocentur ab inferis; quomodo secum trahant luctum, timorem, insaniam, quomodo item agant homines praecipites in scelus, iniecto illis serpente, et infuso veneno; denique quomodo flagellis insectentur facinorosos, et ardentibus facibus eos agitent. Haec enim omnia aptissime et gravissime excogitata sunt ab hominibus sapientissimis, qui magnitudinem irae divinae, et causas humanarum calamitatum diligenter considerarunt. Sunt autem Furiae nihil aliud nisi pravae cupiditates, seu commotiones animorum a recta ratione aversae, quibus impelluntur hi ad odium, invidiam, ambitionem, caedem; illi ad stupra, adulteria, incestus; alii ad alia atrocia et nefaria flagitia, incitati a diabolo.' Sabinus, Ovid, *Metamorphoses* (1584), sig. K8r–v, repr. in Melanchthon, *Opera omnia*, XIX, col. 544.

[31] This preface was printed in numerous continental editions and (without ascription to Melanchthon) in two editions by Bynneman (1570 and 1572) STC 24788 and 24788a.

poems imagined without reason, so much of the theatre that they recommend the sequence of the rest of the story and delight the reader with variety and carry out their duty. For example about the horse, or the fleet changed into nymphs. Some things belong to nature, such as Venus being born out of the sea. The whole poem is devoted to the promotion of virtues in general. For it is the image of man as statesman and commander.[32]

Melanchthon places the traditional renaissance view of Aeneas as the ideal ruler[33] within a context where success is seen to require good fortune as well as merit and perseverance, in which the good can be undeservedly killed, while evil men prosper for a time. He portrays a drama of character, politics and fate, which is enlivened by emotion, natural description and wonder. While rejecting readings which merely extract fragments, he shows that the sense of the whole must be built out of a response to a range of detail, some of it conflicting or distressing.

As well as drawing moral lessons, teachers were expected to use Latin literature to teach rhetoric, by pointing out to their pupils the ways in which authors used vocabulary and figures of speech. The commentaries often assist in this aim by noting particular figures and rhetorical effects.[34] The marginal notes on the *Aeneid* sometimes draw attention to Virgil's imitation of passages from Homer.[35] Melanchthon's preface to Cicero's *De officiis* stresses the contribution which the work will make to the pupils' resources of expression. The reader will obtain both copia of words useful

---

[32] 'Rerum cognitio prudentiam alit, sermones eloquentiam. Ut Virgilius cum Aeneam describit, imaginem quandam viri prudentis facit, qui inter varia pericula, ratione et consilio omnia adversa vincit. Sed addit illi etiam Deos, rerum secundarum gubernatores. Viderant enim poetae magnas res geri ratione, sed Fatis fortunantibus et gubernantibus. Item finguntur indigni casus, ubi contra quam merebatur virtus, quidam pereunt. Sicut Pallas hic apud Virgilium. Sed tamen qui fortuna et secundis rebus facti fuerant audaciores, sicut Euryalus et Nisus. Huiusmodi loci miseriam humani generis deplorant. Est et ubi male meritis tale accidunt, ut qui fortuna abusi sunt, sicut tyranno Mezentio accidit. Item qui secundis rebus insolescunt, ut Nescia mens hominum fati etc. Haec ad iustitiam pertinent. Viderunt enim poetae exitus latronum et tyrannorum semper fuisse cruentos. Sed quia Aeneas fingitur esse princeps, ideo videndum est, quas ei tribuat artes reipublicae gerendae, scientiam belli, iustitiam. Ideo dixit, Iustitiae ne prius miser, belli ne laborem. Item clementiam, Equidem et vivis concedere velim. Et seditionum comprimendarum autoritatem, Tantum pietate virum etc. Accedunt obiter descriptiones affectuum in rebus gerendis. Item locorum et temporum, et morborum, vulnerum, remediorum, quae pertinent ad φυσιολογίαν. Sunt autem fabulae quaedam in poematis sine ratione confictae, tantum ad admirationem theatralem, ut reliqui argumenti seriem commendent, et lectorem varietate quadam delectent, et in officio contineant. Sicut de equo, de classe mutata in Nymphas. Quaedam ad naturam pertinent, sicut Venerem esse mari ortam. Ad mores formandos in genere totum poema. Est enim imago ἀνδρὸς πολιτικοῦ καὶ στρατηγοῦ.' Virgil, *Opera*, with commentary of Melanchthon (Lyons, 1533), sigs. a1v–2r, repr. in *Opera omnia*, ii, 22f.

[33] Sir Philip Sidney, *An Apology for Poetry*, ed. G. Shepherd (Manchester, 1973), pp. 100, 108, 119–20; Craig Kallendorf, *In Praise of Aeneas* (Hanover NH, 1989).

[34] E.g. Terence, *Comoediae*, sigs. C7r–v, D5v, E1r, E2r, E5r; Virgil, *Opera* (1580), sigs. C3v, D2r, I5v.

[35] E.g. Virgil, *Opera* (1580), sigs. I5v–8r, L1r–3r.

for discussing civil affairs and an account of the virtues almost set out as commonplaces for young people.[36] The grammar school literature syllabus offers a progress through the greatest examples of the genres of Latin literature. Terence and the easier letters of Cicero's *Ad familiares* provide phrases for speech and composition and examples of human behaviour. Like them Virgil's shorter poems offer models of structure and argument. Sentences from *De officiis* and Horace, and narratives from the *Metamorphoses*, the *Aeneid* and Roman history give different kinds of moral teaching for reuse and for instruction. Reading *De officiis* also gave pupils access to an important aspect of rhetorical theory, the topics of deliberative oratory. Deliberative oratory focuses on arguments about what is right and honourable and what is useful and expedient.[37] These topics are certainly used by English writers on political subjects but they do not appear elsewhere in the grammar school manuals.

The commentaries reflect the preoccupations of the teachers' manuals. Some of them provide the assistance with vocabulary, syntax and context which the pupils require. Others assist pupils in extracting moral *sententiae* and elegant phrases. They emphasise the moral lessons to be drawn from the texts while also registering their content and narrative structure. They place individual speeches and episodes within the context of the whole work. Some of the commentaries attend to the rhetorical structure of particular speeches, letters or poems, and some label figures of rhetoric. Much of what the commentators choose to notice (certainly the vocabulary, the sententiae, the narratives, the structures and the figures) provides material and models for the pupils' writing. This corresponds with one of Brinsley's aims of grammar school education.

24. To make right use of the matter of their Authours, besides the Latine, even from the first beginning, as of *Sententiae* and *Confabulatiunculae Pueriles*, Cato, Esop's *Fables*, Tullies *Epistles*, Tullies *Offices*, Ovid's *Metamorphosis*, and so on to the highest. To helpe to furnish them with variety of the best morall matter and with understanding, wisedome and precepts of vertue, as they grow; and withall to imprint the Latine so in their minds thereby, as hardly to be forgotten.[38]

---

[36] Melanchthon, *Argumentum in Officia Ciceronis*, in *Opera Omnia*, xvi, cols. 627–30. Of the eleven editions of *De officiis* printed in England between 1573 and 1600, Melanchthon's preface and his notes to the text appear certainly in four (STC 5265.8, 5266.5, 5266.6 and 5266.8) and probably in another three (STC 5265.7, 5266.1 and 5267).

[37] Cicero, *De officiis*, 1.3.9–10, 4.14–5.17, 7.20–10.32, ii.3.9–5.18, 23.83–25.89.

[38] Brinsley, *Ludus*, pp. xvi–xvii.

Latin literature was read to extend knowledge of the Latin language (including its expressive possibilities as demonstrated by the best models), to convey historical and cultural information about the ancient world, to teach moral lessons, and to provide phrases and examples for reuse in pupils' own compositions.

COMPOSITION EXERCISES

The principal forms of written Latin composition practised in the grammar school were letters and themes. Theme, a term found in sixteenth-century English and Latin, designated both the subject set and the composition itself. In modern terms the theme was a type of essay, usually on a moral topic. Sixteenth-century writers might also call it a commonplace or an oration.[39] One or two grammar school syllabi mention declamation, but Brinsley finds this exercise more suitable for universities or for the very best pupils.[40] Brinsley also discusses Latin verse composition but he admits that it is more ornamental than necessary.[41] According to Kempe, letter-writing was initially taught through varying phrases from some of the simpler letters from book xiv of Cicero's *Ad familiares* and through double translation.[42] Later, pupils would be instructed to write letters either within realistic schoolboy situations like those presented in the dialogues, or within situations arising from their reading of classical texts, where the words of their author would provide the main material. Thus the free space of the letter would be filled with matter extracted from reading. Imitation would be assisted by the study of a letter-writing manual. Several of the syllabi specify textbooks which the pupils should read to assist in composition, most frequently Erasmus's *De conscribendis epistolis* for letters, Aphthonius's *Progymnasmata* for themes and other composition exercises and Erasmus's *De copia* for facility and style more generally. Since these three works were also several times printed in England in the sixteenth century, it is reasonable to assume that they were widely used. In this section I shall relate the teaching of these three works to the composition exercises pupils undertook.

---

[39] Kempe, *Education*, sigs. G3r–H1r; Brinsley, *Ludus*, pp. 172–90; Richard Rainolde, *Foundacion of Rhetorike* (London, 1563) STC 20604, repr. Menston, 1972, sigs. a3v–4r, A4r–B1r; Baldwin, *Shakspere's Small Latine*, I, pp. 125, 343, 348–50. At Sandwich the fourth, fifth and sixth classes were instructed to practise the exercises of Aphthonius, Baldwin, p. 343.

[40] Baldwin, *Shakspere's Small Latine*, I, pp. 349–50; Brinsley, *Ludus*, p. 185.

[41] Kempe, *Education*, sigs. G4v–H1r; Brinsley, *Ludus*, pp. 190–8.

[42] Kempe, *Education*, sig. G1r–v; Ascham, *English Works*, pp. 239–46. Compare Brinsley, *Ludus*, p. xiv.

De conscribendis epistolis, first published in 1521 and reprinted over 100 times in the sixteenth century, is divided between chapters on the particular kinds of letter and general chapters in which Erasmus discusses a broad issue, to which he might otherwise have to return frequently. General issues include formulae of greeting, the use of titles, formulae for closing letters, the use of historical examples, fables and proverbs, methods of arguing, amplification and suitable figures of speech.[43] Like other authors of letter-writing treatises, Erasmus first proposes that the three main types of letter should correspond to the three types of public oration, identified in the rhetoric manuals: judicial, deliberative and demonstrative.[44] But he then undermines this structure. First he adds a fourth main type, the familiar letter, then he expands the importance of several of the sub-genres while reducing the deliberative genre to a page and the nine sub-genres of judicial to a couple of pages each.[45] The crude criterion of the length of the discussion of each sub-type suggests that there are five principal motives for letters: encouragement, persuasion, consolation, request and advice.[46] Less important than these five but still significant are six subsidiary purposes: recommendation, providing information, giving thanks, lamenting sorrows (usually one's own), congratulation and offering assistance. These headings are evidently more suited to the genre of the letter and the sixteenth century social context than the three types of classical oration.

Within each of these genres Erasmus first discusses the nature of the genre and the kind of arguments or considerations one might wish to include. In letters of consolation, for example, the student is advised to imagine the feelings of the grieving person in order to work out a way of progressing from expressions of sympathy to stories and ideas aimed at reducing grief. Erasmus then provides examples of letters of consolation in which moral sentences, literary quotations, stories from Roman history and philosophical arguments are elaborately woven together.[47] After the examples Erasmus provides for imitation a collection of phrases suitable to each genre, largely taken from Cicero, Pliny the younger and Poliziano.

This threefold pattern of lines of argument and ideas to consider, worked examples of the genre and useful phrases illustrates the way

---

[43] Erasmus, *De conscribendis epistolis*, pp. 276–300, 330–40, 343–9, 366–99; trans C. Fantazzi, *Collected Works*, xxv (Toronto, 1985), pp. 50–65, 83–94, 108–28.
[44] Ibid., pp. 309–12 (trans. *Collected Works*, xxv, pp. 71–2).
[45] Ibid., pp. 513–41 (trans. *Collected Works*, xxv, pp. 205–25).
[46] Ibid., pp. 324–43, 353–476, 488–509 (trans. *Collected Works*, xxv, pp. 79–90, 97–181, 189–203).
[47] Ibid., pp. 432–65 (trans. *Collected Works*, xxv, pp. 148–72).

in which Erasmus's manual combines thinking about the situation of
the letter with material from commonplace books to produce a finished
letter. The reading of classical texts contributes as a model for the finished
product and as a guide to thinking through the issues involved. Erasmus
begins his discussion of letters of request by noting Servius's analysis of
Juno's request to Aeolus in *Aeneid* I into four elements: that the thing
requested is in your power, that it is just, how the request should be
carried out and the reward that will follow.[48]

The notebook of the Elizabethan schoolmaster John Conybeare contains model letters in Latin and English for pupils to write to their
parents.[49] Edward VI's Latin letter of 2 April 1546 to his tutor Richard
Cox demonstrates a rather mechanical elaboration of a few basic phrases,
altering cases and extending constructions as he repeats. There is an obvious link between this form of composition and the drilling on phrases
which Brinsley recommends.

I thank you for the letters which you wrote me. I ought to thank you for your
letters because in them I see your love, goodwill and generosity towards me.
Your love is great, your goodwill is free and your generosity is acceptable. Your
love is great because while you are away you think about me. Your goodwill
towards me is free because you write to me when you have more important
things to do; and your kindness towards me is acceptable because nothing can
come from you which would not be acceptable to me.[50]

Edward repeats nouns and phrases under the direction of his master to
make the most of his (at this stage) meagre Latin. But the elaboration of
a set of words into phrases of a periodic sentence and into a sequence of
patterned sentences became a commonplace of Elizabethan prose, for
example in Peter Wentworth's speech to parliament in 1576 and in the
soliloquies in Lyly's *Euphues*.[51]

---

[48] Ibid., pp. 465–6 (trans. *Collected Works*, xxv, p. 172).

[49] F. C. Conybeare (ed.), *Letters and Exercises of the Elizabethan Schoolmaster John Conybeare* (London,
1905), pp. 2–3, 8–9, 106–8.

[50] 'Ago tibi gratias pro literis quas ad me scripsisti. Debeo enim agere tibi gratias pro literis, quia
in his video amorem, benevolentiam, et generositatem tuam erga me. Amor tuus est magnus
et benevolentia tua est libera, et generositas tua est acceptabilis. Amor tuus est magnus, quia
cogitas de me absens; et benevolentia tua est libera, quia scribis ad me, cum habeas maiora
ad agendum quam id est; et humanitas tua est acceptabilis mihi, quia nihil potest venire abs
te, quod mihi non acceptabile sit.' J. G. Nichols (ed.), *Literary Remains of King Edward VI*, 2 vols.
(London, 1857, repr. New York, 1964), I, p. 25, quoted in Baldwin, *Shakspere's Small Latine*, I, p. 211.
While Edward's education was obviously a special case, his surviving exercises illustrate a highly
developed practical expression of the theories underlying Tudor grammar school education.

[51] See Introduction above and chapter five below.

In a letter to Cox of June 1546, Edward VI incorporates ethical quotations ('Unexercised wit becomes sluggish' (Vives) and 'I flee idleness like the plague. All evils arise from idleness' (Erasmus)) from his reading into an elaboration of his obligation to write letters in order to practise his Latin.[52] Even at the most elementary stage of Latin composition, varying and the incorporation of moral sentences were the basis from which expression was to be generated.

Aphthonius's *Progymnasmata* are a fourth-century Greek group of writing exercises which were usually presented to renaissance schoolboys in a Latin translation by Rudolph Agricola, with commentary and additional examples chosen by Reinhard Lorichius.[53] The *Progymnasmata* provide a graded sequence of fourteen exercises in composition, beginning with the fable (which consists of a story with a moral attached) and building up to the proposal for a law (a set of arguments in favour of a new law and a refutation of objections).[54] The exercises make use of the early reading material (fables, moral sentences) and add different materials and forms (description, speech for a character) which can later be incorporated into larger compositions.

Within each form Aphthonius provides a definition of the form, a division into different sub-types, a recipe for the content of the form and one or more examples. The commentaries explain the terms of the definition and division (sometimes providing alternatives), refer to examples of the form in classical literature, and provide additional examples, usually marked into subsections to show how the elements of the recipe build up into the finished composition.

Aphthonius's nearest approach to the theme is the thesis, his penultimate exercise. The thesis is defined as an enquiry, investigating an issue through speech. It is divided into civil (concerning active life or city business) and contemplative (concerned with the mind). It consists of a preface, urging or praising a particular course of action, a narration of

---

[52] 'Ingenium inexercitatum torpidum ... Otium seu pestem quandam fugio. Ex otio enim omne nascitur malum.' Nichols, *Edward*, I, pp. 19–20, quoted in Baldwin, *Shakspere's Small Latine*, I, p. 213. There are many other examples in Edward's surviving letters, almost all of which can be regarded as linguistic exercises, e.g. Nichols, *Edward*, I, pp. 17–19, 23, 29, 36.

[53] Aphthonius, *Progymnasmata*, with the commentary of Lorichius (London: Thomas Marsh, 1575) STC 700.3; D. L. Clark, 'The Rise and Fall of *Progymnasmata* in Sixteenth Century Grammar Schools', *Speech Monographs* 19 (1952), 259–63; Manfred Kraus will soon publish a paper updating and enlarging Clark's list of editions.

[54] The full series is: fable, narrative, chreia, proverb, confutation, proof, commonplace, praise, vituperation, comparison, speech for a character (ethopoeia), description, thesis, proposal for a law. One of the subtypes of speech for a character is prosopopeia, speech for an imagined character, which appears in style manuals as a figure of thought, personification. Aphthonius, *Progymnasmata*, sigs. Y8v–Z5v.

what is involved, arguments from the legitimate, the just, the useful and the possible, a series of brief objections answered fully, and a conclusion.[55] The thesis builds on parts of the earlier exercise of the commonplace,[56] but adds the refutation of objections, thus moving in the direction of the full four-part oration. Like Aphthonius's other exercises it serves as a preparation for topical invention.[57]

English writers treated the theme (which we would now see as one of the prototypes for the essay)[58] as an advanced exercise with a fixed structure. Christopher Johnson, the master at Winchester in the 1560s taught the theme as a combination of sententia, developed commonplace and proof.[59] Brinsley expected pupils to follow the structure of the classical oration (exordium, narration, arguments in favour, refutation of opposing arguments and conclusion).[60] Ralph Johnson, writing later in the seventeenth century, provided an equally firm and slightly different structure for the theme in which the refutation is dropped and the topics of the arguments in favour are specified (exordium, narration, cause, contrary, comparison, example, testimony, conclusion).[61] The five middle sections of this structure, derived from the topics of invention, draw on Aphthonius's exercises.

The *Progymnasmata* are intentionally rigid forms, exercising the pupil in simplified versions of different aspects of invention, while consciously building up towards the oration.[62] The *Progymnasmata* strongly promote the idea that the orator can argue on both sides of the case, both in pairings of exercises (confutation then proof; praise then vituperation) and in the examples provided. The first example of thesis argues in favour of marriage, the second against.[63] The *Progymnasmata* also present short forms which can be employed within larger compositions. Description,

---

[55] Ibid., sigs. Cc7r–Dd7v.

[56] The commonplace, defined as a speech which presents the good or bad which inhere in something ('Locus communis est oratio bona aut mala quae alicui insunt argumentans') consists of: introduction, contrary, exposition, comparison, sententia, digression, exclusion of pity, arguments from the legitimate, the just, the useful, the possible, the honourable and what will happen, and conclusion. Ibid., sigs. M4v–7v.

[57] Aphthonius provides the pupil with a small number of subjects to insert in each particular form. In topical invention the student will have to select from material found through all the topics. See chapter two below.

[58] Ian Michael, *The Teaching of English: From the Sixteenth Century to 1870* (Cambridge, 1987), pp. 309–16; Peter Mack, 'Rhetoric and the Essay', *Rhetoric Society Quarterly* 23:2 (1993), 41–9.

[59] Baldwin, *Shakspere's Small Latine*, I, pp. 334–6.   [60] Brinsley, *Ludus*, pp. 174–9.

[61] Ralph Johnson, *The Scholar's Guide* (London, 1665; repr. Menston, 1971), pp. 15–16.

[62] Lorichius's commentary specifies the way in which particular exercises relate to the art of rhetoric or can be used in orations. E.g. Aphthonius, *Progymnasmata*, sigs. A2r, C1r–2r, L3r, M8r, P2v.

[63] Ibid., sigs. Cc7r–Dd1v, Dd5v–7v. Other examples of progymnasmata paired to give opposite views on the same proposition: sigs. I5r–7r, L7v–M3r; I7r–8v, M3r–4v; Q8r–R1r, V4r–6v.

narration and speech in character may be useful within an oration, but they may also find a place in an epic poem or a romance.

William Badger's notebook from Winchester in the 1560s provides examples of his teacher Christopher Johnson dictating classical orations followed by adaptations of the same material to schoolboy compositions.[64] The majority of Edward VI's orations represent a higher level of attainment than we would expect in any grammar school, demonstrating considerable knowledge of rhetoric, obtained according to Baldwin from a study of *Rhetorica ad Herennium*,[65] some knowledge of dialectic,[66] and wide reading in moral philosophy. One of Edward's earlier prose compositions exhibits some of the characteristics of the theme. Nichols quite understandably adds the title 'Virtue is better in deed than in mind'.

Pagan philosophers and doctors of the church agree that Virtue is a certain disposition of mind (*affectus*) which pursues (*imitans*) beautiful, honourable and praiseworthy things, and which avoids disgraceful or disgusting things, and anything which opposes the laws of reason. For this reason all learned men have decided that there is nothing more oustanding, more beautiful or more honourable than this Virtue. If man excels the other animals because of being an animal which participates in reason, then that thing which proceeds from this part of man is the best and most beautiful. However, although everyone affirms this with one voice, that 'Virtue is the highest good' or a great good, still the most learned debate among themselves which part of virtue is to be preferred to the other, as 'whether the action of Virtue or the mental disposition should be considered more praiseworthy and more outstanding'. Therefore this is the theme, which I shall now discuss. In this question or dispute I hold the view that the mental disposition is not more impressive than the action, and I shall prove this through parts. There are two kinds of Virtue, of which one is philosophical, the other theological. And although all the philosophical virtues are also theological, still there are more virtues numbered in theology than in philosophy. For the philosophical virtues are four: prudence, justice, courage and temperance. What? Should one dare compare prudence with justice? Should one dare compare knowledge with courage and temperance? Should one dare make understanding equal with the so beautiful number of the most famous virtues? Rightly, rightly it was said by Cicero, that most beautiful of philosophers: 'The whole praise of virtue consists in action'. Now I shall prove that justice is more impressive than prudence in many ways.[67]

---

[64] British Library MS Add. 4379; Baldwin, *Shakspere's Small Latine*, I, pp. 323, 331.

[65] Baldwin, *Shakspere's Small Latine*, I, pp. 231–4, 241–4. Edward made notes on several of Cicero's orations.

[66] E.g. Nichols, *Edward*, I, p. 102; Baldwin, *Shakspere's Small Latine*, I, pp. 234–5.

[67] '[Actio virtutis melior est habitu.] Omnes quidem et philosophi ethnici et doctores ecclesiastici hoc concludunt, quod Virtus sit affectus quidam imitans decora, honesta, et laudabili; vitans vero turpia, seu obscena, et omnia illa quae pugnant cum norma rationis. Hanc ob causam omnes viri

From the exercise of the chreia, Edward has learned how to present and embellish his quotations. From *De officiis* he has gathered phrases about man's superiority to the beasts and about the virtues generally, the list of the virtues and an authoritative statement of his key argument. His study of that work and the *Sententiae pueriles* has equipped him with a reasonable grasp of Latin vocabulary for ethics. He introduces his subject, defines and divides it before embarking on his arguments. He embellishes the argument with rhetorical questions and verbal patterning. The way in which Edward's writing builds from gathered phrases and pre-existing formal models is illustrated by the notes he made to prepare for an essay on the topic: Love is a greater cause of obedience than fear.

Reasons why love is a greater cause of obedience than fear.
Love is in man on account of the person loved.

Similarity in fathers	in will
Those who fear someone hate him	in goods
Examples of Codrus Curtius	it may remain longer
Themistocles Henry 7	it is more reliable
Richard 3	it draws body and soul

Exordium from the usefulness of the question. Outline of my opinion. Confirmation from the love of the wife. Fear deters from evil but does not encourage towards good. What love did in Alexander Severus; what fear did in Heliogabalus. The death of tyrants. What love did in Themistocles, Epaminondas, Scipio, Metellus Cicero etc.[68]

docti in hoc mundo nihil praestantius, nihil pulchrius, nihil magis decorum judicaverunt, quam illa Virtus. Si enim homo excellat caeteris animantibus, quia est animal ut particeps rationis, tum etiam illa res, quae ab hac parte hominis procedit, est optima et pulcherrima. Quanquam autem hoc omnes univoce affirmant Virtutem esse summum bonum, aut magnum bonum, attamen et doctissimi inter se disceptaverunt, quae pars virtutis sit alteri praeferenda; ut, An actio Virtutis vel habitus sit laudabilior et praestantior. Hoc igitur est thema, de quo iam tractabo. Ego autem in hac quaestione seu controversia has teneo partes, habitum non esse praestantiorem actione, idque per partes probabo. Sunt autem duo virtutum genera, quorum unum est philosophicum, aliud theologicum. Et quanquam omnes philosophicae sunt etiam theologicae; tamen plures in theologia recitantur, quam in philosophia. Philosophicae enim sunt quatuor: Prudentia, Justitia, Fortitudo, et Temperantia. Quid? audetne prudentia se comparare justitiae? audetne scientia se comparare fortitudini et temperantiae? audetne cognitio se equiparare tam pulchro numero virtutum clarissimarum? Recte, recte dictum est a Cicerone illo pulcherimmo Philosopho: Omnis laus virtutis in actione consistit. Iam autem justitiam esse praestantiorem prudentia multis modis probabo.' British Library MS Add. 4724, fol. 14r–v, printed in Nichols, *Edward*, I, p. 99.

[68] 'Rationes. amor maior causa obedientiae quam timor.
amor est in hominem propter amatum.

Similitudo in patribus.	in voluntate.
quem metuunt oderunt.	in bonis.
Exempla Codri. Curtii.	diutius permanet.
Themistoclis. Henr. 7.	Certior est.
Ricardi 3.	trahit et corpus et animum.

In the first stage, Edward lists reasons and examples. Subsequently he distributes some of these materials, together with other phrases and ideas he has later found, into the divisions of a five-part oration. Elsewhere in the same manuscript this outline is expanded, with further changes, into a continuous text.[69] Some of Edward's other essay outlines show him making lists of reasons in favour of a proposition and listing objections followed immediately by replies.[70] These notes can be regarded as preparations for the sections of an oration devoted to proof and refutation respectively, but they also resemble Cecil's collections of arguments for and against particular issues with which we shall be concerned in chapter six.[71]

Erasmus's *De copia rerum et verborum*, one of the most often printed of all humanist texts, is specified by name in twelve of the English syllabi.[72] It offers a method of supercharging texts, either by adding to the words used, by grammatical varying or figures of rhetoric, or by adding to the material at hand, using the methods of rhetorical invention. A simple statement may be made to seem greater by dividing it into its parts, by enumerating the whole sequence of events leading up to an occurrence, by including its causes and the things associated or by describing every detail of its appearance. Erasmus gives elaborate instructions for descriptions of things, people, places and times.[73] He includes a demonstration of copia, showing 195 different ways in which the sentence 'your letter pleased me greatly' can be expressed,[74] leading into more methods of variation and a collection of alternative phrases for various sentiments and occasions; and instructions for assembling a commonplace

---

Exordium ab utilitate quaestionis. Enarratio meae sententiae. Confirmatio per uxoris amorem. timor deterret a malo, non hortatur ad bonum. quid amor fecerit in Alexandro Severo, quid timor in Heliogabalo. Tyrannorum exitus. quid amor in Themistocle, Epaminonda, Scipione, Metello, Cicerone etc.' British Library MS Add. 4724, fol. 214r, printed in Baldwin, *Shakspere's Small Latine*, I, p. 251.

[69] British Library MS Add. 4724, fols. 74r–75v, printed in Baldwin, *Shakspere's Small Latine*, I, pp. 251–3.

[70] British Library MS Add. 4724, fols. 215r, 216r.

[71] The preparation of such notes may have been one of the things that made Edward's training unusual.

[72] Baldwin, *Shakspere's Small Latine*, II, pp. 179–80.

[73] Erasmus, *De copia*, ed. B. Knott, in Erasmus, *Opera omnia*, I–6 (Amsterdam, 1988), pp. 202–15, trans. B. Knott, *Collected Works*, XXIV (Toronto, 1978), pp. 577–89.

[74] Erasmus, *De copia* (1988), pp. 76–82 (trans. *Collected Works*, XXIV, pp. 348–54); H. D. Rix, 'The Editions of Erasmus's *De copia*', *Studies in Philology* 43 (1946), 595–618. If someone were to repeat Rix's work using modern bibliographies and catalogues, his list of 153 sixteenth-century editions would be considerably increased. Against Green's argument ('*Grammatica movet*', see note 6 above) that there were too few English editions for *De copia* to have been widely used one might cite the immense number of continental editions and the normal practice of importing Latin textbooks.

book.[75] Erasmus's last method (accumulation of proofs, specifically commonplaces, examples, comparisons, parallels, maxims and fables)[76] relies heavily on collecting material from reading. Some of the methods of producing copia of things resemble particular exercises (description, character description, comparison) from Aphthonius.

In most of its sixteenth-century editions, *De copia* was accompanied by the commentary of Weltkirchius which in general emphasises the links between Erasmus's work and the rest of the humanist educational programme. Weltkirchius labels and defines tropes and figures which Erasmus assumes his reader knows. In his comment on copia through variety of arrangement (1.30) he describes seventeen figures of words.[77] Together with his later list of figures of thought,[78] this means that the commentary to *De copia* itself contains a list of figures and tropes. Weltkirchius provides references to dialectic books and examples for the eighth and tenth methods, elaboration of circumstances and invention of propositions.[79] I shall discuss the impact of *De copia* below, under amplification.

ELEVEN RHETORICAL SKILLS

The techniques of grammar school training in Latin language, literature and composition overlap and reinforce each other. In this section I shall draw together what pupils learned about reading and composition from the different aspects of their training. In reconstructing in this way I may sometimes draw over-general conclusions from partial or uncertain evidence. I hope that the texts analysed later in the book may give some support to these hypotheses. I shall suggest that pupils accumulated a range of techniques, skills, tools of analysis and forms of knowledge which can be analysed into eleven categories. For the sake of brevity I shall call them skills.

1. Moral sentences

Many of the teaching strategies of the grammar school encouraged pupils to learn and use moral sentences. They were the first reading matter in

---

[75] Erasmus, *De copia* (1998), pp. 258–64 (trans. *Collected Works*, XXIV, pp. 635–41).

[76] Ibid., pp. 215–58 (trans. *Collected Works*, XXIV, pp. 589–635).

[77] Erasmus, *De copia*, with commentary of Weltkirchius (London, 1569) STC 10472, sigs. E4r–6v.

[78] Ibid., sigs. E7v–8v.

[79] Ibid., sigs. N4v–7v, P2r–3v, Q2v–5v. Weltkirchius discusses the topics of invention and refers to the accounts of them by Quintilian and Agricola, sigs. Q6v–7r.

the lower classes of the grammar school, learned by heart as examples of Latin syntax and as guides to conduct. Many of these sentences were taken from pagan authors, but Christian texts, such as the Creed, the Lord's prayer and the ten commandments were used in the same way.

Culmann's *Sententiae pueriles* and the collection of short texts which go under the heading of 'Cato' present pithy sentences giving advice on moral conduct. *Sententiae pueriles* is organised by length of phrase and alphabetically, beginning with a group of two-word phrases:

> Help your friends.
> Keep away from the property of others.
> Keep a secret.
> Be friendly.
> Know yourself.
> Cultivate your relatives.[80]

Phrases of three, four and more than four words are listed, followed by religious phrases suitable for study on holy days.[81] 'Cato' in its popular renaissance edition commented on by Erasmus consists of a set of maxims, giving advice on prudent conduct, mainly from a worldly, pagan point of view, and often on the basis of stoic inspiration.

> Continual practice can achieve all things.
> In adversity we recognise who our friends are.
> Friendship should come before everything.
> Familiarity makes hardship easier to bear.
> A liar needs to have a good memory.
> Do not laugh at anyone.
> All good things agree with peace.
> Nothing is sweeter than liberty.
> Ingratitude is the chief of all vices.
> Nothing is worse than poverty.
> Whoever gives quickly to the person in need, gives twice over.[82]

There is a considerable amount of repetition among the sayings,[83] which must have helped impress them on pupils' minds, as well as some

---

[80] 'Amicis opitulare. Alienis abstine. Arcanum cela. Affabilis esto. Cognosce teipsum. Cognatos cole.' Culmann, *Sententiae pueriles*, sig. A2r.

[81] Ibid., sigs. A3r, A6r, B2r, B8v.

[82] Ibid.: 'Assidua exercitatio omnia potest. Amicos inter adversa cognoscimus. Amicitia omnibus rebus anteponenda. (A6r) Consuetudo omnia dura lenit. (A6v) Mendacem memorem esse oportet. (A8r) Neminem irriseris. (A3v) Omnia bona pace constant. (A8v) Libertate nihil dulcius. (A4v) Ingratitudo vitiorum omnium caput. (A7v) Nihil est tam grave quam paupertas (B5v)'; 'Inopi beneficium bis dat, qui dat celeriter.' *Cato*, D5r.

[83] E.g. 'Sua quemque studia delectant. Suo quisque studio delectatur. Trahit sua quemque voluptas.' Culmann, *Sententiae pueriles*, sig. B1v.

inconsistency.[84] According to Brinsley pupils were drilled on these moral sentences both to test their ability to parse the sentences and to reinforce their understanding of the moral sentiments.[85] This fits in with the humanist aim of teaching virtue and good Latin together.

Since the sententiae are pithy moral axioms largely taken from Greek and Latin authors they also serve as a model for the reading of the authors. According to the pedagogical theorists the classical authors ought to be read for the sake of their wise teaching and elegant expression. These qualities are exemplified by the sententiae which can be extracted from their writings, recorded in a commonplace book (of which more later) and reused in an appropriate situation. The sentences are models for the kind of material the pupil might note down from his reading for reuse in his own compositions.

As well as being expected to extract moral sentences from their reading, pupils in higher classes were provided with reference books like Erasmus's *Adagia*, which collects Latin proverbs and discusses their meaning. The *Adagia* indicates four main uses of the study of proverbs: as philosophy, encapsulating the wisdom of the past in a memorable form; for their value in persuading an audience; for decoration, adding authority, beauty and grace to compositions; and because they assist in understanding the writings of the best authors.[86] Pupils were expected to incorporate quotations and proverbs in their letters and themes.[87] We shall see that Elizabethan speeches are often embellished with pithy sayings from classical literature or from reference books. One of the components of the teaching notebook of the Elizabethan schoolmaster John Conybeare was an alphabetical collection of proverbs, presumably intended for his pupils to read or learn.[88]

Moral sentences also played a role in the composition exercises set out in the *Progymnasmata*, under fable and commonplace, but especially in the chreia.[89] The chreia is defined as 'a brief recollection of something that

[84] E.g. ibid.: 'Audentes fortuna iuvat. Belli exitus incertus. Belli fortuna anceps (A3r), Fortes fortuna adiuvat (A4r), Experientia est providentiae magistra (A7r), Expertus pericula facile expavescit (A7v).'
[85] Brinsley, *Ludus*, pp. 125–30, 142–3.
[86] Erasmus, *Adagia*, in *Opera omnia*, 10 vols. (Leiden, 1703), II, cols. 6B–9A, (trans. M. Mann Phillips, *Collected Works*, XXXI (Toronto, 1982), pp. 14–18).
[87] Brinsley, *Ludus*, pp. 175–6, 182–4.
[88] Conybeare, *Letters and Exercises*, pp. 23–55; W. J. Ong, 'Commonplace Rhapsody: Ravisius Textor, Zwinger and Shakespeare', in R. R. Bolgar (ed.), *Classical Influences on European Culture AD 1500–1700* (Cambridge, 1976), pp. 91–126.
[89] Aphthonius, *Progymnasmata*, sigs. A1 r–v, M4v–6v, N1 r.

someone did or said aptly'.[90] It is intended as an example of clever speech or honourable action which can be held up as an example on its own or incorporated into a larger speech. The chreia consists of a statement ('Isocrates said that the root of learning is bitter but the fruits are sweet')[91] and eight sections: praise of the person speaking or acting, explanation of what was said or done, argument from the cause, contrary, comparison, example, opinion of the ancients and epilogue.[92] Edward VI's notebooks show that he composed chreias and also orations setting out from quotations.[93] Moral maxims are among the central features of humanist education and are everywhere in renaissance discourse.[94]

2. Moral stories

The connection between moral teaching and narrative was impressed on schoolboys by their early study of Aesop's *Fables*, by their training in the composition of fables and by the moral commentary which accompanied their reading of Ovid (and sometimes of Virgil). Several of the grammar school statutes specify Aesop's *Fables* as the first Latin narrative to be read by the pupils.[95] When Brinsley explains that he expects to catechise his pupils on the meaning and use of their reading, he takes Aesop as his example.[96] Among the more advanced reading, commentators treated Ovid's *Metamorphoses* as a collection of moral fables, while episodes from the *Aeneid* were allegorised to produce moral instruction. Nicholas Grimalde's introduction to his translation of *De officiis*, first printed in 1556, proclaims the work's attraction for Elizabethans, valuing Cicero's wise moral and political teaching, the range and effectiveness of the stories, the elegant expression and the large quantity of teaching in such a short book.[97] Pupils were expected to admire *De officiis*, not merely as a source of ethical teaching but also for the way it employed moral exempla.

---

[90] 'Chreia est commemoratio brevis, alicuius personae factum, vel dictum apte referens.' Ibid., sig. C8r.

[91] 'Isocrates doctrinae radicem amaram esse dicebat, fructus vero dulces.' Ibid., sig. C8v.

[92] Ibid., sig. C8r.

[93] Nichols, *Edward*, I, pp. 93–4, 117–24. Both the structure of the oration and Edward's use of the word chreia (p. 119) confirm that this oration is a chreia. Baldwin, *Shakspere's Small Latine*, I, pp. 222, 233. Some of Edward's other orations draw on the chreia, using maxims from Cato and the *Sententiae pueriles*. E.g. British Library MS Add. 4724, fols. 24r–25v.

[94] Crane, *Framing Authority*, pp. 3–4, 7–8, 59–65.

[95] For example, Baldwin, *Shakspere's Small Latine*, I, pp. 119, 146, 149, 154, 165, 297, 305.

[96] Brinsley, *Ludus*, p. 145.

[97] Cicero, *Thre Bokes of Duties*, translated by Nicholas Grimalde (1556), ed. Gerald O'Gorman (Washington, 1990), p. 45.

Fable was the first of the composition exercises outlined in Aphthonius's *Progymnasmata*, linking a narrative with a moral sentence.[98] Lorichius's commentary explains that fables are effective in moving and pleasing an audience. He cites Erasmus's view that fables please because of their witty portrayal of customary behaviour and persuade because they put the truth plainly before people's eyes.[99] Aphthonius and Lorichius take materials for other exercises from mythology. Ethopoeia is illustrated with the lament of Niobe and Libanius's declamation for Medea on the point of killing her children.[100] *De copia* includes fables among the items one might use to embellish a proposition and describes ways to prepare for their introduction and to elaborate both narrative and moral.[101] Weltkirchius adds eight ways of presenting fables (from Aesopic dialogues through poetic narrative and drama to allegory and literary exegesis).[102] Both imaginative works and treatises were expected to provide their readers with moral stories suitable for reuse in their own compositions. Sidney's *Apology for Poetry* regards stories as the most effective form of moral teaching, and therefore as the principal justification for poetry.[103]

3. Narratives

Like moral sentences and stories, narrative was taught both through reading and through composition. Arguments prefaced to individual books or to a whole work always emphasise the narrative structure.[104] Melanchthon praised *De officiis* for the usefulness of the narratives it incorporates.[105] Narratio, defined as a setting out of a deed done,[106] is the second of Aphthonius's *Progymnasmata*. It consists of six elements: the person acting, the thing done, the time about which, the place in which, the method by which, and the reason why. Narrative has four virtues: clarity, brevity, plausibility and propriety in the choice of words.[107]

---

[98] Aphthonius, *Progymnasmata*, sigs. A1r–B8r.
[99] Ibid., sig. A2r–v, citing Erasmus, *De copia* (1988), p. 254.
[100] Ibid., sigs. Z1v–2r, Aa6r–7v.   [101] Erasmus, *De copia* (1988), pp. 254–6.
[102] Erasmus, *De copia* (1569), sigs. T1r–3r.   [103] Sidney, *Apology for Poetry*, pp. 105–13.
[104] See the summaries usually prefaced to each book of Virgil's *Aeneid* in *Opera* (London, 1572, 1580) STC 24788–89 and especially William Canter's synopsis printed with the prefatory material to Ovid, *Metamorphoses* (London: Vautrollier, 1582) STC 18951.5. Sabinus's commentary, printed in the 1584 Cambridge edition, interrupts the text after each fable to summarise the narrative and explain its significance.
[105] 'Plurimum etiam ad dicendum conducunt narratiunculae, quae sunt in hoc opere et multae et variae.' Melanchthon, *Opera omnia*, xvi, col. 631.
[106] Aphthonius, *Progymnasmata*, sig. B8v.   [107] Ibid., sig. B8v.

Lorichius's commentary refers to the use of narrative within the classical four-part oration to set out the circumstances of a case, and adds to Aphthonius's example of Venus and Adonis Ovid's version of the story of Pyramus and Thisbe, and Cicero's narrative of Clodius's decision to assassinate Milo.[108] Erasmus's *De copia* provides instructions for collecting, using and embellishing exemplary stories.[109]

Brinsley's nine questions in his instructions for reading elucidate the narrative context of the sentence being construed.[110] His questions are an elaboration of the topics of narrative listed by Lorichius in his commentary on Aphthonius.

> Narrative is concerned with circumstances which are listed in this little verse: who, what, where, with what help, why, how, when. It can be made more copious if you amplify and dwell on the circumstances and carefully describe the time, the place, the manner, the instrument and lastly the reason for which something was done.[111]

Narrative is treated as a separate composition, as a component in a larger work and as an approach to the analysis of a text.

4. *History*

Schoolboys encountered ancient history as the subject of set texts in Latin literature, as explanatory material in commentaries on poems, as examples of deeds and sayings to be learned and reused, and as occasions for composing letters and declamations. The majority of the grammar school statutes list either Sallust or Caesar or both among the texts to be studied.[112]

Sallust is generally held up as an example of history writing and praised as a stylist, for his clarity, brevity and irony. His approach to history is both ethical and rhetorical. Ethical in that he sees Catiline's rebellion as a consequence of a corrupt individual and the general decay of Roman

---

[108] Ibid., sigs. C1 r–8r. Cicero, *Pro Milone*, 9.24–10.29.
[109] Erasmus, *De copia* (1988), pp. 232–46 (trans. *Collected Works*, xxiv, pp. 606–23).
[110] Brinsley, *Ludus*, p. 123.
[111] 'Narratio consumitur circumstantiis, quae hoc versiculo comprehenduntur: Quis, quid, ubi, quibus auxiliis, cur, quomodo, quando. Fit enim copiosa si circumstantiis amplifices atque dilates, et quo tempore, quoque loco, quomodo, quo instrumento, denique causa factum aliquid sit, diligenter persequaris.' Aphthonius, *Progymnasmata*, sig. C2r.
[112] Baldwin, *Shakspere's Small Latine*, ii, p. 564. Of 29 curricula, Sallust is mentioned 23 times, Caesar 17, of these both are together 14 times. Baldwin (ii, pp. 568, 572) finds very little evidence of Shakespeare's use of Sallust and Caesar; though he evidently made great use of Plutarch, and the English chroniclers, and some use of Livy.

morality; rhetorical because he punctuates and motivates his history with character sketches, moral commonplaces and orations. Sallust provides a storehouse of historical episodes and moral observations very well adapted for pupils to reuse in their own compositions. Like Sallust, Caesar decorates his narrative with speeches. In contrast to Sallust's ethical approach, he emphasises practical policy, especially the value of swift decision-making and resolute action.

Brinsley preferred compilations of the deeds and sayings of the Roman emperors over classical historical texts.[113] At Winchester, Christopher Johnson provided his pupils with summaries of the careers of famous Romans.[114] This suggests that the main purpose of historical reading may have been the provision of quotations and examples for incorporation into pupils' independent compositions.

History provided occasions and materials for pupils' letters, themes and declamations. Many of the declamations in Silvayn's *Orator* present speeches for and against characters from Livy and other Roman historians.[115] The surviving school essays of Edward VI use historical examples to support arguments.[116]

5. *Structures for compositions*

Both in their reading of classical texts and in composition exercises, Elizabethan pupils were confronted with a range of structures of writing. From letter-writing manuals and from the *Progymnasmata* they learned to write texts to different kinds of plan. Commentaries set out the plans of their Latin set texts. The introduction to Hegendorff's commentary on Cicero's *Ad familiares*, printed in Thomas Marsh's London edition of 1574, explains how he has exhibited the structure of each letter, within a range of available genres.

I have written notes on all of Cicero's letters, in which first of all I carefully show the genre of each letter to the best of my ability. Then I clearly teach what matters the *exordium* begins from, where the proposition and narration are, where the confirmation is placed and which arguments support it, where there is a digression from the main topic and what the conclusion of the letter is based on. From all these the whole structure of the letter can easily be noted by young people and many examples provided for their imitation.[117]

---

[113] Brinsley, *Ludus*, p. 176.   [114] Baldwin, *Shakspere's Small Latine*, 1, p. 323.
[115] A. Silvayn, *The Orator* (London, 1596) STC 4182, sigs. B1 r–4v, C1 v–5r, D1 v–5r, F1 r–4r.
[116] E.g. British Library MS Add. 4724, fol. 49r.
[117] 'Ego horis succisivis in omnes Ciceronis epistolas scholia quaedam conscripsi, in quibus primo omnium speciem epistolae cuiuslibet pro mea virili diligenter ostendo. Deinde, quibus ex rebus

Erasmus's *De conscribendis epistolis* provides instructions for a large number of different types of letter. Aphthonius's *Progymnasmata* outlines fourteen forms, which are largely fixed but which are capable of variation.[118] Lorichius's commentary and the examples from classical literature which he provides show that such forms as narration, description and commonplace are frequently incorporated into larger works. The favoured English exercise of the theme is treated in this period as a fixed structure.

To articulate the structure of their object text is one of the main aims of renaissance commentary. In the preface to his commentary on Terence, Melanchthon explains the importance of the structure of comedy.[119] The marginal notes to *Andria* in Marsh's 1583 edition of Terence, which appear to be based on Melanchthon's annotations,[120] pick out the rhetorical structure of Simo's opening speech.

> In the exordium he obtains goodwill from his merits.
> The proposition of his plan
> A narration which explains his son's love-life and his plan about the sham wedding. The narration is amplified on every occasion.[121]

These notes use the rhetorical terms for the sections of the formal oration, which would otherwise have been taught through letter-writing. It is likely that the terminology of rhetorical analysis was taught and reinforced more through commentary on set texts than by the direct study of rhetoric manuals.

6. Rhetorical topics

From the letter-writing manuals and the *Progymnasmata* pupils also learned the rudiments of some types of rhetorical invention. Erasmus's *De conscribendis epistolis* suggested a range of elements to be included in

---

exordium epistolae profluat, ubi propositio, ubi narratio sit, ubi confirmatio consistat, quibus argumentis constet, ubi aliquando a themate digressio fiat, quae sit epilogi ratio, candidem doceo. Ex quibus omnibus facile et tota epistolae dispositio iuventuti innotescere potuit et illi exempla ad imitandum plurima suppeditabuntur.' Cicero, *Ad familiares* (1574), sig. A3r.

[118] See pp. 27–8 above.

[119] Melanchthon's commentary on *Andria* (1528), in *Opera omnia*, XIX, col. 697 (trans. in Baldwin, *Shakespere's Five Act Structure*, pp. 176–7).

[120] Baldwin, *Shakespere's Five Act Structure*, pp. 337–9. Only four English editions of Terence are recorded between 1575 and 1600, of these probably two (I have seen STC 23886; 23885.7 should have the same format) have the commentary; the other two (STC 23887, 23888) are plain texts without notes.

[121] 'Exordii benevolentia a meritis captatur ... Propositio consilii. Narratio quae exponit amores gnati et consilium suum de nuptiis. Est autem amplificata narratio occasionibus omnibus.' Terence, *Comoediae*, sig. C1v (margin).

each type of letter depending on the subject of the letter, its aim and the writer's perception of the addressee. Letters of encouragement are concerned with emotional effect and may employ praise, hope and fear, love and hatred. Letters of persuasion draw on the topics of honour and advantage.[122]

Aphthonius's *Progymnasmata* give students practice in using the topics required for praise and deliberation. Under laudatio, pupils are presented with possible ingredients of praise of a person, university or place, that is to say with the special topics of epideictic rhetoric.[123] Topics associated with deliberative oratory, the legitimate, the just, the useful, the possible occur as elements of the commonplace, the thesis and the proposal for a law.[124]

Cicero provides a sustained discussion of the two key topics of deliberative oratory, the honourable and the expedient, in *De officiis*, one of the most commonly used grammar school textbooks. In *De officiis*, *honestum* (usually translated into English as 'the honourable') comprises the four cardinal virtues: wisdom, justice, courage and temperance.[125] Cicero regards justice as the most important of these virtues.[126] He considers a range of different practical applications of justice and discusses the difficulty of negotiating a just outcome among competing claims.[127] In his earlier work *De inventione* Cicero had allowed, in addition to these four virtues, a second group of honourable qualities in which honour is mixed with advantage: glory, rank, greatness and friendship.[128] When English writers debate the issue of honour, their grammar school education may lead them to understand the word in the strict Ciceronian sense (*honestum*) associated with moral virtue or in the more familiar related sense of worldly prestige and influence. In any case the connection between honour and truthful speech makes it difficult to treat honour as entirely separate from virtue.

None of the textbooks in common use discussed what the Romans considered the more important elements of rhetorical invention: the theory of status, the general topics, and the special topics of judicial rhetoric.

---

[122] Erasmus, *De conscribendis epistolis*, pp. 315–16, 324–29, 365–70 (trans. *Collected Works*, xxv, pp. 73–4, 79–82, 108–10).
[123] Aphthonius, *Progymnasmata*, sigs. O7r–8v, Q7r–8r, R5r–7v, T1v–8v. These also appear under vituperation and description, sigs. V4r, Dd8r.
[124] Ibid., sigs. M5r, Cc7r, Ee4v.   [125] Cicero, *De officiis*, 1.5.15–17.   [126] Ibid., 1.43.152–45.160.
[127] Ibid., 1.7.20–18.60.   [128] Cicero, *De inventione*, 11.55.166–8.

7. Thinking about an audience

Although consideration of the audience is the hallmark of a rhetorical approach to writing, Latin rhetoric textbooks in fact say relatively
little about audiences. In the grammar school syllabus the audience of a
piece of writing is considered in three places: in the letter-writing manual, in the study of classical texts and in the *Progymnasmata*. Erasmus's
De conscribendis epistolis urges a careful consideration of the relation between writer, subject-matter and recipient. The chapter on how to begin
a letter combines advice about introductions with guidance on the process of writing.

> I shall give this one preliminary piece of general advice to young students, that
> when they are going to write a letter they should not at once have recourse to
> rules nor take refuge in books from which they may borrow elegant little words
> and sententious expressions. Rather, they should first consider very carefully the
> topics on which they have decided to write, then be well acquainted with the
> nature, character and moods of the person to whom the letter is being written
> and their own standing with him in favour, influence or services rendered. From
> the careful examination of all these things they should derive, so to speak, the
> living model of the letter. After that has been determined I shall allow them
> to search out passages in the authors from which they can borrow a plentiful
> supply of the best words and sentiments.[129]

Having emphasised the importance of thinking about the person addressed, Erasmus makes detailed suggestions for ways in which one might
seek to make a favourable impression on a remote acquaintance, attempt
to renew a lapsed friendship or prepare to make an awkward request.[130]
Erasmus's advice on obtaining goodwill is based on sections on exordia
from rhetoric manuals,[131] but it is always carefully adapted both to the
genre of the letter and to the social situation of the people involved.
His reflections on his own experience of reassuring friends or winning

---

[129] 'Sed illud unum prius in genere studiosis adolescentibus praecipiemus, ut epistolam scripturi,
non statim praecepta respiciant; aut ad libros, unde voculas, sententiolasve aliquot mutuentur,
confugiant, sed prius res, de quibus scribere constituerint, solertissima cogitatione dispiciant;
tum eius ad quem scribitur, naturam, mores, affectusque omnes perspectos habeant: quantum
etiam ipsi apud eum vel gratia, vel autoritate, vel meritis denique valeant. Eque his omnibus
diligenter pensiculatis, epistolae tanquam vivum exemplar ducant. Quo constituto, tum demum
nihil equidem morabor, quo minus locos aliquot ex autoribus petant, unde tum verborum
optimorum, tum sententiarum copiosam supellictilem possint mutuari.' Erasmus, *De conscribendis
epistolis*, p. 316 (trans. *Collected Works*, xxv, p. 74).
[130] Ibid., pp. 317–23 (trans. *Collected Works*, xxv, pp. 74–8).
[131] *Ad Herennium*, 1.3.5–7.11; Cicero, *De inventione*, 1.15.20–18.26; Quintilian, *Institutio oratoria*, iv.1.

over the uncommitted inform the ideas and phrases he suggests. He is teaching prudence as well as composition.

In reading Latin texts, according to Brinsley, pupils must always bear in mind the person speaking, the subject-matter, the person being addressed and the occasion or purpose of the speech.[132] The question of the relationship between speaker and audience is addressed in another way by the issue of self-presentation, which comes to the fore in the exercise of ethopoeia in Aphthonius's *Progymnasmata*.[133] Ethopoeia is a speech which expresses the feelings and behaviour of a historical person or an imaginary character. Aphthonius provides the example of Niobe lamenting the deaths of her children. Lorichius explains that the exercise is useful in adapting one's expression and material to different emotional states. The calm and prudent man speaks in a different way from someone who is frightened or angry.[134] Self-presentation also becomes a subject for investigation in the exercise of writing a letter appropriate to a named personage from one of the school texts.[135]

8. Amplification

Amplification uses rhetorical techniques to make something seem more important in order to elicit a stronger response from an audience.[136] Amplification was taught primarily through the study of *De copia*, reinforced by teachers' comments on ornaments of style, proverbs, comparisons and the reasons authors had used them in a particular passage. In *De copia*, amplification is the ninth method of generating copia of things. The specific techniques of amplification Erasmus mentions in *De copia* (incremental increase, augmentation through circumstances, comparison, reasoning, pretending not to be surprised, and the piling up of words and phrases with the same meaning) are mostly taken from Quintilian's account of rhetorical amplification in *Institutio oratoria*, VIII.4.[137] Amplification is sometimes achieved by adding synonyms and using many figures of rhetoric together.

In a broader sense all the techniques described in *De copia* serve to raise the level of the style and to make what is described appear livelier and more important. The opening words of the treatise describe the

---

[132] Brinsley, *Ludus*, pp. 123–4.   [133] Aphthonius, *Progymnasmata*, sigs. Y8v–Aa7v.
[134] Ibid., sig. Z5r.
[135] Erasmus, *De conscribendis epistolis*, pp. 231–5 (trans. *Collected Works*, XXV, pp. 24–6).
[136] Quintilian, *Institutio oratoria*, VIII.4; Skinner, *Reason and Rhetoric*, pp. 133–53.
[137] Erasmus, *De copia* (1988), pp. 218–20 (trans. *Collected Works*, XXIV, pp. 592–5).

magnificence and impressiveness of language embellished with copia of words and things.[138] In *De conscribendis epistolis* Erasmus provides a short account of amplification, emphasising the use of comparisons, vivid descriptions and examples, as in *De copia*.[139] Reference books, such as Erasmus's *Parabolae* were used to provide pupils with comparisons and examples suitable for amplification. Teaching and awareness of amplification was reinforced by the marginal notes to classical texts which drew attention to passages involving amplification and pathos.

9. Commonplaces

Commonplaces are pre-prepared passages in an elevated style on particular topics (such as peace, justice or mercy) which Cicero recommends that the orator should keep ready for insertion when the argument or the emotional burden of a speech requires it.[140] Aphthonius's *Progymnasmata* provide instructions for the composition of model commonplaces. Aphthonius defines the commonplace as an oration arguing about the good or bad qualities in something. In this sense it appears to derive from part of the conclusion of the classical oration, in which the prosecuting orator argued that the offence was so serious that no leniency could be shown. Lorichius explains that the aim of the commonplace is to amplify or increase virtue, where good people are concerned, or evil characteristics in the bad. Through them the speaker hopes to inspire the emotions of pity or outrage in the audience.[141] The commonplace consists of a preface (expressing the seriousness of the crime or the need for mercy, as appropriate), argument from contraries, exposition of the case, comparison, argument from a moral maxim, digression, moving or removing pity, arguments from the lawful, the just, the useful and the possible, and a conclusion. Although the commonplace is in principle reversible, all the examples given in the renaissance version of Aphthonius denounce crimes.[142] The commonplace, in this sense, serves as an example of logically generated arguments being piled together to create an emotional effect.[143] Commonplaces resemble extended moral sentences. Among

---

[138] 'Ut non est aliud vel admirabilius vel magnificentius quam oratio, divite quadam sententiarum verborumque copia aurei fluminis instar exuberans . . .' Erasmus, *De copia* (1988), p. 26.

[139] Erasmus, *De conscribendis epistolis*, pp. 343–47 (trans. *Collected Works*, xxv, pp. 90–3).

[140] Cicero, *De inventione*, II.15.48

[141] Aphthonius, *Progymnasmata*, sig. M8v; Skinner, *Reason and Rhetoric*, pp. 113–19.

[142] Aphthonius, *Progymnasmata*, sigs. M4v–O6r.

[143] For a highly suggestive elaboration of the connections between the different meanings of *locus communis*, see Francis Goyet, *Le sublime du 'lieu commun'* (Paris, 1996).

Cicero's philosophical works, *De officiis* and *De amicitia* are particularly rich in descriptions of vices and virtues which could be excerpted as commonplaces and reused.

10. Note-taking and commonplace books

In order to assist them in reusing their reading in classical texts and in preparing commonplaces, pupils were instructed in the technique of the commonplace book. In its simplest form this involved maintaining two notebooks while reading classical texts. The first notebook was used to record new words, difficult words and striking or unusual expressions which the student wished to learn, both for reuse and to assist in reading. The second notebook, the commonplace book proper, was an organised system for retrieving the material (which could include phrases but also longer passages) of one's reading. Each page of the notebook would be headed by the name of a subject, such as Friendship, Justice, Mercy.[144] As the pupil read, he would copy especially striking sentences or paragraphs related to this topic into the commonplace book. When he came to write a letter or a theme, the pupil would have access to a personal dictionary of quotations providing him with material from which to select starting points for arguments or illustrative quotations.

The technique of the commonplace book encourages a particular habit of reading, not only attending to the author's argument but also continually asking oneself whether this phrase or that section is worth copying out, and if so, considering under which heading it should go. This habit of referring passages of text to headings also encourages the reader to compare the views on a particular subject expressed in different sections or by different speakers within the same text. Thus although the general tendency of the commonplace method is to fragment a text into short reusable segments, it can also encourage readers to explore connections and contrasts of ideas within a text, to discover preoccupations and connections beyond the level of the linear plot. Although it is relatively rare to find manuscripts which comprehensively carry out the instructions for compiling a complete commonplace book, many commonplace books were begun and the habits of fragmenting and collecting which they encourage seem to have been widespread in sixteenth-century

[144] Rudolph Agricola, *De formando studio* in *Lucubrationes* (Cologne, 1539, repr. Nieuwkoop, 1967), pp. 198–200; Erasmus, *De copia* (1988), pp. 258–63 (trans. *Collected Works*, xxiv, pp. 635–41); Melanchthon, *De locis communibus ratio*, *Opera omnia*, xx, cols. 695–8. Moss, *Printed Commonplace-Books*, esp. pp. 107–13, 119–26.

reading. Edward VI's notebooks in the British Library and the Bodleian show him collecting phrases from his reading in *De officiis*, *Tusculan Disputations* and *In Catilinam* for possible use in his own compositions.[145]

Attendance at sermons provides one further example of the way in which students were expected to analyse and digest text (in this case spoken text) in their notebooks or mentally. The pupils at Winchester in the 1570s were expected to attend church on Sunday, to take note of the Bible-readings and sermons 'and repeat them when they come home, and the next day be opposed of them in school by the Master or Usher'.[146] Brinsley recommends that while the younger pupils should simply record moral maxims from the sermon, more advanced pupils would be expected to analyse the division and exposition of the scriptural text, showing how the teaching, proofs and examples fitted together.[147] The requirement to give an account of the whole argument encourages an additional emphasis on structure in this form of note-taking.

11. Figures of rhetoric

A few grammar school syllabi declare the aim of studying a rhetoric textbook in the highest form. Slightly more include a handbook of figures and tropes in the list of texts. Conybeare's notebook contains a fourteen-page summary of the tropes and figures extracted from Susenbrotus's *Epitome troporum ac schematum*.[148] T. W. Baldwin assumed that Susenbrotus's work was widely known in sixteenth-century England but L. D. Green has argued that the number of continental editions produced was insufficiently large to justify these claims.[149] Nevertheless it seems probable that pupils in the higher forms of Elizabethan grammar schools had a good knowledge of the tropes and figures, though perhaps a different kind of knowledge than the one assumed by Baldwin. A few of the figures were discussed in Lily's *Brevissima institutio*, which was extensively printed and owned.[150] Some of the most important tropes (including metaphor, metonymy, and synecdoche) are discussed in the first book of Erasmus's *De copia*.[151] In his commentary which almost invariably accompanied the

---

[145] British Library MS Arundel 510, MS Add. 4724; Bodleian Library MS Autogr.e.2; MS Bodl. 899. Baldwin, *Shakspere's Small Latine*, I, pp. 227–33, 238, 251.

[146] Baldwin, *Shakspere's Small Latine*, I, p. 346.   [147] Brinsley, *Ludus*, p. 255.

[148] Conybeare, *Letters and Exercises*, p. 97.

[149] Green, '*Grammatica movet*', p. 77; Baldwin, *Shakspere's Small Latine*, I, pp. 101, 356, 363, 382, 405 etc.; II, pp. 138–76.

[150] Green argues that pupils learned about the other figures of rhetoric through studying Lily ('*Grammatica movet*', pp. 86–91, 102–4, 114–15).

[151] Erasmus, *De copia* (1988), pp. 62–6, 68–72 (trans. *Collected Works*, XXIV, pp. 333–6, 339–41).

numerous sixteenth-century editions of *De copia*, Weltkirchius defines seventeen figures of diction (including repetitio, polysyntedon, comma and colon and lists seven figures of thought (including interrogatio, dubitatio and licentia).[152] Commentaries on school texts often label particular figures of rhetoric and discuss the use to which they are put. Taking these means of transmission together, it seems reasonable to conclude that pupils in the higher classes would have had extensive knowledge of the figures of rhetoric.

Knowing the tropes and figures helped pupils to understand their authors' use of the expressive resources of Latin and enabled them to analyse and imitate their reading. In addition to stylistic enrichment, the figures, which will be discussed in more detail in chapter three, promoted habits of thinking about parallelism, ordering and completeness.[153]

CONCLUSION

In this chapter I have shown that Elizabethan grammar schools encouraged a range of rhetorical skills. Because the schools did not present these skills in a systematic hierarchy, because there are conflicts and gaps, instructors and pupils were able to treat them with different emphases and to choose among them to construct personal styles. Before moving on to consider post grammar school training and different authors' uses of these skills, I shall comment briefly on some limitations of this training, on its attitude to the content of texts and on the connection it promotes between rhetoric and ethics.

Taken together, the skills acquired at grammar school do not constitute the full course in classical rhetoric which has sometimes been assumed by scholars. There are several features of the standard course in classical rhetoric which were either omitted or taught in adapted form. These omissions and adaptations are most apparent in the area of invention. Contrary to Baldwin's assumption that Cicero's *Topica* was implicitly present in several syllabi,[154] there was no general treatment of invention, little discussion of the three kinds of case and consequently no account of the theory of status. Such teaching as there was of the three kinds and the four parts of the oration was delivered in the context of the letter-writing manual. Consideration of the forms of argument was understandably

---

[152] Erasmus, *De copia* (1569), sigs. E4r–6v, 7v–8v.
[153] Jeanne Fahnestock, *Rhetorical Figures in Science* (New York, 1999) especially chapter one.
[154] Baldwin, *Shakspere's Small Latine*, I, pp. 101, 158, 289–90, 371; II, pp. 24–5, 108–28.

deferred to the university course on dialectic. Little attention was paid to the peroration and the doctrine of the three types of style.

Grammar school training was prone to excessive reliance on deadening drills but this was to some extent balanced by the emphasis on playing with different linguistic forms, on acting out dialogues and on writing from an assumed fictional or historical situation. The 'moral sentences' approach encouraged readers to fragment their texts, but this was compensated for by teachers' and commentators' emphasis on structure, narrative and character.

Both as part of moral training and in order to provide material for composition, teachers encouraged their pupils to study the content as well as the linguistic form of their reading matter. Boys were drilled on the moral lessons to be derived from the phrases and stories they read and learned by heart. In their commentaries schoolmasters gave considerable emphasis to the structure and narrative order of the set texts. In studying a fable, whether by Aesop or Ovid, pupils were expected to know about the characters, the narrative sequence and the moral teaching concealed within the fictional shell. Phrases, stories and facts about antiquity were useful both as material for conversation and composition and as guides to conduct. All this contradicts Halpern's claim that grammar school education destroyed the content of the texts it taught in pursuit of style.[155]

The grammar school aimed to combine rhetorical and ethical training. Although a philosopher might see this as a union of contraries, in practice rhetoric and ethics have much in common. Thinking about the particular individual or audience addressed, which is central to rhetoric, takes one close to many issues of social relationships and consideration for others. Taking a wider social perspective, an understanding of a society's moral beliefs is an essential prerequisite of persuasion, since the speaker will often have to persuade an audience that particular actions are good or bad. At the same time the moral maxims and stories privileged in grammar school (on the authority of past generations) define what members of the next generation will regard as good. By learning the everyday ethics (and aesthetics) instilled by the grammar school the writer also learns how to appeal to an audience. The grammar school created the Elizabethan audience.

---

[155] R. Halpern, *The Poetics of Primitive Accumulation: English Renaissance Culture and the Genealogy of Capital* (Ithaca, 1991), pp. 24, 46–9.

2

Rhetoric and dialectic at Oxford and Cambridge

Sixteenth-century England's two universities were of crucial importance in national life. One reason for this was the relatively high age-participation rate. By the last decades of the sixteenth century about 700 pupils annually (or just over one per cent of the male cohort) entered Oxford.[1] They were drawn from the same social groups as those who attended grammar school: sons of prosperous husbandmen and yeomen, burgesses from the towns, country gentry, professional men and the lower ranks of the titled.[2] At Oxford and Cambridge the future élite of the country were educated and became acquainted. University graduates went on to become priests, country gentlemen, school teachers, academics, royal servants, doctors, lawyers and tradesmen, as McConica's study of the records of Corpus Christi College, Oxford (which may not have been representative) indicates.[3] The majority of the writers whose works are discussed in the later chapters of this book were members of the minority of the population who attended Oxford or Cambridge.

The Queen and her councillors took a personal interest in university affairs. Three times in her reign Elizabeth made a formal visitation of one of her universities. Each visitation lasted almost a week and necessitated the transfer of the machinery of government and the highest officers of state to Oxford or Cambridge.[4] Elizabeth and her courtiers took care

---

[1] McConica, *Collegiate University*, pp. 54–55, 723; L. Stone, 'The size and composition of the Oxford Student Body 1580–1909', in Stone (ed.), *The University in Society* (Princeton, 1974), pp. 3–110 (esp. 103); Rosemary O'Day, *Education and Society 1500–1800* (London, 1982), pp. 86–90. A reasonable guess, supported by McConica, would be that Cambridge was about two thirds the size of Oxford in the late sixteenth century. This would bring the age-participation rate to about 1.6 per cent.

[2] McConica, *Collegiate University*, p. 728. The additional expense of university education must have meant that a higher proportion came from rich families (although there were some means of assistance available to the relatively poorer). Matriculation records for the last two decades of the century suggest that the gentry accounted for almost half the entrants. Ibid., p. 722.

[3] Ibid., pp. 666–93.

[4] J. G. Nichols (ed.), *The Progresses of Queen Elizabeth*, 3 vols. (London, 1823), I, pp. 149–89, 206–47; III, pp. 144–67; C. Plummer (ed.), *Elizabethan Oxford* (Oxford, 1887); Penry Williams, 'State, Church

to be well-informed about what was going on in the universities.[5] This was a consequence of the prestige of learning. Humanist theorists and their admirers who founded schools required educated school-teachers. The proponents of the reformation argued for a learned priesthood. The universities alone were equipped to satisfy these demands. Cecil, Dudley and Parker often wrote letters complaining of abuses or directing the Vice-Chancellor or the head of a college about how a particular case should be treated. Special care was taken over the appointment of heads of colleges and, at the beginning of the reign, over the removal of fellows who would not support the Church settlement.[6]

This interference co-existed with a realisation that the universities required a certain freedom of enquiry, removed from the strict supervision of Elizabethan court and religious life. When Grindal and Chadderton complained to William Cecil, as Chancellor of the university about the content of Thomas Cartwright's lectures on Acts, he at first tried to treat the lectures as a matter of academic investigation. Later he was persuaded to take a more interventionist line and Cartwright was stripped of the Lady Margaret Chair of Divinity.[7] The doctrinal difference between Whitgift and Cartwright which emerged in this university dispute was later played out on the national stage, when Whitgift became Archbishop of Canterbury and Cartwright (still in personal correspondence with Cecil) was the most celebrated of the imprisoned puritans.

Recent studies of Oxford in the sixteenth and seventeenth century by James McConica and Mordechai Feingold have changed our view of the arts faculty and of the whole university.[8] They have shown that within official college teaching under the supervision of individual tutors students pursued a rich variety of innovative studies alongside the traditional requirements of the university statutes.[9] McConica shows that from their basis in the study of Latin literature, rhetoric and dialectic, late

---

and University 1558–1603', in McConica, *Collegiate University*, pp. 397–440 (esp. 397–400); Angelo M. Pellegrini, 'Renaissance and Medieval Antecedents of Debate', *Quarterly Journal of Speech* 28 (1942), 14–19.

[5] Williams, 'State, Church and University', pp. 400, 418.   [6] Ibid., pp. 401, 404–12, 423–8;

[7] A. F. Scott Pearson, *Thomas Cartwright and Elizabethan Puritanism 1535–1603* (Cambridge, 1925, repr. Gloucester MA, 1966), pp. 25–39.

[8] J. McConica, 'The Rise of the Undergraduate College', and 'Elizabethan Oxford: The Collegiate Society', in McConica, *Collegiate University*, pp. 1–68, 645–732, esp. 693–721; M. Feingold, *The Mathematicians' Apprenticeship: Science, Universities and Society in England 1560–1640* (Cambridge, 1984), Feingold, *Seventeenth-Century Oxford*, pp. 211–448. There is a discussion of medieval teaching methods in A. B. Cobban, *The Medieval English Universities: Oxford and Cambridge to c. 1500* (Aldershot, 1988), pp. 161–208.

[9] Although we await the 1546–1750 volume of the new *History of the University of Cambridge*, there is evidence to suggest that it will reach similar conclusions.

sixteenth-century Oxford arts students read widely in history, mathematics, physics, ethics, theology, modern languages and Greek.[10] Classical literature, rhetoric and dialectic remained at the centre of official college and university teaching. The pre-eminence of dialectic was reinforced by the obligation on all candidates for degrees to participate in disputations. The requirement of preaching for higher degrees in theology and of declamation in some colleges may have put a similar premium on the mastery of rhetoric.[11]

Typically pupils matriculated at one of the colleges of the university aged fifteen to sixteen after completing their grammar school studies.[12] By the end of the century around forty-four per cent of matriculants went on to take the Bachelor of Arts degree, in theory four years after matriculation. Many of the others attended university for two or three years as gentlemen commoners without ever intending to take a degree. Of those who graduated about twelve per cent went on to take higher degrees, almost all of them in theology.[13]

By the mid-sixteenth century colleges had established their own teaching in the main subjects of the arts faculty, following the requirements of the university statutes but adding lectures, disputations, declamations and even disciplines of their own. Every student entering a college was assigned to a tutor who directed his programme of study.[14] This system allowed for considerable flexibility (within the overarching pattern set out by the statutes) in what individuals studied, depending on their previous attainments, their objectives and the interests of their tutors. Lord Herbert of Cherbury, who took part in disputations at the beginning of his time in Oxford (from 1596) but thereafter devoted himself to languages, music and dancing, recommended that elder sons should taste dialectic and the philosophy of Plato and Aristotle but concentrate on modern languages, geography, politics and science. Sir Henry Wotton (New College, 1584–8) made use of his time at university to study Italian and medicine as well as taking the BA degree. The incomplete diary

[10] McConica, *Collegiate University*, pp. 695–710. That the course students followed was more general and more literary than the statutes provide may be confirmed by the booklists (see note 20 below). In eleven Oxford undergraduate booklists between 1551 and 1578 the most frequent texts are: Cicero, *De Officiis* (9), Cicero *Orations* (8), Erasmus, *De copia* (8), Virgil (6), Aristotle, *Organon* (5), Terence (5), Cicero, *Epistles* (4), Valerius Maximus (4), Agricola, *De inventione dialectica* (3), Horace (3) and Valla, presumably *Elegantiae* (3).
[11] Strickland Gibson (ed.), *Statuta antiqua universitatis oxoniensis* (Oxford, 1931), pp. 345, 381; 'Statuta Reginae Elizabethae' (1570), in *Documents Relating to the University and Colleges of Cambridge*, 3 vols. (London, 1852), I, p. 465; J. M. Fletcher, 'The Faculty of Arts', in McConica, *Collegiate University*, pp. 157–200 (esp. 193–4).
[12] McConica, *Collegiate University*, p. 685.   [13] Ibid., p. 156.   [14] Ibid., pp. 64–6.

of the Carnsew brothers (Christ Church, 1570s) shows them practising letter-writing, constructing syllogisms and studying Sturm, Sallust's *Jugurthine War, Rhetorica ad Herennium,* Foxe's sermons, Caesar's *Gallic War,* logic textbooks by Valerius, Caesarius and Melanchthon, Cicero's *De amicitia,* Aristotle's *Ethics,* Josephus's *Jewish History,* Agricola's *De inventione dialectica* and textbooks of mathematics and anatomy. Within this eclectic reading list one can identify the study of grammar, rhetoric, dialectic, moral philosophy and mathematics as the statutes require, broadened with scientific interests and a considerable amount of history.[15]

In this chapter I shall discuss the teaching of rhetoric and dialectic and the practice of disputation and declamation in Oxford and Cambridge in the late sixteenth century. Alongside the evidence of the statutes I shall consider lists of the books owned by members of the universities dying in residence, student notebooks and records of lecture courses and disputations. As in the previous chapter, I shall conclude by describing logical and rhetorical skills which students could be expected to have acquired.

RHETORIC

University statutes require the study of classical manuals of the whole of rhetoric. At Cambridge where the first of the four years stipulated for the BA was devoted to rhetoric,[16] the set texts were Quintilian, Hermogenes, or any other book of Cicero's speeches.[17] At Oxford the grammar course (lasting two terms out of sixteen for the BA) required Linacre's *Rudiments,* Virgil, Horace or Cicero's *Epistles.* In rhetoric, which was allowed four terms, the texts were Aristotle's *Rhetoric,* the rhetorical works or the orations of Cicero.[18] Sixteenth-century Oxford college statutes provide for lectures in humanity (usually involving Latin poetry, history and rhetoric), Greek and rhetoric.[19] The lists of books owned by members of the university who died in residence suggest a basic reading list in rhetoric at both universities which confirms what the statutes indicate. Cicero's

[15] PRO SP 46.15 fols. 212–20, McConica, *Collegiate University,* pp. 695–9.

[16] *Documents . . . Cambridge,* p. 459.

[17] 'Praelector rhetorices Quintilianum, Hermogenem aut aliquem alium librum oratoriarum Ciceronis. Quos omnes libros vulgari lingua pro captu et intelligentia auditorum explicabit interpretabiturque.' Ibid., p. 457. It is interesting that the lectures are said to include explanations in English even though the students are assumed not to need instruction in Latin, ibid., p. 492. These books are very similar to those specified in 1549.

[18] Gibson, *Statuta antiqua,* pp. 389–90.

[19] McConica, *Collegiate University,* pp. 21, 46, 56, 337–8, 342.

Orations and his rhetorical works, especially the pseudo-Ciceronian *Rhetorica ad Herennium* occur very frequently in the lists. Quintilian's *Institutio oratoria*, Cicero's *De oratore* and Aristotle's *Rhetoric* are less frequent but still found very often. There is a small but significant number of copies of Hermogenes.[20]

The teaching of rhetoric in the universities was closely connected to the study of classical literature, especially oratory. The statutes of both universities allow that rhetoric lectures may be given on Cicero's speeches. These orations are very common in the university booklists. College lecturers in humanity were often expected to lecture on rhetoric texts.[21] The booklists which contain rhetoric books almost always include a good deal of classical literature. Ralph Cholmondely's Oxford notebook collects quotations from Cicero's orations and philosophical works alongside notes on a lecture course on Cicero's *Partitiones oratoriae*.[22] The renaissance rhetoric manuals which are most commonly found in the university booklists, Erasmus's *Ecclesiastes*, Melanchthon and Talon,[23] emphasise rhetoric's role in training pupils to read classical and Christian literature.

Our only known complete text of an Elizabethan lecture course on rhetoric is preoccupied with the implications and problems of rhetoric. In his Oxford lectures on Aristotle's *Rhetoric* John Rainolds assumes that his audience has a complete knowledge of the syllabus of the rhetoric manual. He considers how much the underlying assumptions of rhetoric, as they are presented in the early chapters of Aristotle's *Rhetoric*, are consistent with a Christian outlook and useful in a modern context. Rainolds devotes a good deal of his commentary to attacking Aristotle's ethical assumptions. For Rainolds the *honestum* must always be upheld, especially

---

[20] Taking the Cambridge lists as a basis here, since the edition and indexes are complete, and excluding booksellers' inventories (Pilgrim, Denys, Walters), lists after 1600 and one or two obvious errors, in 173 lists there are: 60 entries for Cicero's *Orations*, 50 for *Ad Herennium*, 37 for Quintilian, 28 for Aristotle's *Rhetoric*, 19 for Cicero's *De oratore* and 16 for Hermogenes. Elizabeth Leedham-Green, *Books in Cambridge Inventories*, 2 vols. (Cambridge, 1986). From the 133 Oxford booklists so far published (up to 1579) in R. J. Fehrenbach and E. S. Leedham-Green (eds.), *Private Libraries in Renaissance England*, 5 vols. (Binghamton, Tempe: 1993–8), II–V, there are 24 entries for Cicero's selected orations, 13 for his selected rhetorics, 18 for Quintilian, 7 for Hermogenes, and 6 each for Cicero's *De oratore* and Aristotle's *Rhetoric*.

[21] McConica, *Collegiate University*, pp. 21, 35, 337–8.

[22] Bodleian Library MS Lat misc e. 114, fols. 2r–49v.

[23] Leedham-Green, *Cambridge Inventories*, without the booksellers (see note 20 above) has 27 entries for *Ecclesiastes*, 13 for Melanchthon's *Rhetoric* (impossible to say which one, but according to Kees Meerhoff *Institutiones rhetoricae* was the most commonly printed on the continent) and 9 for Talon. All three appear in the Oxford lists printed in Fehrenbach and Leedham-Green, *Private Libraries*, but in much smaller quantities.

when it conflicts with the expedient.[24] He attacks Aristotle's description of the happy man, which emphasises doubtful worldly advantages in preference to true happiness which is found in heaven.[25] Rainolds finds that Aristotle's arguments here are based on worldly appearance rather than on truth. He urges his audience to construct their arguments from a Christian ethical position rather than from the worldly wisdom codified by ancient philosophers.[26] Rainolds insists that true nobility has nothing to do with birth or reputation but with the moral choices which people make.[27]

By concentrating on philosophical questions which arise from Aristotle's text Rainolds discusses rhetoric in a way which suits the exercise of disputation. But he also forces his audience to face the moral question within rhetoric. Grammar school education encouraged pupils to collect pithy moral phrases from classical literature and recycle them in their own writing. By picking on Aristotle's summaries of generally held views (intended as starting points for arguments which will persuade audiences of ordinary people),[28] Rainolds questions the implications of the worldly wisdom of the proverbs. Rainolds's lectures were a demonstration of his rhetorical skill, but they also encouraged a critical approach to the assumptions of Elizabethan persuasion.

The notebook of Randolph Cholmondeley, who was at Lincoln College between 1577 and 1580 without taking a degree, contains a complete set of annotations on Cicero's *Partitiones oratoriae*, which looks like a record of a course of lectures.[29] Each section of the text is summarised as a main question, to which the commentary adds the opinions of classical and renaissance authorities, including Quintilian, Agricola, Latomus, Strebaeus and Talon.[30] Although the approach to rhetoric is broadly Ramist,[31] the commentary also includes objections and replies, intended to prepare students for disputations on rhetoric.[32] *Partitiones oratoriae* is used as a means of surveying the whole of rhetorical theory within a reasonably brief compass.

Cholmondeley's notes on Cicero's early orations consist mainly of maxims and comparisons chosen from the speeches and in some cases

---

[24] Lawrence D. Green, *John Rainolds's Oxford Lectures on Aristotle's Rhetoric* (Newark NJ, 1986), pp. 240–5.

[25] Ibid., pp. 282–93.   [26] Ibid., p. 348.   [27] Ibid., pp. 302–4.

[28] Aristotle, *Rhetoric*, 1360b14–1362a12; Green, *Rainolds's Lectures*, pp. 280–344.

[29] Bodleian MS Lat misc e. 114, fols. 33r–70v.   [30] Ibid., fols. 33r–34v.

[31] For example in the enumeration of the parts of rhetoric and in the emphasis on method. Ibid., fol. 33r.

[32] For example, ibid., fols. 33v, 36r.

provided with marginal headings ('Ironia', 'Cicero contra Naevium', 'Sententia', 'Apostrophe ad Iudices', 'Cicero de se').[33] At the beginning of his notes on *Pro Quinctio* he provides a succinct summary of the case, on the basis of Cicero's narratio (III.11–IX.32) and taking some phrases from his original.[34] From *Pro Sexto Roscio* he notes that

Truly if, as is well said by the wise, filial piety is often harmed by a look, what punishment can be found severe enough for one who has killed his parent, for whom all human and divine laws demand that he suffer death himself, if circumstances dictate? (XIII.37)

is a 'proverb and an argument drawn from the lesser to the greater'.[35] Later in the same speech he notes an argument 'from the intention of the lawgivers and from the penalties'.[36] He glosses one of the early sections of *Pro Roscio Comoedo* with a quotation from Quintilian:

When the matter is obvious it is as foolish to make arguments as it would be to bring candles into broad sunlight.[37]

Cholmondeley's notes demonstrate the commonplace book habit of collecting and labelling striking passages together with a good knowledge of rhetorical theory and topical invention.

Although the statutes stipulate no modern textbooks of rhetoric, some are included in the university booklists. Some of these (for example, Lorichius's version of Aphthonius and Erasmus's *De copia* and *De conscribendis epistolis*) represent a continuation of grammar school rhetoric into the university course.[38] This is backed up by evidence in the student notebooks of exercises in letter-writing.[39] Some manuals, notably Erasmus's *Ecclesiastes*, are directed towards preaching, which was both a requirement for higher degrees in theology and a skill which many Elizabethan graduates needed to cultivate. Others, like those of Melanchthon and Talon, represent the northern humanist rapprochement between rhetoric and dialectic. Gabriel Harvey's inaugural lecture *Ciceronianus* (1577) proclaims his intention of following Ramus (and by

[33] Ibid., fols. 24r–25r.   [34] Ibid., fol. 24r–v.
[35] 'Proverbium et argumentum cunctum a minore ad maius', ibid., fol. 25r.
[36] 'A sententiis legumlatorum et poeniis' (to xxv.69), ibid., fol. 26r.
[37] Ibid., fol. 27r, to *Pro Roscio Comoedo*, III.8–9; Quintilian, *Institutio oratoria*, v.12.8.
[38] Printed Cambridge lists have 18 entries for Aphthonius, 35 for *De copia* and 27 for *De conscribendis epistolis*. The corresponding Oxford figures (up to 1579) are 9, 30 and 13. Among modern university rhetorics only *Ecclesiastes* rivals these grammar school texts; among classical manuals only *Ad Herennium*, Quintilian and Aristotle.
[39] PRO SP 46.15, fols. 212–20; McConica, *Collegiate University*, pp. 40–1, 695–9.

implication Agricola and Melanchthon) in commenting on Cicero in a way that combines rhetorical and dialectical analysis.[40]

The university statutes insist on the primacy of Aristotle's dialectic but they tend to omit the medieval accretions to the Aristotelian syllabus, returning to the pure text of the *Organon*, often introduced by a humanist authority. The Cambridge statutes of 1570, in which two years out of four for the BA are devoted to dialectic, ordered the professor of dialectic to lecture on Aristotle's *Sophistical Refutations* or Cicero's *Topica*.[41] The four dialectic lecturers (out of a total of nine) mentioned in the 1547 statutes of Trinity College, Cambridge were required to teach, respectively: an introduction to dialectic; from Porphyry's *Isagoge* to Aristotle's *Prior Analytics*; *Posterior Analytics* or Agricola's *De inventione dialectica*; and Aristotle's *Topica*.[42] The Oxford statutes of 1564/5 required five terms' study of dialectic and prescribed lectures on Porphyry's *Isagoge* or any book of Aristotle's *Organon*.[43]

The university booklists confirm and elaborate this picture. Dialectic texts are far more frequent than rhetoric texts. Excluding the known booksellers from the Cambridge lists, in 173 lists there 89 listings of Aristotle's logic (34 of these in sets of the complete works), 45 of Rudolph Agricola's *De inventione dialectica*, 30 of dialectic texts by Melanchthon, 18 of Caesarius's *Dialectica*, 17 by Ramus and 12 by Seton, whose textbook was explicitly written to be taught at Cambridge.[44] In the 36 lists of texts held by undergraduates or recent graduates at Cambridge, there are 17 copies of Aristotle's logic, 11 copies of Agricola, 5 of Melanchthon's dialectic, 3 of Ramus and 2 of Caesarius. In the 77 Oxford booklists between 1560 and 1590 there are 47 listings of dialectic books by Aristotle, 22 of *De inventione dialectica*, 15 of dialectic books by Ramus, 9 of Melanchthon, and 8 of Caesarius.[45] The booklists suggest that

[40] G. Harvey, *Ciceronianus*, ed. H. S. Wilson (Lincoln NE, 1945), p. 82; Peter Mack, 'Renaissance Habits of Reading', in S. Chaudhuri (ed.), *Renaissance Essays for Kitty Scoular Datta* (Calcutta, 1995), pp. 1–25 (12–13).

[41] *Documents . . . Cambridge*, I, p. 457.

[42] J. G. Mullinger, *The History of the University of Cambridge*, 2 vols. (Cambridge, 1873–74), II, pp. 595–7.

[43] Gibson, *Statuta antiqua*, pp. 376, 389.

[44] All these figures are based on Leedham-Green, *Cambridge Inventories*. The figure for Ramus may be an understatement since there are fewer Cambridge booklists after 1570.

[45] These figures are based on a count I made in the Oxford archives in 1978. The five volumes so far published of Fehrenbach and Leedham-Green, *Private Libraries* include Oxford inventories only up to 1579.

Agricola was more important than other humanist logicians and that
Melanchthon's works were influential in the mid-century, giving way to
Ramus in the 1570s at both universities.[46]

The booklists indicate a considerable interest in the humanist reform
of dialectic.[47] Melanchthon, Ramus, Caesarius and the others followed
the new movement in dialectic originated by Lorenzo Valla and Rudolph
Agricola. Valla and Agricola had stripped away the philosophical com-
plications which attended late scholastic logic and had focused instead
on the use of dialectic.[48] For them dialectic was about how to construct
persuasive arguments in neo-classical Latin. They emphasised the topics of invention, the range of available forms of argumentation (where
Aristotelian logic privileged the syllogism), the logical organisation of
poems, speeches and didactic works, and the use of dialectic to analyse
a text.

Three printed works provide evidence of the way in which Aristotelian
logic was taught or introduced in English universities: John Seton's
Dialectica, later revised by Peter Carter, which was much used in Cambridge from the 1540s; John Case's *Summa veterum interpretum in universam
dialecticam Aristotelis* (1584), an example of the work of one of Oxford's
most famous teachers of the later sixteenth century, and the *Logicae artis
compendium* (1615) by Robert Sanderson (1587–1663). All three represent
compromises between the traditional Aristotelian syllabus and the reformed, humanist dialectic associated with Agricola, Melanchthon and
Ramus.

Seton's text was written to provide a simplified version of Aristotle's account of categories, propositions and forms of argument to accompany
Agricola's *De inventione dialectica*. There are three main books, devoted
to words (that is, introductory definitions, predicables and categories),
propositions (with the addition of sections inspired by Boethius on definition, division and hypothetical syllogism) and syllogisms (with a section
on disputation and other forms of proof). The fourth book is a list of
topics taken from Agricola.[49]

John Case, a former fellow of St John's College, Oxford, continued
to teach, presenting students independently for degrees, after he was
required to resign his fellowship when he married. His *Summa veterum*

---

[46] Some indication of the shift from Agricola and Melanchthon to Ramus is offered by a comparison
of the inventories of two booksellers: Pilgrim (1546) and Denys (1578). Leedham-Green, *Cambridge
Inventories*, pp. 61–70, 326–40.

[47] This is made explicit in Cromwell's injunctions of 1535, D. Leader, *A History of the University of
Cambridge*, vol. 1, *The University to 1546* (Cambridge, 1988), p. 332.

[48] See Mack, *Renaissance Argument*, esp. pp. 37–256.

[49] John Seton, *Dialectica*, with the notes of P. Carter (London, 1572) STC 22251.

interpretum in universam dialecticam Aristotelis (1584) presents the materials of the dialectic course in a way suited to undergraduates. His definition of dialectic maintains a nice balance between the scholastic emphasis on dialectic as the gateway to further study and humanist notions of speaking freely on whatever subject is proposed.[50] He agrees with the humanist logicians that dialectic is concerned with questions (of all types) and that it consists of invention and judgment, though he prefers to cite Aristotle as his authority.[51] He employs technical terms from the scholastic logical theory of supposition, but he cites Rudolph Agricola on the topics of invention.[52] His work is divided into five books: an introduction which provides a rapid outline of definition, division, the proposition and argumentation; predicables and categories; demonstration; topics; and sophisms.

The most successful English logic textbook of the early seventeenth century was *Logicae artis compendium* (1615) by Robert Sanderson, who was reader in logic at Lincoln College, Oxford between 1608 and 1610, later becoming Regius Professor of Divinity and Bishop of Lincoln. *Logicae artis compendium* is divided into three parts (on simple terms, on the proposition and on discourse) and an appendix. It provides a clear and thorough summary of the principal Aristotelian doctrines (the third part deals with forms of argumentation, demonstration, Boethius's version of the topics, and the fallacies). To this Sanderson adds brief accounts of some specifically medieval logical teachings (supposition, ampliation and restriction and exponibles; all within part two)[53] and a discussion of method.

But Sanderson shows his commitment to the humanist approach to logic in his first appendix, on the use of dialectic. It includes instructions for the composition of simple themes, which resemble Melanchthon's method and the *Progymnasmata*;[54] for disputations, both internal and adversarial;[55] for the organisation of sciences and textbooks,[56] and for the logical analysis of all these types of text.[57] Although Sanderson's logic is firmly based on Aristotle its commitment to the use of logic anticipates and advances the emphasis in the Laudian Statutes of 1636 on testing the candidate's ability to formulate a fluent Latin argument.[58]

---

[50] John Case, *Summa veterum interpretum in universam dialecticam Aristotelis* (London, 1584) STC 4762, sig. A2r.

[51] Ibid., sigs. A4v, B1r.   [52] Ibid., sigs. G3v, Dd2v, Ee1r, Ii4v, Kk1r–v.

[53] Robert Sanderson, *Logicae artis compendium*, ed. E. J. Ashworth (Bologna, 1985), pp. 85–96, 119–23.

[54] Ibid., pp. 243–59. Philipp Melanchthon, *De Rhetorica libri tres* (Basel, 1519) sig. B4r; Mack, *Renaissance* Argument, pp. 325–9.

[55] Sanderson, *Logicae*, pp. 261–307. His account of disputation is discussed below.

[56] Ibid., pp. 309–16.   [57] Ibid., pp. 317–28.

[58] Ashworth in Sanderson, *Logicae*, p. xxxiv; Feingold, *Seventeenth-Century Oxford*, pp. 215, 315.

DISPUTATIONS AND DECLAMATIONS

Candidates for degrees at Oxford and Cambridge were obliged to attend and participate in disputations. The Cambridge statutes of 1570 required candidates for the BA to dispute twice in the public schools and to respond twice in college in the four years of residence. For the Master of Arts degree the Bachelors were required to respond three times to a master, to respond twice in disputations in hall, and to declaim once.[59] At Oxford the injunctions of 1535 required students in their second year to respond twice *in parviso* in order to obtain the interim status of *sophista generalis* (the Elizabethan statutes reduced the requirement to one response). The *sophistae* were expected to attend disputations in the schools and participate at least once a term for the remainder of their course.[60] Formal disputations were part of the degree ceremonies in both universities.[61] Attendance at and participation in college disputations was probably required even more frequently.[62] Indeed, as some university exercises became formalities, so college disputations must have become more important in establishing a qualification for a degree.[63]

In his *Logicae artis compendium* (1615), Robert Sanderson provides the best description we have of early modern Oxford disputation. His account allows for some differences between college disputations, ordinary disputations and solemn public disputations. According to Sanderson, the question, which should be a specific proposition,[64] is put by the moderator, or, if there is no moderator, by the opponent. The respondent briefly states his view on the question. In ordinary university disputations he makes a simple statement of his view; in college or public disputations he makes a speech outlining the reasons for taking his position.

Then it is the opponent's turn to speak. In public disputations he begins with an introductory statement. In all cases the opponent then makes his first argument which must be directed against the respondent's

---

59 'Statuta Reginae Elizabethae', in *Documents . . . Cambridge*, I, p. 459. Judith Deitch will shortly publish a study of early modern disputation which will analyse new evidence on disputation at Cambridge.

60 Gibson, *Statuta antiqua*, pp. 344, 378. Fletcher, 'Faculty of Arts', p. 169.

61 Leader, *History of Cambridge*, pp. 98–101; Fletcher, 'Faculty of Arts', pp. 182–4.

62 *Documents . . . Cambridge*, p. 491. McConica, *Collegiate University*, pp. 15, 19, 34, 38, 58, 60.

63 Leader, *History of Cambridge*, pp. 97–9; McConica, *Collegiate University*, pp. 24; Fletcher, 'Faculty of Arts', p. 171.

64 A. C. Clark prints many examples of titles for formal disputations, for example (from 1586): *In vesperiis*: Should one prefer soldiers to learned men? Do incantations have any effect? Does everything depend on opinion? *In comitiis*: Can someone who is not a good man be a good citizen? Is it more difficult to resist anger than pleasure? Can gold be made out of ordinary metals? Clark, *Register of the University of Oxford II*, 4 vols. (Oxford, 1887–9), II, i, pp. 170–205 (171).

conclusion. The respondent replies by repeating the opponent's argument (partly for the benefit of the audience; partly to ensure that both participants direct their arguments to the same point) and by denying it. He may give reasons for his denial.

Then it is the opponent's turn again. He will either press the respondent for a fuller reply or make another argument, this time attempting to establish a point from which he can renew his attack on the respondent's conclusion. In reply to this second argument (and to subsequent arguments) the respondent will first repeat the argument and then either agree to it, or, more likely, deny it. In reply the opponent will either press for a better response, or propose a new argument or declare that the respondent's argument is absurd or self-contradictory. Once again the respondent will either clarify the reasons for his denial or repeat the new argument and either deny or accept it. Once the opponent's line of argument is clear the respondent may argue that the premisses are wrong, that the argument is ill-formed or that a distinction needs to be made in the use of terms.

The disputation will end either when the opponent has won the argument (by persuading the respondent to agree to his main response or by making him contradict himself in his replies) or when an agreed period of time has elapsed without the opponent being able to achieve this.

The role of the moderator is to ensure that the disputation keeps to the prescribed forms, to assist the opponent in formulating arguments or the respondent by correcting, explaining or giving examples, and to conclude the disputation with a decision on the question and a brief summary of the participants' positions.[65]

Other sources suggest some variations on the basic model outlined by Sanderson. When Elizabeth made her visitations to Cambridge in August 1564 and to Oxford in September 1566 and 1592 (outside term in each case) special disputations were presented by each faculty.[66] As far as possible topics of general interest were chosen.[67] In each case the respondent made a longish speech presenting a point of view on one of the questions; four opponents in turn made short arguments directed to one or other of the questions proposed (not necessarily the one chosen by the respondent) and one of the university grandees concluded by giving

---

[65] Sanderson, *Logicae*, pp. 282–307.
[66] Nicholls, *Progresses*, I, pp. 149–89, 206–47; III, pp. 144–67; Plummer, *Elizabethan Oxford*, pp. 109–273.
[67] For example 'Is the monarchy the best form of state?', 'Is it better to eat or drink liberally?', 'Is the authority of scripture greater than that of the Church?', 'Does the Civil magistrate have jurisdiction in church matters?' Cambridge 1562, in Nicholls, *Progresses*, II, pp. 170, 174.

his view on one or both of the questions.[68] All the speeches were prepared in advance and there is no evidence that the respondent was allowed to reply to the opponents. The disputations were evidently one of the main attractions of the visit (the Queen usually attended these disputations, though she often missed sermons that had been put on for her).

On 28 May 1549 and on the three days following, Peter Martyr, Regius Professor of Theology, disputed publicly in Oxford on the nature of the Eucharist. A verbatim account of the disputation was printed at the end of his *Tractatio de sacramento eucharistiae*.[69] At the beginning of this disputation the Vice-Chancellor, Peter Martyr and his first opponent William Tresham made brief introductory statements.[70] The overarching structure of the debate is that Martyr states his views and defends them against opponents. However, at particular moments his opponents express their views or their interpretations of passages of scripture and Martyr then has to oppose them.[71] In other words this debate does not illustrate the firm separation of roles of respondent and opponent which traditional accounts of disputation would lead us to expect.[72]

Several printed sources encourage the view that formal disputations opened with long speeches by the respondent. When John Howson incepted in theology in 1602 he decided to devote all the time available to him to the third question proposed to him *in vesperiis*, 'after the wife has been dismissed, is it permissible to take another?' His speech on this topic, described on the title-page as a 'thesis proposed and disputed' was printed in the same year. After reviewing the principal biblical texts, Howson states the point at issue: that recent theologians have wondered whether the dispensation given to the Jews concerning divorce and re-marriage applies only in the case of adultery or in other cases also.[73] Following a review of the opinions of theologians,[74] he states his view that Christ forbade the divorcing husband from a second marriage, which he supports with six plausible arguments.[75] Then he replies to objections which might be made and in conclusion states that divorce can only be admitted on grounds of adultery and that no second marriage is

---

[68] Ibid., I, pp. 170, 213, 237–43, Plummer, *Elizabethan Oxford*, pp. 131–35, 181–2.

[69] Peter Martyr Vermigli, *Tractatio de sacramento eucharistiae* (London: R. Wolfe, 1549) STC 24673. The disputation is separately paginated as *Disputatio de Eucharistia*. See also J. C. McLelland, *The Visible Words of God: An Exposition of the Sacramental Theology of Peter Martyr Vermigli* (Edinburgh, 1957).

[70] Martyr, *Disputatio*, sigs. a3r–b2v.   [71] Ibid., sigs. b3r–5r, g1v–4v.

[72] Seton states that it is not permissible for the respondent to construct arguments or for respondent and opponent to exchange roles in the course of a disputation (*Dialectica*, sig. O4v).

[73] J. Howson, *Uxore dimissa* (Oxford, 1602) STC 13886, sig. A4r.

[74] Ibid., sigs. A4r–C7r.   [75] Ibid., sigs. C7v–D2r.

permitted.[76] The main focus of Howson's argument is on the citation and interpretation of texts. His conclusions follow from the texts he privileges and he backs them up mainly from other texts. He shows a thorough knowledge of ancient and recent commentary on his texts. Although he makes use of dialectical terminology from time to time, naming fallacies or labelling major and minor propositions, and although there are no references to classical literature, the plan of the speech derives less from models of disputation than from the rhetorical model of introduction, exposition, proof and refutation, and conclusion.[77]

John Rainolds's *Sex theses de sacra scriptura et ecclesia* (1580) publish speeches which he gave as opening contributions to two public disputations held on 13 July and 3 November 1579.[78] Rainolds opens with an elaborate rhetorical exordium, drawing on an anecdote about Cato and a story from Livy. Although the speech frequently employs dialectical structures, he elaborates with classical anecdotes and figures of rhetoric in order to make the strongest possible impression on his audience.

The evidence of the student notebooks confirms that quite elaborate orations were composed as introductory statements in disputations. Daniel Featley's commonplace book contains orations directed to the three questions disputed *in vesperiis* in the arts faculty in 1605 and to the three disputed *in comitiis* in 1606.[79] Featley handles the questions with an array of rhetorical flourishes, literary references and quotations from ancient poetry. The letter book of Robert Batt, who was at Brasenose College, Oxford in the 1580s, contains an oration on the question 'Can restless dreams be prophetic?', which was one of the titles set *in comitiis* in 1581.[80] Batt makes a considerable display of classical learning without

---

[76] Ibid., sigs. D5v–6v.

[77] John Rainolds later published a reply to Howson: *A Defence of the Iudgment of the Reformed Churches. That a man may lawfullie not onelie put awaie his wife for her adulterie, but also marrie another* ([Dort, 1609]) STC 20607.

[78] In view of the dates it is possible that Rainolds is here responding *in comitiis* to the incepting doctors of theology. In that case *Sex theses* would be his two disputations for the Bachelor of Theology degree.

[79] The questions were: Are the arts of peace or war more noble? Whether it is better to be mediocre in all sciences or outstanding in one of them? Does fame favour the best? (1605); Has the invention of gunpowder increased the danger or the safety of the state? Are open perjuries more dangerous to the state than hidden ambiguities? Should Aristotle be reproved for not including a good wife among the goods of the happy man? (1606). Bodleian Library MS Rawl. D 47, fols. 70r, 76r, 84r, 102r, 110v. Clark, *Register*, II, i, pp. 175–6. While the first two questions of 1606 carry a political allusion to the gunpowder plot, the third reflects one of the criticisms which Rainolds made of Aristotle in his lectures on the *Rhetoric*. Green, *Rainolds's Lectures*, p. 306.

[80] 'An sit divinatio per insomnia?', Bodleian Library MS Rawl D. 985, fols. 79v–81r. Clark, *Register*, II, i, p. 170 The *insomnium* is a particular type of dream which reflects the leftover business of the day before as distinct from the prophetic dream.

really arguing a position on the question set. The book contains several other orations which might easily relate to disputations in philosophy (for example 'Is the moveable body the subject of physics?', 'Do virtues inhere by nature?', 'Is it better for a prince to be loved or feared?') as well as two titles which look more like declamation topics: 'Oration against ingratitude' and 'On upholding freedom'.[81] The similarity of treatment implies that rhetorical techniques were as important in disputation as in declamation.

At the same time the pervasiveness of the model of disputation is indicated by the structure of university textbooks. Peter Carter's revisions of Seton's *Dialectica* (first printed in 1563) added restatements of the main definitions and explanations, with diagrams, questions and responses.[82] In John Case's textbooks chapters typically begin with a question, followed by a continuous prose review of others' opinions, leading to a statement of his own view. This view is then set out diagrammatically, sometimes, as in the example below, to clarify the organisation of his discussion, sometimes to distinguish different senses of the terms being used. This is an abbreviated version of Case's chapter on definition.

	Parts	The thing defined, for example, man The copula, is Genus, which is like the matter, animal Differentia, which is like the form, rational
Definition consists of	Species	Description, consisting of genus and property Notation, consisting of accidents Interpretation, expressed by synonyms
	Laws	Equality of definition with thing defined Truth, that the whole essence of the thing is explained Perspicuity, that everything obscure is cleared up by the definition.[83]

---

[81] Bodleian Library MS Rawl D. 985, fols. 65r, 69r, 85v, 88v, 98v.

[82] John Seton, *Dialectica*, with the notes of P. Carter (London, 1563) STC 22250.5.

[83] 'In definitione spectantur: partes, species, leges. Partes: Definitum, a definiendo dictum, quod est vox prima de qua quaeritur, ut homo; Copula, a copulando, quae est verbum substantivum ut est; Genus, quod est quasi materia, ut animal; differentia, quae est quasi forma, ut rationale. Species: Descriptio, quae est oratio constans ex genere et proprio, ut homo est animal risibile; Notatio, quae est oratio constans ex accidentibus, ut, Os homini sublime dedit, coelumque videre iussit; Interpretatio, quae est oratio constans ex synonymis, ut, honestum est quod decere. Leges: Aequalitas definitionis cum definito, ut homo est, ergo animal rationale: animal rationale, ergo et homo; Veritas, quae est, ut, tota essentia rei explicetur, quod sit, si genus et differentia insint; Perspicuitas, ut, omne obscurum a definitione arceatur tam voce quam sensu, ut canis.' Case, *Summa in dialecticam*, sig. B3r.

After stating his view Case places a series of objections (from the opponent) and replies (from the respondent). These are the objections and replies following his explanation that dialectic is necessary to the other arts because the arts cannot be constructed without dialectic:

Opponent
The aims of the other arts can be attained without dialectic. For example Hippocrates can cure without the syllogism, Euclid can draw lines without argument. Therefore Dialectic is not necessary.

Respondent
The other arts are considered in two ways,
either in terms of the method of proving their doctrines by contemplation, and this cannot be done without dialectic,
or in terms of carrying out their procedures by external action, which can be done without it.

Opponent
Dialectic teaches how to deceive, as appears from the criticism of the Sophists, therefore far from being necessary it ought to be rejected.

Respondent
It teaches deception, not in order that you might deceive, but so that through understanding the art of deception you may avoid being deceived.

Opponent
Other arts have definitions, divisions and demonstrations, therefore dialectic is not necessary for this reason.

Respondent
They have them in relation to the material they contain.
They do not have them in relation to form which is established for them only by the dialecticians.[84]

Case's examples outline the general line of argument available in each case. The respondent's replies often depend on distinguishing different senses in which particular words can be applied. By making distinctions

[84] 'Opponens: Fines reliquarum artium acquiri possunt sine Dialectica, ut sanare potest Hypocrates sine syllogismo, Euclides lineas ducere sine argumento, ergo non est necessaria.
    Respondens: Aliae artes considerantur bifariam, vel quoad modum probandi praecepta in illis per contemplationem, et sic sine dialectica acquiri non possunt, vel quoad modum exercendi opera per externum actionem, et sic possunt.
    Opponens: Dialectica docet fallere, ut patet de reprehensione sophistarum ergo non est necessaria, imo potius reiicienda.
    Respondens: Fallere docet, non ut fallas, sed ut fallendi arte percepta, evitetur fallacia.
    Opponens: Aliae artes suas habent definitiones, divisiones, demonstrationes, ergo ob has causas non est necessaria.
    Respondens: Habent quoad materiam quam continent, non quoad formam quam solum dialecticis acceptam referunt.' Ibid., sig. A1v.

of this kind, the respondent is able to allow some force to the objection, while denying that it impugns the point he is actually making. Case's textbooks on physics and ethics also include indications of lines of argument on particular issues. An exchange on a topic close to Rainolds's heart, whether plays should be permitted, brings the whole process into focus in a short compass.

Opponent
Games, dances and plays are said in the text to be of little use. Therefore they should not be permitted. Furthermore they often corrupt morals, they expend money, they direct the minds of the citizens away from necessary things towards trivia. Therefore they should be prohibited. When you add to what I have already said that they are so unnatural as to display men dressed in women's clothes acting as women and dancing disgracefully with others in circles, these things should not be tolerated. Moreover in the primitive church the fathers prohibited these games, defining them as nothing other than rising from tables to games, which was expressly forbidden by God's word. Lastly we have six hundred other better forms of recreation, such as singing hymns, reading moral stories and encouraging bird-like singers along with St Ambrose.

Respondent
I shall reply to these arguments in order. First I affirm that games, dances and plays are of little use in relation to the great matters which are usually discussed in the city. In the second argument I deny the antecedent, for plays (or at least those that I previously defined) do not corrupt morals but correct them, and draw the minds of the citizens not to vain trifles but to ideas useful to life. To the third I say that it is not[85] indecorous, not impious for men to portray the characters of women in plays. The disease of disgrace resides not in clothes but in the mind. The other part of the argument relates to lascivious dancing, not chaste and virtuous dancing. On the fourth argument my opinion is this: the fathers prohibited profane and pagan plays because Jove, Phoebus and other idols were superstitiously celebrated in them. But the honest and praiseworthy plays which I spoke of could not be regarded as rising from the table to games. In the final argument I think I hear an over-severe stoic voice, defining virtue as the absence of excitement. I know that it is holy and delightful to sing hymns and psalms, but tell me, do those who always sing hymns and psalms never eat? Do they never feast? Do they never dance in Corinth with Demosthenes? What more can I say? As King David said, the name of the lord can be praised with songs and dances.[86]

---

[85] Possibly this 'not' is mistaken. Case may mean to say that it is indecorous but not impious.
[86] 'Opponens: Ludi choreae, spectacula res minime utiles in textu dicuntur, ergo non sunt licita. Praeterea saepe bonos mores corrumpunt, opes exhauriunt, animos civium a rebus necessariis ad nugas flectunt, ergo sunt prohibenda. Huc adde quod instar monstri sit videre viros muliebri veste histrionice dissimulantes feminas et cum iisdem in gyrum saltantes turpiter, non sunt ergo toleranda ista. Insuper in primitiva luce ecclesiae patres hac ipsa prohibuerunt, definientes nihil

Case's respondent begins by answering the opponent's arguments in turn. He accepts the opening point but denies the consequence drawn by the opponent. He denies the antecedent of the second argument. He answers the third argument by making distinctions, first between clothing and mind and second between different forms of dancing. To the fourth again he distinguishes between pagan and Christian plays. His reply to the final argument is decorated with repetition and rhetorical question, exploiting the skills of declamation to ridicule the severe logic of his opponent.

Although declamations were less important and less common than disputations, there is abundant documentary evidence that they were given.[87] Oxford notebooks provide some examples of texts of student declamations. John Rogers's notebook includes drafts of a pair of declamations he delivered in October 1582 on the opposing themes: 'Small things grow through harmony' and 'All things grow through discord.' The marginal notes indicate a structure loosely based on the *Progymnasmata*: lengthy exordia with many quotations from classical literature, followed by a division, confirmation from several topics and a conclusion.[88] Cholmondeley's notebook includes two orations on topics suitable for declamation: 'All things fall through cruelty' and 'Control of the tongue is a great part of virtue.'[89] The first page (of six) of the second of these speeches is given over to self-deprecation and praise of his audience. Then he sets out the importance of his theme followed by a series of arguments

---

aliud haec esse quam a mensis ad ludos surgere; at expresso Dei verbo hoc negatur, ergo et illa. postremo sexcenta sunt alia meliora nos recreandi media, ut hymnos canere, fabulas morales legere, aviculas cantatrices cum Divo Ambrosio alere.

Respondens: Singulis his argumentis ordine respondeo, primum ergo affirmo ludos choreas, spectacula res minime utiles respectu maximarum rerum quae in civitate solent nominari. In secundo argumento antecedens nego, nam haec (modo quo antea definivimus) mores non corrumpunt sed corrigunt, animosque civium non ad inanes nugas sed ad utiles vitae ideas trahunt. Ad tertiam dico non indecorum esse, non impium ut viri feminarum personas in scenico theatro fingant. Non enim in veste sed in mente sceleris contagio inest. Altera pars argumenti choreas veneris non Dianae et virtutis urget. De quarto argumento sic sentio, quod patres solum prophana et ethnica spectacula prohibuerunt, quae nomine Iovis Phoebi, aliorumque idolorum superstitiose celebrata fuerunt; at honesta et laudabilia haec, de quibus iam loquimur, agere non est a mensis ad ludendum surgere. In postremo argumento nimis severos stoicos loquentes ut opinor audio, qui virtutem omnis perturbationis vacuitatem esse definierunt. Agnosco quidem hymnos canere sanctum esse et delectabile, sed dicant isti mihi an semper hymnos et psalmos cantant? Edunt nunquam? Epulantur nunquam? Imo Corinthum cum Demosthene nunquam salutant? Quid multis? In ludis et choris laudetur nomen domini ut ait Rex ille propheticus.' J. Case, *Sphaera Civitatis* (Oxford, 1588) STC 4761, sigs. Gg6v–7r.

[87] McConica, *Collegiate University*, pp. 30, 54, 60, 709–11; W. Haddon, *Lucubrationes* (London, 1567) STC 12596; John Rainolds, *Orationes duodecim* (Oxford, 1614) STC 20613.

[88] Bodleian Library MS Rawl. D 273, fols. 157r–163v.

[89] Bodleian Library MS Lat misc e. 114, fols. 150r–153v, 156r–158v.

in favour, embellished by comparisons, classical anecdotes and quotations. This declamation builds on and develops the composition exercises of the grammar school, perhaps in preparation for mock-trials at the Inns of Court.

EIGHT ASPECTS OF UNIVERSITY RHETORIC AND DIALECTIC

1. A complete syllabus of classical rhetoric

In contrast to the grammar schools there is good evidence that university students read or heard lectures on a complete textbook of classical rhetoric, such as Aristotle's *Rhetoric, Rhetorica ad Herennium*, Cicero's *Partitiones oratoriae* or Quintilian's *Institutio oratoria*. In his lectures Rainolds assumed that his audience knew the basic technical details of the whole subject. Some of the modern rhetorics which feature in the booklists, such as the works by Melanchthon, Talon and Valerius,[90] presented a simplified version of the whole syllabus, arranged to fit in with a companion volume on dialectic.

The need to study the whole of rhetoric is reinforced by the choice of Cicero's orations as set texts. Sixteenth-century commentaries on Cicero's orations, which derive from Antonio Loschi's excellent *Inquisitio super xi orationes Ciceronis* composed in the 1390s, analyse the arguments and structure of the oration and identify the rhetorical figures employed, as well as explaining the historical circumstances.[91] It is reasonable to assume that lecturers at Oxford and Cambridge teaching Cicero's orations as a rhetoric text would have adopted the same approach.

2. Declamations and sermons

Declamations and sermons constituted an extension of grammar school composition exercises and gave students the opportunity to display the skills they had learned from their study of rhetoric textbooks and Cicero's

---

[90] Cornelius Valerius, *In universam bene dicendi rationem tabula*, which was also printed in England (London, 1580) STC 24584, appears in three Cambridge and five Oxford booklists. His companion volume, *Tabulae totius dialectices* is found much more frequently.

[91] These include commentaries by Agricola, Latomus, Melanchthon and Ramus, all authors whose rhetorical works were studied in England. For further bibliography see the section on dialectical reading pp. 73–4, notes 130–2 below. Notes in English editions of the sixteenth century are purely textual, but the London editions of the 1580s include subject indexes to the text: historical, philosophical, grammatical and rhetorical. For example, Cicero, *Orationum volumen primum* (London, 1585) STC 5309, jj4r–kk3r. This edition also includes Lambinus's notes on the text of the orations.

orations. Both university and college statutes required declamations for certain degrees. Notebook and printed evidence suggests that declamations were sometimes composed in preparation for formal disputations. Knowledge of classical rhetorical structures and techniques was displayed in the composition of declamations. Several of the student notebooks contain collections of orations and sermons, some the work of the notebook's owner, others copied as models for imitation.

Theology students were required to give sermons, which employed techniques of classical rhetoric alongside biblical exegesis and within a non-classical structure. Erasmus's *Ecclesiastes*, which is found quite frequently in the booklists, provides instruction on biblical interpretation and a comprehensive rhetoric course adapted to the needs of the preacher. Book four adds resources for sermon-writing: phrases and arguments on common subject-matter, such as God, the law and moral virtues.

3. *Logical invention and the topics*

Works of renaissance logic studied in English universities added to their Aristotelian inheritance primarily in the area of invention and the topics. In *De inventione dialectica*, which is mentioned in the statutes and appears quite frequently in the booklists,[92] Rudolph Agricola produced a unified account of the whole process of devising arguments and planning compositions, centred on the topics.[93] He devoted the first book of *De inventione dialectica* to a new version of the topics which emphasised their role in investigating the nature of particular things and ideas. According to Agricola the topics are a list of the possible relationships holding between objects and qualities existing in the world.[94] If someone mentally applies each of the topics in turn to an object or a quality, they are assisted to think of further objects or qualities related to the first one which can then become the basis for arguments.

Agricola suggests that people should practise using the topics by making topical descriptions. He gives the example of 'philosopher' for which he provides first a definition ('man seeking knowledge of human and divine things, with virtue') then the genus to which 'philosopher' belongs ('man'), then the species into which 'philosopher' is divided ('Stoic,

---

[92] Rainolds says that Agricola's book is in everyone's hands and refers his readers to it for clarification. Green, *Rainolds's Lectures*, pp. 258–61.

[93] Mack, *Renaissance Argument*, pp. 117–257.

[94] Rudolph Agricola, *De inventione dialectica* (Cologne, 1539, repr. Nieuwkoop, 1967), pp. 6–9.

Epicurean, Peripatetic etc.') before continuing down the list to efficient causes ('another philosopher, pains, devotion to study'), final cause ('to live well and peacefully') and effects ('writings, improvement of morals, living better, fame'). By making topical descriptions of two objects or qualities which are present in the question one wishes to investigate (Agricola's example is 'should the philosopher marry a wife?') one will discover mediate objects or qualities which connect the two terms of the main question. In this example Agricola finds a connection between the production of children (which is part of the definition of 'wife') and the philosopher's concern with virtue. Therefore one argument in favour of marriage for the philosopher would be that the duty to increase virtue can be met by marrying, producing children and educating them vir- tuously. Marriage will also enable the philosopher and the woman he marries to live virtuously.[95]

Agricola's list of topics includes: topics within the substance (defini- tion, genus, species, difference, whole and parts); related to substance (adjacents, sometimes called adjuncts, actions and subject); causes and effects; place, time and circumstances; accidents (contingents, names, opinions, comparisons, similars and dissimilars); and opposites.

Agricola contends that the person who understands the nature and subdivisions of each of the topics will be able to devise arguments and appeals to the emotions in any subject-matter and for any audience.[96] Later humanist dialecticians, most prominently Melanchthon and Ramus, agreed with Agricola's views on the importance and usefulness of the topics but preferred to provide briefer and simpler accounts of the individual topics.[97] The English university textbooks by Seton, Case and Sanderson (and Thomas Wilson's *Rule of Reason*) give due prominence to the topics and acknowledge the importance of Agricola's approach.[98]

4. Argumentation and the syllogism

Elizabethan students of dialectic learned how to formulate their argu- ments as strict syllogisms and in other forms. The syllogism is the main subject of Aristotle's *Prior Analytics*, which codifies all the valid forms of reasoning from two true propositions (in strictly defined forms) to a

---

[95] Ibid., pp. 368–71.   [96] Ibid., pp. 2–3, 197–201, 378.
[97] Mack, *Renaissance Argument*, pp. 327–31, 339, 351–3.
[98] Seton, *Dialectica* (1572), sigs. S7r–T1r; Case, *Summa in dialecticam*, sigs. Cc1v, Dd2v, Ee1r, Ii4r, Kk1v; Sanderson, *Logicae*, pp. 179–212; Thomas Wilson, *The Rule of Reason*, ed. R. S. Sprague (Northridge, 1972), p. 91.

necessary conclusion. For example, if no just man is cruel and every tyrant is cruel, then no tyrant is a just man.[99] For Aristotle (and for subsequent logicians) the attraction of the syllogism was that the truth of the inference was guaranteed by the form in which the propositions were expressed. If the premisses were both true and the form corresponded to his rules, then the conclusion necessarily followed.

Classical and medieval logicians recognised and taught other, less perfect forms of argumentation: enthymeme (incomplete syllogism), induction (argument from particular instances to general statement) and example (incomplete induction).[100] Renaissance dialecticians acknowledged the pre-eminence of the syllogism but insisted that other forms were often more useful in persuasion in real language.[101] They showed that syllogisms were often expressed in non-syllogistic format and they taught other forms of argumentation, like the stoic hypothetical syllogism ('If it is light, it must be day') with its four different inferences (e.g. 'But it is not light, so it must not be day'). Elizabethan students would have been taught the syllogism in introductory lectures on dialectic and in their courses on Aristotle's *Organon*, but they would have picked up other forms from more recent manuals and from their rhetoric texts.[102]

5. Organisation and method

Building on their knowledge of the topics and the forms of argumentation, most English sixteenth-century university students would have some knowledge of method and the arrangement of knowledge. Sixteenth-century accounts of method derive from three different traditions. In his *Posterior Analytics* Aristotle discussed the organisation of science, from first principles via a chain of syllogistic reasoning to detailed appearances. Another strand of influence derives from Rudolph Agricola who thought that the arrangement of material belonged to dialectical invention. In his view an author needed to determine the overall arrangement of a work bearing in mind content, purpose, audience and occasion.[103] Following on from Agricola, Melanchthon treated method less as overall

---

99 This is Sanderson's example of a second figure syllogism (*Logicae*, p. 131).
100 Boethius, *De differentiis topicis, Patrologia Latina*, LXIV, cols. 1183A–84D; Peter of Spain, *Tractatus*, pp. 55–8.
101 Mack, *Renaissance Argument*, pp. 32, 84–8, 200.   102 Quintilian, *Institutio oratoria*, v.8.7.
103 Agricola, *De inventione dialectica*, pp. 196–7, 413–27, 449–50; Mack, *Renaissance Argument*, pp. 218–25.

organisation than as a simplified technique for discovering and presenting material.[104]

The third strand derives from Ramus, who regarded method as the
third part of logic which organised the arguments discovered through the
topics and arranged in syllogisms as a complete science. He subordinated
all other forms of disposition to the single method, which proceeded
from very general and certain first principles by successive divisions and
definitions to particular phenomena. In later versions of his dialectic
Ramus proclaimed three laws to govern method which state: 1) that only
things which are true and necessary may be included, 2) that all and only
things which belong to the art in question must be included, and 3) that
general things must be dealt with in a general way.[105] Ramus used these
laws of method to attack the teaching of most other authorities. Beside
the single method (from the most general to the most particular) which
is obligatory in science and teaching, poets and orators sometimes use
the method of prudence (from particular things to general conclusions)
in order to persuade an audience which resists.

Elizabethan students would have known at least the general principles
of Aristotelian method and might well have read Agricola, Melanchthon
or Ramus as well. Seton's *Dialectica* includes no section on method as
such, but, as in some medieval textbooks of logic, there are special sections on definition and division which play a part in some versions
of method.[106] Case devotes his third tractate to demonstration and
gives a thorough account of key questions raised by Aristotle's *Posterior Analytics*. He explains the usefulness of definition and the roles of
sense-perception and pre-existent mental principles in the acquisition
of knowledge.[107] He also emphasises the importance of definition and
division, as tools of dialectic and in presenting material.[108] Although
Sanderson's account of method derives from Aristotle, his laws of method
are elaborated from Ramus's.[109] His discussion of the method of handling simple themes (appendix one, chapter one) reflects the influence of
Melanchthon.[110]

---

[104] Philipp Melanchthon, *Erotemata dialectices* (1547), in *Opera omnia*, XIII, col. 573.
[105] Petrus Ramus, *Dialecticae libri duo* (Paris, 1574); W. J. Ong, *Ramus and Talon Inventory* (Cambridge
MA, 1958), no. 254, sigs. D2v–3v, E4v–5r; Petrus Ramus, *Scholae in Liberales Artes* (Basel, 1569,
repr. Hildesheim, 1970); Ong, *Ramus and Talon*, no. 695, col. 31; Vasoli, *Dialettica*, pp. 550–62,
582–9; Mack, *Renaissance Argument*, pp. 338, 349–51.
[106] Boethius, *De divisione*, *De definitione*, *Patrologia Latina*, LXIV, cols. 875D–910B; Peter Abelard,
Dialectica, ed. L. M. de Rijk (Assen, 1970), pp. 535–98; Seton, *Dialectica* (1572), sigs. M3v–N5r.
[107] Case, *Summa in dialecticam*, sigs. Y3r–Cc1r.   [108] Ibid., sig. A2r.
[109] Sanderson, *Logicae*, sigs. P1r–4v.   [110] Ibid., sigs. Q1r–R1v.

6. Distinctions and definitions

Disputation places a high premium on accurate definitions, which can serve as a basis for further inferences, and on distinctions between different uses of a term. Both humanist philology and medieval semantic theories provided techniques for distinguishing meanings, on the basis of context and reference respectively. Some of the scholastic distinctions are discussed in the English renaissance dialectic manuals. Seton treats supposition in a generalised way as a theory of the different ways terms are to be understood in particular and universal propositions.[111] Carter's later commentary includes more advanced distinctions and employs scholastic technical vocabulary.[112] Case uses the scholastic terminology of intentions and lists the different types of supposition in his discussion of universals.[113] Sanderson gives brief, simple accounts of supposition, ampliation and restriction and exponibilia.[114]

Some of the diagrams in Case's textbooks serve to distinguish different senses in which words are used.[115] In his treatise on the topics Case proposes four instruments for directing invention and avoiding errors in disputation: choice, in basing arguments on universal axioms from the best authors; distinction, distinguishing between the different meanings of words so as to concentrate on the matter in question; investigation of differences; and comparison of similars.[116] In his account of disputation Sanderson gives special attention to the usefulness of making distinctions.[117]

7. Tactics for disputation

Disputation requires different forms of organisation from the oration, the sermon or the textbook. English authorities agree that the respondent must always outline the opponent's arguments before replying to them. Rainolds uses a diagram to summarise Aristotle's arguments against the use of emotions in rhetoric before replying to each in turn.[118] Rudolph Agricola's discussion of the organisation of arguments in *De inventione dialectica* recognised that the opponent would sometimes wish to put

---

[111] Seton, *Dialectica* (1572), sigs. I7v–K1v.
[112] Such as 'simple supposition, confused supposition, confused and distributed supposition, immobile supposition' ibid., sigs. K1v–3r.
[113] Case, *Summa in dialecticam*, sigs. A2v, F1v.
[114] Sanderson, *Logicae*, sigs. E6r–F3v, G7r–H1v, Ashworth, pp. xlii–xliv.
[115] E.g. Case, *Summa in dialecticam*, sigs. A1v, C2r.   [116] Ibid., sigs. Cc4v–Dd1r.
[117] Sanderson, *Logicae*, sigs. T6v–V1r.   [118] Green, *Rainolds's Lectures*, pp. 136–9.

arguments which seemed very remote from the point at issue in order to establish a basis from which an effective counter-argument could be made.[119]

Peter Martyr's disputation on the nature of the Eucharist gives some flavour of the tactical arguments involved. Martyr's opening position was that the bread and wine is not transubstantiated into the body and blood of Christ because the Bible speaks of the bread and the wine. Tresham opposed, explaining that if a man can be called dust and ashes then the body and blood of Christ can be referred to as bread and wine. Martyr replied that the bread and wine must be taken literally but that figurative interpretations will come into the argument later. Tresham then introduced the key text from Matthew, where Christ says: 'This is my body.'[120] Martyr had to argue that this statement must be taken figuratively.

Tresham's first move evidently anticipates Martyr's response to the key text. Although his argument that the words 'bread and wine' can be used figuratively to refer to the body and blood of Christ is a weak one (and may itself diminish the impact of transubstantiation), it forces Martyr into a response which insists on the literal meaning of words. By a disputational trick Tresham forces Martyr to oppose the form of interpretation he will later need to insist on.

Sanderson provides advice for both parties in a disputation. The opponent needs to keep the overall aim and the detailed plan of his argument in mind at all times (method), to find mediums of argument through the topics and to know how to support whatever part of an argument the respondent contests.[121] Understanding of comparisons and similarities will suggest propositions which may obtain assent from an unwary respondent.

The respondent needs to see the implications of propositions apparently unconnected to the subject under debate, and must be able to reject arguments which are either ill-formed or based on misleading premisses.[122] Crucially the opponent must be able to distinguish between different senses in which words are used. To help with this Sanderson provides laws of distinction and a list of ten common distinctions.[123] He believes that in this part of disputation scholastic logic is much more effective than humanists allow, commenting that one properly used scholastic

[119] Agricola, *De inventione dialectica*, pp. 446–50.   [120] Martyr, *Disputatio*, b3r–4r.
[121] Sanderson, *Logicae*, pp. 289–94.   [122] Ibid., p. 298. Seton, *Dialectica* (1572), sig. O5v.
[123] Sanderson, *Logicae*, pp. 302–6.

technical term is worth pages of Cicero and Lipsius.[124] Above all the respondent must avoid agreeing to something that is false, denying something true, absurdity and self-contradiction.[125] The respondent must always be cautious, avoiding saying more than he needs to or making concessions which can later be used against him.[126] In order to succeed in disputation students must cultivate ingenuity, modesty and candour.[127] Seton and Wilson suggest that the role of opponent exercises skill in invention, while judgment, the testing of the formulation of arguments, is the province of the respondent.[128] Case adds that it is essential to avoid being annoyed by the aggressive remarks of an adversary.[129]

8. Dialectical reading

In *De inventione dialectica*, Rudolph Agricola outlined the method of dialectical reading. In analysing a passage of classical literature one must first discover the question to which the arguments of the text are directed, both the general question of the whole work and the particular issue being addressed in a given section. By comparing the question with propositions made in the text it will be possible to work out whether the proposition supports or opposes the question and how it relates to other propositions in the text. This will enable chains of inference to be reconstructed. Some propositions will be capable of being formed into syllogisms on the main question, while others will be devoted to proving subordinate points or minor propositions. Once the underlying argumentative framework of the passage has been reconstructed, the topics through which each argument is linked to its conclusion can be inferred and labelled.[130] Agricola illustrates each stage of his account of dialectical reading with examples from classical literature. His commentary on Cicero's *Pro lege Manilia*, composed at the same time as *De inventione dialectica*, serves as an example of a reconstruction of the argumentative structure of a classical text.[131]

---

[124] Ibid., p. 303.   [125] Seton, *Dialectica* (1572), sigs. O5v–6v; Wilson, *Rule of Reason*, p. 155.
[126] Sanderson, *Logicae*, pp. 299, 301; Seton, *Dialectica* (1572), sig. O6r; Wilson, *Rule of Reason*, pp. 155–6.
[127] Sanderson, *Logicae*, p. 283.
[128] Seton, *Dialectica* (1572), sig. O4v; Wilson, *Rule of Reason*, p. 153.
[129] Case, *Summa in dialecticam*, sig. Dd4v.
[130] Agricola, *De inventione dialectica*, pp. 353–62; Mack, *Renaissance Argument*, pp. 227–33.
[131] Agricola, *De inventione dialectica*, pp. 461–71; Peter Mack, 'Rudolph Agricola's Reading of Literature', *Journal of the Warburg and Courtauld Institutes* 48 (1985), 23–41; Marc van der Poel, 'The "Scholia in orationem pro lege Manilia" of Rudolph Agricola', *Lias* 24 (1997), 1–35.

Elizabethan Rhetoric

The idea of logical analysis of texts proved to be one of the most enduring innovations of humanist dialectic. Melanchthon and Ramus followed Agricola's lead both in their logic textbooks which frequently analysed passages from literary texts and from scripture in order to teach the use of dialectic, and in their commentaries on classical literature.[132] Sanderson's appendix 'De analysi logica' outlines rules to follow and issues to bear in mind in uncovering different kinds of logical structure. He also provides examples of classical texts to analyse as instances of themes, problems and entire sciences.[133]

Given the variety of studies pursued in the Elizabethan university (particularly by those gentlemen commoners who had no intention of graduating) and the range of textbooks listed in the inventories it would be wrong to assert that all students acquired all these skills. Nevertheless it seems likely that rhetorical doctrines and dialectical analysis were widely employed in reading classical texts. The inventories show the persistence of grammar school textbooks alongside the classical rhetoric manuals and orations required by the university statutes. The same notebooks which demonstrate the variety of individual reading show their authors composing letters and declamations (and analysing the logical structure of sermons). Anyone who planned to graduate must have acquired skills in invention and criticism of arguments, in forming and analysing syllogisms, in defining, in distinguishing different applications of words and in arranging a series of arguments.

While disputation remained the crucial test of argumentative skill, in Elizabethan universities it became more closely linked to rhetoric. Students followed a course of rhetoric which was comprehensive, which was linked to the analysis of classical texts and the composition of new ones, and which was closely connected with dialectic, both in reading texts and in disputation. In dialectic pupils were taught to define and distinguish, to invent arguments, to shape them correctly and to organise persuasive discourse on a large scale, either as arguments from first principles or as strategies for debate. Following the humanist model, dialectic was treated as a useful practical skill. In the final chapters of the book we shall consider the impact of dialectical training on examples of Elizabethan political and religious argument.

[132] Kees Meerhoff, 'Logique et éloquence: une révolution Ramusienne?', in K. Meerhoff and J. C. Moisan (eds.), *Autour de Ramus* (Montreal, 1997), pp. 87–132; Peter Mack, 'Ramus Reading: The Commentaries on Cicero's *Consular Orations* and Vergil's Eclogues and Georgics', *Journal of the Warburg and Courtauld Institutes* 61 (1998), 111–41.
[133] Sanderson, *Logicae*, pp. 317–29.

University training in rhetoric and dialectic was essentially propaedeutic, pursued for the sake of studies in history, ethics and natural philosophy. Dialectic was connected with further studies particularly through disputation. At the end of his treatise on the topics, Case decides to include topics of ethics and physics because students will need to take part in disputations on these subjects.[134] Students should keep a list of axioms for these subjects in the memory ready to be compared with theses which may be put to them. Studies of ethics, physics and history in turn aimed to be preparations for a lifetime of reading and reflection, whose results would be marshalled and presented according to the methods inculcated at grammar school and university. In the next three chapters we shall consider middle stages in this process of application of learned techniques: the role of vernacular handbooks of rhetoric and dialectic and the adaptation of Latin patterns of eloquence to the structures of English; the everyday rhetoric of notebooks, letters and narratives; and the transmission of moral instruction in the informal lifelong reading of histories, conduct manuals and romances.

---

[134] Case, *Summa in dialecticam*, sigs. Kk2r–Ll3v.

3

English-language manuals of rhetoric and dialectic

ENGLISH MANUALS AND THE LATIN EDUCATIONAL CONTEXT

Given that the English manuals have received far more attention in the scholarly literature than the Latin textbooks used in school and university, it needs to be stated at the outset that only four of the twenty were printed more than twice in the sixteenth century.[1] Thomas Wilson's *Rule of Reason* was printed seven times between 1551 and 1580, his *Art of Rhetoric* eight times between 1553 and 1585, William Fulwood's *Enemie of Idleness* ten times between 1568 and 1621 and Angel Day's *The English Secretary* nine times between 1586 and 1635.[2] By contrast, George Puttenham's *Arte of English Poesie*, upon which so many theories of Elizabethan culture have been erected,[3] was printed only once in 1589, and the elder Henry Peacham's *Garden of Eloquence* once in each of its editions (1577 and 1593).

Any educationally based account of the English manuals must therefore concentrate mainly on Wilson, Fulwood and Day. These are the only English-language manuals which can have exercised much influence in transmitting doctrine. Other manuals may help us understand the way in which rhetorical teachings were received and adapted.

I shall argue that there is one important exception to this rule. Sherry, Peacham, Puttenham (in his third book), Wilson (in the third book of

---

[1] In arriving at the figure of twenty I have included Abraham Fleming's *A Panoplie of Epistles* (London, 1576) STC 11049, because of the 'epitome of precepts'. I have excluded John Browne's *The Marchants Avizo* (London, 1589) STC 3908.4, which had at least two other sixteenth-century editions, because it contains only eight model letters and no instructions for letter-writing. Had I included Browne I should also have had to include Nicholas Breton's *A Poste with a Madde Packet of Letters* (London, 1602) STC 3684, which includes more than eighty fictional letters.

[2] All these figures are taken from the *Short Title Catalogue*. The English-language manuals are surveyed in Howell, *Logic and Rhetoric* and Skinner, *Reason and Rhetoric*, pp. 51–67.

[3] For example, Whigham, *Ambition and Privilege*; Patricia Parker, *Literary Fat Ladies: Rhetoric, Gender, Property* (London, 1987); Rebhorn, *Emperor of Men's Minds*.

his *Rhetoric*) and Day (in his last eight editions)[4] all produced versions of an English style manual. The material which these treatments share (the bulk of the manual) therefore went through twenty-one editions. All these style manuals are based on each other and on a succession of renaissance Latin adaptations of the classical Latin style manual, found principally in *Rhetorica ad Herennium* book IV and Quintilian's *Institutio oratoria*, books VIII and IX.

All the English manuals fit in with the syllabus of the Latin-medium school and university courses. The twenty English-language manuals to which I have already referred cover six types of teaching. Fulwood's *Enemie of Idleness*, Abraham Fleming's *A Panoplie of Epistles* (1576) and Day's *English Secretary* are letter-writing manuals.[5] Sherry's *A Treatise of Schemes and Tropes* (1550, and with some changes 1555), Peacham's *Garden of Eloquence*, the third book of Puttenham's *Arte of English Poesie* and the bulk of John Hoskins's manuscript *Directions for Speech and Style* (1599) are manuals of style. Richard Rainolde's *Foundacion of Rhetorike* (1563) is a translation of Aphthonius's *Progymnasmata* with newly composed English orations.

These three groups clearly represent English versions of standard grammar school textbooks. They are firmly based on (mostly Latin) continental models. The letter-writing manual which forms the larger part of Angel Day's *The English Secretary* depends for its definitions and instructions on Erasmus's *De conscribendis epistolis*. Fulwood's *Enemie of Idleness* is an adaptation of *Le style et manière de composer . . . toute sorte d'epistres* (Lyons, 1566), itself an adaptation of Erasmus.[6] The 'epitome of precepts' which precedes Fleming's *A Panoplie of Epistles* (1576) is a translation in dialogue form of Christopher Hegendorff's *Methodus conscribendi epistolis*.[7]

---

[4] The dedicatory epistles (and the *Short Title Catalogue*) suggest that there are three versions of *The English Secretary* from 1586 (STC 6401), 1592 (STC 6402) and 1599 (6404). The latter two versions are considerably different from the first edition (changes in phrasing, additional comments, new examples, new sections on figures and tropes, and the secretary's duties) but only slightly different from each other. My account is based on the edition of 1599.

[5] On these manuals see K. G. Hornbeak, 'The Complete Letter-Writer in English', *Smith College Studies in Modern Languages* 15 (1934), 1–150; Jean Robertson, *The Art of Letter Writing* (London, 1942); G. W. Pigman, III, *Grief and English Renaissance Elegy* (Cambridge, 1985), pp. 12–16, 20–2, 131–4; Lynne Magnusson, *Shakespeare and Social Dialogue: Dramatic Language and Elizabethan Letters* (Cambridge, 1999), esp. pp. 3–4, 61–88, 114–30. The distinction between Day's 'gentleman's' manual and the merchants' manuals of Fulwood and Browne, which Magnusson asserts, is undone by her own examples (pp. 128–9).

[6] Robertson, *Art of Letter Writing*, pp. 13–14.

[7] The 'epitome of precepts' exists as a separate quire in four of the extant copies, including British Library 92 d. 25. Some of the translated letters by Cicero, Isocrates, Pliny, Erasmus, Ascham and

A fourth group, the manuals of the whole of rhetoric, correspond to the university textbook of rhetoric. Leonard Cox's *Arte or Crafte of Rethoryke* (1532) was a translation of Melanchthon's *Institutiones rhetoricae* with new examples. Thomas Wilson's *Arte of Rhetorique* draws on a range of classical and renaissance sources. Most of the definitions are taken from *Rhetorica ad Herennium*, Cicero's *De inventione*, Quintilian, and Melanchthon's *Elementorum rhetorices libri duo*, but Wilson also makes use of Erasmus's *De conscribendis epistolis* and *De copia*, and, for the discussion of emotional persuasion, Rudolph Agricola's *De inventione dialectica*.[8] Dudley Fenner's *Arte of Rethorike* (1584, 1588)[9] translates, and Abraham Fraunce's *Arcadian Rhetorike* (1588) adapts, the Ramist rhetoric manual.

Also associated with the university arts faculty is the fifth group, the manuals covering the whole of dialectic. Within a broadly Aristotelian framework, Wilson's *Rule of Reason* combines a section on judgment derived from Melanchthon's *Erotemata dialectices* with a section on invention taken from Rudolph Agricola and Boethius. Thomas Blundeville's *Logike* (1599, 1617, 1619) translates and adapts the same treatise by Melanchthon. Ralph Lever's *The Arte of Reason, rightly termed, Witcraft* (1573, but probably composed before 1551) was based mainly on Aristotle.[10] Ramus's *Logic* was translated by McIlmain (1574, 1581) and Fenner (1584, 1588) and adapted in Abraham Fraunce's *Lawyer's Logike* (1588). Finally, the preaching manuals are translations of two Latin texts associated with the theology faculty: Niels Hemmingsen's *The Preacher* (1574, 1576) and Andreas Gerardus (Hyperius)'s *The Practice of Preaching* (1577).[11]

The English manuals correspond to the types of textbook employed in school and university teaching. They are mostly derivatives of continental renaissance Latin originals. In their prefaces the English authors and translators show themselves to be fully attuned to the aims of humanist education. Peacham's remarks on the need to join eloquence and knowledge correspond very closely to comments by Erasmus, Sturm and

others in the anthology which makes up the bulk of the work are also taken from Hegendorff. Fleming, *Panoplie of Epistles*; Hornbeak, 'Complete Letter-Writer', pp. 14–16; W. G. Crane, *Wit and Rhetoric in the Renaissance* (New York, 1937, repr. Gloucester MA, 1964), p. 109.

[8] Thomas Wilson, *The Art of Rhetoric*, ed. Peter E. Medine (University Park PA, 1994), pp. 160–4; Agricola, *De inventione dialectica*, pp. 199, 378–80, 383–4. References to Erasmus are given in notes 39–40 below.

[9] *Short Title Catalogue* gives five editions of Fenner's combined work, *The Artes of Logike and Rethorike*, but since four of these are from the same printer in Middleburg in 1584, and since there are few copies of any of the four, it seems fair to treat them as variants of a single edition.

[10] Howell, *Logic and Rhetoric*, pp. 57–63.

[11] Preaching manuals and their continental sources are discussed in Debora Shuger, *Sacred Rhetoric* (Princeton, 1988).

Ascham.[12] The manuals are also presented as part of a wider process of making textbooks of learned subjects available in English, which will assert the dignity of the English language and contribute to its future development.[13] In 1550 Sherry claimed that his translation of the figures of rhetoric into English would help not only pupils who lack first-class teachers but everyone else as well, since everyone understands better what is written in their native language.[14] In the following year Wilson made it clear that he saw *The Rule of Reason* as part of an international project of making the tools of learning available to those who had not studied Latin and Greek.[15]

The presentation in English of doctrines of rhetoric and dialectic could be seen as a logical extension of the humanist project. Since the humanists aimed to make rhetoric and dialectic useful in reading and writing, what could be more useful than extending their reach into the vernaculars? Wilson's work fitted in with a broader tide of linguistic nationalism. By making important educational works available in English, scholars hoped to improve the usefulness of English. The struggle to acquire vocabulary and structures in which to express the content of learned subjects would expand the possibilities of the language. At the same time the new technical vocabulary associated with rhetoric and dialectic would increase awareness of what could be done in the language and prepare the way for more successful imitation of classical and continental writing.

Yet Wilson's careful summary of the whole of logic made his work especially suitable for the use of students who wished to confirm their understanding of Latin texts or, as we might say in the vernacular, who wanted a crib. There is some evidence in the student booklists and in the ownership marks in surviving copies that a few copies of Wilson's textbooks were used by university students.[16] Sherry implies that schoolboys may prefer to read, or may need the help of, a style manual in English. The references to Latin examples which we find throughout the style manuals make more sense if we assume that schoolboys and students used them in addition to the audience of those outside institutions of

[12] Henry Peacham (the elder), *The Garden of Eloquence* (London, 1577, repr. Menston, 1971) STC 19497, sig. A2r–v. Compare Ascham, *The Scholemaster*, in *English Works*, pp. 265–6, Erasmus, *De ratione studii*, pp. 113–14.

[13] 'No learned nation hath there been but the learned in it have written of schemes and figures, which they would not have done except they had perceived the value.' Richard Sherry, *A Treatise of Schemes and Tropes* (London, 1550), facsimile repr. ed. H. W. Hildebrandt (Gainesville, 1961), sig. A5r.

[14] Ibid., sigs. A4v–6v.   [15] Wilson, *Rule of Reason*, pp. 1–2.

[16] Leedham-Green, *Cambridge Inventories*, I, pp. 313, 317, 333.

Latin learning. Hoskins composed his manuscript English rhetoric manual, *Directions for Speech and Style*, for the benefit of his friend's son, who
had left university and begun to study at the Inns of Court.[17] Although
Puttenham states that his chief purpose is the 'learning of Ladies and
young Gentlewomen or idle courtiers desirous to become skilful in their
owne mother tongue', he also regards his teaching as sufficiently worthwhile to dedicate his book to his notoriously well-educated Queen and
her chief minister.[18] The English manuals correspond so closely to the
categories of textbook established by the grammar school and university
syllabi that they could have been used both to extend the usefulness of
humanist education outside the circle of Latin learning and to reinforce
the understanding of those within it.

So far I have shown that the English manuals of rhetoric and dialectic
were based on continental (mostly Latin) models, corresponded to grammar school and university textbooks, endorsed the aims of the humanist
reform of education and were part of the project of translating textbooks
of learned subjects into English. Only four of them were at all successful
as publications.

All four English-language manuals reflect grammar school and university
teaching. William Fulwood's popular letter-writing manual, *The Enemie
of Idleness*, provides instructions for composing a range of letters useful in
everyday life, for example: 'How to request counsel of an advocate', 'How
one friend should write to another, comforting him for his loss', 'How
to visit our friend with letters, not having any great matter to write'.[19]
For each type he offers a three or four item list of contents, which he
confusingly calls a 'style', and appends a model letter.

How to request a temporal benefit
As concerning the manner how to demand temporal things, as a book, a horse
or such like, the letter must be divided into four parts.

First, we must get the good will of him to whom we write, by praising his
liberality, and principally of the power and authority that he hath to grant the
thing that he is demanded.

---

[17] John Hoskins, *Directions for Speech and Style*, ed. H. H. Hudson (Princeton, 1935), pp. 2–3, 31.
[18] George Puttenham, *The Arte of English Poesie*, ed. G. D. Willcock and A. Walker (Cambridge, 1936), pp. 158, cxii, 2.
[19] William Fulwood, *The Enemie of Idleness* (London, 1582) STC 11479, sigs. D5v, F6v, K5v. For ease of reading I have modernised the spelling in most of the quotations from sixteenth-century English rhetoric manuals.

Secondly, we must declare our demand and request to be honest and necessary, and without the which we cannot achieve to our determinate end and purpose. Thirdly, that the request is easy to be granted, considering his ability, and that in a more difficult thing his liberality is ordinarily expressed.

Fourthly, to promise recompense, as thanks, service etc.[20]

Although this is not a copy of Erasmus's much longer instructions for letters of request, it makes the same points: that the request should be within the donor's power, that it should be just, that recompense should be promised, and that the donor's liberality should be praised.[21] After the instructions he provides an anthology of model letters. In the third book, consisting of invented letters and replies, Fulwood takes some pleasure in letting the correspondents give radically different views of an incident. Thus a mother writes to reprove her widowed daughter for her dishonourable behaviour, but the daughter replies with an aggrieved account of her efforts to elude a persistent suitor.[22] Fulwood's exchanges sometimes raise moral issues, as when a letter to a prince requesting clemency for a friend is answered by a letter on the superior claims of justice.[23] Fulwood imitates classroom practice in inventing letters for historical situations (as when Cicero, writing to reprove Catiline, assures him that he speaks with great affection)[24] but he also enjoys the dramatic situation created by an exchange of letters. He explains that the letters of famous authors translated in book II serve to inspire courageous readers to the imitation of different styles.[25]

Angel Day's *The English Secretary* is more ambitious, providing not only instructions for the contents and structure of letters but also a handbook of tropes and figures and a conduct manual. In the order of types of letter discussed and in the principal comments on each type Day generally summarises Erasmus's *De conscribendis epistolis*. As a consequence he directs the letter-writer's attention to the social situation implied in each letter. In letters of exhortation, for example, the main topics to be employed are 'either of praise or mislike, of hope of reward, or fear of evil to follow, of love to well-doing or of hate unto badness, of emulation of other's praise, glory or reputation, of expectation thereon depending, of examples, or of entreaty'.[26] After discussing the nature of praise and envy, Day, still

[20] Ibid., sig. E1 r–v.   [21] Erasmus, *De conscribendis epistolis*, pp. 465–7.

[22] Fulwood, *Enemie*, sigs. Q1 v–3r.   [23] Ibid., sigs. R6r–7v.   [24] Ibid., sig. I2r.

[25] Ibid., sig. M7r–v. Fulwood uses simple familiar letters of Cicero as his model for the familiar and domestic letter, sigs. K3r–5v.

[26] Angel Day, *The English Secretary* (London, 1599) STC 6404, facsimile repr. ed. Robert O. Evans (Gainesville, 1967), sig. G4v. Compare Erasmus, *De conscribendis epistolis*, pp. 324–9, 340. Hornbeak draws the same conclusions as I do, 'Complete Letter-Writer', pp. 17, 20–23.

summarising Erasmus, invites his reader–writer to consider the recipient of the letter.

To apply now this praise in exhorting or counselling any one, it behoveth we first conceive what disposition, habiliments or other matter of value are in him whom we have to deal with, furthering or convenient to such a purpose, whereunto we would exhort or persuade him and the likelihood of the same greatly to put forth or commend; or if before time he have behaved himself any ways well, we shall encourage him in praising of that already done; and in showing that the more excellent the thing is, the more difficult it is to be attained, for *Difficilia quae pulchra*, and yet the difficulty not so great as the praise, glory and recordation thereof, shall thereby afterwards be returned honourable.[27]

The summary is not elegantly composed or easy to follow but it is worth reading because of the well thought out Erasmian material it conveys. Like Erasmus, Day gives summaries of more general rhetorical teaching, for example on the topics of deliberative oratory and the handling of emotion.[28] For each type, he provides at least one example (not translated from Erasmus) with marginal notes which point out (usually in roman type) the topics of the letter and (in italic type) the figures of rhetoric employed. Occasionally Day adds comments on the style of the letter he has just composed. Thus, on a letter of a son seeking reconciliation with his angry father, Day comments:

The style of this Epistle is vehement because the passions of him from whence it came were vehement, and is deduced as you see from the nature of *Reconciliatorie*, which as well for the submissive and lowest terms it beareth, as also for the urgent petition therein contained, I have rather chosen to place among the *Petitorie*. The part of *honest* herein delivered is passed in words meekest and of great obedience, wherein he studieth by all possibility to mitigate towards himself the too much severity of his father. The *Exordium* is carried by *Insinuation*, expressing the vehement affects and surcharged conceits of a mind more than ordinarily grieved.[29]

In Day's hands, in contrast to Fulwood's, the technical vocabulary of rhetoric is shown to be a subtle tool for analysing the texture and effect of a passage of writing. Day occasionally refers to grammar school texts, sometimes addresses the issue of composing letter-declamations on each side of an issue and often touches on issues concerning the role of education and parents' expectations of their children.[30] Some of Day's letters resemble school composition exercises, for example the description of a city, the praise of learning, the persuasion to marriage and the death

---

[27] Day, *English Secretary*, sig. G4v. Compare Erasmus, *De conscribendis epistolis*, pp. 324–6.
[28] Day, *English Secretary*, sigs. E4r–v, G3v–H1r.   [29] Ibid., sig. N4r–v.
[30] Ibid., sigs. D4v, H1v–I1v, K2v–3v, L2v–4r.

speech.[31] Both Fulwood and Day suggest that letters of reply should begin by setting out the main points of the letter received.[32]

Thomas Wilson's manuals emphasise the connections between rhetoric and dialectic. In *The Art of Rhetoric*, he frequently comments on rhetoric's need of the logical topics for invention, arguing that a perfect knowledge of logic is required before anyone can benefit from rhetorical training.[33] His comparison between the two arts concentrates on their similarity, locating the difference mainly in issues of style and audience.

> Both these arts are much like, saving that Logic is occupied about all matters, and doth plainly and nakedly set forth with apt words the sum of things by way of argumentation. Again of the other side Rhetoric useth gay painted sentences and setteth forth those matters with fresh colours and godly ornaments and that at large.[34]

The Rule of Reason provides a complete course in dialectic, based on Aristotle's syllabus but with important humanist inflections. Wilson gives prominence to the topics, taking the definition of topic, the list of topics, the diagram and some of the treatment of individual topics from Rudolph Agricola but supplementing this with maxims from Boethius.[35] Wilson takes great care in explaining the method of topical invention,[36] which he illustrates with worked examples.[37] He provides a complete account of the syllogism and the other forms of argumentation. His discussion of definition, division and eight topics for handling a simple question recalls Melanchthon on method.[38]

The Art of Rhetoric covers the whole syllabus of the subject. Wilson adds in material on the topics of exhortation and comfort, taken from Erasmus's *De conscribendis epistolis*.[39] His discussion of amplification is based on Erasmus's *De copia*, which he also uses for some aspects of style (especially for evidentia, similitudes, examples, fables and comparisons).[40] His account of disposition recalls Agricola's summary of

---

[31] Ibid., sigs. D4v–E1v, E2r–3r, H4r–I1v, I3v–K1r.

[32] Fulwood, *Enemie*, sig. M8r; Day, *English Secretary*, sig. H3v.

[33] Wilson, *Rhetoric*, pp. 49, 65, 145; R. H. Wagner, 'Wilson and his Sources', *Quarterly Journal of Speech* 15 (1929), 525–36; Wagner, 'Thomas Wilson's *Arte of Rhetorique*', *Speech Monographs* 27 (1960), 1–32; Peter E. Medine, *Thomas Wilson* (Boston, 1986), pp. 55–74.

[34] Wilson, *Rule of Reason*, p. 11; Medine, *Wilson*, pp. 41–54.

[35] E.g. Wilson, *Rule of Reason*, pp. 90–1, 93, 99–100; Agricola, *De inventione dialectica*, pp. 9, 25, 26, 57–9, 62–5. Wilson's definition of logic (*Rule of Reason*, p. 8) is taken from Agricola, *De inventione dialectica*, p. 193.

[36] Wilson, *Rule of Reason*, p. 89.   [37] Ibid., pp. 135–53.   [38] Ibid., pp. 37–45.

[39] Wilson, *Rhetoric*, pp. 79–103 and Medine, *Wilson*, notes, p. 262; Erasmus, *De conscribendis epistolis*, pp. 400–29, 432–5.

[40] Wilson, *Rhetoric*, pp. 147–60, 203–5, 213–22, 231–2 and Medine, *Wilson*, notes, pp. 271–5, 286–7, 291–2, 298. Some of the material from *De copia* is used via *Ecclesiastes*.

the different factors the writer must consider in determining the structure of a text.[41]

Wilson explains the role which moral sentences play in amplification and appends two pages of apothegms which he only breaks off by referring to Heywood's *Proverbs*, 'worthy immortal praise', where plenty are to be had in print.[42] His rhetoric is illustrated with specially composed or translated declamations in each of the principal rhetorical genres.[43] Wilson's practical bent is also illustrated in the important place in his textbook which he devotes to humour. Taking seriously the third of the orator's duties ('except men find delight, they will not long abide; delight them, and win them; weary them and you lose them forever'),[44] Wilson spices his manual with asides and amusing stories. He devotes a separate and quite lengthy section to the method of arousing laughter, in which the precepts from *De oratore* are illustrated with Wilson's own retellings of funny stories of classical and native origin.[45]

THE ENGLISH STYLE MANUAL

I have already suggested that the English manuals of style (Sherry, Puttenham, Peacham and Hoskins), none of which was much printed on its own, might best be considered, along with the accounts of the tropes and figures in Wilson's *Rhetoric* and Day's *English Secretary*, as versions of a single archetext: the renaissance English style manual. With minor variations, these manuals treat the same set of figures. Later ones copy from and adapt the earlier ones. They all rely on a series of renaissance Latin style books which adapt the classical sources for the uses of the grammar schools of northern Europe. In order to understand the English-language style manuals one has to begin by looking at renaissance Latin adaptations of classical treatments of the tropes and figures.

Where classical accounts listed large numbers of figures, sometimes with lengthy discussions of each, divided into only three classes (tropes, figures of thought, figures of diction), Erasmus in *De copia* (1512) highlights a group of figures especially useful for producing copia of words.[46] He provides a particularly thorough account of different types of metaphor, but also considers antonomasia, metaphor, allegory, onomatopoeia, metonymy, synecdoche, hyperbole and a range of figures

---

[41] Wilson, *Rhetoric*, pp. 51–2, compare Agricola, *De inventione dialectica*, pp. 449–50; Mack, *Renaissance Argument*, pp. 224–5.
[42] Wilson, *Rhetoric*, pp. 149–51.   [43] Ibid., pp. 57–9, 61–4, 66–70, 79–100, 103–19, 126–8.
[44] Ibid., p. 47.   [45] Ibid., pp. 164–83.   [46] On *De copia* more generally, see chapter one above.

of pronunciation (for example, interrogatio, irony, admiratio, dubitatio, exclamatio and occupatio). Under copia of things he discusses description, amplification, commonplaces, examples and proverbs. The *Tabulae de schematibus et tropibus* (1516) of Peter Schade (?1493–1524), better known under the Latin name of Mosellanus, provides a more articulated division of the figures than that found in the classical authorities, with brief definitions of each and examples from the best authors. As a result of reading *De copia*, Mosellanus adds comparison, example and icon to the list of figures, divides metaphor into seven types and considers enigma, proverb, irony, sarcasm, wit and contradiction as forms of allegory.[47]

Melanchthon's *Institutiones rhetoricae* (1521) follows Mosellanus in emphasising metaphor and allegory. He adds comparison and example to the tropes.[48] Among rhetorical schemes, he gives special prominence to anaphora (beginning each of a series of phrases with the same word) and antistrophe (closing each with the same word). Within the rhetorical figures he introduces a new subdivision of figures of amplification, including interpretatio, incrementum, climax, antithesis, antimetabole, synoeciosis and epanados.[49]

Susenbrotus's *Epitome troporum ac schematum*, first printed in 1540, draws on the work of Erasmus, Mosellanus and Melanchthon. It follows Melanchthon's reorganisation of the figures and aims to supplant Mosellanus in the textbook market by providing additional examples of each figure.[50] Where Mosellanus had listed 98 figures and Melanchthon around 70, Susenbrotus increases the number, with occasional repetition,[51] to 132. On the whole he prefers Greek terminology in naming the figures, though he always gives Latin terms (sometimes several of them) as well. Within each entry he allows himself the space to explain fully and to give several examples from classical poetry, oratory and scripture. Susenbrotus regards the style manual as essentially an aid to reading, since only by explaining the rhetorical artifices employed by the author can a teacher impart the meaning of a classical text to his pupils.[52] He gives careful explanations of many figures which are used mainly in poetry. This is Susenbrotus's account of metaphor.

---

47 P. Mosellanus, *Tabulae de schematibus et tropibus* (London, 1573) STC 21810.3, sigs. B3r–4r, 4v–5v.
48 Philipp Melanchthon, *Institutiones rhetoricae* (Hagenau, 1521), sig. D1v.
49 Ibid., sig. E1r–v. This is an attempt to absorb the lessons of *De copia* within the style manual.
50 Joannes Susenbrotus, *Epitome troporum ac schematum* (Zurich, undated), sig. A2v, printed in facsimile in J. X. Brennan, 'The *Epitome troporum ac schematum* of Joannes Susenbrotus: Text, Translation and Commentary' (unpublished PhD thesis, University of Illinois, 1953).
51 For example, prosopopeia, Susenbrotus, *Epitome*, sigs. E2v, F3r.   52 Ibid., sig. A2r.

A metaphor occurs when a word is transformed from its proper and genuine significance to another but related one. This trope is by far the most beautiful: as 'I see' for 'I understand'; 'I grasp it' for 'I comprehend it'; 'to swallow' for 'to overcome' or 'to put up with'; 'I look up to' for 'I esteem'. Likewise if you should say a man of odious and insipid loquacity 'brays' or 'babbles'. Furthermore a word is changed from its proper meaning to another either by necessity, as when we say that vines 'gemmate', the fields 'thirst', the fruits 'labour', the fields 'luxuriate'. Or for the sake of emphasis and greater significance, as 'incensed by wrath', 'inflamed by desire', 'fallen into error'. Or, finally, for the sake of ornament, as 'a light of language', 'splendour of birth', 'the tempest of the public assemblies', 'rivers of eloquence', 'the spring and soil of all glory', and 'the corn fields undulate', that is they are being moved etc.[53]

Though hardly as full as Quintilian, Susenbrotus gives a clear explanation of the concept with many examples from ordinary speech. He borrows his definition and some examples from Erasmus's *De copia*, his division from Quintilian.[54] Susenbrotus's account of synecdoche ('when one thing is understood from another in any way whatever') explains many examples of poetic uses of language, especially from Virgil. The explanation and the examples are mainly from *De copia*.[55] Metonymy too is illustrated mainly with poetic alterations of name. Susenbrotus copies the divisions of the figure from Weltkirchius's commentary on *De copia*.[56] The final section of the book, on rhetorical schemes of amplification, derives much of its content (for example, sections on descriptions of character, persons, things, places and times, division and enumeration, proverb, comparison and example) from *De copia*, though the descriptions of many of the particular figures are based on the versions in *Rhetorica ad Herennium* and Erasmus's *Ecclesiastes*.[57]

---

53 'Metaphora est cum vox a propria ac germana significatione ad alienam sed cognatam transfertur. Tropus longe pulcherrima ut, video pro intellige, perspicio pro cognitum habeo, devoro pro vinco et perfero, suspicio pro admiror. Item si hominem odiosae atque insulsae loquacitatis rudere aut blaterare dicas. Porro vox a propria significatione ad aliam transfertur, vel necessitatis causa: ut cum vites gemmare dicimus, sitire agros, fructus laborare, luxuriare segetes; vel emphaseos ac maioris significantiae gratia, ut incensus ira, inflammatus cupiditate, lapsus errore; vel denique ornatus causa ut lumen orationis, generis claritas, concionum procella, eloquentiae flumina, fons ac seges gloriae, et segetes fluctuant, id est moventur etc.' Susenbrotus, *Epitome*, sig. A5r (trans. Brennan, *Epitome troporum*, slightly altered).

54 Quintilian, *Institutio oratoria*, VIII.6.4–18, esp. 6; Erasmus, *De copia* (1988), pp. 62–4 (trans. *Collected Works*, XXIV, pp. 333–4); Brennan, *Epitome troporum*, p. 110. It is noticeable that Susenbrotus omits Erasmus's discussion of seven sources of metaphor, which Mosellanus (*Tabulae*, sig. B3r–v) and some English authors include.

55 Susenbrotus, *Epitome*, sigs. A5r–v; Brennan, *Epitome troporum*, p. 110; Erasmus, *De copia* (1988), pp. 70–2 (trans. *Collected Works*, XXIV, p. 341). On this occasion Susenbrotus follows Erasmus's logical division of types of synecdoche.

56 Susenbrotus, *Epitome*, sigs. A5v–6r; Brennan, *Epitome troporum*, p. 110; Erasmus, *De copia* (1569), sig. D8r–v.

57 Susenbrotus, *Epitome*, sigs. F3r–G3r; Brennan, *Epitome troporum*, p. 140.

Most of the English versions of the style manual translated and adapted from all these classical and renaissance Latin versions as well as copying the previous English ones. Thus under the heading of transumption, Wilson writing in 1553 made use of Richard Sherry's *Treatise of Schemes and Tropes* (1550), who was himself there following Susenbrotus.[58] Henry Peacham's *Garden of Eloquence* (1577, revised in 1593) used Susenbrotus, Sherry and Wilson.[59] Puttenham adds new English names and many examples of his own to the account of the figures in *The Arte of English Poesie* (1589), but the framework of his entries usually comes from Susenbrotus.[60] Day (1595) normally works directly from Susenbrotus.[61] John Hoskins's manuscript *Directions for Speech and Style* (c. 1600) is particularly alert to changes in stylistic fashion. One crucial example of this is his cautious endorsement, in comparison with Peacham's enthusiasm, of the figure of sententia (embellishment with proverbs).[62]

Sherry follows Susenbrotus when he takes the view that no eloquent writer can be perceived as he should be without knowledge of the figures.[63] The tropes and figures are as frequent in English authors as in classical texts and they are especially useful in interpreting scripture.[64]

Many things might I bring in to prove not only a great profit to be in them but that they are to be learned even of necessity, for as much as not only profane authors without them may not be well understand, but also they greatly profit us in the reading of holy scripture, where if you be ignorant in the figurative speeches and tropes, you are like in many great doubts to make but a slender solution, as right well do testify Castalio Vestimerus and the noble doctor St Augustine.[65]

Knowledge of the tropes and figures will save students time and make them better readers.

For as like pleasure is not to him which goeth into a goodly garden garnished with divers kinds of herbs and flowers and there doth no more but behold them, of whom it may be said that he went in for nothing but that he would come out, and to him which beside the corporal eye pleasure knoweth of every one the name and property, so verily is there in reading good authors and in sundry sorts of men that do it.[66]

---

[58] Wilson, *Rhetoric*, pp. 200, 284–5; Sherry, *Schemes and Tropes*, sig. C5r–v; Susenbrotus, *Epitome*, sig. A7r (metalepsis).

[59] William G. Crane (ed.) 'Introduction' to Henry Peacham (the elder), *The Garden of Eloquence* (London, 1593, STC 19498, facsimile repr. Gainesville, 1954), pp. 11–15.

[60] On allegory, for example, compare Puttenham, *Arte* (1936), pp. 186–91 with Susenbrotus, *Epitome*, sigs. A7v–B2r.

[61] On zeugma, Day, *English Secretary* (sig. Kk3v) translates Susenbrotus (*Epitome*, sig. B6v).

[62] Hoskins, *Directions*, pp. 38–40; Peacham, *Garden* (1593), sigs. Cc3r–4r.

[63] Sherry, *Schemes and Tropes*, sig. A6v.   [64] Ibid., sig. A7r.

[65] Ibid., sig. A7r–v.   [66] Ibid., sig. A8r–v.

Peacham claims that knowledge of the figures is both delightful and necessary:

the knowledge of them so necessary that no man can read profitably or understand perfectly either poets, orators or the Holy Scriptures without them; nor any orator be able by the weight of his words to persuade his hearers, having no help of them.[67]

In his second edition he makes a great deal more of the connection between figures, emotional persuasion and the power conferred on the orator by the combination of wisdom and eloquence.[68] In *The English Secretary* Day marked the tropes and figures used in his model letters to assist his readers in analysing the models and in using figurative ornaments in their own letters. After 1595 he removed the need for his readers to purchase a separate manual of figures by including one of his own.[69]

In all the English manuals the main emphasis in every case is on identifying a name (sometimes with alternative names), giving an explanation of the figure and providing examples. Sometimes the figure is subdivided, with explanations and examples of each type, and sometimes there is a comment on the use of a figure (which may be advice on when not to use it). Sherry's account of metaphor follows Mosellanus with additional material from *De copia*.

Metaphora, Translatio, translation: that is a word translated from the thing that it properly signifieth unto another which may agree with it by a similitude. And among all virtues of speech this is the chief.

None persuadeth more effecteously, none showeth the thing before our eyes more evidently, none moveth more mightily the affections, none maketh the oration more goodly pleasant, nor copious.

Translations be diverse

1. Some from the body to the mind as: I have but lately tasted the Hebrew tongue, for newly begun it. Also I smell where aboute you go, for I perceive.
2. From the reasonable to the unreasonable, as Virgil in his *Georgic* applied the counsels and fashion of wars, belonging to men, to bees.
3. From the unreasonable to the reasonable. What whinest thou? What chatterest thou? That one taken of a wolf, that other of a [mag]pie.
4. From the living to the not living. The mouth of the well, the fatness of the earth. The land will spew them out.
5. From the not living to the living. Cicero flourisheth in eloquence.
6. From the living to the living. The Jews winched against Moses.

[67] Peacham, *Garden* (1577), sig. A3r. [68] Peacham, *Garden* (1593), sigs. AB3v–4r.
[69] Day, *English Secretary*, sig, Ii4v.

7. From the not living to the not living. The words flow out of his mouth. He is good for a green wound.[70]

Sherry's account of membrum (a phrase which needs another phrase to complete it) is based on Susenbrotus.

Colon, *membrum orationis*, a member of the reason, is so called when a thing is showed perfectly in few words the whole sentence not showed, but received again with another part, thus: Thou didst both profit thine enemy, and hurt thy friend. This exornation may be made of two parts only, but the perfectest is made of three, thus: Thou didst profit thine enemy, hurt thy friend, and didst no good to thy self.[71]

Peacham's version of this figure combines the definitions from Sherry and Susenbrotus, and translates a different example from Susenbrotus.

Membrum, when in few words the construction is ended, but not the sense also, or thus, when the oration is pronounced with three or four members, either coupled or uncoupled thus. See what a great offence and adversity thou hast brought to thyself, by one wicked deed, thou hast consumed thine inheritance, cast thy parents into sorrow, driven away thy friends, defiled thy name and provoked God to anger.[72]

Peacham adds examples from the Bible and a comment of his own on the use of the figure.

This is a very pleasant exornation, if so be that it standeth by equality of number, and also it serveth much to sharpness, for both these figures, as well in blaming as in commending, do in manner strike the mind with often strokes.[73]

Day treats membrum and parison as the same figure. His account is based on Susenbrotus but omits Susenbrotus's interesting comments on the use of the two figures.

Membrum or Parison, when one or more members do follow in equal sentences, as thus: 'See now by one fault how many mischiefs thou hast heaped to thyself,

---

[70] Sherry, *Schemes and Tropes*, sigs. C4v–5r; Mosellanus, *Tabulae*, sig. B3r–v.
[71] Sherry, *Schemes and Tropes*, sig. D5r. Susenbrotus describes it as follows: 'Membrum, colon, est cum duo vel plura membra, vel absque nexu vel cum eo copulata proferuntur, hoc modo Vide quantum infelicitatis uno crimine tibi conscivisti, patrimonium prodegisti, parentes in luctum coniecisti, amicos abalienasti, famam contamnasti, deum ad iram provocasti. Item, Et inimico proderas et amicum laedabas et tibiipsi non consulebas. Hoc schema cum in se orationis membra continet, quae ex pari fere numero syllabarum constant. ἰσοκωλία sive Compar nominatur. [after examples of isocolon] Maxime probantur quae tribus constant membris, quanquam nihil vetat et duobus uti vel pluribus. Haec schematis gratiam amittunt, si sunt longiora, numero et brevitate commendantur. Omissio item coniunctionum addit gratiam, acrimoniam et vehementiam, (Susenbrotus, *Epitome*, sig. D4r).
[72] Peacham, *Garden* (1577), sig. I4v.   [73] Ibid., sig. K1r.

thou hast consumed thy patrimony, grieved thy parents, estranged thy friends, defamed thy stock, undone thy kindred and heaped mischief a thousandfold to thyself more than can be avoided' or thus with copulation: 'neither hast thou herein dealt discreetly for thyself, nor respected thy friends, nor regarded thy being, nor studied of the evil, nor cared for the good that might happen, but leaving all at random, thou hast done what in thee lieth to work all our undoing'.[74]

Basing himself on the description and example in *Rhetorica ad Herennium*, Sherry combines a simple account of epanaphora with a comment on its usefulness.

Epanaphora, Repeticio, repetition, when in like and diverse things we take our beginning continually at one and the self-same word, thus: To you this thing is to be ascribed, to you thank is to be given, to you this thing shall be honour. In this exornation is much pleasantness, gravity and sharpness, and it is much used of all orators and notably setteth out and garnisheth the oration.[75]

All the figures of repetition are useful in amplifying and rendering style more impressive and more capable of conveying emotion. Wilson describes the more complicated repetition involved in climax or gradatio.

Gradation is when we rehearse the word that goeth next before and bring another word thereupon that increaseth the matter, as though one should go up a pair of stairs and not leave till he come at the top. Or thus: Gradation is when a sentence is dissevered by degrees, so that the word which endeth the sentence going before doth begin the next. 'Labour getteth learning, learning getteth fame, fame getteth honour, honour getteth bliss forever.'[76]

Wilson's explanation explores the effect of the figure; the opaqueness of the description is clarified by the example. While many of the figures involving repetition and alteration of word-order are described relatively briefly, figures associated with amplification, which mostly entered the manuals through Susenbrotus's use of Erasmus,[77] are explained and exemplified more fully. Here Peacham divides examples into true and fictional and explains the effect of the figure on the audience:

Paradigma is the rehearsal of a deed or saying past and applying it to our purpose, whereof there be two kinds, the one true, which is taken from histories, chronicles and memory of deeds done, and it is of great force to persuade, move and enflame men with the love of virtue and also to deter them from vice and not used only to confirm matters, but also to augment, enrich and garnish them

[74] Day, *English Secretary*, sig. Ll1v.   [75] Sherry, *Schemes and Tropes*, sig. C8r.
[76] Wilson, *Rhetoric*, p. 228.
[77] Erasmus, *De copia* (1988), pp. 202–15, 230–58; Susenbrotus, *Epitome*, sigs. E4v–5v, F3r–4r, F6v–7r, G2r–3r.

with much comeliness ... Fained examples are taken from poets' inventions and fables attributed to brute creatures, as to beasts, birds, fowls, fishes and also to trees, rivers, mountains. This kind bringeth a great delectation to the hearers but especially to the simple sort who delight a great deal more to hear fond fables than grave matters, yet being aptly applied they also delight the wise and learned and have been always by learned men well allowed and liked of.[78]

While Peacham, following Erasmus, treats example as a figure, a comment in the first book of Puttenham's *Arte of English Poesie* makes the connection between example, political education and the invention of subject-matter for speeches.

There is nothing in man of all the potential parts of his mind (reason and will except) more noble or more necessary to the active life than memory, because it maketh most to a sound judgement and perfect worldly wisdom, examining and comparing the times past with the present ... Right so no kind of argument in all the oratory craft doth better persuade and more universally satisfy than example, which is but the representation of old memories and like successes happened in times past.[79]

Figures related to example (paradigm) such as prosopographia, topographia and chronographia connect the style manual back to fable, description and other composition exercises. This is Day's account of prosopopeia, based on Susenbrotus but with his own examples, which are composition exercises in their own right.

Prosopopeia, when to things without life we frame an action, speech or person fitting a man, as if we should say of virtue as of a living person that 'her ways were sweet and replenished with all manner of delight, that she putteth her self forth to the worthiest to be received, and to the most honoured to be embraced'. Or fain the ghosts from out their graves to prescribe good examples or to rebuke the vices of men. Or our country to accuse us of our negligent regard unto it in these or such like speeches: 'Unkind people and Citizens whom I have engendered in my bowels, nourished with my paps, fostered with my delights, why do you thus ungratefully not only abstain to tender me, but give me an open prey to my foes to suppress me: yea which is most loathsome of all others become proper murderers and parricides of your own parentage and family, cruel destroyers of your own patrimony, and wretched renders and tearers of your mothers' bowels, without all regard and pity.'[80]

Some of the other figures of amplification, such as division and comparison, introduce logical method and topical invention into the style

[78] Peacham, *Garden* (1577), sigs. U2v–3r; Erasmus, *De copia* (1988), pp. 232–44; Susenbrotus, *Epitome*, sigs. G2v–3r.
[79] Puttenham, *Arte* (1936), p. 39.
[80] Day, *English Secretary*, sigs. Ll3v–4r. Susenbrotus, *Epitome*, sig. F3r–v.

manual.[81] Some explanations offer readings of the texts cited as examples. In discussing the use of comparisons in amplification, Sherry cites and explains a comparison by Isaiah.

To like use serve examples and similitudes, as in Isaiah: The ox knew its owner and the ass the manger of its master, but Israel hath not known me [1, v.3]. The example of the ox and the ass is not used for this to prove that the hebrews did not know their god, but that the impiety and foolishness of that nation should be amplified. The same may be applied to proof after this manner. If the ox and the ass acknowledge their masters, of whom they are nourished and do serve them, how much more convenient is it that man should acknowledge his maker and nourisher and serve him both in mind and body?[82]

Among Peacham's examples of chronographia, descriptions of times, is a description of midnight, translated into prose from the *Aeneid*, on which Peacham comments:

The poet describeth the night to amplify the dolour of Dido, for Dido could find no rest when everything on earth received rest.[83]

After Erasmus and Susenbrotus the style manuals lay strong emphasis on proverbs and pithy sayings (sententiae). Peacham describes paroemia among the tropes.

Paroemia, a saying much used and commonly known, and also very excellent for the novelty, to which two things are required, one that it be notable, renowned and much spoken of and a sentence in every man's mouth, called of the Latins, an adage and of us Englishmen, a proverb, the other that it be pretty, feat and witty, that is to say, that it may be discerned by some note and mark from common speech and also commended by antiquity and learning.[84]

At the end of the book he devotes almost two pages to a classification of pithy sayings under the figure of *gnome*. In the revision of 1593, Peacham describes three figures in this area: paroemia, apodixis and *gnome*.[85] Hoskins notes the predominance of this figure and expresses some reservations about rhetorical fashions.

Sententia, if it be well used is a figure – if ill and too much, it is a style, whereof none that writes humourously or factiously nowadays can be clear. For now there are such schisms of eloquence that it is enough for any ten years that all the bravest wits do imitate some one figure which a critic has taught some great personage. So it may be that within this two hundred years we shall go through

---

[81] Day, *English Secretary*, sigs. Mm1 r–v, Mm3r; Susenbrotus, *Epitome*, sigs. F4v–6r.
[82] Sherry, *Schemes and Tropes*, sig. E5v.
[83] Peacham, *Garden* (1577), sig. P2r; Virgil, *Aeneid* IV, 522–8.   [84] Ibid., sig. D2v.
[85] Peacham, *Garden* (1593), sigs. F3r–4r, N3v–4r, Cc3v–4r.

the whole body of rhetoric ... I have used and outworn six several styles since I was first Fellow of New College ... It is very true that a sentence is a pearl in a discourse, but is it a good discourse that is all pearl?[86]

Another fashionable trope useful in amplification and closely related to topical invention is antithesis. Peacham's account adds quotations from St Paul to a description, division and comment based on Susenbrotus.

Antithesis is a proper coupling together of contraries, and it is either in words that be contrary or in contrary sentences. Contrariety of words thus: I have loved peace and not loathed it; I have saved his life and not destroyed it ... 1 Cor 3. We are fools for Christ's sake, but we are wise through Christ; we are weak, but you are strong ... Contrariety of sentences, among the wicked, simplicity is counted as foolishness and craftiness high wisdom; flattery is friendship and faithfulness made fraud ... This exornation is very eloquent and to be compared with the best and none more used of orators in varying and garnishing an oration than it.[87]

Peacham records the effectiveness and popularity of the figure without pejorative comment. Puttenham is more censorious. He translates antitheton as the encounter, 'by reason of his contentious nature' and remarks on its previous and current use.

Isocrates the Greek orator was a little too full of this figure and so was the Spaniard that wrote the life of Marcus Aurelius, and many of our modern writers in vulgar use it in excess and incur the vice of fond affectation. Otherwise the figure is very commendable.[88]

Such observations and similar comments by Hoskins make the style manuals a rich source for individual reactions to stylistic fashions. These writers use the figures as critical tools for describing contemporary styles and comparing them with their antecedents. An intense rhetorical self-awareness is focused through the process of labelling and exemplifying figures, and contrasting their uses. Here Hoskins discusses the use of two figures related to antithesis, synoeciosis and contentio. All but two of the examples have been omitted.

Synoeciosis is a composition of contraries, and by both words intimateth the meaning of neither precisely but a moderation and mediocrity of both; as *bravery* and *rags* are contrary, yet somewhat better than both is *brave raggedness* ... This is a fine course to stir admiration in the hearer and make them think it a strange harmony which must be expressed in such discords; therefore this example shall conclude:

---

[86] Hoskins, *Directions*, pp. 38–9.   [87] Peacham, *Garden* (1577), sig. R1 r–v.
[88] Puttenham, *Arte* (1936), pp. 210–11.

There was so perfect agreement in so mortal disagreement, like a music made of cunning discords.
This is an easy figure now in fashion, not ever like to be so usual.
Contentio is contrary to the former. That was a composition of terms disagreeing; this is an opposition of them, as:
There was strength against nimbleness, rage against resolution, fury against virtue, confidence against courage, pride against nobleness . . .
This figure Ascham told Sturmius that he taught the Queen of England, and that she excels in practice of it; and indeed it is a figure fit to set forth a copious style. This figure serves much for amplification.[89]

In a few cases the style manuals attempt to introduce improvements to aspects of the rhetorical approach to style. For example, Puttenham allows himself a lengthy and at times rich discussion of the determinants of an individual style before agreeing with the traditional and restrictive analysis of three levels of style dependent on diction and subject-matter.[90] Some writers attempted to clarify the organisation of the sometimes rather random-looking list of tropes and figures. We have seen that Melanchthon subdivided tropes into tropes of word and phrase; and schemes into grammatical and rhetorical, this latter group subdivided into rhetorical figures of words, phrases and amplification. This scheme was followed by Susenbrotus, Peacham in his first version and Day. In his second edition, Peacham attempted to introduce further subdivisions among the rhetorical schemes, as follows:

1. Rhetorical Schemes	Repetition
	Omission
	Conjunction
	Separation
2. Figures moving passions	Exclamation
	Moderation
	Consultation
	Permission
3. Figures of Amplification	Distribution
	Description
	Comparison
	Collection[91]

This attempted reform focuses on the effect of each of the figures, in the way it affects the grammar of the sentence (the rhetorical schemes), in

---

[89] Hoskins, *Directions*, pp. 36–7.   [90] Puttenham, *Arte* (1936), pp. 148–53.
[91] Peacham, *Garden* (1593), sigs. C1r, C2r, G4v–H1r, I1v, I2v–3r, I4v, K3r–v, R4r–S2r; B. M. Koll, *Henry Peachams The Garden of Eloquence* (Frankfurt, 1996), pp. xlviii–xcvii.

the aim of the orator in using it (figures moving passions) or in the type of enrichment achieved (figures of amplification). In spite of this attempt at clarification the lists in each sub-group remain quite miscellaneous and there are many figures whose placing within one group rather than another seems quite arbitrary. Further simplification is attempted in the English Ramist rhetorics, which copy their Latin originals in reducing the tropes to four (metonymy, irony, metaphor and synecdoche) and the figures to nineteen. The figures are subdivided into figures of repetition and figures of sentences, themselves subdivided into forms of exclamation, types of asking and ways of answering. The Ramist rhetorics are very rich in examples from poetry.[92] Sometimes the English authors increase the confusion of the received order, as when Peacham describes the same figures in different places.[93] He corrects this in his second edition.

ADAPTATION TO ENGLISH

We must now turn to the question of the extent to which the renaissance Latin style manual was adapted to suit the English language. Certain of the figures established in the Latin style manual have no possible application in English, yet they appear in some of the English style manuals. The figure of anatiptosis, also called enallage, involves alteration of grammatical features such as case, gender, number, mood and tense. Some at least of these transformations are not applicable in English, but nevertheless this figure was included in some English manuals, for example by Sherry and Peacham:

Anatiptosis, *Casus pro casu*, when one case is put for another, as methink it is so. Anatiptosis, when we put one case for another, called also Enallage. Thus, I give you this gift with hearty good will . . . the accusative for the dative . . . Enallage of gender, when we put the neuter for the masculine or feminine, or any one of them for another [and tense, number, mood].[94]

Sherry and Peacham struggled to find English examples (Peacham's example is certainly not acceptable). Puttenham included the figure, at the same time pronouncing it inapplicable to English.

---

[92] Dudley Fenner's *The Artes of Logike and Rethorike* (Middleburg, 1584) STC 10766 presents examples almost exclusively from the Bible, but Abraham Fraunce in *The Arcadian Rhetorike* (London, 1588) STC 11338 quotes a range of poetry in Greek, Latin, Italian, French, Spanish and English (usually from Sidney, whereas his *Lawier's Logike* (London, 1588) STC 11343 takes its English poetic examples mostly from Spenser).

[93] In *Garden* (1577) Peacham describes aposiopesis at sigs. E4r and N1v; zeugma at sigs. E4v–5r and K2v–3r; and asindeton and polysindeton at sigs. G4r–v and I4r–v.

[94] Sherry, *Schemes and Tropes*, sig. B8r–v; Peacham, *Garden* (1577), sigs. H3r–4r.

Enallage, your figures that worke auricularly by exchange were more observable to the Greeks and Latines for the braveness of their language over that ours is for the multiplicitie of their grammaticall accidents [cases, moods, tenses, genders] . . . We having no such variety of accidents have little or no use of this figure. They call it Enallage.[95]

These English versions appear to be taken directly from Susenbrotus,[96] though anatiptosis also appears among the grammatical figures listed in Lily's *Grammar*, which was taught in most grammar schools. The same figure appears under a slightly different name in Quintilian.[97] Since this figure is unthinkable in English, its presence in some of the English manuals, if it is not a mere mistake, must reflect the intention that the English manuals could be used as guides to the reading of Latin authors and perhaps even for Latin composition.

A more important figure, or pair of figures, which appears in all the English manuals is homeoptoton or homeoteleuton, meaning similar cases or similar endings in a series of words. Sherry defines as follows:

Homioptoton, *similiter cadens*, fallyng all alike is when in the same construction of words there be two words or more which be spoken alike in the self same cases, thus: Thou praisest a man needy of virtue, plentiful of money. Cicero for Flaccus: There is in them no variety of opinion, none of will, none of talk. Homoioteleuton, *similiter desinens*, ending all alike, when words or sentences have alike ending, as: Thou darest do filthily, and studiest to speak bawdily. Content thyself with thy state, in thy heart do no man hate, be not the cause of strife and hate.[98]

Angel Day condensed the two into one figure.

Homeoteleuton, or *similiter cadens*, when words and sentences in one sort do finish together, as thus: Weeping, wailing, and her hands wringing . . . Or thus: Thou livest maliciously, speakest hatefully, and usest thyself cruelly.[99]

Day's phrase 'in one sort' expresses his understanding that English words which end similarly are likely to be the same parts of speech. This is particularly true in the case of the examples he chooses, adverbs and present participles. Other authors take the process of adapting this figure even further. Wilson anglicised the figures as follows:

Like Ending and Like Falling
Then the sentences are said to 'end like', when those words do end in like syllables which do lack cases. 'Thou livest wickedly, thou speakest naughtily' . . . Sentences also are said to 'fall like' when diverse words in one sentence end in like cases,

[95] Puttenham, *Arte* (1936), p. 171.   [96] Susenbrotus, *Epitome*, sigs. C2v–3r.
[97] Quintilian, *Institutio oratoria*, ix, 3.6–10.   [98] Sherry, *Schemes and Tropes*, sig. D5v.
[99] Day, *English Secretary*, sig. Ll1v.

and that in rime. 'By great travail is got much avail; by earnest affection, men learn discretion.'[100]

Wilson adds a good deal of advice on when these figures are most pleasing and on the danger of their over-use.

Divers in this our time delight much in this kind of writing, which being measurale used delighteth much the hearers; otherwise it offendeth, and wearieth men's ears with satiety. St Augustine had a goodly gift in this behalf, and yet some thinks he forgot measure and used overmuch this kind of figure . . . Tacitus also showeth that in his time the judges and sergeants-at-the-law were given to use this kind of phrase both in their writing and also in their speaking.[101]

In his discussion of usage Wilson refers to Latin authors because he expects that readers of his English manual will want to exploit their newly acquired rhetorical knowledge in reading Latin. Puttenham goes one step further than Wilson, noting the origin of the figure in similarity of cases but identifying its use with rhyme.

Omoioteleton or the Like Loose. The Greekes used a manner of speech or writing in their profes, that went by clauses, finishing in words of like tune, and might be by using like cases, tenses and other points of consonance, which they called Omoioteleton, and that is wherin they most approched to our vulgar ryme.[102]

All Puttenham's examples of this figure are set out as verse. With homeoptoton or homeoteleuton then, a grammatical feature essentially unsuited to English is included in the manuals in order to translate the Latin text and to assist in reading and writing Latin. At first English equivalents are found involving different grammatical properties. Later the figure is adapted to describe an important feature of English verse which is unknown to classical Latin rhetoric.

Some Latin figures are altered to suit the needs of English. Among the defects of word-positioning Susenbrotus includes paroemeon, which he defines as 'when many words beginning with the same letter are placed together excessively', as in 'Machina multa minax minatur maxime muris', which he regards as ludicrous.[103] Peacham adapts this

Paroemion is a figure of speech which beginneth diverse words with one and the same letter, making the sentence more ready for the tongue, and more pleasant to the ear.[104]

Puttenham finds the figure pleasing and poetically useful.

---

[100] Wilson, *Rhetoric*, p. 226.   [101] Ibid., p. 227.   [102] Puttenham, *Arte* (1936), p. 173.
[103] Susenbrotus, *Epitome*, sig. C3v: 'cum multa voces ab eadem litera incipientes, ex ordine collocantur'.
[104] Peacham, *Garden* (1593), sig. I1r. Compare Peacham, *Garden* (1577), sig. G3v.

Parimion. Ye do by another figure notably affect the eare when ye make every word of the verse to begin with a like letter . . . It is a figure much used by our common rhymers and doth well if it be not too much used.[105]

Since alliteration is a frequently occurring feature of English verse and prose and since Latin provides a label, albeit a pejorative one, some of the English manuals adopt the name, reposition the figure and extol its usefulness. In this case the Latin manual is essentially rewritten to produce a figure which corresponds to a recurring feature of English usage. Hoskins alters paronomasia (in which slight alterations are made in words to make them resemble other words) to make it do duty for alliteration.[106] Puttenham uses epinome to describe the refrain which is a feature of English poetry.[107] Whereas Roman rhetoric had treated allegory as an extended form of metaphor because it involves a longer term translation of meaning of a term or a narrative, some English manuals understood this extension to apply to the poetic conceit, in which an expression of similarity is drawn through a succession of words or phrases. For Puttenham the poetic conceit is a form of allegory.[108]

Some figures of Greek and Latin rhetoric have a considerably altered value when applied to English. Among the grammatical figures are several concerned with alteration of word order: hyperbaton (change in order of words), anastrophe (reversal of normal word-order) and hysteron proteron (reversal of logical order). Because of the relative lack of inflections English syntax is far more dependent on word-order than Latin syntax. In almost every line of Latin poetry word-order is manipulated to meet the needs of quantitative metre. Alterations in word-order in English are much less frequent and therefore have a much greater effect in directing emphasis and in calling the reader's attention to the form of words employed.

Most of the English style manuals include these figures involving change in word-order but they do so either merely to list the figures or to express their hostility to them.[109] In 1577 Peacham comments that

---

[105] Puttenham, *Arte* (1936), p. 174.

[106] Hoskins, *Directions*, pp. 15–16. Compare Susenbrotus, *Epitome*, sigs. D4v–5r, *Rhetorica ad Herennium*, IV.21.29, Quintilian, *Institutio oratoria*, IX.3.66–74.

[107] Puttenham, *Arte* (1936), p. 225.

[108] Ibid., p. 186. Sometimes the adaptation of Latin terms to English conditions may be thought to go too far. Puttenham twice decides to treat tautologia as excessive alliteration, rather than redundant repetition (pp. 173, 254).

[109] Of those not mentioned below, Sherry defines each of the figures without examples or comments (*Schemes and Tropes*, sigs. B7v–8r), Wilson has only a short paragraph on word-order (*Rhetoric*, p. 232) and the Ramist rhetorics omit the figures.

changes in word-order obscure the meaning of phrases;[110] in 1593 he omits the figures altogether. Puttenham explains that there are many sub-types of disorder under the general heading of hyperbaton, or 'the Trespasser',

> whereof some are onely proper to the greekes and latines and not to us, other some ordinarie in our maner of speaches, but so foule and intollerable as I will not seeme to place them among the figures, but do raunge them as they deserve among the vicious or faultie speaches.[111]

Even Day, who normally follows Susenbrotus, omits hyperbaton and calls anastrophe 'a preposterous inversion of wordes, besides their common course', choosing examples which illustrate ungrammatical order rather than rhetorical emphasis.[112] For once the authors of the English manuals are very conscious of the strangeness of the figure. They are so concerned to resist the threat to English structure that they fail to mention the usefulness of what is, after all, hardly an uncommon device in English writing.

Wilson and Puttenham both thought that rhetorical terminology would need to be firmly based in the English language if English people were to remember, understand and use it. But the English equivalents they devised failed to replace the received terminology, which combined Latin and Greek words in ways conducive to duplication and ambiguity. One reason for the failure was that many of the people who would have needed to adopt English terms were already more familiar with the classical terms in which they had been drilled in the course of their humanist education.

Some features of Latin are used to expand the possibilities of writing in English. A common feature of Latin writing but one which exists in English as a result of Latin influence is zeugma, when words (especially verbs) can be left out of one phrase or sentence because they are present in a parallel sentence. Sherry's definition associates the figure with Linacre's Latin grammar.

> Zeugma, *iunctio*, joining, as Linacre saith is when in like sentences a certain common thing which is put in the one and not changed in the other is not expressed, but left out: as in Virgil: Before I forget Cesar, either the Parthian shall drink of the flood Araris, or Germany of Tigris: here is left out shall drink.[113]

---

[110] Peacham, *Garden* (1577), sigs. F3v–4r.   [111] Puttenham, *Arte* (1936), pp. 168–9.

[112] Day, *English Secretary*, p. 82.

[113] Sherry, *Schemes and Tropes*, sig. B7r. The flood *Araris* is the river Saône in France. Sherry alludes to line sixty-two of Virgil's first eclogue: 'aut Ararim Parthus bibet aut Germania Tigrim'.

Sherry's slightly opaque definition of this trope is most easily understood as a translation of Susenbrotus (who was quoting Linacre):

Zeugma occurs when in similar clauses something common placed in one is required unchanged in others.[114]

The three kinds of zeugma which Sherry goes on to describe are taken directly from Susenbrotus and Linacre. Day's examples show the extent to which a certain kind of English prose style can embrace such a Latinate figure.

His looseness overcame all shame; his boldness fear; his madness reason, where all the clauses are concluded under this one verb, *overcame.* Or thus: *What availeth it to shrine so much this vaine beauty, which either by long sickness, extremity of old age, infinite sorrows and cares, or a thousand mishaps beside, is every day in danger to be utterly erased.*[115]

It is doubtful whether the second example can really be called zeugma in that no verb which is logically required is omitted. Day thinks of it as zeugma because a number of agents share the same verb and because placing the verb at the end of the sentence is unusual in English and normal in Latin.

Like some of the other figures mentioned above, zeugma was included in Lily's Latin grammar, the standard textbook of the English grammar schools, alongside other figures involving omission of parts of speech and changes in 'normal' grammatical rules of precedence and agreement. These figures, together with the practice of composing in Latin and instructions on word-order for Latin composition like those printed by Brinsley,[116] must have contributed to changes in the way in which pupils wrote English. One example of a familiar Latin construction, not identified as a figure of speech, leading to an additional pattern in English prose is the *quantum . . . tantum* construction, which emerges in Hal's soliloquy at the end of scene ii of *Henry IV Part One* as:

> By how much better than my word I am
> By so much will I falsify men's hopes.
> (lines 205–6)

As a group the English style manuals present a different emphasis within the figures from their classical originals. These changes of emphasis

---

[114] 'Zeugma est quando in similibus clausulis commune aliquid in una positum, in aliis non mutatum desideratur.' Susenbrotus, *Epitome*, sig. B6v.
[115] Day, *English Secretary*, sig. Kk3v.   [116] Brinsley, *Ludus*, pp. 159–62.

derive from the work of Erasmus, Melanchthon and Susenbrotus. Among the tropes most attention is given to metaphor and to allegory, which is usually treated as a grouping of types of wit and irony.[117] As in classical rhetorics, considerable attention is given to a group of figures involving repetition of a particular word, such as anaphora, antistrophe, symploce, epanados, epizeuxis, anadiplosis and climax. Repetition of structure is recognised in figures in which adjacent phrases have similar syntax or length, as in colon and parison. Another group centres on notions of contrariety: contentio, antimetabole and synoeciosis. A large set of figures represent the speaker's approach to words or audience, for example exclamatio, apostrophe, aposiopesis, correctio and occupatio. The idea of creating a self-projection for an imaginary or absent person underlies the important figure of prosopopeia.[118] English manuals give special emphasis to figures involving rhetorical questions, such as addubitatio and communicatio. Lastly, in connection with Erasmus's *De copia*, most of the non-Ramist English manuals emphasise figures and techniques connected with amplification, including comparisons, descriptions, examples and proverbs.

In the first place the manuals are translations of Latin handbooks, providing an English version of a text which was useful in itself and which grammar school pupils were supposed to read (and probably did read) in Latin. Secondly, and as part of that function, they were guides to Latin rhetoric to assist people in reading and composing Latin. Thirdly they were guides to rhetoric for people who only wanted to read and write in English. To that end some of the figures were adapted to the needs of English. Fourthly, they were part of the process of absorbing the perceived advantages of Latin into English.

The bilingual situation of the educated Elizabethan underlies the tensions between these different roles. An Elizabethan civil servant or clergyman was educated in Latin. He would compose scientific works, occasional letters and arguments against continental theologians in Latin. He might prefer to read the Bible in Latin. But he would compose the bulk of his correspondence, arguments against puritans, most sermons and all parliamentary speeches in English. English versions of Latin texts would sometimes have helped him. His own use of English would have

---

[117] Sherry, *Schemes and Tropes*, sig. C7r–v, Puttenham, *Arte* (1936), pp. 186–91, Peacham, *Garden* (1577), sigs. D1r–4v. The source for this seems to be Susenbrotus, *Epitome*, sigs. A7v–B2r.

[118] In the style manuals (both Latin and English) prosopopeia (personification) covers all aspects of what Aphthonius called ethopoeia (speech for a character). See discussion of Aphthonius in chapter one above, pp. 27–9, 40–2.

been much altered by his Latin training. The other readership for such manuals wanted to imitate men like this. They wanted a book which reflected the Latin manuals they could not read and which assisted them in reading English versions of classical authors and in writing an educated, that is Latinate, register of English.

4

Everyday writing: notebooks, letters, narratives

Most Elizabethans had their strongest and most frequent contact with writing in the form of personal notes and memoranda, letters and legal documents. The composition of many of these documents involved questions of organisation and self-presentation, also sometimes of style, which registered rhetorical competences. We have seen that grammar school education taught pupils to collect sentences and examples in notebooks. Puritans encouraged note-taking as a way of absorbing and reflecting on the teaching of sermons. Margaret Hoby's *Diary* which records her prayers and church attendance frequently refers to writing in her 'sermon book' notes of sermons she has heard a day or two before.[1] An increasingly centralised and bureaucratic decision-making process demanded collection of written evidence and retention of copies of letters. The victims of religious persecution (Catholic or Protestant) wrote narratives to strengthen the courage and hatred of their co-religionists. Since the materials available are so diverse and have rarely been studied before,[2] this chapter will concentrate on a few, possibly atypical examples. At the same time, it is these materials which bring us closest to the experiences and thought-processes of individual Elizabethans.

My study of particular notebooks, letters and narratives will illustrate the impact of the rhetorical skills developed in the grammar school. Moral sentences, arguments, comparisons and political axioms found in books and sermons were collected in notebooks and reused in letters. As well as collecting fragments from texts, Elizabethans took notes of the overall structure of sermons and texts. They copied out letters to serve as models of content, organisation and style appropriate to particular

---

[1] M. Hoby, *The Private Life of an Elizabethan Lady: the Diary of Lady Margaret Hoby* (Stroud, 1998), pp. 15, 16, 27, 32, 40.
[2] Two pioneering studies of Elizabethan letters have been published: Frank Whigham, 'The Rhetoric of Elizabethan Suitors' Letters', *PMLA* 96 (1981), 864–82; Magnusson, *Shakespeare and Social Dialogue*, esp. pp. 35–57, 87–113.

circumstances of practical life. They used notebooks to assemble arguments, sketch outlines, and draft letters and orations. Letters written in particularly delicate circumstances prompted the use of more self-conscious devices of style. Letters and narratives were inflected to present their writers as truthful or friendly or to elicit particular responses from their audiences. Narratives were crafted to present moral or spiritual teaching or to provide support for arguments. Some of these features correspond to particular elements of grammar school teaching; others represent combinations of such elements or adaptations to the expectations of other genres.

NOTEBOOKS

A surprising number of notebooks and miscellaneous manuscripts from the Elizabethan and Jacobean period survive.[3] Their contents are intriguingly various. Folger MS V.b. 198, edited in 1997 by Jean Klene as *The Southwell-Sibthorpe Commonplace Book*, contains poems and letters by Lady Anne Southwell, Ralegh, Henry King, receipts and accounts, moral sentences, lists of the predicables and categories, inventories of clothes, books and possessions, notes on a sermon and book eight of St Augustine's *City of God*, extracts from a bestiary and an essay.[4] Folger MS V.a. 321, edited in 1983 by A. R. Braunmuller as *A Seventeenth-Century Letter-Book*, contains letters by the Earl of Essex, Queen Elizabeth, Francis Bacon, Ben Jonson, George Chapman and many others (named and anonymous), orations, petitions, narratives, warrants, the 'Oath of Association' of 1584 and the House of Commons' 'Petition of Right' of 1610.[5] British Library MS Harley 5353, edited by R. P. Sorlien in 1976 as *The Diary of John Manningham*, which will be the main point of reference in this section, contains poems, *imprese*, stories and jokes told by fellow students and relatives, items of news, recipes for medicines, paradoxes by Donne, comparisons, and notes on sermons heard and books read.[6] Although

---

[3] There is an admirable list of university notebooks, which are a different class from most of those studied here, in Hugh Kearney, *Scholars and Gentlemen* (London, 1970), pp. 193–9; W. T. Costello, *The Scholastic Curriculum in Early 17th Century Cambridge* (Cambridge, 1958) studied some of them.

[4] Jean Klene, C.S.C. (ed.), *The Southwell-Sibthorpe Commonplace Book* (Tempe, 1997) RETS 7th series, vol. 20.

[5] A. R. Braunmuller (ed.), *A Seventeenth-Century Letter-Book* (Newark NJ, 1983).

[6] R. P. Sorlien (ed.), *The Diary of John Manningham of the Middle Temple 1602–1603* (Hanover NH, 1976), p. 2. None of the examples I shall refer to is a commonplace book in the strict sense, discussed in chapter one above, of a collection of quotations organised under headings. This is true of many manuscripts described as commonplace books, including all those included in the microfilm collection *Commonplace Books from the Huntington Library*. If, as it appears, comparatively few manuscript commonplace books were substantially filled with classified quotations, opinions about the impact of commonplace collecting will need to be amended.

Manningham was a student at the Inns of Court when he wrote the manuscript, it has no apparent connection with his law studies. As a whole the contents of each of these volumes can be explained only by saying that some individual thought all the items worthy of preservation for some purpose. My argument will be that the choices about what to include and how to extract reflect the preoccupations and practices of rhetorical education.

One of the main functions of the notebook was to collect impressive phrases for reuse. This was encouraged by Elizabethan teachers, partly as a first step to the compilation of commonplace books proper but also as a way of deriving benefit from reading. Many of the entries in Manningham's diary are funny stories, witty observations and striking comparisons. Manningham probably expected to find such passages instructive and amusing as well as useful in his own conversation and writing. Some of his sermon notes are similar to these entries, collecting maxims, comparisons and witty phrases. The impulse to record moral similes such as

Honor is like a buble, which is raysed with one winde and broken with another.
Thankefullness is like the reflex of the sunne beame from a bright bodie[7]

also informs selections of sententiae, maxims and quotations like

God made some riche, and some poore, that twoe excellent virtues might flourish in the world, charitie in the riche, and patience in the poore.
Pride is the sting of riches. *Tolle superbiam, et divitiae non nocebunt.*
Themistocles said there was no musicke soe sweete unto him as to heare his own prayses.[8]
Aliud est incepisse, aliud perfecisse.[9]
Yf syn enter into the heart it becomes like a denn of theeves, and like a cage of uncleane birdes.[10]

Sometimes Manningham appears to be recording religious maxims, which could be used either as quotations or to support arguments in his own writings.

There is a tyme for all to dye; and this act of dying is done by us, and upon us. It is a sentence which comprehendeth all though all apprehend not it.[11]
The lawe stretcht noe further then the outward action, but Christ layes it to the secret thought.[12]

[7] Sorlien, *Manningham's Diary*, p. 37.
[8] Ibid., p. 61: 'Take away pride and riches will do no harm.'
[9] Ibid., p. 67: 'It is one thing to have begun, another to have finished.'
[10] Ibid., p. 204.   [11] Ibid., p. 203.
[12] Ibid., p. 204.

Notes of this kind illustrate the 'commonplace-book' tendency to extract fragments from texts. Manningham's notes on reading John Hayward's recently published *An Answere to the First Part of a Certaine Conference concerning Succession... [by] R. Dolman* (London, 1603) STC 12988 consist almost entirely of verbatim extracts.[13] Some sense of the structure of the work is given by copying out the chapter titles and some of the divisions within a chapter.[14] The notes concentrate on political principles which may serve as axioms.

The world is nothing but a greate state, a state is noe other then a greate familie, and a familie noe other then a great body; as one God ruleth the world, one maister the familie; as all the members receive both sence and motion from the head, which is the seate and tower both of the understanding and will, soe it seemeth noe lesse naturall that one state should be governed by one commaunder.[15]

Generally custom doth not onely interpret lawe but correcteth and supplieth where there is no lawe.[16]

Quae praeter consuetudinem et morem maiorum fiunt, neque placent, neque recta videntur (A. Gellius).[17]

Opinion is partiall and report erronius, yet those the guides of the multitude.[18]

Occasionally he notes a rhetorical principle or records a clever comparison.

Notorious points the more wee proove, the more we obscure; you doe but gild gold in labouring to prove it.

All this bundle of wordes is like a blowne bladder full of winde but of no weight.[19]

Manningham's quite substantial notes on Lancelot Andrewes's sermon on John 16, verse 7 serve mainly to capture the movement of Andrewes's

---

[13] In fact the author of the *Conference About the Next Succession to the Crown of England* (STC 19398) circulated on the continent in late 1593, which supported the claim of Lady Arbella Stuart, was the English Catholic writer Richard Verstegan. At the time it was widely thought that the true author was the Jesuit Robert Persons. Sorlien, *Manningham's Diary*, pp. 322–3, 401–2. Manningham's notes focus on principles of politics rather than on the controversy about the succession.

[14] For example Sorlien, *Manningham's Diary*, pp. 237, 238, 239. Compare John Hayward, *An Answere to the First Part of a Certaine Conference concerning Succession... [by] R. Dolman* (London, 1603) STC 12988, fols. B1r–v, C2v, D3r–4r.

[15] Sorlien, *Manningham's Diary*, p. 238. Compare Hayward, *Answere to Dolman*, fol. B4r.

[16] Sorlien, *Manningham's Diary*, p. 239. Compare Hayward, *Answere to Dolman*, fol. D3v.

[17] Sorlien, *Manningham's Diary*, p. 239. Compare Hayward, *Answere to Dolman*, fol. D4r. 'What arises outside custom and the habits of our ancestors neither pleases nor seems right' (Aullus Gellius, *Noctes Atticae*, xv.11.2). Manningham copies the Latin maxim from the marginal note in preference to the English translation in Hayward's text.

[18] Sorlien, *Manningham's Diary*, p. 241.

[19] Ibid., p. 237. Compare Hayward, *Answere to Dolman*, fols. B1v, B3r.

chief argument.[20] Occasionally a comparison or a pattern demands to be recorded.

> Expedient it was that Christ should depart from them, howe good soever his presence was unto them. Wee knowe that bread is the strength of mans hart, yet sometymes it may be expedient to fast; our bloud is the treasury of our lyfe, yet sometymes it is expedient to loose it; our eyesight is deare and precious unto us, yet sometymes it is expedient to sitt in a darke roome.[21]

The impulse to collect fragments accounts for many of Manningham's notes, but they often also summarise the structure of a sermon he has heard.[22] Recording an anonymous sermon on Jonah 3, verses 4 and 5, he notes:

> He divided his text into Jonahs sermon to the people of Nineveh, and the peoples repentaunce at the sermon; the former consists of mercy, 'yett fourty dayes', and justice, 'and Nineveh shall be destroyed'; Gods patience and his judgment. he might have sayd, as the prophet David sayd, 'My song shall be of mercy and judgement'.
> 4 things in the effect of the Sermon; fayth in beleving God, and that was not fruitles. 2. fasting, and that was not frivolous. 3. their attyre, and that was not costly, but sack cloth. 4. their number, that was not small, from the greatest to the lowest.[23]

Manningham records the preacher's division of his text and his four main conclusions. While setting down the structure of the sermon, he still notes some of the preacher's phrasing. The second sentence of the first paragraph either notes the preacher's use of correctio or makes an aside improving the phrasing of the sermon to make it fit another Bible text. Elsewhere Manningham is willing to comment critically on the preacher's logic.

> To peremptory to conclude before his premises.[24]

Many of Manningham's notes on structure must have been taken directly from the divisions announced by preachers after their exordia,[25]

---

[20] Sorlien, *Manningham's Diary*, pp. 61–6. The text given in the *XCVI Sermons* is dated to Whitsun 1611 and probably differs from the text Manningham heard in 1602; most of the phrases and arguments Manningham records have counterparts in the printed edition, but in some cases it is difficult to say whether a difference reflects Manningham's summarising or Andrewes's revision. This sermon is reprinted in Lancelot Andrewes, *Sermons*, ed. G. M. Story (Oxford, 1967), pp. 242–62.

[21] Sorlien, *Manningham's Diary*, p. 64.   [22] For example ibid., pp. 68, 101, 134, 152, 165, 211.

[23] Ibid., p. 71.   [24] Ibid., p. 137.

[25] Andrewes's initial division of 1 Timothy 6, verses 17–19 is quoted in chapter eight below, p. 273.

but he sometimes introduced number and order to a paragraph of arguments.[26] Some other notebooks go further than Manningham in recording organisation. British Library MS Harley 3230 is a theological notebook belonging to Henry Addyter, worked on intensively between 1585 and 1593 with further sporadic entries made twenty years later.[27] It began as a commonplace book with quotations organised under theological headings.[28] Later it incorporated notes from books and sermons,[29] English translations of psalms,[30] a draft letter,[31] and commentaries on the Creed,[32] the ten commandments,[33] the Lord's prayer[34] and the books of the New Testament.[35] The link with Ramism is made clear by the inclusion of tree diagrams of the programme of education and the contents of rhetoric and dialectic.[36] Beneath the heading 'Quid sit theologia' and a tree diagram of the parts of theology, a substantial logical commentary on Psalm 19 begins with a dialectical analysis of the first eleven verses set out as a Ramist diagram.[37] John Rogers's student notebook analyses a sermon by Tobie Mathew in a way that seems parallel to Manningham's analysis (and probably depended on the preacher's division of his material).

Notes of a sermon preached before the judges by doctor Mathew in oxon the 29th of June 1581
Text Proverbs cap 24 vers 21 22 23 24
My sonne feare the lord and the king and meddle not with them that are seditious.
to the 25th verse   here are two parts to be observed:
    1) a general charge to all the good sons of Solomon, in these words: my sonne feare the lord and the king
    2) a particular instruction to the wise, in these words: it is not good to have respects of any person in judgement etc.

---

[26] For example he selects and numbers some of the comparisons between the church and a vine (or a vineyard) made by John Spenser. Sorlien, *Manningham's Diary*, p. 91; John Spenser, *God's Love to his Vineyard* (London, 1615) STC 23096 sold as *A Learned and Gracious Sermon*, sigs. B2r–3v. There is some evidence that the posthumously printed sermon is a revised version of the one Manningham heard in October 1602, but many of the phrases and ideas are identical and it seems unlikely that markers of organisation would have been removed in revision.
[27] British Library MS Harley 3230, fols. 186v (name), 1v, 7v, 11v, 34v, 51r, 57v, 93v, 98v, 99v (dates).
[28] E.g. ibid., fols. 4r, 5r, 6r, 7r.   [29] E.g. ibid., fols. 9r, 14r, 65v.   [30] Ibid., fols. 80v–82v.
[31] Ibid., fol. 80r.   [32] Ibid., fols. 23r–35v.   [33] Ibid., fols. 38r–51v.   [34] Ibid., fols. 52r–58r.
[35] Ibid., fols. 83r–170r, with various interruptions. The individual sections of the commentary are dated, perhaps indicating that the text was heard or delivered as a series of lectures.
[36] Ibid., fols. 2r, 172v, 178r.
[37] Ibid., fols. 4v–5r, transcribed in Mack, *Renaissance Argument*, pp. 368–9. Tree diagrams of the books of the Bible and the individual psalms were published in Stephanus Szegedinus, *Tabulae Analyticae* (London: Richard Field, 1593) STC 15015.3, but in Psalm 19 the printed analysis agrees with Addyter's only in the analysis of the effects of the law, sig. B3v.

a charge is:
1) an appellation: my son
2) a commandment: fear the lord and the king
3) a prohibition: and meddle not with those that are seditious
4) a reason: for their destruction shall rise suddenly and who knoweth the ruin of them both.[38]

Many notebooks and miscellaneous manuscripts contain copies of letters. Letters by famous people might have been copied for historical interest or because of the glamour associated with fame.[39] A person might keep copies of some of his own letters as reminders or as evidence in case of subsequent problems. Alternatively letters might be kept as models for future imitation. The Devon schoolmaster John Conybeare's notebook includes Latin letters suitable for his pupils to copy in writing to their parents and model letters for other purposes.[40]

Folger MS V.a. 321 contains a large number of letters by named people, either famous or familiar to the presumed compiler, but it also contains many unassigned letters. Some of the letters of request or recommendation are expressed in such non-specific terms that they could be reused unaltered. While biographical speculations can be made to account for some of these letters, they will not explain all of them. Most of the anonymous letters (and many of the named ones) are better regarded as examples of types of letter which were frequently needed. Many of the letters are letters of advice, from a father to his sons, from a father to a daughter, from Egerton to Essex, from William Cecil to Robert Cecil, and even a satirical letter of advice.[41] Many of the letters are petitions, for the release of a prisoner, for relief, for a job, for the right to accompany the King to a cockfight.[42] One group of letters concerns a duel,[43] another a range of situations connected with courtship.[44] A letter of consolation is followed by a letter rejoicing at a recovery.[45] One writer criticises a schoolmaster for the weaknesses of his pupil's Latin. In the next letter the schoolmaster disposes a series of maxims to reject the complaint.[46]

Some of these letters look more like stylistic exercises than anything which could actually have been sent. Others would serve as models

---

[38] Bodleian Library MS Rawl. D 273, fol. 178.
[39] For example Braunmuller, *Letter-Book*, letters 1–9 relate to the actions of the Earl of Essex; letter 96 gives an account of the last battle of the *Revenge*; letter 53 copies a forged letter from the Emperor of China to Queen Elizabeth.
[40] Conybeare, *Letters and Exercises*, pp. 1–9, 106–9; Braunmuller, *Letter-Book*, p. 9.
[41] Braunmuller, *Letter-Book*, letters 1–2, 10, 29–30, 83, 123.
[42] Ibid., letters 11, 15–16, 24–8, 38, 42, 85, 87, 138–9.   [43] Ibid., letters 17–21, 63–4.
[44] Ibid., letters 34–7, 39–41, 46–50, 112–13, 134.   [45] Ibid., letters 32–3.
[46] Ibid., letters 99–100.

more easily than as personal mementoes. Some of the documents are grouped as evidence to support a petition to be admitted to a retirement institution.[47] They would have been useful to the petitioner as a record and to anyone else seeking similar benefits as a model. The letter Chidiock Tichbourne wrote his wife on the eve of his execution might serve as a historical document, an object for compassionate meditation or a model of consolation.[48] The major types of letter specified in the manuals (encouragement, persuasion, consolation, request, recommendation, thanks and advice) are all included. Apart from the anthologies found in letter-writing manuals (such as Fulwood's *Enemie of Idleness* and Fleming's *Panoplie of Epistles*) the closest analogue to the Folger collection is Nicholas Breton's very successful *A Poste with a Madde Packet of Letters* (1602) which provides fictional examples of many of the most useful types of letter, with many moral sentences and some attempts at elevated style. Although this collection could possibly have been used for teaching, the emphasis on love-letters and the instances of comic rejoinders suggest that the main function of the book was entertainment.[49]

Besides letters and notes on texts heard or read, notebooks can also contain personal memoranda, listing actions to be undertaken or outlining reasons in preparation for composing a document or taking part in a discussion.[50] Among Nathaniel Bacon's papers are lists of actions which his father asks him to undertake,[51] and a list of reasons why the lease he was granted by John Calthorpe should be continued under the heir James Calthorpe.

Reasons for the demande of the continuance of my lease for 13 yeres.

In primis the consideracion on my behalfe given to John Calthorp and either litle or no consideracion on the contrary parte.

Item I and others from whome I claymed had byne longe tyme in possession of the lease and therefore the takinge or sekinge of a lease over my hedd deserveth the lesse favor.

---

47 Ibid., letters 91–5.   48 Ibid., letter 12. This letter is discussed further below.

49 Nicholas Breton, *A Post with a Madde Packet of Letters*, in *The Works in Verse and Prose of Nicholas Breton*, ed. Rev. A. B. Grosart, 2 vols. (1879, repr. New York, 1966), II, pp. 1–27 (separately paginated).

50 For further discussion, see the account of William Cecil's memoranda in chapter six below. My point here is that equivalents for Cecil's memoranda of high politics exist at the humbler level of estate management and family affairs.

51 A. Hassell Smith, et al. (eds.), *The Papers of Nathaniel Bacon of Stiffkey*, 4 vols. (Norwich, 1979–2000) Norfolk Record Society vols. 46, 49, 53, 64, I, pp. 219–20. Nathaniel Bacon writes memoranda of actions to perform, I, pp. 57–9, 172, 198, 271–3. The catalogue of the library presumed to be Nathaniel Bacon's includes several books on rhetoric (*Ad Herennium, De oratore*, Aristotle, Quintilian) and dialectic (Case, Ramus); Fehrenbach and Leedham-Green, *Private Libraries* I, pp. 79–135.

Item in respecte of Mr James Calthorps credit for that he hath obtayned the inheritance of John Calthorp, my lease either oughte to have his contynuance for 13 yeres or otherwise recompence at Mr James Calthorps hands . . .

Item the symplicitie of John Calthorp together with his manor of delivery to James and smalenes of consideracion to James as afore asketh favour for John and none for James and so mete it is that James see Johns covenaunte discharged to me.[52]

Nathaniel Bacon's arguments are based on comparisons (of consideration paid), on time of occupancy, on the principle that obligations are inherited as well as assets, and on the person of the testator. It appears that Nathaniel is listing and strengthening his arguments in preparation for a meeting or for composing a more formal document. One stage on from the assembly of arguments is the drafting of outlines and drafts of speeches, letters and poems. Other notebooks provide evidence of different stages in these drafts. In Bodleian Library MS Rawl. D 47, an Oxford student's notebook, Daniel Featley (1582–1645) gives a draft of a Latin funeral oration for John Rainolds delivered in 1607, when Featley was an MA and one of the younger fellows of Corpus Christi College, of which Rainolds was president. Immediately before the draft oration there is a set of notes.

Lim Meth pro funer or in ob Rain
   1° deploratio mortis eccles Acad nos patr. pater opt Polus ossa Exite lachry levi dolor osequ const sublatam thes caelo dign dicdi argtum via felices Hook lacertus R cap Juellus anuli corona capit guil ferat si [vita] omnes pupilli facti sumus nervo Acad oculo corpus [christum] cap. oratio luct et squalore obsit
   2° Descript virtut In vita 1 doctrina, lectio men ingen translat libri seni unbr Edw Sandr et Parr Juell Hook Thren 2 humilit cum comes Essex et alii infinos audiunt . . .[53]

This methodical outline (*limus methodicus*) provides a series of topics and some phrases and images suitable for the speech. Its relationship to the oration can be suggested by quoting the opening sentences.

Ergo hac miserae et afflictae Christi sponsae languentis et debilitate Academiae, depositis rebus nostris et extrema iam spe pendentibus restabat unum ut Rainoldus quo illa maxime confidebat, haec mirifice gloriabatur istae se erigebant et sustentabant, de quo cogitantes quem intuentes omnium quas excepimus acerbitatum memoriam deposuimus cum omnium animos et studia ad se convertisset, ab omnium complexu divelleretur. O spem fallacem fragilemque

---

[52] *Nathaniel Bacon Papers*, II, pp. 190–1.
[53] Bodleian Library MS Rawl. D 47, fol. 128r. The text is given incomplete and untranslated because of the difficulties of transcription and interpretation caused by the ungrammatical structure and the abbreviated words. I have inserted square brackets where I am most uncertain of my reading.

vitam, et inanes contentiones nostras, quae in medio spatio saepe franguntur, et corruunt et ante in ipso cursu obruuntur, quam portum conspicere potuerunt. O legem inconstantiae rerum humanarum constantissimam. 'Omnes eodem cogimur; omnium versatur urna serius ocyus; sors exitura' est.[54] O querelam iniustitiae nostrae iustissimam. 'Virtutem incolumem odimus, sublatam ex oculis quaerimus invidi.'[55] Ecclesia lacerto fracto laxata est, Academia oculo effosso deformata est, corpus vero nostrum (Heu quanto cum dolore dicendum est), corpus inquam nostrum capite amisso concidit, et velut recenti doloris ictu etiamnum palpitat. Ecclesia maeret quia filium dilectissimum et athletam fortissimum, Academia squalet quia alumnum gloriossissimum, quid nos fratres par est facere qui charissimum patrem amisimus? Sic nos Pater optime fessos deseris? In aeternum? Histrio Polus[56] ut verum dolorem imitaretur filii ossa et urnam in scenam dicitur intulisse en fratres non in re ficta, sed seria, non filii, sed patris ossa et exanime cadaver qui tam multa tractavit dicendi argumenta fit ipse dicendi argumentum, hic iacet per quem res et spes meae et vestrae steterunt, et cuius famam non capit orbus, eius corpus haec vilissimum arca continet thesaurum caelo dignissimum in terra. Exite lachrymae exite qui vobis antehac commeatum obstruxerat commeavit.[57]

The first six sentences are devoted to a somewhat generalised lament for Rainolds's death (*deploratio mortis*). The seventh sentence laments the

---

[54] Horace, *Odes*, II.3.24–6.   [55] Ibid., III.24.31–2.

[56] Aulus Gellius, *Noctes Atticae*, VI.5. I am grateful to Marc van der Poel for these three references.

[57] 'And so in this weakness of both the miserable and dejected drooping bride of Christ and the University, while our affairs are brought low and now hanging in their last moment of hope, there remained one thing (to make our situation worse), namely that Rainolds, the man in whom the Church had great confidence and the University glorified greatly, and in whom both of them used to encourage and support themselves, the man about whom thinking and at whom looking we have set down the memory of all the sorrows which we have received, separated himself from the embrace of all, after he had converted the souls and enthusiasms of all to him. O deceptive hope and fleeting life, and our foolish hopes, which are often dashed in the mean time and collapse and are overwhelmed on their voyage before they can catch sight of the harbour. O most constant law of the inconstancy of human affairs. "We are all forced to the same end; sooner or later everyone's urn revolves; Fate will come to pass." O most just complaint of our injustice. "Envious as we are, we hate virtue when it is safe and want it back when it has been taken away from our sight." The Church is in mourning because its arm is broken; the University is deformed because its eye has been torn out; but our own Corpus (alas, with how much sorrow must it be said) I say our Corpus has fallen with its head removed and still threshes about as if with the wound of recent sorrow. The Church mourns because it has lost its most beloved son and strongest fighter. The University is in mourning because it has lost its most glorious alumnus. What should we brothers do who have lost our most dear father. Best of Fathers, do you desert us in our weariness? For ever? The actor Polus in order to imitate true sorrow is said to have brought the bones and urn of his son on stage. See brothers, not a staged event but a real one, not a son's but the bones and inanimate cadaver of a father. He who discussed so many subjects of speaking has now himself become a subject of speech. Here lies the man on whom your and my affairs and hopes relied. Although the world does not contain his fame, this box contains his most wretched body on earth, a treasure worthy of heaven. Fall tears, fall. The one who before has stopped your passage now moves you to fall.' Bodleian Library MS Rawl. D 47, fol. 129r–v, quoted in Latin for the sake of comparison with the outline.

loss suffered by church, university and his colleagues (*eccles Acad nos*). Sentences seven and eight juxtapose the father the college misses with the best of fathers (*patr. pater opt*). The tenth sentence compares the Roman actor Polus's method of imitating grief (*Polus ossa*) with the real grief of the fellows before Rainolds's body. The eleventh calls on them to shed their tears (*Exite lachry*). So the shape of the finished speech corresponds to the order of topics in the outline.

At the same time there are changes in the order presented in the outline. The idea that Rainolds's body is a treasure worthy of heaven occurs in the penultimate sentence of the extract but in the outline (*thes caelo dign*) it comes much later. In the same way the sixth sentence of the extract anticipates the ideas that the university has lost its eye and Corpus Christi College its head (*Acad oculo corpus [christum] cap.*) from later in the outline. These anticipations rule out the possibility that the *limus methodicus* was composed after the oration to serve as some kind of aide-mémoire for the orator, for in that case the speech and the outline would have had exactly the same order of topics. It suggests moreover that the outline was a preliminary division of the material, subject to revision and amplification (most notable here in the rhetorical elaboration of the implications of Rainolds's death in the first few sentences) as the full oration was composed. Since the oration in Rawl. D 47 has some, but relatively few, deletions and insertions, it is likely that it was a second or third draft of the speech to be delivered. As the text proceeds there are more deletions and abbreviations so it is unlikely to have been the finished fair-copy. Featley's manuscript contains other examples of the *limus methodicus* for orations and disputation speeches.[58] They resemble the outlines which Edward VI made before drafting his orations, though I assume that as an MA Featley's speech-writing was not under the direct tutorial supervision practised on Edward.

Notebooks like these provide some indications about Elizabethan processes of planning compositions. So far as one can see at this preliminary stage of research, writers of orations or letters would first collect a list of appropriate arguments, then attempt to arrange a selection of them according to a pre-arranged format, perhaps into three sections or some variant of the four-part oration. This skeleton (often in the form of numbered headings) would then be elaborated into a more continuous note-form draft in which some indications for introductions, comparisons and phrases would appear (often in the form of one- or two-word cues). The

[58] For example Bodleian Library MS Rawl. D 47, fols. 139r, 185r.

note-form draft would help in the composition of a full draft. Individual ideas and arguments would be elaborated; some sections would be subjected to more thorough-going rhetorical amplification; changes would be made in the ordering of material. The first full draft would itself then be subjected to different stages of amplification and rewriting. This hypothesis suggests that a combination of oral and written practices underlay practical processes of composition. The skeleton plan and the process of redrafting evidently depend on the technology of writing, but the use of one-word cues to recall phrases and ideas suggests oral habits of mentally improvising sections before attempting to record them fully in writing.

On the basis of five notebooks and a few loose sheets I have argued that Elizabethans used notebooks to extract striking phrases from, and to analyse the structure of, texts they read; to collect model letters for imitation; to assemble lists of arguments and to plan and draft their compositions. I hope that my examples have also shown the interest of these almost unstudied notebook materials. A thorough analysis of the kinds of such manuscripts, their typical contents and their structure would tell us a great deal about how Elizabethan people thought, read and wrote.

LETTERS

Where renaissance letters of friendship are characterised by considerable freedom in structure and content, as the letter-writing manuals observe, practical letters devoted to the conduct of business tend to convey expected content in a standard form. When Elizabeth, Countess of Bath recommends a maid to Mrs Kirkham in March 1594, she first commends her diligence and honesty, claiming that she would have kept her if she had been able to, then she enumerates her skills, her level of pay and the type of clothing she expects. The letter closes with personal salutations and a request to be informed of any subsequent reasons for dissatisfaction.[59] 'A letter for the preferring of a Servant' from Nicholas Breton's *A Poste with a Madde Packet of Letters* (1602) follows a very similar shape. The latter dispenses with the exordium in praise of the recipient's generosity (which would be expected in a letter of request from an inferior) and begins by narrating the recipient's need of a servant. The bulk of the letter is devoted to praising the honesty, confidentiality and diligence of the bearer. The petition that the bearer be employed is combined with expressions of friendship and obligation:

[59] W. C. Trevelyan (ed.), *Trevelyan Papers, Part III* (London, 1872), Camden Society first series vol. 105, p. 27.

if therefore at my request you will entertaine him, I doubt not but you will thank me for him; for I was glad I had so trusty a servant to commend to you, and hope to heare he will much content you.[60]

Both this model letter and the Countess of Bath's real one reflect the letter-writing manuals' instructions for letters of recommendation. Fulwood explains that such a letter should begin by praising the addressee for liberality and benevolence; then it should secure goodwill for the intended beneficiary by praising him. Thirdly it should make the request honestly and modestly, avoiding the mistake of asking for something excessive or inappropriate. The letter should conclude with promises of service and obedience.[61] For noblemen a different form of letter is recommended: a salutation giving the writer's name and titles, praise of the person to be preferred; reasons for the request and a promise to recognise the recipient's goodwill in obtaining the benefit.[62]

According to Angel Day letters of request should begin by praising the addressee, then recall the nature of his or her relationship with the writer, as a reason why the request should be granted. After showing that the request is honest, lawful and within the power of the addressee, the writer should explain how the request can be carried out and express his gratitude for the favour and his willingness to return it.[63] Nathaniel Bacon uses these topics in drafting a group of letters in August 1575 requesting stone for some building work from Edward Paston (both by direct request and by canvassing the support of Paston's relatives). He emphasises the link of neighbourly friendship between them, the surplus of stone available to Paston, the great benefit Paston would be doing him and the goodwill Paston (and his relatives) might expect in return.[64]

When in 1577 Sir Thomas Gresham writes to Nathaniel Bacon to congratulate him on the birth of his first son, he first expresses his pleasure that God has sent his daughter a boy, then regrets his inability to attend the christening and names a deputy, sets out the provision he has made for a present, and closes with further commendations to the parents.[65] Four years earlier Lady Anne Bacon's congratulations on the birth of Nathaniel's daughter had made the same points.[66]

In his brief letter to Sir Henry Goodyer commiserating with him on the death of his wife, John Donne emphasises his fellow-feeling in grief and his certainty that Sir Henry is 'well provided with Christian and

---

[60] Breton, *A Post*, letter 12, in *Works*, II, pp. 12–13.   [61] Fulwood, *Enemie*, sig. C8r–v.
[62] Ibid., sig. M3r–v.   [63] Day, *English Secretary*, sigs. N2r–3r.
[64] *Nathaniel Bacon Papers*, I, pp. 170–1.   [65] Ibid., I, p. 254.   [66] Ibid., I, pp. 81–2.

learned and brave defences against all human accidents',[67] in a similar
way to Dorothy Moryson's consolation of an unknown correspondent
on the death of her husband.

Good Madam: I have bene most sorie to heare of your late hard happe . . . but
good Lady suche is the worlde, and godes ordinaunce for us that lyves in it, to
passe many cares and afflictions, whereof I have had deepely my parte; it is his
mercifull school for his children, to make them seeke after the joyes of heaven,
which he hathe ordeyned for them. And so Mr Morrison, he is happier then
those he hathe lefte behinde him.[68]

Donne and Dorothy Moryson both use the topics which Fulwood recommends: expressions of shared sorrow, commonplace arguments of
consolation and promises of future assistance.[69] Angel Day lists consolatory arguments about the frailty of human life, the inevitability of
suffering and its use in drawing people to heaven.

The best way to expell the griefe thereof is by meditation of our estates, the
condition wherein we live, the inevitable force of that which is befallen us,
which because wee are worldlinges must nedes in like sorte betide us, howe
neare thereby wee may bee drawne in contempte of earthlie vanities, . . . that
troubles are sent unto us from God, to call us thereby home unto him, . . . that
by such meanes we are discerned to bee his children . . .[70]

Letters like these were essential to the maintenance of family life and the
conduct of business. By following well established norms they conveyed
a sense of order and reassurance. Originality in letters of this type would
be a sign of anxiety, of uncertain or inappropriate sentiments on the part
of the writer. In other letters more general considerations from rhetoric
and dialectic assist writers in selecting arguments and determining the
shape of the letter.

   Many of the less firmly structured Elizabethan letters are dominated
by instructions (for example on matters of estate management), by family news and gossip and by advice. Many such letters pass from family news to rumours about court promotions, national events or even
disasters abroad. Rhetorical education had some impact on passages
in letters dispensing moral advice, attempting persuasion or presenting
apologies.

   John Chamberlain's famous letters to Dudley Carleton are largely
concerned with family news and court gossip, but from time to time

[67] Edmund Gosse, *The Life and Letters of John Donne*, 2 vols. (London, 1899), I, p. 128.
[68] Braunmuller, *Letter-Book*, letter 32, p. 150.
[69] Fulwood, *Enemie*, sig. F6v.   [70] Day, *English Secretary*, sig. R2v.

Chamberlain from his position of detached observation permits himself to advise his younger, more conventionally ambitious friend. When Carleton is in Paris in 1602, Chamberlain advises him not to put himself forward for a vacancy in the service of Sir Robert Cecil.

> If you were once in his service, what usage soever you found, there is no starting but that you are lodged; whereas now it is *integrum* for you to take what way you list: and that may serve for *ultimum refugium*, and I hope for better at your hands then a bare service: the place you are in will make you knowne, and there wilbe always meanes to further you to his favor. Yf there be not extreme cause to the contrarie I wold wish you to continue a while as you are, for I assure you both court and countrie take notice of you and geve you your due: therefore you must not *succumbere oneri* but go on cherefully to the journies end.[71]

Chamberlain mingles arguments from advantage and honour. If Carleton were under Cecil he would have to remain there, whereas at present it remains honourable for him to follow his own path. Chamberlain presents the advantageous course of remaining where he is as devoted and cheerful persistence. Against the potential discomforts of service with Cecil, Chamberlain offers evidence of present success and the hope of future distinction. Even if eventually Carleton works for Cecil, Chamberlain wants him to enter that service at a higher level and with more hope of independent advancement. The Latin tags serve to emphasise arguments from honour and philosophy and to advance ultimate rest over present security.

When Nathaniel Bacon in 1572 complains to his father that his father-in-law, Sir Thomas Gresham, has installed new tenants on land that he thought was his to bestow, Sir Nicholas replies that such wrongs are commonplace and must be borne uncomplainingly for the sake of future benefits.

> Sonne, I have receyved your letter dated the second of this monethe wherby I understond a straunge dealing, but this is not the first, for my self was as yll dealt withall in the beginning and worse. Where no good fayth is kept there owght to be no trust. I pray God all assuraunces be faythfully performed concernyng the inheritaunce of the land. You shall do well hereafter when you come next up to London to remember me to cause the assuraunce to be over loked agayne . . . but howsoever these thinges be, you must for a tyme endure it without fynding any fawlt and to seke in humble and curteouse maner by suyte to recover that which in honestie and trothe perteynes to you. The rest that is to be done shalbe done by me.[72]

---

[71] N. E. McClure (ed.), *The Letters of John Chamberlain*, 2 vols. (Philadelphia, 1939), I, pp. 163–4.
[72] *Nathaniel Bacon Papers*, I, p. 44.

Sir Nicholas is careful to reassure his son that he is in the right, both by a plain condemnation ('straunge dealing') and an appended maxim ('Where no good fayth is kept there owght to be no trust'). Honesty and truth support Nathaniel's position. Together with his expression of fellow-feeling in the experience, these ethical statements prepare the way for the more prudential part of the letter, which advises Nathaniel to take care of future expectations rather than indulging immediate anger. Documents must be checked; a proper display of forbearance and humility must be made. Above all, Nathaniel should leave it to his father to arrange an agreement.

Sir Nicholas assumes the right to instruct his son, rather than to persuade him of the course he should adopt, but he employs the language of grammar school moral philosophy and the topos of shared suffering to reassure him of his support. Sir Nicholas acts as a purveyor of practical wisdom but he asserts that such wisdom merely provides the means to achieve what is morally right.

Logical argument plays a larger part than maxims in letters which seek to persuade a superior or an equal. When Nathaniel Bacon requests that the Dean of Norwich should write a letter confirming that Bacon has purchased the rights to a wood to deter a tenant who has locked the gates to prevent him from removing timber, he is careful to minimise the inconvenience to the Dean and Chapter ('I see not howe it can be any ways hurtfull unto yow'; 'you shall do but that by your letter whiche you have done in the Chapter'). He stresses his wish to avoid contention ('I were lothe to contende with him onlesse I should be dryven therunto') and the minor concession requested to bring it about ('His mynd shalbe but a litle yeilded unto'). In order to reassure the Dean that the Chapter has not wronged the tenant by selling Bacon the wood, he recounts an incident which serves as a confirmation from the greater (one of the topics of argument).

Presently after your sale of the woodes made unto me, I offered (and settynge no pryce) to sell him one of those woodes, and that which is fitteste for him and which lyeth next his howse, and he refused the offer and made lyght of it. Nowe what likelyhood is ther that this man would have delt with both those woodes when he refused both the better wood and which laye aptest for his howse? This wyll some what answer his complaintes.[73]

Bacon uses argument both to persuade the Dean to write the letter and to provide him with justification of the Chapter's treatment of their tenant.

[73] Ibid., I, p. 181.

He argues that since the tenant was not interested in a purchase more favourable to him he would also not have wanted the less favourable one. He recognises that the Dean is under no obligation to write the letter but he tries to convince him that to do so would be advantageous (in keeping the peace).

In the early 1570s Nathaniel Bacon tried to persuade his father-in-law to allow Anne, his daughter, (the marriage had taken place but remained unconsummated) to live in the household of Sir Nicholas Bacon. Asking Sir Thomas Gresham's agent Anthony Stringer to raise the question, he outlines the arguments in favour (the support of Anne's stepmother and Bacon's father and stepmother, and the advantage to Anne of being educated in her husband's family) but devotes more space to refuting objections. He denies that he intends to begin sexual relations with her before the time agreed and insists that the agreements made can be maintained. He assures them that Anne will be well-treated and that she will be allowed to return to Sir Thomas whenever he wishes.[74]

Sir Thomas Egerton took on a far more difficult task in July 1598, when he urged the Earl of Essex to end his discontented exile from the court after the incident in which the Queen had boxed his ears before the Privy Council.[75] The letter is organised in four parts: humbly explaining his reasons for writing, setting out the damage Essex's present course of action causes to the state and to himself, proposing the remedy that he submit to the Queen and return to court, and concluding apologetically. Egerton begins the letter by alluding to the proverbial maxim that an onlooker often sees more of the game than the players.[76] He emphasises that he does not presume to advise so experienced a counsellor but out of affection tells him his thoughts. The bad consequences of Essex's absence from court are amplified in a series of patterned arguments.

In this course you hold, if you had enemies, you do that for them which they could never do for themselves; your friends you leave open to scorn and contempt; you forsake yourself, overthrow your fortunes, and ruinate your honour and reputation; you give that comfort and corage to the forrayne enimye as greater thay can not have, for what can be more pleasing or welcom news unto them then to heare that her Majestie and the realme are maymed of so worthie a

---

[74] Ibid., I, pp. 10–11.

[75] R. C. Bald, *John Donne: A Life* (Oxford, 1970), pp. 103–4; James, *Society, Politics and Culture*, pp. 444–6. On Egerton see the important studies of Louis A. Knafla, 'The Law Studies of an Elizabethan Student', *Huntington Library Quarterly* 32 (1969), 221–40 and *Law and Politics in Jacobean England: The Tracts of Lord Chancellor Ellesmere* (Cambridge, 1977).

[76] 'Lookers-on see more than players', F. P. Wilson (ed.), *Oxford Dictionary of English Proverbs*, 3rd edn (Oxford, 1970), pp. 483–4: citing examples from Puttenham and Francis Bacon.

member, who hathe so often and so valyauntlie quayled and daunted them; you forsake youre countrie when it hath most neede of your counsell and helpe; lastlie you fayle in your indissoluble dutie which you owe unto your most gratious soveraigne.[77]

Egerton draws on commonplaces of prudent conduct to condemn Essex's action. He harms his friends, fortune, honour and reputation. He encourages personal and national enemies, weakens his country and fails in his duty. By exaggerating Essex's military reputation Egerton both supports his argument about foreign enemies and mollifies the letter's recipient. Essex's offence is amplified by being divided into different aspects. The parison with anaphora ('you give comfort to your enemy . . . you forsake your country . . . you fail in your duty') emphasises the seriousness of each. Then Egerton gathers the arguments together. The first four may seem small in the light of philosophy, but the last two are duties which have to be acted on. In order to make the remedy appear less unpalatable, he introduces it with a pair of moral maxims.

Bene cedit qui cedit tempore: and Seneca sayth, *Lex si nocentem punit, cedendum est iustitiae; si innocentem, cedendum est fortunae*. The medicine and remedy is not to contend and strive, but humbly to submit and yield.[78]

Policy, duty and religion require Essex to submit to his sovereign. There can be no dishonour in yielding, but the failure to do so is dishonourable and impious. Essex's duty is to conquer himself, which is where true valour and fortitude lie. Egerton deploys the key terms of virtues and duty to argue in favour of submission, before apologising and deferring to Essex's superior understanding. Outside these apologies this letter is both elaborate in style and forthright in expression. Its courtesy and craft leave no doubt of the response required.

   Essex's reply is polite without relinquishing superiority. In order to defend himself he must answer Egerton's arguments, which he incorporates in a series of rhetorical questions.

In this course doe I any thing for myne enemyes? . . . Or doe I leave my Frendes . . . Or doe I overthrowe my Fortune . . . Or doe I Ruynate myne honor?[79]

---

[77] Braunmuller, *Letter-Book*, letter 1, pp. 54–7.

[78] 'He yields well who yields in good time.' 'If the law punishes the guilty it must be accepted as justice; if it punishes the innocent, it must be accepted as an example of fortune.' Braunmuller, *Letter-Book*, letter 1, p. 58. There is a slight connection to the maxim 'Legem nocens veretur, fortunam innocens'. [Cato], *Libellus*, sig. D6r.

[79] Braunmuller, *Letter-Book*, letter 2, p. 62.

Reasons tending to a negative answer follow each of the questions so that Essex can conclude:

No, no, I gyve every of these considerations his dewe right, and the more I weigh, the more I fynde my self Iustified from offendeinge in any one of them; As for the last two obiections, that I forsake my countrey when it hath most neede of me, and fayle in that indissoluble dutye which I owe to my soveraigne; I answere, that if my Countrey had at this tyme nede of my publique service, her Maiestie that governs it, wolde not have dryven me to a private lyfe.[80]

Essex repeats Egerton's arguments partly to show that he has answered all the arguments against him and partly to provide an occasion for expressing his own view of events. This emerges particularly in the way he picks up Egerton's argument about duty. Essex agrees that the duty of allegiance is indissoluble but argues that the duty of attendance is different.

I owe her Maiestie the office: dutie: of an Earle Marshall of England; I have bene content to doe her the service of a Clarke, but I can never serve her as a villain or a slave; But yet you say I must gyve way to tyme, So I doe, for nowe I see the storme come, I have put my self into harbor.[81]

Essex considers himself dispensed from the obligation of personal service since the Queen has treated him in a manner unfitting to his position. He uses the topic of duty to introduce the injury to his sense of honour which is the chief theme of the rest of the letter.

I pacientlie beare and senciblie feele all that I then receyved when the Scandall was gyven me, nay, when the vylest of all indignities was done unto me; Dothe religion enforce me to sewe? dothe god require it? is it impietie not to doe it? why? can not princes erre? and can not subiectes receyve wrong?[82]

Egerton has urged him to accept wrongs philosophically; Essex answers that he does so in retiring from public life, but insists on, and amplifies the feeling of wrong done to him. Like Egerton he divides the effect of the wrong done him into separate propositions, linked by rhetorical questions; but he adds to the effect by choosing forceful and offensive epithets. He concludes his reply by reminding Egerton of his opening proverb. As a looker on, Egerton may see more, but he only sees while Essex suffers. Egerton may see more, but Essex undoubtedly feels more.[83] Where Egerton had deployed widely accepted topics of deliberation to advise him, Essex uses the formal obligation to respond to each argument

---

[80] Ibid., letter 2, p. 65.   [81] Ibid., letter 2, pp. 65–6.
[82] Ibid., letter 2, p. 66.   [83] Ibid., letter 2, p. 69.

to create an occasion for a more personal expression of emotion. Egerton follows the letter-writing manuals' advice about praising and deferring to superiors. Because Essex needs to be no more than polite in return, his response is more forceful. But it is also less controlled, more dangerous and easier to dismiss. Egerton's tight argumentative structure, humble self-presentation and elaborate style minimise the awkwardness of his assignment, treating it almost as a textbook problem in ethics; Essex's proud frankness accentuates the clash of wills.

John Donne was well aware of the difficulty of his task in writing to Sir George More in February 1602 to announce his clandestine marriage to Anne More.[84] His first letter tries to justify his conduct by explaining the strength of their affection and the reasons for their secrecy. He presents a persona of honesty and pragmatism, arguing that although More has the power to ruin them, forbearance will serve his interest better. With only a slight display of deference he aims for frankness.

Sir, If a very respective fear of your displeasure, and a doubt that my lord (whom I know, out of your worthiness, to love you much) would be so compassionate with you as to add his anger to yours, did not so much increase my sickness as that I cannot stir, I had taken the boldness to have done the office of this letter by waiting upon you myself to have given you truth and clearness of this matter between your daughter and me, and to show you plainly the limits of our fault, by which I know your wisdom will proportion the punishment.[85]

In seeking to justify and diminish his fault, he greatly underestimated Sir George's anger. Donne was dismissed from his post as secretary to Sir Thomas Egerton and imprisoned. Three weeks later, after his release, Donne chose to present himself in a more penitent and sympathetic way.

If these weights oppressed only my shoulders and my fortunes and not my conscience and hers whose good is dearer to me by much than my life, I should not thus trouble you with my letters; but when I see that this storm hath shaked me at root in my Lord's favour, where I was well planted and have just reason to fear that those ill-reports which malice hath raised of me may have troubled hers, I can leave no honest way untried to remedy these miseries, nor find any way more honest than this, out of an humble and repentant heart, for the fault done to you, to beg both pardon and assistance in my suit to my Lord . . .

Now I beseech you that I may [write to your daughter], since I protest before God it is the greatest of my afflictions not to do it. In all the world is not more true sorrow than in my heart, nor more understanding of true repentance than in yours.[86]

[84] Gosse, *Life and Letters of Donne*, I, pp. 100–2; Bald, *John Donne*, pp. 128–39.
[85] Gosse, *Life and Letters of Donne*, I, pp. 100–1.   [86] Ibid., I, pp. 112–13.

Donne's humility here is deepened by his understanding of the ruin of his worldly fortunes and partly motivated by the (mistaken) hope that More's intercession could rescue them. Still he finds words to acknowledge his error, proclaim his repentance and assure Anne's father of the depth of his concern for her situation. The second letter is studded with the grave words so evidently absent from the first: miseries, 'humble and repentant heart', afflictions, sorrow, repentance. By contrast, Queen Elizabeth's even more awkward protestation to James VI of her innocence in the matter of his mother's execution focuses entirely on her emotions and her rules of behaviour.

> My dear Brother, I would you knew (though not felt) the extreme dolor that overwhelms my mind, for that miserable accident which (far contrary to my meaning) hath befallen . . . I beseech you that, as God and many more know how innocent I am in this case, so you will believe me, that if I had bid aught, I would have bid by it. I am not so base minded that fear of any living creature or Prince should make me afraid to do that were just; or done, to deny the same. I am not of so base lineage, nor carry so vile a mind.[87]

Elizabeth hopes that rather than giving way to an emotional response, James will accept her arguments. Since she is willing to admit that Mary deserved death and since she would not be afraid to admit responsibility if she had ordered Mary's death, according to Elizabeth, it follows that she must be innocent. In her anxiety to proclaim her firmness and nobility, she seems to be unaware that her entire excuse depends on words of her own which could easily be interpreted in an opposite sense. It may have been precisely her insecurity that drove her to claim innocence of a deed she covertly intended. Fortunately for Elizabeth, James appears to have understood what remedy to exact for his qualified grief and where his future interests lay.

Classical rhetorical theory suggests that in oratory the grand style is the source of the strongest emotional effects. In letters, by contrast, emotion is often expressed most strongly through simple expressions. Donne's elaborate presentation of his need to write to Anne is less moving than the consistent affection of Thomas Knyvett's greetings to his wife.

> Sweet harte I am forst yet to send the shaddowe of my selfe, the true affection of a substance that loves you above all the world. My busines I hope wilbe dispatcht presently and god willing I will be with you before you are aware . . . Thus in

---

[87] G. B. Harrison (ed.), *The Letters of Queen Elizabeth I* (New York, 1935, repr. Westport, 1968), p. 188.

haste intreating the to be merry and the more merry to think thou hast him in thy armes that had rather be with you than in any place under heaven; and so I rest thy dear loving husband for ever.[88]

Chidiock Tichbourne's final letter is more elaborate than this (itself among Knyvett's more metaphysical salutations) and the circumstances make it grander, but its strongest emotional force arises from the everyday greeting and the way Tichbourne adapts the language of prayer to commend his wife and friends to God.[89]

The most loving wife alive I commend me to thee, and desier god to blesse the with all happines. Pray for thy dead husband and be of good comforte . . . God of his infinite goodnes and mercie, give the alwayes his grace to remain his true and most faithful servaunt, that through the merittes of his bitter and blessed passion thou maiest become an inheritrix of his kingdom with the blessed weomen in heaven . . . Farewell lovinge wyfe, farewell the dearest to me in all the earth. Farewell for ever in this worlde. Farewell.[90]

In *The Enemie of Idleness* Fulwood recommended simple language and brevity for passages of commiseration.

Commiseration must be made of sweete pitiful and humble language, like to a Comedie, and must be briefe, for it is inough if a man do but somewhat move the audience to pitie.[91]

NARRATIVES

In everyday Elizabethan life a person might be called on to give a narrative as part of a judicial or quasi-judicial investigation or as part of routine official supervision of some venture. In some of the publicly supported voyages, for example, one member of the ship's company acted as registrar of the decisions made and actions taken, on behalf of the Privy

---

[88] B. Schofield (ed.), *The Knyvett Letters 1620–1644* (Norwich, 1949), Norfolk Record Society vol. xx, pp. 56–7.

[89] The more elaborate prayers of the later Elizabethan period are never as effective as Cranmer's short collects composed for the 1549 Book of Common Prayer, often on the basis of continental originals. See Peter Mack, 'Rhetoric and Liturgy', in D. Jasper and R. C. D. Jasper (eds.), *Language and the Worship of the Church* (Basingstoke, 1990), pp. 82–109 (93–102).

[90] Braunmuller, *Letter-Book*, letter 12, p. 114. Tichbourne's mastery of rhetorical patterning is demonstrated in his famous *Elegy*, also composed before his execution; Norman Ault (ed.), *Elizabethan Lyrics* (London, 1925), p. 114.

[91] Fulwood, *Enemie*, sig. C4v.

Council. As with the system of grammar school monitors, the identity of the registrar was not always known to the rest of the officers.[92] Alternatively someone might wish to produce a narrative to strengthen the faith of their associates, by illustrating the wickedness of their religious persecutors, or to encourage participation in a venture, by depicting the wealth on offer. In all these cases the authors of the narratives had to find ways of presenting their accounts as credible and themselves as honest.

In 1582 the servant Hugh Rist made a deposition in the case for separation of Sir Gawen and Lady Roberda Champernowne, on the grounds of her adultery. Responding to a written list of questions, he stated that one evening within the previous three years, Sir Gawen Champernowne had gone with John Gatchell to Exeter to the court sessions, Gatchell had returned late at night, had woken Rist who was sleeping in the Lodge and had asked him to show him to Lady Roberda's bedroom to fetch some documents.

And when Gatchell knocked at the chamber dore, and that it was knowen that Gatchell was there the chamber dore was opened streight waye, and Gatchell and this deponent went both in the chamber and the sayd Gatchell went to the bed side betwene to the Courteyne and the bed where the sayd Ladie Laye, and then this deponent went to his chamber agayne, and Left the sayd Gatchell there, and before this deponent was past downe over the stayres he heard the chamber dore made fast and the sayd Gatchell before his going into the chamber desired this deponent of all Love that he would not tell his the sayd Gatchells wife of his retourne home agayne, and about two or three of the clocke the same morninge would take his horse and ride to exeter agayne and would tell this deponent That he would be at exeter before his master was upp.[93]

By limiting his account to what he has himself observed, and by providing circumstantial detail which makes it more plausible, Rist, or the clerk noting his evidence, hopes to win credit which will extend to his other testimony. Later Rist says that Gatchell has called on Lady Roberda at night 'three or four times' in the previous three years but maintains that he only took him to her chamber on this one occasion. To a later question, Rist describes a subsequent occasion, 'aboute two yeres and a half agonne' on which he and Gatchell discussed the affair.

[92] E. S. Donno (ed.), *An Elizabethan in 1582: The Diary of Richard Madox* (London, 1976), Hakluyt Society, series 2, vol. CXLVII, pp. 25–7; Baldwin, *Shakspere's Small Latine*, I, p. 311.

[93] Bridget Cusack (ed.), *Everyday English 1500–1700: A Reader* (Edinburgh, 1998), p. 125, edited from Devon Record Office, Manuscript Chanter 861.

In the way as they went this deponent went unto Gatchell my ladie meaning the sayd Ladie Robarda is much in your mowth I thincke you doe somewhat with her that you ought not to doe And the sayd Gatchell at the first sayd noe there is no such thinge, No sayd this deponent, Howe chaunce then the dores be opened unto you whensoever you comme, I cannot beleve but there is somme matter betwene you, well sayd Gatchell to this deponent you are one, that I dare trust . . . but if you bewraye me I am utterlie undone, quod this deponent I warrant you I will never bewraye you Then said Gatchell in deed the truthe is I have occupied my Ladie meaning the sayd lady Robarda, and I canne have my pleasure of her whensoever I will If my master be oute of the waye, but it was Long before I could gett her good will.[94]

Rist attempts to win credence for his much more damaging report of Gatchell's confession by his lifelike reconstruction of the conversation and by the potentially dangerous admission that he previously gave his word that he would not betray the confidence. Rist's reports of Gatchell's reluctance to tell, his protestation that he courted Lady Roberda for almost a year and his later offer to compensate secrecy all add to the plausibility of the narrative, though all could easily be inventions.

In August 1577, Nathaniel Bacon informed his father Sir Nicholas, who was Lord Keeper and a prominent member of the Privy Council, that two English ships, operating under a licence from the King of Spain, had been attacking Dutch fishing boats near the Norfolk coast.[95] On 27 August, the Privy Council wrote to Nathaniel requiring him, together with another Justice of the Peace, to investigate the circumstances and, if there was proof, to take bonds from any apparent offenders to appear before the council itself.[96] This letter was accompanied by a more detailed letter of advice from his father. According to Sir Nicholas, Nathaniel should do his best to apprehend the offenders and seize ships and goods before any warning could be given. He should question 'men of the best credite that you canne get' and should ask detailed questions about the number, manner of seizure and value of any ships taken, comparing the answers given by the principals with those of their mariners and servants.[97] He urges his son to take good testimony and, 'if the profe fall out according to th' enformacion', to attend the council in person with his evidence. To this end he offers to pay the expenses of the journey.[98]

Sir Nicholas hopes that wise and discreet handling of this case will bring his son credit among the Lords of the council, but he also warns

---

[94] Ibid., p. 126.   [95] *Nathaniel Bacon Papers*, I, pp. 200, 205–6.   [96] Ibid., I, pp. 208–9.
[97] Ibid., I, pp. 209–10.   [98] Ibid., I, pp. 210, 215.

him of the need to secure corroboration for everything he does (from a second Justice who will sign the depositions and from witnesses of good credit), since he may need to refute counter-accusations from the defendants. In response to this advice Nathaniel took notes of his conversations with Roger Carew, who was accused of the piracy, and took depositions from a range of witnesses, especially gentlemen and property owners.[99] The depositions relate a large number of facts and circumstances (how many prizes and of what value, where they were captured, how many were wounded in the fight, what amount of fish was on board, what meat was supplied to the ships for the soldiers) which are usually checked against another testimony. For example the statements which Edmund Dowsing the ship's cook makes about the sale of iron pots captured from a Scottish ship and the supply of beef are confirmed by statements from the buyer of the pots (though he admits to a much smaller number) and the supplier of the beef.[100] Although some notable factual claims are left unresolved (Copleston claims the prizes were first taken to Scarborough; Dowsing that they went to Burnham and Grimsby),[101] the accumulation of circumstances helps confirm both the general reliability of the witnesses and the main contention, that two Dutch ships were captured by English sailors, operating under a Spanish licence.

All the depositions were intended to accompany and justify the account of their own actions which Nathaniel Bacon and Ralph Shelton sent to the Privy Council around 6 September. This is a rather flat and cautious document, explaining that ships have been detained and individuals bound over to appear before the council and asking for further instructions. It also lists actions not taken because they were not in the commission and explains why Shelton and Bacon have been unable to apprehend Hubbart, whom they call the principal offender.[102] The Justices leave the council to infer the nature of the offences committed from the attached depositions, which they have written in the name of the witnesses. The Justices present themselves as passive collectors of information.

Shortly before writing to the Privy Council, Bacon wrote a more personal and more vivid account of events to his father.

Upon some enquirie after our cominge we found that Hubbart had newly received £160 for one of the Flemish prises with the fish therin, whereof one £100 was paid by one Roger Carewe, captain, brother to that Henry Carew

99 Ibid., i, pp. 211–16. 100 Ibid., i, pp. 214–15.
101 Ibid., i, pp. 213, 214. 102 Ibid., i, pp. 216–18.

of whom I wrot, the other £60 by one Bottleson of Cambridgeshire, and with this mony he was gone about an houre before to his ship to make paiment therof unto his souldiers . . . The warraunt was delivered [to the ship], and the aunswere herto was that Hubbart was not ther, but some of them wold within a while comme a land. We staied, but none came . . . [Roger Carew went to the ship and brought the answer that Hubbart would come later] The number of them was so great as no force was to be used, and so ther was no remedie than but of necessitie to hold our selves contented with the aunswere . . . This Roger Carew even to our faces used very ill wordes, and especially to me (for that he saw by my meanes this staie of them shold be mad), and the wordes were sutch as I knowe, yf the Counsell shold be advertised of them, he shold receive some sharp rebuke for it. But I purpose rather to forbeare so to do, least it shold be thought I seake by him to sting some freinde of his, or otherwise to reveng my privat injury more than redresse of the cause.[103]

To his father, Nathaniel can afford to be more frank about the conclusions he has reached and the frustrations and affronts he has endured. To the council he must present himself as measured and neutral, detached from any personal feelings when the public good is at stake. A few days later Sir Nicholas sent his son the original of a letter he had received from Sir Francis Walsingham, asking him to burn the letter once he has read it.[104]

For the offenders, bothe Hubberde and the two Carews are bound to be answerable unto the law. My Lords doe carrye themselves the more myldely in the punisshing of the seyd offenders in respect of Her Majeste's present offence against the Prince of Orange, wherof I hoped ther woold have growen some qualyficatyon (which at this present, consydering in what termes thinges stande in the Lowe Contryes, mygth greatly have stoode him in steede) but I see Her Majesty is bent otherwyse . . . I leave to your Lordship's grave consyderatyon howe hardely yt agreeathe with pollecye at this tyme to dyscowntenaunce the Prince of Orange when the gevyng of him of a lyttle cownetenaunce were lykely to remove a verry dayngerowse ennemy farther of from Her Majesty. But he that gydethe prynces' hartes wyll not have yt so.[105]

After his son's labours, Sir Nicholas thinks that he owes him a credible explanation of the reasons of state which have ensured that none of the pirates remain imprisoned. Walsingham's own letter will be more persuasive and will give more idea of the reluctance with which the decision was accepted than any summary could. While the bureaucratisation of state business makes possible this direct testimony, at the same time ordinary rhetorical considerations of self-presentation suggest that revealingly critical sentiments ought not to be allowed to remain on record.

[103] Ibid., I, pp. 212–13.   [104] Ibid., I, p. 224.   [105] Ibid., I, p. 223.

In October 1590, the High Court of the Admiralty began to hear a complaint of Thomas Middleton against Robert Hallett, contending that a smaller ship, the *Conclude*, had been deprived of its share of the proceeds of the capture in the Caribbean earlier that summer of the Spanish ship *Buen Jesus* by Hallett, who captained the prize on its return to England, on behalf of the larger ship involved, the *Harry and John*.[106] While it was agreed that there had been no written agreement allocating a share to the *Conclude*, Middleton called witnesses from several ships to establish that the *Conclude* had been involved in the capture, and that the sharing of the flags of the *Buen Jesus* between the *Conclude*, the *Moonlight* and the *Harry and John* and the formation of a prize crew from all three ships confirmed the verbal agreement (contested by Hallett) to share the prize.[107] Thomas Harden, a seaman aboard the *Moonlight*, a small ship which had made an agreement to consort with the *Harry and John*,[108] gave evidence of the *Conclude*'s participation in the fight.

In the morning when the lighte appeared the spanish shippe was assaulted both by the *Harry and John* and the *Conclude* and the *Moonlight* being all togeather, and forced by them to yealde unto them, And uppon yealdinge every of those thre shippe the *Harry and John*, the *Conclude* and *Moonlight* entered of theire men on borde the said prize in theire boates and were quietly possessed thereof amongst them as theire prize and had the pilladge on borde amongst them of this examinates knowledge being masters mate of the said shippe the *Moonlight* at the takinge of the said prize in company of the two other shipps aforesaid. Affirminge that the *Conclude* was the best sayloer of all the said shipps and first mett with the said prize in the nighte as he thinketh for that the company thereof first tould the *Harry and John* of the said prize to be a heade of them.[109]

Harden insists on the collaboration of the three ships in capturing the *Buen Jesus*. He adds circumstantial detail to enhance the plausibility of his testimony and to support his claim that all three ships participated in the capture. As a further indication of his caution and trustworthiness, he qualifies his statements that the *Conclude* was the first to sight the Spanish vessel and that she carried a light as a signal for the other English ships. He claims that since all three captains agreed to put a combined crew onto the prize, he had assumed that there must have been an agreement to share the prize.[110] Hugh Harding, who was master of the *Conclude*

---

[106] This is the name given in the depositions; more formally the ship was known as the *Hopewell*. D. B. Quinn (ed.), *The Roanoke Voyages*, 2 vols. (London, 1955), Hakluyt Society series 2, vols. CIV–CV, II, p. 580.

[107] Hallett subsequently left former members of the *Conclude*'s crew in the Azores, perhaps in order to weaken their claim on a share. Quinn, *Roanoke Voyages*, II, pp. 640, 642, 645, 686.

[108] Ibid., II, p. 584.   [109] Ibid., II, p. 633.   [110] Ibid.

confirmed that he had carried a light overnight and provided versions of conversations with the other masters. He claimed that there was an agreement to divide the spoils, noting that the masters had also agreed to divide two chests of sugar and the flags from the *Buen Jesus*.[111] In the absence of a written agreement, Harding marshals signs indicating other forms of collaboration between the captains of the three vessels. He uses circumstantial details to establish the fundamental point of his ship's participation in the capture.

The defence denied the existence of any agreement.[112] In their cross-questioning, they sought to divide members of the crew of the *Conclude* from other witnesses. They asked witnesses about the relative size of the Spanish ship and the three English vessels. Then they asked if the *Buen Jesus* would have yielded to the *Conclude* alone, or to the *Harry and John* and *Moonlight* without the *Conclude*.[113] Finally they called members of the crew of the *Buen Jesus* to testify that their ship was captured only because of the superior strength of the *Harry and John* and that they would not have yielded to the two smaller ships.[114]

Where the plaintiffs used the circumstances of the fight and signs of agreement to support belief in their version of events, the defence relied on arguments from relative strength and probability. Since the two minor vessels were too weak to harm the Spanish ship, and since the Spanish ship yielded largely or exclusively to the larger ship, only the larger ship deserves the spoils. This argument prevailed with the court.[115]

Where legal questioning encourages cautious, plain testimony, reports intended to encourage further exploration call for bolder claims and more elaborate expression. Arthur Barlowe's report of the first voyage to Virginia in 1585 makes the best of the coastal swampland.

The soile is the most plentifull, sweete, fruitfull and wholsome of all the world: there are above foureteene severall sweete smelling timber trees, and the most part of their underwoods are Bayes, and such like: they have those Okes that we have, but farre greater and better.[116]

Barlowe amplifies through comparison and enumeration of details. Summarising his impressions of the people, the topos of the golden age proves irresistible.

---

[111] Ibid., II, pp. 643–5.   [112] Ibid., II, p. 685.
[113] Ibid., II, pp. 657–9, 662–3.   [114] Ibid., II, pp. 697–702.
[115] Ibid., II, p. 712. Quinn suggests that both the Spanish witnesses and the master of the *Moonlight* may have been paid off by John Watts, the owner of the *Harry and John*. *Roanoke Voyages*, I, p. 70.
[116] Ibid., I, p. 106.

We were entertained with all love, and kindnesse, and with as much bountie, after their manner, as they could possibly devise. Wee found the people most gentle, loving and faithfull, voide of all guile and treason, and such as lived after the manner of the golden age. The earth bringeth foorth all things in aboundance, as in the first creation, without toile or labour.[117]

Barlowe writes to arouse the curiosity and enthusiasm of his audience. His paradisal tone is repeated in Ralph Lane's account of Virginia and his attempt to place the first colony in 1585–6.

The Territorie and soyle of the Chesepians (being distant fifteene miles from the shoare) was for pleasantnes of seate, for temperature of Climate, for fertilitie of soyle, and for the commoditie of the Sea, besides multitude of beares (being an excellent good victual, with great woods of Sassafras, and Wall nut trees) is not to be excelled by any other whatsoever.[118]

Lane emphasises the pleasingness of land and climate, its provision with ample and easily obtained food resources. Detail and comparison amplify the advantages of the place. The real hardships faced by the colonists (which prompted them to accept Drake's offer of a return voyage) have to be suppressed in the interest of the future enterprise.

By contrast, persecution narratives, which are just as strongly directed to an audience, exaggerate the cruelty and cunning of the persecutors. The man or woman of right religion must be presented as victimised and mistreated in order to increase hatred of the opposing faith, and as brave, firm and ultimately successful in order to encourage co-religionists. Thomas Mowntayne's autobiography manages to fulfil these expectations within an exciting and edifying narrative.[119]

Soon after Mary's accession to the throne, Mowntayne was summoned by the Bishop of Winchester to be interrogated about his beliefs. Mowntayne was firm and polite in the face of the Bishop's threats, making long speeches, which he reports as if verbatim, on the benefits of the Protestant religion.[120] His interrogators are presented as inhumane and corrupt.

Than sayd Sir Richard Sothewell, 'To the racke with them! to the racke with them! sarve them lyke eretyckes and traytors as they be; for one of these knavys ys able to undoo a hole syttye.' Thys was spoken at afternone, and soudaynly he fell aslepe as he sate at the borde.[121]

---

[117] Ibid., I, p. 108.   [118] Ibid., I, p. 257.

[119] Printed from British Library MS Harley 425 as 'The Troubles of Thomas Mowntayne' in J. G. Nichols (ed.), *Narratives of the Days of Reformation* (London, 1859), Camden Society original series vol. LXXVII, pp. 177–217.

[120] Nichols, *Narratives*, pp. 178–84.   [121] Ibid., p. 188.

With the same arbitrariness, Mowntayne was sent to the Marshalsea prison, then to the Tower and back to the Marshalsea, where late one evening he was told that the next day he would be sent to Cambridge Castle.

Shorte warnynge I hade; but there was no remedye. In the mornynge I made me redy by tymes, and rekenyd with my keper; went downe and toke my leve of al my felowe prysonars with the reste of my frendys, movynge them and exortynge them, as the tyme dyd serve, 'to be constante yn the truthe, to serve God and feare hyme, and to be obedyent unto the deathe, and not to resyst the hyere powers'.[122]

After he had prayed with his fellow prisoners, six horsemen took him northwards. On the journey he was well fed and housed, but he refused the offer of good treatment in return for conformity as firmly as he resisted threats.[123] The morning after he arrived at Cambridge Castle he was told to prepare to be executed, but he refused because he had received no trial and had been shown no death warrant. Instead he remonstrated with the keeper about the wickedness of the sin he was about to commit and showed him many examples of the punishment of sin. The keeper was so moved by Mowntayne's private sermon that he begged forgiveness from God and promised to help him in any way he could.[124] After being freed from Cambridge on a fortunate technicality and after narrowly evading recapture on several occasions, he eventually escaped to Flanders, where he remained until Elizabeth's accession.

Mowntayne's autobiography is full of direct speech, illustrating the wicked arbitrariness of his persecutors and the courageous holiness of his own speech. At every turn he finds sympathisers and helpers, who warn him of an impending search or conceal him from the authorities. Mowntayne's words are effective and they build godly communities around him. He avoids self-congratulatory references to the help he receives from providence, but the message of his narrative is that those who are brave in their witness without foolhardiness will receive assistance when they least expect it.

The staples of grammar school rhetorical education enabled everyday Elizabethan writing to perform its tasks. Moral sentences were recorded in personal notebooks and reused in letters to reassure the recipient, to confirm that both writer and audience participated in a community

---

[122] Ibid., p. 190.   [123] Ibid., pp. 191–4.   [124] Ibid., pp. 199–202.

of values. Notebooks recorded stories for use in letters and conversation and collected examples from the reading of history. Narratives were crafted to enhance the reliability of the speaker (through amplification of details or through cautious limitation of claims), to support arguments and to illustrate moral principles. The structures of sermons and books were analysed in notebooks. Model letters (again collected in notebooks) provided sentiments, expressions and structures appropriate to many of the situations of everyday social intercourse (recommendation, request, congratulation, consolation). The topics of deliberative oratory were employed in letters of advice. The composition of letters and narratives was dominated by ideas about self-presentation and the reaction of an audience. Ideas about style influenced the selection of quotations and comparisons, and the phrasing of key passages.

University training in topical invention helped Nathaniel Bacon find the arguments which he listed in his notebook before using them in letters. The case of the *Harry and John* illustrated a clash between the implications of circumstantial evidence and arguments about the probable effect of differences of strength. Essex replied to each of Egerton's arguments in turn before developing his own commonplaces of honour and offence.

Through these learned techniques people acquired a repertory of arguments and phrases for performing the different roles which social situations required. The Countess of Bath recommended a servant and Dorothy Moryson consoled her friend in terms which recall the English letter-writing manuals and behind them Erasmus's *De conscribendis epistolis*. When Donne's self-presentation as a man divided between loyalties failed to move his father-in-law, he switched to the more conventional language of regret and devotion. Sir Thomas Egerton drew on conventional notions of epistolary humility before creating an argumentative context in which the commonplaces of honour and duty urged Essex to abandon his pique.

Skilful manipulation of these verbal forms and ethical axioms achieved practical goals and advanced careers. By convincing the High Court of the Admiralty that the *Buen Jesus* only surrendered because of the involvement of the *Harry and John*, Robert Hallett deprived the owners and crew of the *Conclude* of any reward for their share in the exploit. Sir Nicholas Bacon hoped that his son Nathaniel's effective investigation of a case of piracy would win him favour with the Privy Council, a result independent of the question of punishing the shipowners involved.

Mowntayne's strength of witness found him helpers in dangerous places and encouraged his fellow Protestants.

Rhetorical training provided Elizabethans with ways to use their classical reading to construct arguments in practical life. In the next chapter we shall see how the same forms and materials shaped contemporary English romances, histories and conduct manuals. These popular genres in turn reinforced and broadened the impact of grammar school moral and rhetorical teaching.

5

Histories, conduct manuals, romances

The attraction of the idea of education was so great in sixteenth-century England that many forms of vernacular writing justified themselves primarily as vehicles for moral teaching. Sir Philip Sidney's principal claim for poetry, which he sees as embracing all forms of fiction, is that it is a more effective form of moral teaching than history or philosophy.[1] History, conduct manuals and romances are the most often printed genres of secular writing in English in the sixteenth century. My argument in this chapter will be that these three popular genres of Tudor vernacular writing are linked and that both in subject-matter and in form they draw on the resources of rhetorical education. I shall show that histories, conduct manuals and romances share six common features: moral stories, ethical sentences, techniques of amplification, speeches and letters, debate, and shared themes. All these common features are connected with and illuminated by the procedures of Tudor rhetorical education.[2] Most are features of grammar school teaching, which provides both material (moral sentences, stories, commonplace themes) and methods for storing, varying and presenting it. Texts in all three genres reuse material from earlier writings and in turn present subject-matter for further reuse. This means that passages from a romance may derive part of their meaning from debate with sections of a conduct book or a chronicle and vice

---

[1] Sidney takes several phrases and arguments from North's translation of Amyot's introduction to Plutarch's *Lives*: 'These things it doth with much greater grace, efficacy, and speed than the books of moral philosophy do; forasmuch as examples are of more force to move and instruct than are the arguments and proofs of reason, or their precise precepts, because examples be the very forms of our deeds, and accompanied with all circumstances . . . Examples tend to the showing of them in practice and execution, because they do not only declare what is to be done, but also work a desire to do it, as well in respect of a certain natural inclination which all men have to follow examples.' T. North, *Plutarch's Lives of the Noble Grecians and Romans*, 8 vols. (Oxford, 1928), I, p. xvi. Compare Sidney, *Apology for Poetry*, pp. 106–7.

[2] Works on moral philosophy and romances (but not histories) are discussed in the general context of rhetoric in Crane, *Wit and Rhetoric*; R. Helgerson discusses romance and history (as well as geography, religion and law) in *Forms of Nationhood* (Chicago, 1992).

versa. The authors of these works, including the three who have been
accorded a place in the literary canon, Sidney, Lyly and Elyot, make
extensive use of the resources of content and expression cultivated in the
grammar school. In fact one is missing something important about their
writing if one does not attend to their exploitation of techniques and
materials which they share with all the other writers of prose of informal
moral instruction. In the last section of this chapter I shall compare views
about friendship and counsel in works from all three genres to show how
shared material was used for different purposes.

Since histories, conduct manuals and romances are repertories of
technique as well as of moral teaching, grammar school and university
training can be thought of as encouraging attention to the way in
which rhetorical skills are used. Some features of these texts invite a
reading which emphasises the Tudor taste for debate, speech-making
or amplification. Because they foregrounded certain techniques and
ethical principles, endorsing some, playing with and debating others,
histories, conduct manuals and romances promoted particular values and presented certain forms of argument as models of effective
persuasion.

Although my argument concerns genre, a matter of some importance to Tudor writers, a meaningful comparison can only be conducted
through a selection of individual texts. In order to avoid prejudicing my
argument by choosing only examples from within the literary-historical
canon, I have tried to pay some attention to publication history as at
least a loose guide to contemporary reception.[3]

In history, the principal examples will be Edward Hall's *The Union
of the Two Noble and Illustre Families of Lancaster and York* (1548), which
from now on I shall call his *Chronicle*, as is customary, and *The Mirror for
Magistrates* (1559). Hall's *Chronicle* was printed three times as an independent work (though it incorporated large sections from Polydore Vergil,
Fabian and Sir Thomas More) and a further time as part of Grafton's
Chronicle at Large (1569).[4] Much of it was also reused in the three sixteenth-
century editions of Holinshed's *Chronicle* (1577). Holinshed and Grafton
are both multi-volume folio works which must have been very expensive.
Even the separate folio of Hall is very much at the upper end of the
market. Not counting the suppressed edition of 1555, there were seven

---

[3] Initial manuscript circulation remained important for some romances, but in the second half of
the sixteenth century histories and conduct manuals were primarily, and romances were largely,
written for publication in print.
[4] Grafton's frequently-printed *Abridgement of Chronicles* is very brief and contains little of Hall.

sixteenth-century editions of *The Mirror for Magistrates*, originally edited by William Baldwin, which even in its expanded edition was much less substantial, and presumably less expensive, than the chronicles. Some account must also be taken of English translations of classical historians, notably Sir Thomas North's version of Plutarch's *Lives* (1579), which was printed twice in the sixteenth century.[5]

The most celebrated English conduct manual is Sir Thomas Elyot's *The Book Named the Governor* (1531) which was printed eight times in the sixteenth century, though some passages were suppressed in Elizabethan editions.[6] There were three sixteenth-century editions of Sir Thomas Hoby's English translation of Castiglione, *The Book of the Courtier* (1561) and a further three of the Englishman Bartholomew Clerke's Latin translation, *De curiali sive aulico libri quatuor* (1571), which was probably preferred by the intellectual élite.[7] William Baldwin's *A Treatise of Morall Philosophie* (1547) which consists mainly of a series of moral aphorisms organised by subject and by the philosopher to whom they are attributed, was one of the best-sellers of the sixteenth century, with a total of seventeen editions.[8] Elyot produced a briefer collection of philosophers' sayings, *The Banquet of Sapience* (1539), which was printed six times. The currency of both these volumes must owe something to their similarity to standard grammar school texts like 'Cato's' *Distichs* and the *Sententiae pueriles*. Translations of the two versions of Antonio de Guevara's forged work on the life, sayings and letters of the emperor Marcus Aurelius were also very successful.[9] Lord Berners's *Golden Boke of Marcus Aurelius* (1535) was printed fifteen times and Sir Thomas North's *Diall of Princes* (1557) three times. Xenophon's *Cyropaedia*, some of Plutarch's *Moral Essays* and Erasmus's *Institutio principis christiani* are important sources for all these works.[10]

5 According to the *Short Title Catalogue*, there was also a variant issue of each edition. On histories see F. J. Levy, *Tudor Historical Thought* (San Marino, 1967); A. Patterson, *Reading Holinshed's Chronicles* (Chicago, 1994); D. R. Kelley and D. Harris Sacks (eds.), *The Historical Imagination in Early Modern Britain* (Cambridge, 1997); there is no recent study of Hall.

6 On Elyot, see S. E. Lehmberg, *Sir Thomas Elyot: Tudor Humanist* (Austin, 1960); John M. Major, *Sir Thomas Elyot and Renaissance Humanism* (Lincoln NE, 1964); P. Hogrefe, *The Life and Times of Sir Thomas Elyot, Englishman* (Iowa City, 1967); Skinner, *Reason and Rhetoric*, pp. 72, 75–87. On courtesy manuals more generally, see Ruth Kelso, *Doctrine of the English Gentleman in the Sixteenth Century* (Urbana, 1929); John E. Mason, *Gentlefolk in the Making* (Philadelphia, 1935).

7 J. W. Binns, *Intellectual Culture in Elizabethan and Jacobean England* (Leeds, 1990), pp. 258–64.

8 William Baldwin, *A Treatise of Morall Philosophie (1547)*, facsimile of the 1620 edition, ed. R. H. Bowers (Gainesville, 1967); John N. King, *English Reformation Literature* (Princeton, 1982), pp. 358–66.

9 W. Nelson, *Fact or Fiction: The Dilemma of the Renaissance Storyteller* (Cambridge MA, 1973), pp. 35–6.

10 These sources would mostly have been used in Latin or Greek but there were two editions of an English translation of the *Cyropaedia* (1552, 1567) STC 26666–7. That no Greek–Latin edition was

My discussion of conduct manuals will draw mainly on Elyot's *Gover-nor*, Baldwin's *Treatise* and Berners's *Golden Boke*.

Among romances John Lyly's *Euphues* (1578) and *Euphues and his England* (1580) set the model for the revival of the genre and were very popular, twelve editions of the first and ten of the second appearing before the end of the sixteenth century.[11] The extensive manuscript circulation of the unprinted original version[12] and the success in the following century of the revised version made it seem important to refer to Sir Philip Sidney's *Arcadia* (1590), although there were only four printed editions in the sixteenth century.[13]

The distinction between fictions, conduct manuals and rhetoric text-books becomes blurred in some cases as rhetoric manuals too take on the task of informal moral education. The invented examples in Angel Day's *The English Secretary* describe historical events like those in Hall and Elyot, relate a death speech like the ones in Guevara and Hall, and discuss friendship and explain the arguments against abduction in a way very pertinent to *Euphues* and *Arcadia*.[14] Day's final section 'Of the partes, place and Office of a Secretorie' is a conduct manual.[15] Nicholas Breton's *A Poste with a Madde Packet of Letters* (1602) in the form of a fictional collection of letters provides moral teaching, stylistic models, expressions of emotional states and amusing epistolary narratives.[16] It plays with grammar school forms and themes for recreational reading.

MORAL STORIES

The fundamental shared premiss of histories, conduct manuals and ro-mances is that narratives, whether historical or fictional, embody teach-ing. In some cases this teaching is practical. Noblemen are advised to

printed in England before 1613 may suggest that its importance has been overstated. Philemon Holland's complete translation of Plutarch's *Moralia* appeared in 1603, though separate essays were translated earlier. Jacques Amyot's French version of the *Moralia*, which English readers may well have used in preference to the Greek, was available from 1572.

[11] On Lyly and prose romance more generally, see G. K. Hunter, *John Lyly: The Humanist as Courtier* (London, 1962); R. Helgerson, *The Elizabethan Prodigals* (Berkeley, 1976); P. Salzman, *English Prose Fiction 1558–1700* (Oxford, 1985); Arthur Kinney, *Humanist Poetics* (Amherst, 1986); G. M. Logan and G. Teskey (eds.), *Unfolded Tales* (Ithaca, 1989).

[12] Described in Henry Woudhuysen, *Sir Philip Sidney and the Circulation of Manuscripts 1558–1640* (Oxford, 1996), pp. 299–355.

[13] I discuss the rhetoric of other romances in 'Rhetoric in Use: Three Romances by Greene and Lodge', in P. Mack (ed.), *Renaissance Rhetoric* (Basingstoke, 1994), pp. 119–39.

[14] Day, *English Secretary*, sigs. F1v–G1r, E2v–3r, L3r–M2r, M4r–v.

[15] Ibid., sigs. Nn1r–Rr1r, Jonathan Goldberg, *Writing Matter* (Stanford, 1996), pp. 265–72.

[16] Breton, *Works*, II, e.g. pp. 6–13. On Breton's influence see Hornbeak, 'Complete Letter-writer', pp. 29, 33–49.

read history in order to extend their knowledge of military tactics or ladies are invited to read romances to learn about the stratagems of their admirers.[17] More often in all three genres the narratives serve as examples of moral behaviour, depicting the punishment of vice and the reward of virtue.

Tudor translators and historiographers justify the writing of history by claiming that it secures the memory of what has happened in the past,[18] that it teaches moral and political lessons,[19] and that it supplies examples which can be used in other forms of writing.[20] In his *Methode of Wryting and Reading Histories*, Blundeville urges his readers to note down weighty examples in a commonplace book under the heading of the lessons they illustrate. By this means examples will be ready to be inserted into one's own writing.[21]

For Hall, in the dedication of his *Chronicle*, history is the means by which fame defeats oblivion. The function of history is moral teaching, especially the education of the prince.

If no man had written the goodness of noble Augustus, nor the pity of merciful Trajan, how should their successors have followed their steps in virtue and princely qualities; on the contrary part, if the cruelty of Nero, the ungracious life of Caligula had not been put in remembrance, young princes and frail governors might likewise have fallen in a like pit, but by reading their vices and seeing their mischievous end, they be compelled to leave their evil ways and embrace the good qualities of notable princes and prudent governors. Thus writing is the key to induce virtue and repress vice; thus memory maketh men dead many a thousand year still to live as though they were present; thus Fame triumpheth upon death and renown upon Oblivion, and all by reason of writing and history.[22]

By means of the written word the virtues and vices of past princes influence the conduct of their successors. The writing of history, by securing memory and immortalising fame, is therefore the principal means of

---

[17] Lorna Hutson *The Usurer's Daughter* (London, 1994), pp. 106–11 shows that in romances amorous and military stratagems served as models for prudent behaviour.

[18] 'An history is the recorder of times past, the light of verity, the mistress of man's living, the president of memory, the messenger of antiquity.' Alexander Barclay, 'Preface', Sallust *Jugurthine War*, trans. Barclay [?1520] STC 21626, sig. A6r. 'There is neither picture, nor image of marble, nor arch of triumph, nor pillar, nor sumptuous sepulchre, that can match the durableness of an eloquent history.' Jacques Amyot, 'Preface', North, *Plutarch's Lives*, I, p. xv.

[19] North, *Plutarch's Lives*, I, pp. ix, x, xiii–xviii, xxiv.

[20] Ibid., I, pp. xvii–xix, Thomas Blundeville, *The True Order and Methode of Wryting and Reading Hystories* (London, 1574) STC 3161, sig. A2r.

[21] Blundeville, *Methode of Wryting and Reading Hystories*, sigs. H2v–4r.

[22] Edward Hall, *The Union of the Two Noble and Illustre Families of Lancaster and York* (London, 1809), hereafter *Chronicle*, pp. v–vi.

providing moral education to princes. Hall amplifies his praise of history by combining anaphora, colon and personification in his concluding sentence. In his *Chronicle* he often comments on the morality of historical actions, both in order to interpret events and to point lessons for his readers. After Henry of Richmond has expressed to Thomas Mowbray, Duke of Norfolk, his anxieties about Richard II's treatment of the nobility and asked him to advise the King to act differently, Hall describes Mowbray's reaction.

When the Duke of Norfolk had heard fully his device, he took it not in good part, but reckoned that he had gotten a prey by the which he should obtain greater favour of the King than ever he had, and so he at the time dissimuled the matter (as he was in deed both a deep dissimuler and a pleasant flatterer). And after when he had opportunity and saw his time, he was very glad (as tell tales and sycophants be, when they have anything to instil into the ears and heads of princes) to declare to the king what he had heard, and to aggravate and make the offence the greater, he much more added but nothing diminished.[23]

Most of what Hall writes in this paragraph consists of inference from the later development of the quarrel. In order to justify his reconstruction of Mowbray's thinking he compares it to the usual behaviour of flatterers and sycophants. Since Mowbray falls into these categories (themselves based on moral treatises and fictions but commonly extended to life) he must have thought and acted in roughly this way. At the same time the labelling of Mowbray's thinking means that Hall's readers are presented with a historical example of such behaviour to guide their interpretation of other events and to be reused in their own writing. In his final sentence Hall portrays Mowbray as employing rhetorical amplification, since he adds plausible material to his report of Richmond's speech in order to increase the offence to Richard.

After describing (and indeed amplifying with the addition of vivid detail) Queen Margaret's melancholy reaction to the defeat of the Lancastrians at the Battle of Barnet, Hall suggests another way for her, and his audience, to consider her situation.

This Queen Margaret might well consider and think that these evil adventures chanced to her for the most part for the unworthy death of Humfrey Duke of Gloucester, uncle to her husband. Of the which mischance, although she were not the very occasion and provoker, yet she greatly offended in that she consented thereto, and did not save his life, when she ruling all other might conveniently have stayed and letted it. For surely he being alive and having

<hr>

[23] Ibid., p. 3.

the moderation and governance of the commonwealth, King Henry had never wavered in so many hazards and jeopardies of his life as he did. I would desire of God that all men would in equal balance ponder and indifferently consider the causes of these misfortunes and evil chances, the which being elevate in authority, do mete and measure justice and injury, right and wrong, by high power, blind authority and unbridled will.[24]

Hall suggests that her suffering was caused, and probably deserved, by her failure to save Duke Humfrey's life. Through ethopoeia he invites Margaret to consider how different the outcome might have been if she had acted differently. He outlines arguments to persuade his readers both that Margaret might have been able to save Duke Humfrey and that his survival would have made a difference. Once this connection has been made, Hall points the general lesson to all rulers. Margaret's pitiable state becomes an example, elaborated through doubling and isocolon, to teach the need to administer justice fairly. It is also a political lesson about the advantages to the state of figures of moderation.

The moral implication of political history is presented even more overtly in the *Mirror for Magistrates*, which breaks roughly the same historical span as Hall's *Chronicle* into a series of exemplary tragedies, in the manner of Lydgate's *Fall of Princes*.[25] William Baldwin's preface 'To the nobility and all other in office' explains that the aim of the *Mirror for Magistrates* is to admonish rulers to act justly.

For here as in a looking glass you shall see (if any vice be in you) how the like hath been punished in other heretofore, wherby admonished, I trust it will be a good occasion to move you to the sooner amendment.[26]

Richard II puts it very clearly in his tragedy.

> And therefore Baldwin sith thou wilt declare
> How princes fell, to make the living wise,
> My vicious story in no point see thou spare,
> But paint it out, that rulers may beware
> Good counsayle, lawe, or vertue to despyse.[27]

---

[24] Ibid., pp. 297–8.
[25] At one point the interlocutor Ferrers tells Baldwin to go through the chronicles marking up the stories to be noted. Some of the prefaces list monitory stories which will not become the subject of separate tragedies. William Baldwin, et al., *Mirror for Magistrates*, ed. L. B. Campbell (Cambridge, 1938), pp. 91, 131. See also J. L. Mills, 'Recent Studies in *A Mirror for Magistrates*', *English Literary Renaissance* 9 (1979), 343–54; Lawrence D. Green, 'Modes of Perception in the *Mirror for Magistrates*', *Huntington Library Quarterly* 44 (1980–1), 117–33; Andrew Hadfield, *Literature, Politics and National Identity* (Cambridge, 1994), pp. 81–107.
[26] Baldwin, *Mirror for Magistrates*, pp. 65–6.   [27] Ibid., p. 112, lines 22–6.

The lesson will be driven home more strongly by amplifying all the details of Richard's fall. Each story illustrates the consequences and the punishment of a particular vice. In some cases the title of the tragedy names the vice. Robert Tresilian falls for 'misconstruing the laws and expounding them to serve the prince's affections', Richard II for 'evil governance', and James I of Scotland for 'breaking his oaths'.[28]

Many of the lessons in *The Mirror for Magistrates* are expressed as moral epigrams. In the case of Richard II, rulers are instructed to 'beware good counsayle, lawe or vertue to despyse'. The moral comments also serve to present the stories as examples suitable for reuse. For this purpose the details of the narratives are as important as the morals, because they add plausibility to the historical event which endorses the authority of the maxim. As well as serving as a repertory of lessons and persuasive examples, cumulatively the stories provide a picture of late fourteenth- and fifteenth-century England dominated by warring nobles and insecure rulers. The nightmare memory of a powerful, unrestrained warlord class is the justification for the centralised Tudor monarchy, hence the reiteration of these stories in Polydore Vergil, Thomas More, Hall, the *Mirror for Magistrates* and Shakespeare's history plays.

Sir Thomas Elyot specifies educative stories and moral sentences as among the chief benefits to be derived from reading *The Governor*.

I desire only to employ that poor learning that I have gotten to the benefit [of my country] and to the recreation of all readers of any noble or gentle courage, giving them occasion to eschew idleness, being occupied in reading this book, enforced throughly with such histories and sentences whereby they shall take, themselves confessing, no little commodity.[29]

The Book Named the Governor is divided into three books. The first discusses the advantages of monarchy and proposes a scheme of education for noblemen responsible for local government, whom Elyot terms magistrates. The second and third books contain a number of essays (some of which stretch across several chapters) on the virtues required in a ruler. These essays usually consist of a definition, quotations from philosophers and stories from literature or history illustrating aspects of the virtue (including its contrary vice). Moral narrative takes its place within a structure like that of the grammar school theme. On the virtue of placability for example, Elyot first defines (where someone has occasion for

[28] Ibid., pp. 73, 111, 155.
[29] Sir Thomas Elyot, *The Book Named the Governor*, ed. S. E. Lehmberg (London, 1962), p. 14. The older edition by Henry Croft, 2 vols. (London, 1880) has useful notes to the source materials but is rare and unwieldy.

anger but prefers forgiveness) and praises, then quotes Cicero, amplifies
the contrary (anger), and quotes Ovid, before relating and commenting
on a number of historical examples of the evils of anger and the benefits
of clemency.[30] Among these examples is the earliest occurrence of the
now well-known story of the Lord Chief Justice imprisoning the future
Henry V, with these comments:

> Now here a man may behold three persons worthy excellent memory. First a
> judge, who being a subject, feared not to execute justice on the eldest son of his
> sovereign lord, and by the order of nature his successor. Also a prince and son
> and heir of the king, in the midst of his fury, more considered his evil example and
> the judge's constancy in justice, than his own estate or wilful appetite. Thirdly,
> a noble king and wise father, who contrary to the custom of parents, rejoiced
> to see his son and the heir of his crown to be for his disobedience by his subject
> corrected.
>
> Wherefore I conclude that nothing is more honourable, or to be desired in a
> prince or nobleman than placability.[31]

In *The English Secretary* Angel Day retells the story as an example of
courage on the one part and obedience on the other which might be amplified in an epistle laudatory.[32] Throughout his work Elyot uses historical
examples to derive lessons in a way that confirms his praise of history as
the most useful reading for noblemen.[33] In his later defence of history,[34]
Elyot finds that the educative function of history is equally well served
by fiction.

> But if by reading the sage counsel of Nestor, the subtle persuasions of Ulysses,
> the compendious gravity of Menelaus, the imperial majesty of Agamemnon, the
> prowess of Achilles, and valiant courage of Hector, we may apprehend anything
> whereby our wits may be amended and our personages be more apt to serve our
> public weal and our prince, what forceth it us though Homer write leasings?[35]

In his *Apology for Poetry* Sidney understands teaching as the purpose of
poetic narrative, but argues that the teaching is all the more effective
for being concealed within a story.[36] In *Euphues and his England*, Euphues
concludes the lengthy story of Callimachus and the hermit, which he
has told during the sea voyage, by stating the lessons of the story: only
travel in order to improve your mind morally.[37] The main narrative of

---

[30] Elyot, *Governor* (1962), pp. 111–15.   [31] Ibid., p. 115.   [32] Day, *English Secretary*, sig. F IV.
[33] Elyot, *Governor* (1962), p. 39.   [34] Ibid., pp. 228–31.   [35] Ibid., p. 231.
[36] 'With a tale forsooth he cometh unto you, with a tale which holdeth children from play, and old
men from the chimney corner. And, pretending no more, doth intend the winning of the mind
from wickedness to virtue.' Sidney, *Apology for Poetry*, p. 113.
[37] John Lyly, *Euphues and his England*, in *Works*, ed. R. W. Bond, 3 vols. (Oxford, 1902), II, p. 30.

Euphues is arranged so that at the end of the plot, when he is rejected by Lucilla, Euphues reproaches himself for neglecting the moral advice which he was given at the beginning of the book by Eubulus, the old Neapolitan gentleman. By this device Lyly is able to moralise the story both at the beginning, when Euphues rejects the advice, and at the end when he endorses it.[38]

The overall narrative of Sidney's *Old Arcadia* is less obviously didactic, because the worthy princes are eventually pardoned for several deceitful and immoral acts which love drives them to commit.[39] Sidney draws incidental morals, as when at the beginning of book four he notes that everlasting justice uses folly to overturn worldly wisdom.[40] Nor do the heroes avoid criticism, though such criticism is placed in the mouths of characters who are themselves criticised.[41] Sidney's letter of dedication claims that *The Old Arcadia* is not for severe eyes, 'being but a trifle and that triflingly handled'.[42] It appears also that some of the most immoral actions of the heroes are omitted in the more epic revision of *The New Arcadia*,[43] while other more heroic deeds are added. It is in *The New Arcadia*, too, that Palladius's understanding of military stratagems is attributed to his reading of histories.[44] While the teaching function of stories remains a fundamental expectation for Sidney, *The Old Arcadia* takes a sympathetic, comic view of the consequences of sexual attraction.

In all three genres we have seen a strong link between stories and their moral or practical teaching for the audience. In most cases the teaching is the justification for the story, though the truth or prestige of the story also helps validate the teaching. Where Sidney and Elyot argue

[38] Ibid., I, pp. 187–94, 241.

[39] 'So uncertain are mortal judgements, the same person most infamous and most famous, and neither justly.' Sir Philip Sidney, *The Countess of Pembroke's Arcadia (Old Arcadia)*, ed. J. M. Robertson (Oxford, 1973), p. 416, quoted in Blair Worden, *The Sound of Virtue: Philip Sidney's Arcadia and Elizabethan Politics* (New Haven, 1996), p. 17. Worden eventually identifies a quite definite Christian Stoic political and ethical teaching, pp. 319, 331–40, 351.

[40] Sidney, *Old Arcadia*, p. 265.

[41] Philanax's accusations are excessively vehement in themselves but also qualified by comments which suggest that he seeks revenge. Ibid., pp. 386, 391, 398.

[42] Ibid., p. 3.

[43] For example the treacherous devices by which Musidorus elopes with Pamela, Musidorus's decision to violate Pamela's virtue in spite of his oaths, Pyrocles's false promises to Basilius and Gynecia and his sexual encounter with Philoclea. Ibid., pp. 185–96, 201–5, 220–3, 235–43. Changes which improve the moral standing of the princes are listed in W. Ringler jr (ed.), *The Poems of Sir Philip Sidney* (Oxford, 1962), p. 375. For the view that the revisions are ambivalent in their effect, see Catherine Bates, *The Rhetoric of Courtship in Elizabethan Language and Literature* (Cambridge, 1992), pp. 122–33.

[44] Sir Philip Sidney, *The Countess of Pembroke's Arcadia (New Arcadia)*, ed. V. Skretkowicz (Oxford, 1987), p. 35.

that fiction is as effective as fact for the purpose of moral teaching, the historians generally argue that true examples give force to abstract precepts. Nevertheless the historians frequently use the resources of rhetoric to interpret actions and to amplify the significance of their stories.

The association between stories and moral teaching is established early and repeated frequently in the grammar school syllabus. Aesop's *Fables* are approved as early reading material because of the moral lessons they teach. The method of the fables is generalised to other forms of reading in Brinsley's *Ludus Literarius*, where it is said to be both an aim of education to acquire, and one of the procedures of teaching to note down, moral lessons which arise from narratives.[45] In composition, several of the early exercises in the *Progymnasmata* are concerned with the connection between a story and its significance. In the fable, the moral must be given after the fable and linked to the story.[46] In the narrative the reason for the action must be provided.[47] In the chreia examples must be found to illustrate the significance of a saying or an action.[48] Grammar school training encourages both a moral reading of narrative and the use of exemplary stories to back up arguments. The moral of the narrative is often articulated through proverbs and ethical axioms.

MORAL SENTENCES

William Baldwin's *A Treatise of Morall Philosophie*, which consists almost entirely of moral sentences attributed to philosophers and arranged according to topic,[49] finds that there are three principal ways to teach moral philosophy, by rules, by proverbs and by comparisons and examples.

The second kind of teaching is by proverbs and adages, which kind of philosophy most commonly is used, in which they show the contraries of things, preferring always the best: declaring thereby both the profits of virtue and the inconveniences of vices, that we, considering both, may imbrace the good and eschew the evil.[50]

William Cecil composed a sententious memorandum of advice to his son around 1567 which consists almost entirely of moral sentences. He presents it as a sort of ten commandments of practical life. Much of his advice appears to be derived from standard ethical sources such as Isocrates's *Ad Demonicum*.

---

[45] Brinsley, *Ludus*, pp. xvi–xvii, 145.   [46] Aphthonius, *Progymnasmata*, sig. A1v.
[47] Ibid., sig. B8v.   [48] Ibid., sigs. C8v, D1v.
[49] As does Sir Thomas Elyot's much briefer *The Bankette of Sapience* (London, 1534) STC 7630.
[50] Baldwin, *Treatise of Morall Philosophie*, sig. B3r. Compare Isocrates, *Ad Demonicum*, 12.

1. Use great providence and circumspection in the choice of thy wife, for from thence may spring all thy future good or ill . . . Beware that thou spend not above three of the four parts of thy revenue . . . For gentility is nothing but ancient riches. So that if the foundations sink, the Building must needs consequently fail.
2. Bring thy children up in learning and obedience yet without austerity; praise them openly; reprehend them secretly; give them good countenance and convenient maintenance, according to thy ability; for otherwise thy life will seem their bondage . . . Suffer not thy sons to pass the Alps, for they shall learn nothing but pride, blasphemy and atheism . . .
4. Let thy kindred and allies be welcome to thy table, grace them with thy countenance, and ever further them in all honest actions, for by that means thou shalt so double the bond of nature as thou shalt find them so many advocates to plead an apology for thee behind thy back . . .
8. Towards thy superiors be humble yet generous . . . towards inferiors show much humility and some familiarity, [which] gains a good report . . . for high humilities take such root in the minds of the multitude . . .
9. Trust not any man too far with thy credit or estate . . .
10. Be not scurrilous in conversation nor stoical in thy jests . . . [The latter] may pull on quarrels and yet the hatred of thy best friends. Jests when they savor too much of truth leave a bitterness in the mind of those that are touched.[51]

Edward Hall often uses proverbs and moral axioms to interpret the historical events described in his *Chronicle*. After describing an action in which the Duke of Clarence had been tricked into attacking a stronger French force, with the loss of many lives, including his own, Hall comments:

I lament the folly and foolishness of this duke and I marvel at his unwitty doing and rash enterprise that he would adventure his life and hazard his company leaving behind him the archers which should have been his shield and defence. What may be said, he desired honour and lost his life; he coveted victory and was overcome. Thus is the old proverb verified which sayeth, if sheep run wilfully among wolves they shall lose either life or fell.[52]

He explains the Duke's actions through character (folly and foolishness) and vice (ambition, desire of honour) and derives lessons about tactics (never leave the archers behind) and moral conduct (do not seek honour rashly). Hall uses isocolon (equal phrase length) and congeries (addition of words and phrases with the same meaning) to amplify his summary

---

[51] L. B. Wright (ed.), *Advice to a Son* (Ithaca, 1962), p. 9–13. Compare Isocrates, *Ad Demonicum*, 15, 20, 22, 30. There is a useful discussion of this document and of Cecil's approach to educating both his sons in Crane, *Framing Authority*, pp. 122–7.

[52] Hall, *Chronicle*, p. 106.

of Clarence's conduct.[53] The moral lesson is generalised and justified by reference to a proverb advising caution and restraint of the will. The capture and execution of the Duke of Exeter in one of the towns belonging to the Duke of Gloucester, whom he had betrayed, is moralised and generalised through a proverb.

So the common proverb was verified, as you have done, so shall you feel. Oh Lord I would wish that this example of many highly promoted to rule might be had in memory . . . to the entent that they by these examples should avert their minds from ill doings and such ungodly and execrable offences.[54]

By attaching the proverb to the event Hall both confirms the validity of the generalised observations about human conduct which are encapsulated in proverbs, and, imitating the pattern of the fable in the *Progymnasmata*, amplifies the event and makes it available for reuse as an example.

Many of the moralising passages in *The Mirror for Magistrates*, usually at the beginning and end of the individual poems, express the lessons of the tragedies as axioms. 'Thomas, Duke of Gloucester' concludes:

> For blood axeth blood as guerdon due,
> And vengeance for vengeance is just reward,
> O righteous God, thy judgements are true,
> For look what measure we other award,
> The same for us again is prepared:
> Take heed ye princes by examples past,
> Blood will have blood, either first or last.[55]

The *Mirror for Magistrates* also provides a platform for more general political and moral teaching.[56]

Sir Thomas Elyot regarded histories and sentences as the most useful teaching of *The Governor*.[57] In his discussion of the benefits of poetry, he collects examples of moral sentences from the Latin poets.[58] Elyot quotes three maxims to show that reason, society and knowledge demand the virtue of justice.

Reason bid[s thee] do the same thing to others that thou wouldest have done to thee. Society (without which man's life is unpleasant and full of anguish) saith, 'Love thou thy neighbour as thou dost thyself' . . . Knowledge also, as a perfect

---

[53] This is part of Erasmus's ninth method of achieving copia of things, which is taken up by the style manuals. *De copia* (1988), p. 220 (trans. *Collected Works*, XXIV, p. 594); Susenbrotus, *Epitome*, sig. E4r.

[54] Hall, *Chronicle*, p. 19.   [55] Baldwin, *Mirror for Magistrates*, p. 99, lines 197–203.

[56] For example the tragedy of Owen Glendower contains a lengthy aside on the nature of true nobility. Ibid., pp. 122–3, lines 43–56.

[57] Elyot, *Governor* (1962), p. 14.   [58] Ibid., pp. 47–9.

instructrice and mistress, in a more brief sentence than yet hath been spoken, declareth by what mean the said precepts of reason and society may be well understood and thereby justice finally executed. The words be these in Latin, *nosce teipsum*, which is in English know thyself.[59]

Festina lente plays a significant role in Elyot's account of prudence,[60] and quotations from the philosophers form an important part of all his essays on virtues. North's dedication of his 1557 translation of Guevara's *The Diall of Princes* to Queen Mary focuses on the moral teaching expressed in grave sentences.

There is no author (the sacred letters set apart) that more effectually setteth out the omnipotency of God, the frailty of men, the inconstancy of fortune, the vanity of this world, the misery of this life and finally that more plainly teacheth the good which mortal men ought to pursue and the evil that all men ought to fly than this present work doth. The which is so full of high doctrine, so adorned with ancient histories, so authorized with grave sentences and so beautified with apt similitudes.[61]

Both his work and Berners's *Golden Boke of Marcus Aurelius* largely consist of moral sentences amplified and explained.[62]

At the beginning of *Euphues*, Lyly summarises the main movement of the plot with a proverb:

It hath been an old said saw, and of not less truth than antiquity, that wit is better if it be the dearer bought, as in the sequel of this history shall most manifestly appear.[63]

Eubulus's speech, Euphues's reply and Lyly's moralisation of the dialogue consist largely of moral axioms, amplified with comparisons and examples.

Is it not far better to abhor sins by the remembrance of others faults than by repentance of thine own follies? ... The more I love the high climbing of thy capacity, by so much the more I fear thy fall ... Be merry but with modesty; be sober but not too solemn; be valiant, but not too venturous. Let thy attire be comely but not costly, thy diet wholesome but not excessive.[64]

---

[59] Ibid., p. 164.   [60] Ibid., pp. 80–1.

[61] A. de Guevara, *The Diall of Princes*, trans. Sir Thomas North, selections ed. K. N. Colvile (London, 1919), pp. 4–5.

[62] A. de Guevara, *The Golden Boke of Marcus Aurelius*, trans. Lord Berners (London, 1535) STC 12436, sigs. G3v–H1r. There is a reprint of this text in J. M. Gálvez, *Guevara in England* (Berlin, 1916).

[63] Lyly, *Works*, I, p. 185.

[64] Ibid., I, pp. 189–90; compare Shakespeare, *Hamlet*, I.iii.70–1. G. K. Hunter, 'Isocrates's Precepts and Polonius's Character', *Shakespeare Quarterly* 8 (1957), 501–6.

Lyly decorates his axioms with patterns of alliteration, isocolon and parallel structures.[65] Sidney uses moral axioms more sparingly than Lyly, but still the principal speeches of the *Old Arcadia* are founded on pithily expressed moral commonplaces. The following are all taken from the first page of Philanax's speech opposing Basilius's planned retirement.

> Wisdom and virtue be the only destinies appointed to follow.
> Either standing or falling with virtue a man is never in an evil case.
> It is weakness too much to remember what should have been done.
> No destiny nor influence whatsoever can bring man's wit to a higher point than wisdom and goodness.
> Who will stick to him that abandons himself?[66]

It is an important point of the *Old Arcadia* that however true they are, such axioms are not effective ways of persuading minds overwhelmed by passion. The importance of moral axioms in all three genres reflects their use at school as paradigms of syntax, which were learned by heart, as the quarry to be extracted from the reading of texts and collected in commonplace books and as a component of several school writing exercises (*progymnasmata*).

TECHNIQUES OF AMPLIFICATION

Writers of romances, histories and conduct manuals employ a more elaborate writing style at moments of emphasis or where an emotional response is sought from the audience. Amplification may involve: detailed description in order to bring a scene to life; comparisons, either providing further examples or building something up by showing that it is greater than parallel cases; or dense use of figures of speech, especially metaphors and figures involving repetition of words and patterning of phrases. As well as marking important passages, amplification was also a method of varying received source material and an opportunity to display skill.

---

[65] Hoskins, *Directions*, p. 16, comments on Lyly's use of alliteration (which he wrongly calls paronomasia) and the way he combines it with other patterns of repetition: 'In those days Lyly, the author of *Euphues*, seeing the dotage of the time upon this small ornament, invented varieties of it; for he disposed the agnominations in as many fashions as repetitions are distinguished. By the author's rhetoric, sometimes the first word and the middle harped one upon another, sometimes the first and the last, sometimes in several sentences, sometimes in one; and this with a measure of *compar*, a change of contention, or contraries and a device of similitude, in those days made a gallant show. But Lyly himself hath outlived this style and breaks well from it.'

[66] Sidney, *Old Arcadia*, p. 7. Compare John Webster, *The Duchess of Malfi*, ed. J. Russell Brown (Manchester, 1976), v.ii.287–8; Russell Brown provides a table of Webster's borrowings from *Arcadia* and other sources at pp. 214–16.

For Hall, as for other humanist historians, eloquent writing is an important attribute of history, because a well-written work will increase the fame and memory of the actions, and because appropriate style will increase the impact of the examples on the readers. Hall's most common stylistic resource is a fairly mindless doubling of epithets, but he also employs isocolon and repetition to drive home a point (as in the example quoted above in which he comments on the foolhardiness of the Duke of Clarence) and combines linked and varied examples with anaphora and colon in deliberately weighty passages (as in the discussion of the value of history quoted above). The opening of his 'Introduction to the History of Henry IV' is rich in patterning, elaboration and examples.

What mischief hath insurged in realms by intestine division, what depopulation hath ensued in countries by civil dissension, what detestable murder hath been committed in cities by separate factions, and what calamity hath ensued in famous regions by domestical discord and unnatural controversy, Rome hath felt, Italy can testify, France can bear witness, Beame can tell, Scotland may write, Denmark can show and especially this noble realme of England can apparently declare and make demonstration. For who abhorreth not to express the heinous facts committed in Rome, by the civil war between Julius Caesar and hardy Pompey by whose discord the bright glory of the triumphant Rome was eclipsed and shadowed? Who can reherce what mischiefs and what plagues the pleasant country of Italy hath tasted and suffered by the seditious factions of the Guelphs and Ghibellines? . . . But what misery, what murder, and what execrable plagues this famous region hath suffered by the division and dissension of the renowned houses of Lancaster and York, my wit cannot comprehend nor my tongue declare neither yet my pen fully set forth.[67]

The first sentence is organised around a series of patterned descriptions answered by isocola naming a range of countries. An example of discord in each of the named countries is then elaborated as a patterned question, leading up to a longer question appropriate to England, where division has been most notable. This paragraph amplifying the disastrous effects of discord leads on to an almost equally patterned paragraph on the benefits which follow from union.[68] Apart from illustrating Hall's skill and knowledge the section serves to announce the overarching structure of *The Union of the Two Noble and Illustre Families* and to validate this structure by showing that it is an instance of pattern which is found throughout history and as part of human nature. Hall's closing description of Henry V is another obvious high point of the *Chronicle*, marked with an elaborate gradatio with isocolon.

---

[67] Hall, *Chronicle*, p. 1.   [68] Ibid., p. 2.

This Henry was a king whose life was immaculate and his living without spot. This king was a prince whom all men loved and none disdained. This prince was a captain against whom fortune never frowned nor mischance once spurned. This captain was a shepherd whom his flock loved and lovingly obeyed. This shepherd was such a justiciary that no offence was unpunished nor friendship unrewarded.[69]

Hall provides what the situation demands, an amplified encomium of the ideal prince, but the praise is so generalised and so all-embracing that it seems more like a rhetorical commonplace written as an exercise than a tribute to, or a conclusion about, Henry. On other occasions amplification takes the form of detailed description, even where parts of that description have to be constructed by the historian, as in the example of Queen Margaret's reaction to defeat at Barnet, referred to above.[70] Sometimes Hall has to balance the need to amplify a particular scene against his critical approach to his sources. He reports several accounts of the death of Richard II, differing on the form of death and the degree of Henry IV's responsibility, including one which prompts him to provide a detailed description (including dialogue) of the fight leading up to Exton's killing of Richard and Exton's words of remorse. He invites the reader to judge between the competing versions.

Thus have I declared to you the diversities of opinions concerning the death of this unfortunate prince, remitting to your judgement which you think most true, but the very truth is that he died of a violent death and not by the dart of natural infirmity.[71]

Hall reinforces the credibility of his account by appealing to his readers to make their own judgment of plausibilities. They must draw their own conclusions from the competing accounts. But he also sets a firm limit to conjecture, perhaps trusting that the readers will accept the limit in return for the freedom he allows within it. Whether Richard starved, was poisoned or died by the sword, it was an unnatural death for which Henry has to take responsibility. Therefore his death requires the emotional intensification created by the vividly described scene, even if some aspects of that scene are conjectural.[72] Just as a lawyer might construct a detailed depiction of a murder to persuade a jury, Hall elaborates the circumstances of the death which dominates the course of his history, in order to intensify its emotional impact.

In the earlier tragedies of *The Mirror for Magistrates* amplification is mainly achieved through patterned language. Sackville's 'Induction',

[69] Ibid., p. 112. [70] Ibid., p. 297. [71] Ibid., p. 20. [72] Ibid., pp. 19–20.

added in 1563, employs allegory, personification, enargeia and ecphrasis to create a suitably hellish atmosphere for Buckingham's speech.[73] The 'Complaint of Henry Duke of Buckingham' is amplified with comparisons, similes and several detailed descriptions of parallel stories.[74]

Sir Thomas Elyot amplifies his essays on particular virtues with exemplary stories and quotations from philosophers. Typically these stories are organised topically, exploring the parts of a virtue, its consequences or causes, and the opposed vice. Elyot uses a more elaborate style to drive home the conclusion to be drawn from an example. After translating at length a story of Augustus's mercy to Cinna, taken from Seneca's *De clementia*, he adds an apostrophe which amplifies the action by enumerating the difficulties Augustus faced.

> O what sufficient praise may be given to this noble and prudent Emperor, that in a chamber alone, without men, ordnance, or weapon, and perchance without harness, within the space of two hours, with words well couched, tempered with majesty, not only vanquished and subdued one mortal enemy, which by a malignity, engendered of a domestic hatred, had determined to slay him, but by the same feat excluded out of the whole city of Rome all displeasure and rancour toward him, so that there was not left any occasion whereof might proceed any little suspicion of treason, which otherwise could not have happened without slaughter of people innumerable.[75]

Each detail which Elyot provides has the effect of increasing first the difficulty and then the success of what Augustus achieved. At each point an implicit comparison magnifies the action, which is then crowned by the explicit contrast with other methods of achieving the effect. The passage could almost be a textbook example of amplifying by describing the way in which something was brought about and looking into the causes, Erasmus's second and third methods of producing copia of things.[76] *The Golden Boke of Marcus Aurelius* uses syntactical patterns, paradox and extreme comparisons to elaborate and draw attention to moral commonplaces.

> I swere by the goddis immortall that the day of my tryumph being in the chariot, I was as pensive as I might be. O Rome, cursed be thy folly and wo be to hym that hathe brought up in the so moche pryde. And coursed be he that hath invented so greatte pompe in the. What greatter or more unegall lyghtnes can be, than that a Romayne capitayne, bicause he hath conquered realmes, altered peasibles, distroyed cities, caste downe fortresses, robbed the poore, enryched tirantes,

---

[73] Baldwin, *Mirror for Magistrates*, pp. 298–317.   [74] Ibid., e.g. pp. 321, 326, 333, 335.

[75] Elyot, *Governor* (1962), p. 118; Seneca, *De clementia*, 1.9.1–12.

[76] Erasmus, *De copia* (1988), pp. 200–1 (trans. *Collected Works*, XXIV, pp. 575–6).

shedde moche bloode and made infinite wydowes, shulde for recompence of
all these domages be receyved with great triumph? . . . remembringe the infinite
treasures yl gotten, and heryng lamentations of the wydowes sorowfully wepinge
for the deathe of their husbandes, and callynge to mynde our manyfolde frendes
deed, though I reioyced me openly, I wepte droppes of blooud secretely.[77]

The combination of the imagined scene of triumph and the recollected
details of the actions that earned the triumph make this an unusually
effective elaboration of the theme of the vanity of worldly glory. Guevara
and Berners use apostrophe, rhetorical question, enumeration of details,
antithesis and parison to elevate the style of this passage.

  Where other writers reserve the elaborate style to mark passages of
particular resonance, for Lyly comparison, example and balanced constructions are the ordinary currency of his expression. His style is particularly rich in comparisons from natural history. While this invites the
reader to attend to the crafting of almost every sentence, it also encourages a detached view of supposedly emotional outpourings.

Ah Euphues into what a quandry art thou brought? In what sudden misfortune
art thou wrapped? It is like to fare with thee as with the Eagle, which dieth
neither for age, nor with sickness, but with famine, for although thy stomach
hunger yet thy heart will not suffer thee to eat. And why shouldest thou torment
thyself for one in whom is neither faith nor fervency? O the counterfeit love of
women.[78]

Lyly here employs rhetorical question, simile, antithesis, alliteration and
apostrophe, but among so many figures, the reader responds to the final
exclamatio with detached questioning rather than emotional sympathy.
Most of Sidney's intensely figured passages are in his characters' set
speeches, which will be considered in the next section, but he can use
balanced phrases to mark the onset of a set piece, as in the description
of the peasants' rebellion from the *Old Arcadia*:

These words being spoken, like a furious storm, presently took hold of their well
inclined brains. There needed no drum where each man cried; each spake to
other, that spake as fast to him; and the disagreeing sound of so many voices
was the only token of their unmeet agreement. Thus was their banquet turned
to battle, their winy mirths to bloody rages, and the happy prayers for the duke
to monstrous threatening his estate; the solemnizing his birthday tended to the
cause of his funerals.[79]

Sidney employs similitude, climax, parison, synoeciosis, zeugma and
contentio to elevate the style of this passage. The skilfulness of the

[77] Guevara, *Golden Boke*, sig. Cc3r–v.   [78] Lyly, *Works*, I, p. 240.   [79] Sidney, *Old Arcadia*, p. 128.

harmonious balancing of phrases is as striking as its inappropriateness to the chaotic scene. The aristocratic prose looks down at the peasants' actions, preventing their rebellion from being seen as either serious or threatening. In a slightly earlier description of Philoclea's reaction to discovering that the Amazon Cleophila is in fact a man, the amplification is achieved through comparison with amplification of circumstances, contentio and isocolon. Sidney's slight unbalancing of the parallels results in prose which is critically alert as well as witty.

The joy which wrought into Pygmalion's mind while he found his beloved image wax little and little both softer and warmer in his folded arms, till at length it accomplished his gladness with a perfect woman's shape, still beautified with the former perfections, was even such as, by each degree of Cleophila's words, stealingly entered into Philoclea's soul, till her pleasure was fully made up with the manifesting of his being, which was such as in hope did overcome hope. Yet did a certain spark of honour arise in her well disposed mind, which bred a starting fear to be now in secret with him in whose presence, notwithstanding, consisted her comfort – such contradictions there must needs grow in those minds which neither absolutely embrace goodness nor freely yield to evil. But that spark soon gave place, or at least gave no more light in her mind than a candle doth in the sun's presence.[80]

Sidney brings out both the joy and the danger of the moment. The balances and contrasts are as strongly present in the ideas as in the phrasing of the paragraph: the transformation from stone to woman compared with the revelation that a woman is a man; hope that is more than hope; fear that is comfort; a candle against the sun. He nails the moral confusion of the situation with a precision combined with lightness which anticipates Jane Austen.

While it would be foolish to maintain that each of these writers used the same techniques of amplification for identical purposes, apart from Lyly, who does so continually, all from time to time deliberately elevate the level of their prose, with, for example, apostrophes, comparisons, figures of repetition or detailed and vivid descriptions. Using Erasmus's *De copia* and *De conscribendis epistolis*, amplification was one of the major topics of grammar school teaching. Pupils were taught to amplify by using additional ornaments or tropes and by going into detail, adding examples and making comparisons. Writers could expect their readers to notice and evaluate their use of such techniques. Equally writers could use them in ways which went beyond the normal expectations of emphasis and emotional effect.

[80] Ibid., pp. 120–1.

SPEECHES AND LETTERS

Tudor histories and romances frequently contain formal speeches to explain the reasons for actions and to show the author's skill in finding expressions and arguments to suit the situation. Among conduct manuals, some, like Elyot's *Governor*, express their ideas mainly through brief essays, while in others, such as Castiglione's *Courtier* and *The Golden Boke of Marcus Aurelius*, most of the teaching comes in the form of speeches and letters. The speeches in Guevara's *Golden Boke of Marcus Aurelius* are concentrated around Marcus Aurelius's deathbed.

O what lyttel thoughte we take in this lyfe untylle we falle grovelynge with our eyes uppon dethe ... The vanities of us that are vayne is so agreable to us that whanne we begynne to lyve we ymagyne that our lyfe wylle endure a holle worlde, and whanne it is ended hit semeth us to be but a puffe or a blaste of wynde. And bycause than sensualitie peyneth for sensibylitie, and the fleshe for the flesshe, reason guyded with them that be mortall tellethe me that it peyneth not with the departynge. If I have lyved as a brute beaste, hit is reason that I dye as a discrete manne ought to do. I dyenge, this day shall dye all my sycknes, hungre shall dye, colde shall dye, all my peines shall dye, my thought shall dye, my displeasure shall dye, and every thinge that gyveth peyne and sorowe. This daye the night shall be taken away and the sonne shyne brighte in the skie. This daye the ruste shall be taken fro myn eies and I shall see the sonne clerely.[81]

Guevara takes the occasion of the death speech to deliver warnings to the living about their thoughtlessness and about the vanity of life. In the fifth sentence of the extract an almost liturgical use of antistrophe reassures the reader about the intended meaning, but earlier repetition and apparent parallelism leads to a development of the argument. Although, with epanados (repetition of a word), sense pines for sense and flesh for the flesh, yet reason, reversing their proposition while repeating the verb, can tell us not to fear death. Living like an animal can be a prelude to a fuller understanding of death. The apparent resolution of the early part of the extract is transformed by metaphor and contentio into the full resolution of the end.

The Mirror for Magistrates consists entirely of speeches of confession. Classical historians such as Thucydides, Livy and Sallust, as well as school exercises provide a precedent for the composition of speeches for particular historical personages and situations. The speeches which Hall composes, and which are the rhetorical high points of his *Chronicle*, are often detached from the speaker, as though he is composing an oration for

---

[81] Guevara, *Golden Boke*, sigs. Yiv–2r.

the situation rather than for the person. Hall's general view of Edward IV is largely positive, after making allowance for the necessity of war, and his inclination to lust and avarice.[82] Even so, the elaborate writing and the moral content of his death speech come as something of a surprise.

My welbeloved, and no less betrusted friends, councillors and allies, if we mortal men would daily and hourly with ourself revolve and intentively in our hearts engrave, or in our minds gravously ponder, the frail and fading imbecillity of our human nature and the caduke fragility of the same, we should apparently perceive that we being called reasonable creatures, and in that predicament compared and joined with angels, be more worthy to be nuncupate and deemed persons unreasonable, and rather to be associated in that name with brute beasts . . . For while health in us flourisheth or prosperity aboundeth, or the glosing world laugheth, which is he so reasonable of us all that can say (if he will not err from the truth) that he once in a week remembered his fatal end . . . Such is the blindness of our frail and fragile nature, ever given to carnal concupiscence and mundane delectation, daily obfuscate and seduced with that lothargious and deceivable serpent called hope of long life that all we put in oblivion our duty present and less remember the politic purveiance for things to come. For blindly we walk in this frail life till we fall groveling with our eyes suddenly upon death. The vanities of this world be to us so agreeable that when we begin to live we esteem our life a whole world, which once overpassed it showeth no better but dust, driven away with a puff of wind.[83]

In this speech Hall appears to be reworking the classical commonplaces. The dying man understands the nature of the world and warns his friends to take more account of last things and to order their affairs better for their death. He raises the level of diction and adds parallel words and phrases (congeries) wherever possible. It reads like a self-conscious exercise in copia, loading a commonplace outline with a heavy freight of instances and epithets. The absence of Christian consolation suggests that Hall may be consciously varying and elaborating the last words of eminent pagan philosophers, such as Socrates or Marcus Aurelius. He may even have in mind the speech from *The Golden Boke of Marcus Aurelius* quoted above. In the context of the primarily political preoccupations of the *Chronicle*, it reminds the reader of a different scale of concerns, to which princes and ordinary citizens are equally subject. Angel Day includes a death speech in one of the examples of letters descriptory in *The English Secretary*:

And for my selfe, stand ye all assertained that having long since poyzed in equall ballance the long continuance of a fraile, wretched and travelled life, the most part wherof is caryed away in sleepe, sorrowe, griefe, sickenesse, daunger, and

---

[82] Hall, *Chronicle*, p. 341.   [83] Ibid., p. 339.

the residue also never freed of care and all maner of disquiet, with the hope of an everlasting joy, happines, rest, peace and immortall residence, I finde no reason whie I should at all affect the toyle of such earthlie tediousnesse.[84]

The second half of *The Golden Boke of Marcus Aurelius* is devoted to a collection of letters on such subjects as friendship, the vanity of honours, and consolations for exile and for the death of husband and child. Letters, some of them based on Guevara, also bulk large in the post-narrative sections of Lyly's *Euphues*.[85] Lyly provides models of many of the textbook forms of letter: moral advice, consolation, congratulation, advice to a son and enticement of a lover. Euphues addresses Philautus on the vanity of court life and the need to prepare for death by renouncing sin. To Eubulus he offers rather harsh consolation on the death of his daughter; to Botonio congratulations on his good fortune in being banished from the court.[86] Euphues's letter to Alcius criticising him for wasting his time at university and advising him about how to do better recalls two of the model letters in Fulwood's *Enemie of Idleness*.[87] *Euphues and his England* contains exchanges of letters between Philautus and Euphues, and between Philautus and Camilla, which resemble letters from the manuals on love and friendship.[88]

Philanax's speech to Basilius on the folly of his planned retirement becomes in *The New Arcadia* (with only minimal alteration) a letter which Kalander shows Musidorus.[89] Sidney provides Pyrocles (dressed as the Amazon Cleophila) with a virtuoso speech to end the peasants' rebellion. At first Cleophila seizes the attention of the mob with her striking and unusual action.

An unused thing it is, and I think heretofore not seen, O Arcadians, that a woman should give public counsel to men; a stranger to the country people; and that lastly in such presence a private person, as I am, should possess the regal throne. But the strangeness of your action makes that used for virtue which your violent necessity imposeth. For certainly a woman may well speak to men who have forgotten all manly government; a stranger may with reason instruct such subjects that neglect due points of subjection.[90]

Having taken command by emphasising the strangeness of the situation, she asks them whom they are rebelling against. Since of all the people in the lodges it can only be her, she offers them her life rather than that

[84] Day, *English Secretary*, sigs. E2v–3r (E3r: 1599 gives F3r).
[85] Bond, 'Introductory Essay' in Lyly, *Works*, I, pp. 154–6.   [86] Lyly, *Works*, I, pp. 306–16.
[87] Ibid., I, pp. 316–19; Fulwood, *Enemie*, pp. 101–3, 209–15.
[88] Lyly, *Works*, II, pp. 123–41, 143–54; Fulwood, *Enemie*, pp. 244–8, 274–81; Day, *English Secretary*, sigs. M4v, U1r–2v, Bb4r–Cc3r.
[89] Sidney, *Old Arcadia*, pp. 6–8; *New Arcadia*, pp. 20–2.   [90] Sidney, *Old Arcadia*, p. 129.

they should attempt anything against their Duke. The surprise which this interpretation of events produces enables her to amplify the wickedness and folly of any attack on their Duke.

> No, no your honest hearts will neither so gratify your hateful neighbours, nor so degenerate from your famous ancestors. I see in your countenances, now virtuously settled, nothing but love and duty to him who for your only sakes doth embrace the government. The uncertainty of his estate made you take arms; now you see him well, with the same love lay them down. If now you end, as I know you will, he will take no other account of you but as of a vehement, I must confess over vehement, affection.[91]

Once she has calmed the people she provides a flattering interpretation of their action which they are only too pleased to live up to, and to get away with. Cleophila succeeds because she understands the necessity of taking the initiative and the order in which the commonplaces should be applied. Her success prompts Sidney to some fairly contemptuous remarks about the reliability of the masses and some lessons about handling rebellion.

> And, indeed, no ill way it is in such mutinies to give them some occasion of such service as they may think in their own judgements may countervail their tresspass . . . But [the subordinates] that were most glad to have such a mean to show their loyalty, dispatched most of [the leaders] with a good rule: that to be leaders in disobedience teacheth ever disobedience to the same leaders.[92]

In a self-consciously teacherly mode, Sidney provides a general rule for the contents of the speech to pacify a crowd and a maxim to explain the actions of the peasants. In all three genres letters and speeches provide opportunities to display skill in all aspects of rhetoric as well as a chance to explore motivation. Several of the letters found in conduct manuals and romances related directly to the model letters provided in letter-writing manuals and collections of letters. Schoolboys were directed to write letters or compose speeches appropriate to particular historical circumstances.

DEBATES

Where unopposed speeches explain someone's thoughts and demonstrate the author's rhetorical skill, debates explore conflicts of ideas and

---

[91] Ibid., pp. 130–1. Important as the speeches are in *Arcadia*, *pace* Hutson (*Usurer's Daughter*, pp. 88, 97) the princes' skill with language does not replace their valour; like many medieval romance heroes they are skilful with words as well as strong.

[92] Sidney, *Old Arcadia*, pp. 131–2.

illustrate the practice of dialectic. Hall uses debate to dramatise character and to order opposed principles. At the siege of Rouen, Henry V received twelve ambassadors from the city.

Amongest whom one learned in the civil law, more arrogant than learned and yet not so arrogant as indiscreet, said these words. 'Right high and mighty Prince, right noble and puissant King, if you will with yourself diligently consider wherein consisteth the glory of victory and the triumph of a conqueror, you shall plainly perceive that the type of honour is in the taming of proud men, overcoming of valiant soldiers, and subduing of strong cities and populous regions, and not in slaying Christian people by hunger, thirst and famine, in which consisteth neither manhood, wit, nor policy. Alas regard you your honour and see yonder great multitude of miserable people crying for meat and weeping for drink and dying for lack of succour and relief.'[93]

These considerations lead the ambassador to suggest that the King should allow the poor to leave the city in order to obtain mercy from God, and should then assault the city, which will bring him glory if he succeeds. Hall's evident disapproval of the orator does not prevent him from devising a competently patterned and emotional speech. When Henry has thoroughly pondered the tone and implications of the speech, he replies.

Think you, O Fantastical Frenchmen, that I am so ignorant and so brutal that I cannot perceive your double dealing and crafty conveyance. Judge you me so simple that I know not wherin the glory of a conqueror consisteth. Esteem you me so ignorant that I perceive not by what crafts and warlike policies strong enemies are to be subdued and brought to subjection ... The Goddess of war called Bellona (which is the correctrice of princes for right witholding or injury doing, and the plague of God for evil living and untrue demeanour amongst subjects) hath these three handmaids ever of necessity attending on her, blood, fire and famine, which three damsels be of that force and strength that every one of them alone is able and sufficient to torment and afflict a proud prince ... To save mine own people (which is one point of glory in a captain) and to preserve the town which is my lawful and just inheritance, and to save as many of you as will not willingly be destroyed, I have appointed the meekest maid of the three damsels to afflict and plague you until you be bridled and brought to reason, which shall be when it shall please me and not at your appointment.[94]

He goes on to explain that his treatment of the inhabitants ejected from the city into no-man's-land has been far more humane than that of their fellow citizens. Henry's speech here is eloquent and inventive. The introduction uses disjunctio to reject the deceitfulness and the pretension to teaching in the Frenchman's approach. Then he employs the allegory

---

[93] Hall, *Chronicle*, p. 84.   [94] Ibid., p. 85.

of Bellona and her handmaids to insist that starvation is one of the ter-
rors of war, again using parallel constructions to emphasise the strategic
choices available to him. The brilliance of Henry's rhetorical solution
also highlights the importance of the military lesson. Unlike the Duke
of Clarence who was seduced into a foolhardy attack by the promise of
glory, Henry weighs the alternatives, preferring a victory which does not
put his own people at risk. Where the inexperienced and treacherous
ambassador makes a superficial appeal to glory and pity to seek an advantage, Henry understands, and knows how to use, the violence and
suffering involved in war.

The longer debate between Henry Chichele, who was Archbishop
of Canterbury, the Earl of Westmoreland and the Duke of Exeter on
whether to undertake a war against France exhibits a clash of different
kinds of argument. For the Archbishop both glory and legal right (as
well as the hidden motive of distracting the King from religious reform)
demand a war with France. Westmoreland argues that geographical
contiguity and the history of Scottish submission and rebellion make it
more prudent to conquer Scotland first. Exeter replies that one should
deal with the cause rather than the symptom; if French support were
removed, there would be no trouble from Scotland. He confirms this
argument from the chronicles, before using the example of Cato's words
to the Roman senate to argue that the fertility and wealth of France make
it a prize worth obtaining.[95]

Lyly's *Euphues* opens with a pair of opposed speeches: Eubulus's advice to Euphues, and Euphues's rejection of that advice. Eubulus ad-
mires Euphues's promise and is appalled by his upbringing. He warns
him against the temptations of Naples and urges him to restrain his
impulses.[96] To ground his reply Euphues argues that there can be many
different opinions on moral issues and matters of taste. Then he responds to Eubulus's arguments in turn, starting with an attack on his
assumptions about Euphues's situation.

Now whereas you seem to love my nature and loath my nurture, you bewray your
own weakness in thinking that nature may any ways be altered by education,
and as you have examples to confirm your pretence, so I have most evident and
infallible arguments to serve for my purpose. It is natural for the vine to spread;
the more you seek by art to alter it, the more in the end you shall augment
it . . . Though iron be made soft with fire, it returneth to his hardness; though
the falcon be reclaimed to the fist, she retireth to her haggardness; the whelp of

---

[95] Ibid., pp. 50–6.   [96] Lyly, *Works*, I, pp. 187–90.

a mastiff will never be taught to retrieve the partridge, education can have no show where the excellence of nature doth bear sway.[97]

Euphues refers Eubulus's approach to his individual case back to the underlying issue of nature versus education, allowing him to employ a series of comparisons from natural history. By induction these lead back to a general statement ('education can have no show where the excellence of nature doth bear sway') which can form the basis of a rebuttal of Eubulus. Next Euphues attacks Eubulus's comparison with wax, by substituting other comparisons ('Can the Aethiope change or alter his skin? or the Leopard his hue?').[98] Once he has established the primacy of nature, Euphues contests Eubulus's view of Naples, relying on the argument from relativity, which he deployed at the outset, to insist that he and other young men like the entertainments on offer in Naples. Even were Naples corrupt, a rare nature would be able to survive it, just as many plants prosper in a hostile environment. He concludes with the distinction of persons. Since old men always reject the enjoyments of youth, it is pointless for either of them to attempt to persuade the other.[99] Euphues's ready wit enables him to find arguments to support his rejection of unwelcome advice. Lyly comments that fertile wits are always satisfied with their own opinions and unwilling to listen to different views.[100] The debate provides a moral warning which the reader can attend to, as well as demonstrating that, since skilful arguers can find reasons to support vice, virtue is more important than intelligence and education.

At the end of the book, when Euphues has understood his folly and adopted a Christian viewpoint, he features in a debate with Atheos, in which he succeeds in converting his opponent to Christianity.[101] In *Euphues and his England* a dinner-party concludes with a triple disputation, in which Surius and Camilla debate the cause of love, while Martius and Flavia discuss whether it is wise to allow young men and women to mingle and Philautus and Frances consider which of secrecy or constancy is the more important quality in a lover.[102] Euphues as moderator resolves the arguments. Since virtuous love is founded on 'Time, Reason, Favour and Virtue', men must show their good faith through constancy, secrecy, confidence and trust, while women must demonstrate patience, jealousy, liberality, fervency and faithfulness. Having

---

[97] Ibid., I, p. 191.   [98] Ibid., I, p. 191.   [99] Ibid., I, pp. 191–4.
[100] Ibid., I, pp. 195–6. Bates emphasises the open-endedness of debate in *Euphues* and draws attention to unresolved debates in the entertainments for Elizabeth (*Rhetoric of Courtship*, pp. 61–83, 97–109).
[101] Lyly, *Works*, I, pp. 291–305.   [102] Ibid., II, pp. 163–80.

established these general principles, Euphues then adjudicates each of the particular disputations.[103] By adapting the form of the university disputation, in which the presiding master would resolve several different questions, Lyly's debate combines elegant conversation, modelled on *The Courtier*, with overt instruction about conduct. Lyly feeds his audience's taste for argument and controversy, but maintains a firm moral control on the conclusions to be promulgated. Although argument can make a case for the worse action, it can also clarify an issue and persuade of a truth.

Near the beginning of both versions of *Arcadia*, Sidney presents a debate between Musidorus and Pyrocles. Musidorus reproaches his cousin for wishing to remain in Arcadia instead of continuing with their heroic grand tour. Since only a great cause can change the behaviour of a virtuous mind, and since Pyrocles has recently abandoned his quest for knowledge, appeared troubled and sought solitude, the implication (which Musidorus leaves unstated) is that something must be wrong.[104] With detailed and carefully organised logical arguments he elaborates a simple question: what is the matter?

Pyrocles attempts several replies: at first he responds to Musidorus's compliments with an even more elaborate one of his own which is intended to interrupt the logic of the latter's case; then he suggests that it might be advantageous to leave off acquiring knowledge ('which you call the bettering of my minde') to prevent straining the mind, and in order to contemplate ('who knows whether I feed not my mind with higher thoughts?'); next he praises solitariness; and after a pause in which he sighs, he praises Arcadia in ludicrous terms:

Do you not see the grass how in colour they excel the emeralds, everyone striving to pass his fellow – and yet they are all kept in equal height?[105]

The point of the speech is the confusion of its organisation and its content. Pyrocles was unable to select and order the arguments with which he might have defended himself because of his state of tension, and because he was unwilling to own up to his real motivation. As Pyrocles spoke, Musidorus planned a logical response, the main points of which Sidney sketches for us:

For having in the beginning of Pyrocles's speech which defended his solitariness framed in his mind a reply against it in the praise of honourable action (in showing that such a kind of contemplation is but a glorious title to idleness; that in action a man did not only better himself but benefit others; that the

[103] Ibid., II, p. 182.   [104] Sidney, *Old Arcadia*, pp. 13–14.
[105] Ibid., p. 15; Sidney, *New Arcadia*, p. 51.

gods would not have delivered a soul into the body, which hath arms and legs (only instruments of doing) but that it were intended the mind should employ them; and that the mind should best know his own good or evil by practice; which knowledge was the only way to increase the one and correct the other; besides many other arguments which the plentifulness of the matter yielded to the sharpness of his wit), when he found Pyrocles leave that, and fall to such an affected praising of the place, he left it likewise, . . . [106]

and replied instead with an *ad hominem* response in which he trailed the word 'lover' to see how Pyrocles would react.

This scene shows us logic in action, as compliment, as evasion but also as something which may be discarded in favour of an approach which is directed more to the emotions. Musidorus's expression is shaped by his logical and rhetorical education, but that education also offers him a set of masks, from which he can choose according to how he perceives his respondent or his audience. In this dialogue Musidorus represents humanist educational orthodoxy.

The *tour-de-force* of debate in Sidney is the trial scene in the *Old Arcadia*, in which Philanax accuses each of the princes, each in turn replies, and Euarchus presents his judgment.[107] Philanax's accusation against Pyrocles is organised as a full four-part oration, making skilful use of logic and figures to present Pyrocles's actions in the most unfavourable light. Against this Pyrocles presents a plain but incomplete account of his relations with Basilius and Gynecia, while confessing to the rape of Philoclea in order to absolve her of responsibility. The successive reconstructions of events and motivations by accuser, accused and judge offer the readers a sequence of reversals each of which throws new light on the events they have watched unfold. Euarchus sifts the arguments of fact and interpretation on both sides before condemning the princes. This condemnation is itself reversed when Basilius recovers from the sleeping draught. The narrative of the scene is exciting and full of reversals, but much of the pleasure for the audience arises from watching each participant's exploitation of the resources of argument and expression.[108]

Debates offer a contrast of viewpoints, a portrayal of argumentative and rhetorical strategies and a comparison of rival principles. Their

---

[106] Sidney, *Old Arcadia*, p. 16, *New Arcadia*, p. 52.

[107] Sidney, *Old Arcadia*, pp. 386–415, analysed from the point of view of dispositio in Kinney, *Humanist Poetics*, pp. 284–5.

[108] W. Ringler points out that the dénouement contains a major flaw. The princes were condemned for the rape of Philoclea and the abduction of Pamela, but they are absolved when it turns out that Basilius is alive. Ringler argues that Sidney had begun the process of removing this difficulty when he altered the oracle at the beginning of the *New Arcadia*. Sidney, *Poems*, pp. 378–9.

inclusion in histories and romances indicates a taste for competitive argument, to which writers wished to respond. Disputation was the main form of intellectual exercise practised at Tudor universities. Show debates were often staged as entertainments for visiting dignitaries. Legal disputations and mock trials were important forms of teaching in the Inns of Court. Hall and Sidney both incorporate the point by point refutation of an opponent's position, as well as allowing for extra-logical forms of persuasion. Lyly follows the model of university disputation more closely.

SHARED THEMES

Texts from all three genres discuss the same themes. Programmes of education and discussions of the method of choosing teachers feature in *The Governor*, *Euphues* and *The Golden Boke of Marcus Aurelius*.[109] *Euphues* includes an adapted translation of Plutarch's treatise on education, which Elyot also translated separately, and which is absorbed into Kempe's *The Education of Children in Learning*.[110] The topic of education leads on to the controversy over the impact of nature and nurture.[111] Death and consolation bulk large in all the texts. All present death as a moment of moral insight, when the vanities of the world are stripped away and when warnings can be delivered about the true nature of life and the importance of virtue. Among political themes, Guevara and Elyot agree on the primacy of justice,[112] and Hall and *The Mirror for Magistrates* warn of the dangers to the state in corrupt administration of justice.[113] In *Old Arcadia* the princes find justice hard to uphold as a virtue and difficult to attain through legal processes. Pyrocles in particular, who finds diplomatic lying very easy, is outraged by the lies of judicial oratory.[114] Lyly, Elyot and Guevara are hostile to the vanity of court life and to flatterers,[115] but Elyot attributes some importance to the appearance of majesty and Hall insists on the need to take notice of noble counsellors.[116]

---

[109] Elyot, *Governor* (1962), pp. 15–40; Lyly, *Works*, I, pp. 260–83; Guevara, *Golden Boke*, sigs. D1v–F1v.
[110] Sir Thomas Elyot, *The Education or Bringing Up of Children* (London, 1533); Kempe, *Education* both repr. in R. D. Pepper (ed.), *Four Tudor Books on Education* (Gainesville, 1966), pp. 1–48, 181–240.
[111] Lyly, *Works*, I, pp. 187–96; Sidney, *Old Arcadia*, pp. 13–16; *New Arcadia*, pp. 49–52; Guevara, *Golden Boke*, sigs. D1v, X1r–v.
[112] Guevara, *Golden Boke*, sig. Z1r, Elyot, *Governor* (1962), p. 159.
[113] Hall, *Chronicle*, pp. 9, 298; Baldwin, *Mirror for Magistrates*, pp. 73, 77, 111, 268.
[114] Sidney, *Old Arcadia*, pp. 202–3, 228–9, 391–4.
[115] Lyly, *Works*, I, pp. 282, 321; Elyot, *Governor* (1962), pp. 154–8; Guevara, *Golden Boke*, sigs. Z3v–4r.
[116] Elyot, *Governor* (1962), pp. 99–103; Hall, *Chronicle*, pp. 3, 46–7.

The way in which the three genres re-articulate shared stories and sentences can be illustrated by considering the themes of friendship and counsel. Sir Thomas Elyot devotes four chapters of *The Book Named the Governor* to the subject of friendship. Citing Aristotle's *Ethics* and Cicero's *De amicitia*, he explains that friendship is a virtue which can only exist between good men of roughly equivalent social rank who share tastes and manners. The best friends are beneficent, liberal and constant.[117] Then Elyot illustrates friendship with three stories in which a friend is ready to die to save his friend, the last of which is the fifteen-page novella of Titus and Gisippus, adapted from Boccaccio's *Decameron*.[118] Gisippus puts male friendship before marriage, allowing his friend Titus to marry his betrothed Sophronia, because he recognises that Titus's passion for her is greater and because he realises that while other brides could be found he could never replace such a friend.[119] The interest of the narrative lies in the lengthy punishment of Gisippus's deceptive act of altruism. He is expelled from Athens. Reduced to penury in Rome he is not even recognised by the man for whom he sacrificed happiness. Only when he is on trial for his life does Titus acknowledge him and attempt to die in his place. Where Boccaccio was content to restore Gisippus to life and to Titus's affections, Elyot feels the need to add the worldly restoration of Gisippus's property and position in Athens, achieved through Titus's military valour.

Resuming his argument Elyot condemns ingratitude, which he treats as the contrary of friendship, with further definitions and exemplary stories. Finally, taking examples, quotations and stories from Plutarch's essay 'How to tell a friend from a flatterer', he describes the choice of friends and the dangers of flatterers.[120] In Elyot, as in Plutarch, the idealisation of the sharing and trust of friendship leads to anxiety about betrayal, false friendship and bad influence.

Guevara's comments on friendship are scattered more widely through the speeches and letters of *The Golden Boke*.[121] Phrases from Elyot and Guevara are collected among many others in the chapter 'Of Friends, Friendship and Amitie' (IV.3) in Baldwin's *Treatise of Morall Philosophie*:

---

[117] Elyot, *Governor* (1962), pp. 132–4; Cicero, *De amicitia*, v.17–vii.24. Classical ideas of friendship are usefully surveyed in H. Hutter, *Politics as Friendship* (Waterloo, 1978).

[118] Elyot, *Governor* (1962), pp. 136–51; Boccaccio, *Decameron*, ed. V. Branca, *Opere*, IV (Milan, 1976), x.8, pp. 900–20. Hutson, *Usurer's Daughter*, discusses Elyot's use of the story, pp. 57–64, 84–5.

[119] Elyot, *Governor* (1962), pp. 136–49, esp. pp. 139–41, 144–5.

[120] Ibid., pp. 154–8; Plutarch, 'How to tell a friend from a flatterer', *Moralia*, IV, 48–74 (48–50, 52–3, 59–60). Compare Isocrates, *Ad Demonicum*, 1.24.

[121] E.g. Guevara, *Golden Boke*, sigs. D4v–E1v, Bb2v–Cc2v.

Where any repugnancy is, there can be no amity, since friendship is an entire consent of wills and desires.

Therefore it is seldom seen that friendship is between these persons: namely a man sturdy of opinion inflexible and of sour countenance and between him that is tractable, with reason persuadable and of kind countenance and entertainment.[122]

The friend in all things trusteth to his friend, first regarding who is his friend.[123]

He that promiseth and is long in fulfilling is but a slack friend.[124]

In *The Mirror for Magistrates*, Hastings laments the trust he placed in Catesby, using sententiae to analyse history, moralising his experience of personal treachery into a general lesson about true and false friendship.

> A Golden Treasure is the tried friend.
> But who may gold from counterfeits defend?
> Trust not too soon, ne al too light mistrust.
> With th' one thyself, with th' other thy friend thou hurtst.
> Who twyneth betwixt and steereth the golden mean,
> Nor rashly loveth, nor mistrusteth in vain.[125]

'Maister Dolman', the author of Hastings's tragedy appears to be drawing both on Plutarch's strategies for testing supposed friends and on Seneca's warnings against suspecting friends without good reason,[126] summed up in one of Baldwin's axioms: 'Prove not a friend with damage, nor use thou him unproved.'[127]

Lyly's *Euphues* presents heterosexual attraction as a danger to male friendship. Shortly after travelling to Naples and meeting Philautus, Euphues elaborates the benefits of friendship, in words that are largely taken from Baldwin's *Treatise of Morall Philosophie*.[128] Lyly organises familiar commonplaces into such balanced phrases that readers appreciate the skilful writing, well aware of the distance between Euphues's words and his commitments.

I have read (saith he) and well I believe it, that a friend is in prosperity a pleasure, a solace in adversity, in grief a comfort, in joy a merry companion, at all times an other I, in all places the express image of mine own person; insomuch that

---

[122] Baldwin, *Treatise of Morall Philosophie*, sig. L8r; Elyot, *Governor* (1962), p. 133.

[123] Baldwin, *Treatise of Morall Philosophie*, sigs. L7v–8r; Guevara, *Golden Boke*, sig. E1r.

[124] Baldwin, *Treatise of Morall Philosophie*, sig. M1v; Guevara, *Golden Boke*, sig. Bb4r. Baldwin also borrows Guevara's comparison between the qualities of a friend and those of a good horse: *Treatise of Morall Philosophie*, sig. M1r; Guevara, *Golden Boke*, sig. E1r.

[125] Baldwin, *Mirror for Magistrates*, p. 281, lines 337–42.   [126] Seneca, *Ad Lucilivm epistulae morales*, 3.

[127] Baldwin, *Treatise of Morall Philosophie*, sig. M1r.

[128] Lyly, *Works*, I, p. 197; Baldwin, *Treatise of Morall Philosophie*, sig. L7v; Elyot, *Governor* (1962), p. 134.

I cannot tell whether the immortal Gods have bestowed any gift upon mortal men, either more noble or more necessary than friendship.[129]

Lyly uses the sentences Baldwin had collected from Cicero, Guevara and Elyot but he shows that they are ineffective in their goal of teaching Euphues to cultivate virtuous and lasting friendships. He immediately warns us that a friendship based on so little acquaintance cannot be expected to last,[130] so that we are well prepared for the outcome of Euphues's soliloquy opposing love to friendship.

Shall I not then hazard my life to obtain my love? and deceive Philautus to receive Lucilla? Yes Euphues, where love beareth sway, friendship can have no show. As Philautus brought me for his shadow the last supper, so will I use him for my shadow till I have gained his saint. And canst thou wretch be false to him that is faithful to thee? Shall his courtesy be cause of thy cruelty? Wilt thou violate the league of faith, to inherit the land of folly?[131]

Lyly's ingenious patterning of sound and syntax enables him to sum-marise the conflict concisely. The rapidity of Euphues's choice and the wit of Lyly's writing encourage a detached judgment from the reader. The phrasing of Euphues's questions show us that he will choose Lucilla and that this is a mistake. Immediately after Lucilla rejects Euphues, he and Philautus resume their old friendship.[132] Sexual rivalry is strong enough to expose the platitudes of *amicitia*, but male friendship, now founded also on shared hatred, is longer-lasting and more comfortable. Although there are also maxims to warn us against false friends, Euphues's suc-cessive reversals of affection expose the emptiness of the aphorisms of friendship and the ease with which they can be exploited opportunisti-cally. In *Euphues and his England*, Philautus's lack of success in his courtship of Camilla prompts him to seek to regain Euphues's friendship, carelessly lost in a passage of banter. They exchange letters on the nature of true friendship,[133] and Philautus realises the advantage of having a friend with whom to discuss the progress of his love. However the the friends are eventually separated by Philautus's decision to remain in England and his marriage to Frances.

The friendship of Pyrocles and Musidorus is the underlying premise of the whole plot of the *Old Arcadia*.[134] When Pyrocles falls in love with

---

[129] Lyly, *Works*, I, p. 197. Compare as the paragraph proceeds with Baldwin, *Treatise of Morall Philosophie*, sigs. M1r, L7v and Cicero, *De amicitia*, VI.20.

[130] 'Whosoever shall see this amity grounded upon a little affection will soon conjecture that it shall be dissolved upon a light occasion', Lyly, *Works*, I, p. 197; Guevara, *Golden Boke*, sigs. D4v–E1r; Baldwin, *Treatise of Morall Philosophie*, sig. M1v.

[131] Lyly, *Works*, I, pp. 209–10.   [132] Ibid., I, p. 245.

[133] Ibid., II, pp. 141–54.   [134] Sidney, *Old Arcadia*, p. 10.

Philoclea he wants Musidorus's advice before putting into practice his plan of dressing up as an Amazon 'both to perform the true laws of friendship and withal to have his counsel and allowance'.[135] Friendship obliges Musidorus to tell Pyrocles that his behaviour is falling short of his usual standards, to warn him against the dangers of love and to dissuade him from his shameful plan.[136] But friendship also overcomes Musidorus's strong ethical sense, obliging him, in spite of all the reasons against, to support his friend in what he feels compelled to do.[137]

When Musidorus too falls in love and disguises himself as a common shepherd, friendship enables the two princes to share their suffering.[138] The experience of sexual love reinforces their appreciation of friendship.

> They recounted to one another their strange pilgrimage of passions, omitting nothing which the open-hearted friendship is wont to lay forth, where there is cause to communicate both joys and sorrows – for, indeed, there is no sweeter taste of friendship than the coupling of their souls in this mutuality either of condoling or comforting.[139]

This sharing of joy and sorrow is not a substitute for the love they both feel for their mistresses, though it is the occasion for a certain amount of hugging and kissing,[140] but a method of maintaining their spirits and enhancing their devotion. Once Musidorus decides to act on his passion by encouraging Pamela to elope, he comes to feel a conflict between the wish to remain in Arcadia in order to support his friend and the desire to make certain of his love by removing his mistress to a place of safety.[141] But when Musidorus offers (not altogether wholeheartedly) to abandon his plan for the sake of 'the holy band of true friendship', Pyrocles insists that in his friendship Musidorus's own interests take precedence.[142] In this he follows the teaching of Plato and Seneca, though Musidorus's plan sets in motion many of the crimes for which the princes are later condemned. In the last scene of the *Old Arcadia*, Pyrocles and Musidorus, like several of Elyot's exemplary friends, each seek to die in order to preserve the other's life.[143] In Arcadia, where there are two princesses, friendship is enhanced by the experience of love. Both friendship and love overcome the dictates of reason and the rules of virtue. For some of the philosophers that would make the princes flatterers rather than true friends.

---

[135] Ibid., p. 12.   [136] Ibid., pp. 13, 18–20, 24.   [137] Ibid., p. 25.   [138] Ibid., pp. 42–3.
[139] Ibid., p. 168.   [140] Ibid., pp. 43, 171.   [141] Ibid., pp. 173, 185.
[142] Ibid., pp. 174–5.   [143] Ibid., pp. 412–14; Elyot, *Governor* (1962), pp. 135, 148–9.

Friends are supposed to give good counsel,[144] of which princes need the benefit. In Guevara's *Golden Boke*, Marcus Aurelius advises his son to make a distinction between his friends and his counsellors. For pleasures he should keep company with young people but for advice on serious subjects like military affairs, diplomacy, legislation and appointments, he should consult the old and experienced. The prince's personal friends may not be his best counsellors; or, to reverse the implication, his true friends (the elderly counsellors) may be defined by virtue and reason rather than by affection and shared interests. Marcus tells his son that the prince should always take counsel in important and difficult matters, listening to a range of different opinions and taking note of the difficulties pointed out as well as the solutions. But counsellors should always be listened to critically and with an awareness of where their own interests lie. Marcus Aurelius claims that he never afterwards listened to someone whose advice had been motivated by self-interest.[145] When one of the senators asked him why he gave his time to all types of people, he replied that people with lordship over many should not make themselves available only to a few.

I have redde in bokes and have proved it by my selfe that the love of subiectes, the suretie of the prince, the dignitie of thempire, and the honour of the Senate, do conserve the prince, not with rigour but with gentyll conversation.[146]

The people owe obedience to the prynce, and to do his persone great reverence and fulfyll his commaundementes, and the prince oweth egall iustice to every man and meke conversation to all men.[147]

Sir Thomas Elyot's principal discussion of counsel occurs in the final chapters of *The Governor*, because he believes that 'the end of all doctrine and study is good counsel'.[148] Consultation is the occasion on which whatever has gone wrong in the commonwealth can be investigated and put right. Consultation concerns the future but must investigate the past and the present. It is concerned with possibility, honour, expedience and time.[149] Elyot assimilates consultation to the topics of deliberative oratory and to the institution of parliament. He draws out two points for particular emphasis and exemplification: that everyone should be

---

[144] 'The greatest reward that one friend may do to another is in great and weighty matters to succour him with counsel.' Baldwin, *Treatise of Morall Philosophie*, sig. I5r; Skinner, *Reason and Rhetoric*, pp. 70–4.

[145] Guevara, *Golden Boke*, sigs. Aa1v–3r.   [146] Ibid., sig. H4r.   [147] Ibid., sig. I2r.

[148] Elyot, *Governor* (1962), p. 238.

[149] Ibid., p. 237. These resemble the topics of deliberative oratory discussed in Cicero's *De inventione* and *De officiis*.

heard and that the general good should always be preferred to particular interests.[150]

Elyot considers counsel from the prince's point of view in his discussion of affability which he regards, perhaps following Guevara, as one of the noble qualities which the Governor should seek to develop.

Affability is of a wonderful efficacy or power in procuring love. And it is in sundry wise, but most properly, where a man is facile or easy to be spoken unto.[151]

Elyot elaborates the virtue of affability with examples of the effect of its contrary, pride, in alienating support and losing kingdoms. The example of Marcus Antoninus[152] secretly consulting plain speakers in order to amend his faults leads to a series of examples of the damage caused to rulers by the restraint of free speech. Elyot claims that if Julius Caesar had encouraged free speech and easy access not only would he not have alienated his friends, but he would also have been warned about the conspiracy by those who knew of it but were unable to approach him. Affability, resort to counsel and the allowance of free speech enable a kingdom to be kept and improved.[153]

Many of Guevara and Elyot's ideas about counsel (and some of their phrases) are presented as aphorisms in Baldwin's *Treatise of Morall Philosophie*.

Glorious is that commonwealth and fortunate is that prince that is lord of young men to travail and ancient persons to counsel.[154]

Though the determination might be done by a few, yet take counsel of many; for one will show thee all the inconveniences, another the perils, another the damages, another the profit and another the remedy. And set thine eyes as well upon the inconveniences that they say as upon the remedies they offer.[155]

It becometh a King to take good heed to his counsellors, to find who follow their lusts, and who intend the common weal, that he may then know whom for to trust.[156]

Hall teaches the advantages of wise counsel by positive and negative examples. Richard II fell because of his corrupt counsellors,[157] but the ideal

---

[150] Elyot, *Governor* (1962), pp. 238, 240. These remarks may be motivated by Elyot's exclusion from the royal council at the time of Henry VIII's divorce. Lehmberg, *Sir Thomas Elyot*, p. x.

[151] Elyot, *Governor* (1962), p. 107. Compare Isocrates, *Ad Demonicum*, 20, 31.

[152] Croft shows that Elyot follows Patrizi's misattribution of this story, which Lampridius told of Alexander Severus. Elyot, *Governour* (1880), II, pp. 45–6.

[153] Elyot, *Governor* (1962), pp. 108–11.   [154] Baldwin, *Treatise of Morall Philosophie*, sig. I1r.

[155] Ibid., sig. I5r. This is slightly compressed from Guevara, *Golden Boke*, sig. Aa2r–v.

[156] Baldwin, *Treatise of Morall Philosophie*, sig. I1r. Compare sigs. I4v–I5v with Elyot, *Governor* (1962), pp. 237–8.

[157] 'Such a governor was King Richard II, which of himself being not of the most evil disposition, was not of so simple a mind nor of such debility of wit, nor yet of so little heart and courage

king, Henry V, dispensed with his 'old flatterers and familiar companions' and chose men of 'gravity, wit and high policy' to advise him.

He, not too much trusting to the readiness of his own wit, nor to the judgements of his own wavering will, called to his counsel such prudent and politic personages, the which should not only help to ease his charge and pain in supporting the burden of his realm and empire, but also incense and instruct him with such good reasons and fruitful persuasions that he might show himself a singular mirror and manifest example of moral virtues to his common people and loving subjects.[158]

Hall here seems to endorse Marcus Aurelius's advice to his son in Guevara. He amplifies good counsel by depicting Henry's consultation in action in debates about policy. In *The Mirror for Magistrates*, flattery corrupts good counsel, leading to the fall of prince and advisor.[159] The Earl of Warwick is praised for always putting the good of the common weal first, and thus obtaining the love of the common people.[160] The tragedy of Collingbourne, executed for composing a rhyme about Richard III and his advisors becomes the occasion for a defence of free speech.

If king Richard and his counsellors had allowed, or at least winked at, some such wits, what great commodity might they have taken thereby. First they should have known what the people misliked or grudged at (which no one of their flatterers either would or durst have told them) and so might they have found mean, either by amendment (which is best) or by some other policy to have stayed the people's grudge: the forerunner commonly of rulers destructions. *Vox populi vox dei* in this case is not so famous a proverb as true: the experience of all times doth approve it. They should also have been warned of their own sins.[161]

The *Old Arcadia* sets a much lower value on public opinion but the duty of one prince to provide good advice to another is what drives Euarchus to visit Arcadia.[162] Basilius's folly in abandoning the government of Arcadia and retiring to a solitary place is twice attributed to his unwillingness to take counsel.[163] He sets aside Philanax's well-founded opposition to his course of action, just as Pyrocles was unable to agree to Musidorus's reasons for desisting from his sensual weakness.[164] Friendly counsel is ineffective against pride or love, but it ameliorates the worst effects of misfortune. In their dialogue in prison, Pyrocles and Musidorus successfully console themselves against their immediate troubles by considering

but he might have demanded and learned good and profitable counsel, and after advice taken, kept, retained and followed the same. But howsoever it was, unprofitable counsellors were his confusion and final perdition.' Hall, *Chronicle*, p. 47.

[158] Ibid., p. 46.   [159] Baldwin, *Mirror for Magistrates*, pp. 103, 112.   [160] Ibid., p. 209.
[161] Ibid., p. 359.   [162] Sidney, *Old Arcadia*, pp. 357–9.   [163] Ibid., pp. 6–8, 358.
[164] Ibid., p. 19.

providence and the life beyond death.[165] In the *New Arcadia* too, the inability of reason to overcome love is balanced by the success of reason in Pamela's rejection of Cecropia's atheism.[166]

Euphues begins with Euphues's rejection of Eubulus's well-meant advice, but the disaster which befalls Euphues has the effect of endorsing the value of the counsel. Euphues becomes the example from the contrary which confirms the argument. In the 'Cooling Card for Philautus and all fond lovers' which follows the main narrative, Euphues claims that his own experience provides the authority to confirm his advice.

If my lewd life, Gentlemen, have given you offence, let my good counsel make amends; if by my folly any be allured to lust, let them by my repentance be drawn to continence.[167]

For the remainder of the book and its sequel, Euphues is a giver of advice rather than an active man, but there is some incongruity in Euphues's last letter, full of sententious advice about marriage, sent from him in his solitary melancholy to his happily married friend.[168]

The Book Named the Governor contributes to a long-lasting vogue for writings about friendship.[169] Elyot's celebration of the virtue of friendship, expressed in terms largely taken from *De amicitia* and linked with his discussion of good counsel, contributes to an argument about the place of classical education in the training of the political élite.[170] In Elyot's view reading Latin literature will prepare young men to become good friends, by training them about friendship and by providing them with ethical and historical materials for conversation and shared study, and will thereby make them the most fitting counsellors for the prince. Where Guevara distinguished between the wise older men who would give counsel (and therefore be the prince's true friends) and the younger boon companions, Elyot wants to train the young men (who will continue to practise the skills of the warrior and the aristocrat)[171] to become friends and counsellors. The anxiety about flattery and false friendship is as much a matter of politics as of moral misdirection.

---

[165] Ibid., pp. 370–4.   [166] Sidney, *New Arcadia*, pp. 355–63.

[167] Lyly, *Works*, I, p. 247.   [168] Ibid., II, pp. 223–8.

[169] Compare Montaigne, 'De l'amitié' and Francis Bacon, 'Of Friendship', 'Of Counsel'.

[170] While I have come to agree with Hutson's emphasis on the link between propaganda for humanist education and celebration of friendship, I construct the connection somewhat differently. Educated Elizabethans argue about the nature of friendship and the risks of flattery but persuasive communication does not become friendship's defining characteristic (Hutson, *Usurer's Daughter*, pp. 2–3, 11, 77–8, 87–8).

[171] Elyot, *Governor* (1962), pp. 59–69, 91–4.

Baldwin makes available the essence of Elyot's, Guevara's and Cicero's ethical teaching. *The Mirror for Magistrates* and Hall's *Chronicle* apply the political lessons. Although he concurs with Elyot's praise of education and his celebration of male friendship, Lyly's wish to write an engaging story prompts him to expose the emptiness of the associated sententiae. Euphues knows all the right maxims but they have no impact on his conduct. Disgust at the behaviour of Lucilla leads him back to Philautus. Lyly emphasises the conflict between male friendship and heterosexual unions. Sidney's princes are warriors with dynastic obligations as well as grand tourists. Their moral axioms have no force against the promptings of love. Sidney shows that once the princes evade the absolute embrace of virtue, their moral thinking is clouded with contradictions.[172] Friendship provides companionship but also encourages false loyalties and crime. Good fortune and providence save his heroes, the princesses and the state from the consequences of their actions. Where histories and conduct manuals enable a celebration of educated friendship, romance entertains questions about how moral axioms are affected by emotions, deceptive appearances and changes of circumstance.

CONCLUSION

Histories, conduct manuals and romances, as genres of moral and political teaching, drew content, small-scale structures and techniques of expression from rhetorical education. This inherited subject-matter consisted primarily of stories (including histories) and moral sentences. Many of these 'histories and sentences' derive from Cicero, Plutarch and Guevara's forgeries concerning Marcus Aurelius, but they are made available through texts (including translations) in all three genres. Inherited material was passed from Elyot to Baldwin to Lyly and onwards for reuse in other writers.

Rhetorical teaching provided a number of methods for presenting inherited material. All our authors use forms of amplification to mark important passages and to increase the impact of stories and lessons. The texts are rich in enargeia, comparisons, examples and patterned syntax. Hall, Lyly and Sidney anticipate an audience with a taste for elaborate and copious writing. Many of the texts contain speeches, letters, debates and fables which exploit the forms taught at grammar school and university. Elyot's *Governor* contains many essays on moral topics which

---

[172] Sidney, *Old Arcadia*, pp. 120–1 (quoted at note 80 above).

apply the techniques of rhetoric and dialectic to subject-matter derived mainly from Cicero and Plutarch. Erasmus's *Adagia* was a formal model as well as a source of proverbs and stories.

Histories record the stories and sayings which form the material of the conduct manuals. The conduct manuals provide moral lessons, sometimes in the form of narratives, sometimes of axioms, which rest on the accumulated experience of a nation or a civilisation. At the same time the education of the political élite, which is the aim of the conduct manual, provides the justification for collecting records and composing histories. Furthermore the axioms and commonplaces of conduct manuals provide histories (certainly in the cases of Hall's *Chronicle* and the *Mirror for Magistrates*) with norms for analysing events. The mind-set formed by the conduct manual selects events worthy to be recorded and provides the teaching which the narrated events illustrate and confirm.

The building blocks of rhetorical education ensure that this system is less uniform and rigid than this analysis might initially suggest. In the first place many maxims of conduct are available and there is a degree of conflict among members of the whole set. Secondly, although narratives are treated as necessarily meaningful, pupils have also been trained in extracting different meanings from narratives, either by amplifying some parts of the story and reducing the impact of others, or by connecting them to different axioms or different topics of argument.

Histories and conduct manuals make ethical materials available for reuse in letters, speeches and treatises but a culture of competitive varying and of debate encourages the use of these materials to argue different types of case. At the same time only those with a knowledge of the axioms and the stories are entitled to participate in debate, and these materials, although they admit of some contradictions, are selected to conform with the interests of the élite. Conflicts about particular interpretative points or courses of action will be contained within the élite and by norms of sociability.

For Elyot fiction is as effective a form of moral teaching as history; for Sidney it is superior because more capable of being idealised (this perhaps underestimates the extent to which history is idealised). Both treat fiction as if it were a version of history. But in the practice of romance writing however much space is devoted to letters of advice, moral maxims and improving stories, the obligation to delight is a stronger motive than in histories and conduct manuals. In *Euphues* and *Arcadia* this impulse to delight is expressed at the stylistic level in boldness of expression and comparison, but also at the level of plotting in novelty, surprise and reversal. These features all have the capacity to destabilise moral commonplaces and to question the limits on ethical discourse. Although Euphues is careful to moralise his story, his actions undermine platitudes about friendship and draw attention to the fact that the border between apparent friendship (a treacherous form of flattery) and its true version is permeable and hard to define. Catherine Bates has pointed out that some contemporary writers misread the ending of *Euphues and his England* assuming that Philautus had succeeded in overcoming Camilla's virtuous resistance.[173] Pyrocles and Musidorus manage to remain heroes while breaking many of the norms of virtuous conduct,[174] while the ending of the *Old Arcadia* (like the incompleteness of the *New*) poses more questions than it answers. At the same time individual letters, speeches and phrases from both romances could be (and were) quarried for orthodox moral teaching.

Within the space defined by the rhetorical discourse of moral teaching, Lyly and Sidney (and in varying degrees such successors as Lodge, Greene and Nashe, encouraged by the market for printed books) elaborated fictions which interrogated the norms of civil conduct. They acknowledged the weakness of reason struggling against emotion and the difficulty of distinguishing between truth and appearance. Montaigne's rethinking of practical ethics is based on the application of an individual intelligence to an intertextual farrago of materials rather similar to those disseminated in England in histories, conduct manuals and romances.

[173] Bates, *Rhetoric of Courtship*, pp. 94–5.
[174] Worden, *Sound of Virtue*, pp. 18–20, 319 notes the way in which ethical precepts are 'questioned, contradicted and jested with', before revealing their force.

6

Political argument

Both in its educational institutions and in publications like Elyot's *Book Named the Governor* and Baldwin's *Treatise of Morall Philosophie*, Tudor humanism aimed to form men who could apply rhetorical skills and moral understanding to the problems of practical life. The Elizabethan Privy Council was dominated by moderately-born university-educated men like William Cecil, Nicholas Bacon, Walter Mildmay and Francis Walsingham who sat alongside hereditary peers and who were served by secretaries of state and ambassadors who shared their own background. The Privy Council considered large numbers of logically argued written reports. On important issues its members debated carefully worked out positions before reporting their proposals to the Queen. The culture of argument, which has been described in earlier chapters, prescribed the methods and provided the criteria of political decision-making.

Both the materials presented to the Privy Council and its processes of argument have generated a rich documentary record. In this chapter I analyse the argumentative and rhetorical procedures employed in letters of political advice (mainly from diplomats overseas), in William Cecil, Lord Burghley's political memoranda composed throughout his career, in speeches and notes from Privy Council debates and in the Earl of Essex's *Apology*, a long political pamphlet connected with debates in the Privy Council in 1597 and 1598 about a possible peace treaty with Spain. Parliamentary oratory and debate, which is related in subject-matter and personnel but which survives in different types of record, will be the subject of the next chapter.

Because these materials have never previously been analysed from the point of view of argument and rhetoric it seems important to discuss examples of each type of document in turn. Privy Council debate was dominated by logical techniques learned at university and by the topics of deliberative oratory outlined in rhetoric textbooks and in Cicero's *De officiis*. But techniques of grammar school rhetoric such as moral sententiae, comparisons, narratives and imagery are often employed to support an argument or to influence the approach to an issue.

DIPLOMATIC LETTERS

Elizabethan and Jacobean envoys abroad were expected to provide the Privy Council with responses to particular questions and to report on more general political developments. They also often give advice about the course of action most favourable to the Queen's interests and about the instructions which they might be given to further those aims. The envoy's double duty of describing the situation at the court in which he resides, usually on the basis of rather indirect knowledge, and of advising the council necessarily involves him in a good deal of analysis and persuasion. The geographical distance involved also ensures that the letter was the main channel of communication between envoy and employer.

Thomas Wilson (?1525–81) whom we have already met as the author of the English-language manuals *The Rule of Reason* (1551) and *The Art of Rhetoric* (1553) undertook diplomatic missions abroad between 1567 and 1577. He was elected to each of the parliaments between 1563 and 1581 and frequently spoke in favour of the Privy Council line.[1] I have selected three paragraphs from two letters to Walsingham written during Wilson's second mission to the Netherlands in 1577, when the alliance between the Prince of Orange and the States General (together with Philip II's bankruptcy) forced the Spanish governor, Don John of Austria, to make considerable concessions to the Dutch rebels, including the withdrawal of the Spanish army from the Netherlands.[2] In his letter of 5 February 1577, Wilson weighs up the prospects for a peace agreement.

I can not yet saie that there is any assured hope of peace, neyther wil I thenke it to bee peace, tyl the Spanyards have geaven over their fortes, and are marchynge homewards by lande, and out of this Cowntrie. But so farre unlike it is that they are yet goinge, as they fortifie at Mastrike by twoe companies in cowrse daie and nyght, they spoyle the pune towns about Liege, they have lastly taken a proper town called Eyndoven in Brabant not farre frome Bolduc, and threaten to beseige Boldic it selfe excepte they wil yeelde to them, they are not determined to goe by lande, and scante tenn myllions will not satisfie their demaundes for paie behynde, neyther wil don John harken to the returne of Counte Buren, the Prince of Orenge sonne. And yet notwithstanding, the Emperors Ambassadors to doe good offices for peace, the Bishoppe of Liege also, and Octavio Gonzago,

---

[1] Medine, *Wilson*, pp. 75–105.
[2] Geoffrey Parker, *The Dutch Revolt* (Harmondsworth, 1985), pp. 169–98.

both specially sent frome don John hether to deale for quietnes. And the commone speache is, that a peace wilbee concluded afore this weeke bee ended, which I praie God maie be, so it be safe and sownde, but I wil not beleve that any peace shalbee, til I see it fullie concluded, and the Spaniards actuallie retired.[3]

At the outset Wilson states the question he is considering and the final test which he will apply. Peace will not be certain until the Spanish army actually withdraws. Then he adduces evidence against the prospect of peace: the Spanish continue with their military action; the soldiers will not leave until they are paid; and Don John shows no sign of releasing Count Buren. All these arguments can be related through the topics of invention to the peace treaty. Military actions are *contraries* of peace; the lack of pay will be a *cause* of continued violence and the detention of Count Buren will be a *cause* of war for his father. Wilson merely states the evidence, but in each case a series of propositions (some of them general maxims of conduct) can easily be inferred to link the evidence with the conclusion. For example, the failure to release Count Buren can be seen as an indication that peace will not be made, if we add the following propositions implicit in the context: the Prince of Orange is the leader of the Dutch Protestants; the leader must be involved in the peace deliberations; the father's concern for his son is paramount; no peace can be made until the essential demands of both sides are met.

After listing the reasons against the likelihood of peace, Wilson provides three indications in favour: the intervention of the Emperor's ambassadors, the activity of two named envoys from Don John and the testimony of 'commone speache'. Although Wilson expresses his hope for peace, he remains cautious. Peace will require both a fully concluded treaty and the withdrawal of the Spanish army. A few months later, on 8 June 1577, when peace had been agreed and the Spanish army had begun to withdraw, Wilson again wrote to Walsingham about the meaning of Don John's behaviour.

Truthe it is don John seekes by al meanes to be populare, and hath so wel caried himself [with] courtesie to al in general, with his aptnes to geave audience, and his willingness to applie himself to the humour of the States and other suppliantes particularlie, using great liberalitie therwithal to verie manie, and constancie in his doinges, that manie of the greatest yea and most of the meaner sorte are enchanted in his love, and hyghlie esteeme hym above al others. And yet this moche must I thenke that he is thus apparantlie good for necessitie, because he can not otherwise brynge that to passe whiche he hath in his mynde

[3] Public Record Office, State Papers (hereafter PRO SP) 70.143.1076, dated 5 February 1577.

to doe, seemyng now to be somewhat wearie of this his cunninge dealinge, because he is overmoche controuled by the States, yea almost commanded by them. First the Burgesses of Anterpe, being sette on by the States here are verie earnest to have the Almaines sowldiers discharged and the Castil to bee defaced, whereof the first is in hande to bee donne by order from hense, and the second resteth in deliberacyon. Moreover the 9 nations of Bryssels here, have verie latelie exhibited their bil, by Mons Montcigny, Counte Lalainges brother, for the Spanyardes, Italians and others their adherents to bee presentlie removed from [the] person of don John, whiche hath greatlie trowbled his le[isure]. Such men are thought to be of his arriere Conseil, and do direct his doings to their harm as they fear.[4]

Wilson begins by listing adjuncts and actions which indicate Don John's intention of achieving popularity. His courtesy, accessibility, flexibility, liberality and constancy (almost in the words of Elyot's advice to governors) have endeared him to his subjects. But for Wilson this show of benevolence can only be a stratagem ('And yet this moche must I thenke that he is thus apparantlie good for necessitie'). Given Wilson's assumption of underlying Spanish cunning, any flexibility on Don John's part is interpreted as a sign of hidden malice. This interpretation is amplified with an inference about the manner of his courtesy ('seemyng now to be somewhat wearie of this his cunninge dealinge') and a detailed description of the degree to which his subjects are prepared to press him. Wilson sets out his interpretive framework before reporting recent events. The citizens of Antwerp demand the removal of troops and the destruction of fortifications. The nine nations require the removal of some of the foreign advisors at his court. In response to Don John's flexibility the Netherlanders demand further reductions in Spanish military power and influence. For Wilson these requests show both how far Don John has gone to create a favourable atmosphere and how close to exasperation he must be. Wilson's argument here shows how easily the meaning of actions can be reinterpreted once a strong assumption is interposed. Every concession Don John makes becomes further evidence of his malice. Wilson was always suspicious of Spanish motivations when the interests of Protestants were involved but Don John's reputation and his initial instructions from Spain, which the Protestants claimed to have intercepted,[5] provided additional justification for his view.

Later in the same letter, Wilson turned to consider the position of William of Orange, the leader of the Protestants in the northern provinces

---

4 PRO SP 70.145.1237, dated 8 June 1577 (last sentence supplied from *Calendar of State Papers Foreign 1575–77*, p. 589 [hereafter CSP]).
5 *CSP Foreign 1575–77*, p. 515.

of the Netherlands. William was ambivalent about the peace treaty, since he feared that once peace had been made Don John would attempt to impose Catholicism throughout the Spanish Netherlands. But at the same time William did not wish to lose the political advantages which followed from his alliance with the States General, many of whom were Catholics.[6] In raising the issue of the prince, Wilson understood that his own commitment to the Dutch Protestants was greater than that of the Queen and many of the Privy Council.[7]

Whose case must at this time be advisedlie pesed, and some resolution taken thereupon, whiche [if] he grawnte maie bee for the best. I can saie no more than I have done heretofore. The Prince must of necessitie geave hymself over to some greater personage than himself for his lesser strengthe or els yeelde al to the Kinges mercie. Of this I am fullie perswaded, that lacke what course the Queenes majestie wyl have hym to take, he wil most willinglie folowe the same and bee altogether at her highnes devocyon. Some what must be donne, or els some willbe undoone. And in my symple iudgement an overture made of parte takinge under the colour of peace makynge, woulde do moche good and geave a terror to the proudest of them. Yea such a bolde dealinge would cawse others to joyne with us, that now stande as neuters, lackynge stil what wee wil dooe. There is no trustinge suspected frendes at this tyme, but playne dealinge indeede, with a protestacyon to make peace, wilbe the best assurance. And valiant workynge never wanted good fortune, yea by hardynesse, the courage of an enemie maye the sooner be abated, and like it is, since England hath shewed her fire, which heretofore hath been famouse and fortunate, especiallie in foreyne countries. And I praise God that I maye rather see Englande invade then, I bee invaded, as Scipio fought Carthage, to brynge Hannibal out of Italie, and as Demosthenes persuaded the Athenians rather warre upon Philippe in Macedone, than to suffer him to warre upon them in their own countrie. But these determinacions I do leave to others of more skil and better judgement.[8]

Wilson tries to disguise his support for English intervention in favour of the Protestants. He expresses William's situation as a dilemma. The Prince must seek the support of either the King of France or Queen Elizabeth. Therefore he will prefer the Queen, whatever conditions she may impose. Having established the Queen's freedom of manoeuvre,

---

[6] In a letter to Walsingham of 10 February 1577, Wilson claimed to detect signs of the States General manoeuvring for a peace without William's assent. He believed that William would never agree to a peace which allowed Catholicism to be reimposed. *CSP Foreign 1575–77*, pp. 514–15.

[7] One indication of this is the difference in tone between Wilson's letters to Burghley and to Walsingham. On the same day as the paragraph below, Wilson wrote to Burghley that he saw no likelihood of William taking part in the peace settlement unless the Queen became involved. *CSP Foreign 1575–77*, p. 589.

[8] PRO SP 70.145.1237, dated 8 June 1577.

Wilson urges the need for action with a generalised exhortation almost in the form of a proverb ('Some what must be donne, or els some willbe undoone'). The disaster invoked presumably refers to the fate of the Protestants, though this is not stated. After establishing the need for action he introduces his solution, 'an overture made of parte takinge', but this is then moderated, 'under colour of peace makynge'. Rather than specify the form of support for the Prince which he envisages, Wilson amplifies the advantages of boldness in making enemies fearful and strengthening allies. He uses a maxim of the active life ('There is no trustinge suspected frendes at this tyme') to develop the image of swift decisive action, though again he is careful to qualify 'playne dealing' with 'with a protestacyon to make peace'. He dare not depart from the rhetoric of prudence, even as he develops the commonplace of resolution, firm and successful action.

He attempts to resolve the paradox of combining action and honour with prudence by implying that action will have practical benefits. He supports this claim with a maxim ('valiant workynge never wanted good fortune') and a generalisation from history. It is likely that resolution will carry the day without the need for fighting, but if there is fighting we shall be following the best precedents in the ancient world by putting foreign territory at risk rather than our own. The examples of Scipio and Demosthenes bring cultural weight to the case he is arguing. The passage concludes with a pretence at modest even-handedness. It is for others to decide the best course of action. The positive argument for intervention depends on grammar school resources: amplification, maxims of conduct and instances from ancient history.

Among a series of letters to Burghley and Walsingham, Wilson includes a letter to the Queen, in which he relates a meeting in which he and Don John complimented the Queen (whose portrait Wilson showed him) and agreed that the difficulties between England and Spain in arranging the peace could be resolved if Don John and the Queen could meet.[9] In spite of his wish to report the compliments, Wilson evidently found this an awkward conversation to sustain since he immediately writes of the untrustworthiness of Spanish envoys and justifies deceiving them.

Where they cannot prevail by open and apparent actions they will work by covert and douce means intermingling honey and sugar with their drugs of poison and

---

9 'He wished that he might have the hap once to see her. Told him that the two noble natures meeting together could not but agree in all goodness and virtue, and the one better understand the other than by messengers or ambassadors.' *CSP Foreign 1575–77*, p. 596.

destruction. His speech tends to this end, that she be very circumspect how to
trust and never to believe words but the effect of words. It is good even to give
like measure,

He that speaks me fair and loves me not
I will speak him fair and trust him not.

Cretisendum semper cum Cretense and as the common speech is *fallere fallentem non est
fraus.*[10]

After these classical *sententiae* permitting deception, he cites a range
of historical examples and a Latin maxim (with paronomasia), this
time referring to the dangers of trusting people of different religion
('Ubi non est eadem fides, ibi est nulla fides'), to argue that there
cannot be any long term peace between Don John and William of
Orange.[11]

Late in his career, unable to attend court in person, Burghley used the
same secular maxim as Wilson (and the topics of deliberative oratory)
to give his son Robert advice on the awkward balance between morality
and advantage in politics. In 1593 the Earl of Bothwell had offered to
help the English in return for their support in regaining his position with
King James.

The matter you write of concerning the answer to be made by Lock is very
picquant for difficulties on both sides, wherin the rule of christian philosophy
consisteth in difference betwixt *utile* and *honestum*. And yet *utile incertum*, and yet
honestum certum. But if *honestum* were reciproche, it were to be preferred with more
constancy. In private men's causes *cretisare cum cretensi* is allowable. Thus you see
how I begin to wander before I dare affirme anything. If my hand were free
from payne I would not commyt thus much to any other man's hand, and yet
you may impart my words to her Majestie without offence.[12]

Burghley states the dilemma in terms derived from the rhetorical tradition of deliberative oratory (also discussed in *De officiis*). The Christian in
politics has to balance arguments of practical effectiveness (*utile*) against
honour and morality (*honestum*). In this case the moral argument (not to
take part in stratagems against a friend) is clear, the advantage, given
Bothwell's unreliability, uncertain. And yet Burghley is reluctant to give
up the possibility of strengthening the Protestant position in Scotland.
How much easier the choice would be if everyone were honourable!
And in private behaviour it is quite allowable to lie to someone who

[10] Ibid., p. 597. Compare Erasmus, *Adagia*, I.ii.29.   [11] *CSP Foreign 1575–77*, p. 597.
[12] Letter from Burghley to Sir Robert Cecil, 21 May 1593, Thomas Wright (ed.), *Queen Elizabeth and
her Times: A Series of Original Letters*, 2 vols. (London, 1838), II, p. 425. Read, *Lord Burghley and Queen
Elizabeth*, p. 484.

deceives you. Classical moral axioms provide him with justifications for compromising his Christian ethical principles.

Ralph Winwood (?1563–1617) was active in diplomacy mostly under King James I. He was educated at Oxford between 1577 and 1592.[13] The exchange of letters which follows is taken from a mission to the Netherlands which he undertook in 1609 in connection with the dispute about the succession to the Duchies of Cleves and Juliers. These were important for the control which they held over Rhine communications between Holland and the Protestants of Southern Germany.[14] In his first letter Winwood outlines the situation confronting the Protestant pretenders to the dukedoms, explains that he expects to attend a conference in Dusseldorf and asks the council for further instructions.

And now I wilbe bold by your Lordships good favour to crave your further direcions in the different of Cleves: a cause of that importance that if it be carried with iudgement and resolucion will much eclipse the brightnes of the sea of Roome, and asmuch abate of the greatnes of the howse of Austria . . .

[He expects to be called to a conference at Dusseldorf.]

Though what resolucion wilbe taken cannot be divined, yet solidely to proceede for the good of the common cause, and the honour of the Princes, which professedly undertake the Defence of the just Pretendante, the Counsayles in reason ought to tend to this course: that the Princes pretending doe summon by their letters the Archduke Leopaldus to quitte Juliers which unjustly he doth possesse: and the Magistrate and people of the towne, to yeeld themselves to the obedience of their Lawfull Princes; which if they shall refuse to doe, the Princes must be so well prepared presently to beseidge the towne, and to that purpose now they leavy both horse and foote, by stronge hand to recover their right, which by reason they cannot obtayne. If no man come in to the defence of the towne the quarrell is determined, and the Princes are established in their rightfull possessions. And who wilbe so hardy to come in, when it shalbe declared that what the Princes doe, they doe by th'advice of their Majesties of France and great Brittany, the united Provinces, and the Princes protestant of Germany. All other marchanding courses wilbe to th'advantage of the adverse part, whose desire is to draw the dispute into length . . . [15]

Winwood first establishes the importance of the case by explaining that if it is managed well it will lessen the influence of Rome and the power of the Hapsburgs. Then he makes an argument: the Protestant cause and the honour of the Kings involved requires decisive action. He then elaborates the manner in which this will be achieved, gives the cause of

---

[13] *Dictionary of National Biography*, XXI, pp. 704–7.
[14] Geoffrey Parker, *Europe in Crisis 1598–1648* (London, 1979), pp. 125–7, 152–3.
[15] PRO SP 84.66, fols. 286v–288r, dated 25 September 1609.

the future Catholic retreat (the overwhelming combination of France, Britain, the Netherlands and the German Protestants) and dismisses less decisive alternative actions ('all other marchanding courses') because of their unworthiness and their lack of success (topic of opposites).

Throughout the letter Winwood presents a clear idea of the instructions he would like to have. Hesitation will permit the Catholic powers to drag matters out and establish a candidate favourable to their interest. Like Wilson before him he holds out the prospect that a threat alone, provided it is well concerted and strongly made, may be enough to resolve the situation, without the need for fighting.

The Privy Council replied to this letter on 4 October 1609. It agreed that if Winwood was invited and if he heard that the French and Dutch were sending envoys, he could confer with them at Dusseldorf.

Wherein because the matter it self is of such Condition and Consequence as no man can yet discern what will be the surest way to the end, and because it is the part of all wise Princes before they do particularly engage themselves in matters of this Consequence (which is like to draw no less after it than a general War in Christendom) to examine narrowly and equally every part and Circumstance that depends upon it, it hath pleased his Majestie to command us to lay before you many things, wherein he desires to be satisfied before he can give you leave to conclude what Nature or Proportion he resolves to bear therein.[16]

The Privy Council seizes on Winwood's initial proviso ('though what resolucion wilbe taken cannot be divined') to insist on a more measured approach. Where he hoped for virtually unopposed success, the council emphasises the dangers of taking up an aggressive stance on a sensitive issue. The council's topics for the importance of the case (general war in Christendom) are directly opposed to his (the prospect of Protestant gain). The council emphasise circumspection and consideration, where he extols resolution, but nevertheless it is willing, provided appropriate assurances can be given, to consider undertaking a role and a proportion of the cost.

The Privy Council wishes to be satisfied that there are no other pretendants with worthwhile claims and that the Princes Pretendant will continue in their commitment to arbitrate between their opposed claims. The council also wishes to know who else has agreed to support the claims of the Princes and what particular assistance is required.

---

[16] Edmund Sawyer (ed.), *Memorials of Affairs of State collected from the Winwood Papers*, 3 vols. (London, 1725), III, p. 76.

his Majestie thinks you may well disclaim from any more power at this time then to confirm that his Majestie is resolved to aid them as far as shall be fit for him, when he shall understand from thence what is their resolution, and what likelihood there is that his Majesty shall receive no dishonour by engaging himself for his Friend's Quarrel.[17]

'Dishonour' here implies material loss as well as loss of face. James's support is conditional both on the actions of others and on his calculation of the likelihood of success. The letter concludes with the reminder that the King cannot lightly use the 'vail and cloak of Religion' to disturb the peace of Europe.

These points are taken up by Winwood in his reply that although he will follow his instructions, he hopes to be excused for his thoughts. He wishes that James could have given him more freedom of action since the legitimacy of the claims of the two Princes Pretendant is not in dispute. This gives him another opportunity to outline his strategy.

The reason of this my desier is this: because it is heere generally receaved that this resolucion, ioyntly taken and publickly declared, is the surest and most compendious way to determine the quarrell and to settle the Princes in peaceable possession of their right, without drawing sword or blood, which is the cause the Princes doe intreate the mediacion of their Majesties and the cause for which they sende their Ministers. I confesse my weake iudgement will not serve me to believe that if this resolucion be once declared, and assured to be put in execution if neede requier, the Emperour, King of Spaine or Archdukes, eyther ioyntly or severally will farther move in this matter. By this course, his Majestie's honour, which doth bear the greatest share in this cause, the cause being mixti generis, not only of State but of religion, is in safety and out of danger. For if this resolucion be taken, the cause of religion will prevail, whereof his Majestie is the Patron and Protectour, but if the Proposition be made and not accepted, yet his Majestie's honour is preserved, or rather improoved, whenas the world must take notice the cause doth fall not by his default.[18]

Winwood's response aims to convince the council that a strong English commitment will determine the issue without the need for fighting. While avoiding a definite statement, he implies that the other Protestant powers have already reached the same conclusion. At the same time he affects modesty and assures the council that the King will be able to extricate himself with his honour intact if the project fails. He picks up the issue of honour from the council's reply and reinterprets it, arguing that even if the other powers fail to support the Princes Pretendant, James's commitment will enhance his honour as a champion of Protestantism. He

[17] Ibid., III, p. 77.   [18] PRO SP 84.66, fols. 294–5, dated 20 October 1609.

refrains from answering the council's direct questions about the positions taken by the other states and the nature of the help required. However he seizes on a sentence in the council's letter which refers to quarrels between the two princes to describe the consequences of failing to assist them.

> And if I may without offence freely deliver what I thinke: I feare the cause will fall and these Princes fayle of their pretencions for want of good conducte in themselves, and resolucion in their friends.
> The two Princes who manage this cause are both yong and unexperienced; the iealousies betweene them are greate and apparent; neither are they, as yet, assisted by men of State, for counsayle, or of warre for command.
> They onely are possessed of Duisseldorp, which is a poore and weake place, subiect to surprize, if Leopoldus, who is accompanied with the best commanders which have followed the Archdukes warres, shal have the boldnes to attempt that enterprise.
> The other townes, which are all unfortified, refuse garrison; the Countries, both Juliers and Cleves, doe professe they will espouse no mans quarrelle and, to avoyde a warre, they will render themselves primo occupanti.[19]

Winwood can easily find propositions to prove the weakness of the princes once his argumentative strategy demands it. Now Winwood's central argument is that without a resolute alliance the duchies will be seized by the Catholic powers. Arguments for the princes' weakness are drawn from their persons, their councillors, the places they hold, from the comparison with the resources of their opponents and from the attitude of the subjects they hope to rule. In the two sections quoted Winwood has outlined the benefits which will follow from intervention and the disasters that will befall the princes if they are left unsupported. If the Emperor is left to judge the issue, he will install Catholic candidates; if the princes are not assisted, they will fail; what course remains but intervention?

> I have helde it my duetie to represent these particularities of this busines, whereof what the importance is, your Lordships best can iudge. If the matter be carried with resolucion, there is much honour to be gotten, and that without chardge or danger. What the Orator said of pronuntiacion, that it was the first, the second, the thirde parte in the arte of Rhetoricque, the same may be sayd of resolution in the cariage of a busines of this nature.[20]

Where the letter from the Privy Council emphasised risk and expense, Winwood counters with resolution. Where his previous letter had stressed

---

[19] Ibid., fol. 295.
[20] Ibid., fol. 296. The story about Demosthenes appears in Cicero, *De oratore*, III.56.213, Quintilian, *Institutio oratoria*, XI.3.6 and Wilson, *Rhetoric*, p. 241.

the importance of the issue for protestantism, his reply to the council picks up their concern with honour and expense, while attempting to link the cause of religion with the King's honour. Like Wilson, Winwood uses maxims of state and classical anecdotes to drive home the point he wishes to support. It is noticeable that he makes much more use of arguments connected with the actual political and strategic situation in outlining the difficulties facing the princes than in arguing for their likely success.

In 1609 Charles Cornwallis, then the resident ambassador in Spain, was instructed to assure Philip III that James I had not hindered the negotiations for the Twelve Years Truce between Spain and the United Provinces but had rather encouraged it.[21] It appears that James had noticed an unexpected coldness on the part of Spain. On 7 April Cornwallis wrote back to the council to say that he had put that point of view strenuously and that on any just estimate James's actions had been the pattern of kingly virtue.

But the knott consisteth not in that poynte. Soe experienced an Estate as this cannot be ignorant that both your Majestie and the Kinge your next neighbor are to receyve much contentment in this conclusion, as whereby a countrie that would have added so much strengthe to this Monarchie (alreadie soe extraordinarilie powerfull) is to be aparted from it, and soe great a preparation and continuall readines of an armie and munition in partes soe neare unto your owne gates, by that meanes removed. The hardenes resteth in another poynte. For howsoever for the time the nurse that wanteth milke is by necessitie made contented to rocke the cradle, till the childe doe sleepe, yet well she knoweth that uppon awakinge she must provide to give other and more ample satisfaction. I have within these two dayes mett with the true conceipte that is here enclosed in the secrett of their bosomes. The united Estates (I finde) they accompte but as the stales, Your Majestie and your neighbor Kinge the Fowlers, the Estates the artisans, Your Majesties the architects and modellers, the Estates the subscribers with their handes, Your Majesties the contrivers in your heades. Soe that for conclusion they reckon the conditions yours, though the frute be theirs, and for this yeeld none other thankefullnes then is usually given to the phisition that adviseth in a gangren a cuttinge of of a putryfied or irrecoverable member, for the givinge ease and securitie to the rest of the bodie.[22]

Cornwallis explains that the Spanish had hoped that their friendships with the French and British would have enabled them to subdue the Dutch. Given that this hope had been disappointed and that Britain could be seen to have benefited from the Truce, James must look for

[21] On the background and consequences of the truce, see Parker, *Europe in Crisis*, pp. 132–5.
[22] PRO SP 94.16.61, dated 7 April 1609.

nothing from Spain other than hostility when opportunity presents itself, unless some other means of reconciliation can be found.

The letter presents an interesting combination of *realpolitik* and comparison with everyday life. At first Cornwallis focuses on the deliberative topic of advantage. The Spanish are experienced enough to realise that as a result of the peace they have lost wealth and the English no longer face enemies and weapons at their gates. Spain sees no reason to be grateful to the British for helping achieve something which was in the British interest. Far from thinking that James hindered the peace, they regard it as the culmination of a plan which he inspired.

Cornwallis regards comparison with everyday life as the most appropriate device for achieving such a fundamental reorientation of the British understanding of how the Spanish view their actions. Partly it is a matter of explaining that things appear to the Spanish in a different light, but more importantly Cornwallis needs to convince the council that his new interpretation of attitudes is more plausible. The comparison with the wetnurse is both arresting and enigmatic. The peace with the Dutch is presented metaphorically as a temporary measure, forced on the Spanish by necessity, which will have to be paid for later in the broader political contest. The later comparisons with hunting, building and projecting are simpler in themselves and explained more fully and plainly, but they also carry the greatest burden of persuasion. It will be difficult for James's councillors to imagine themselves, in the way that Cornwallis claims the Spaniards see them, as the originators of the Dutch revolt. The final comparison with the doctor who advises amputation is easier to assimilate. Like the previous comparisons it presents Britain in the role of contriver rather than actor, but it insists on the necessity of the action while exploiting the amputee's understandable lack of enthusiasm. Since the Spanish have agreed to peace out of necessity, those who helped them achieve the peace must not expect gratitude, especially if the Spanish see them as the ultimate beneficiaries. Although Cornwallis is careful to emphasise that this view is a misinterpretation of James's virtuous conduct, his comparisons enable him to explain how such a view might seem persuasive to the Spanish.

CECIL'S MEMORANDA

Among the vast quantity of letters and documents composed by William Cecil, Lord Burghley are a considerable number of memoranda, summarising a situation, or listing action to be taken or evidence for and against a particular course of action.[23] Some of these memoranda are lists of actions to be undertaken, for example on the first day of the reign or in order to prepare the country for invasion.[24] Others are drafts of instructions to ambassadors or summaries of information relating to a particular issue, the revolt of the Dutch against the Spanish, for example.[25] It is not always easy to distinguish between memoranda of these types and the more exploratory or more argumentative ones with which I shall mostly be concerned here. In 1569 Cecil composed a memorandum which he later sent to the Duke of Norfolk, listing perils and remedies in the present situation of the realm.

Perils

A Conspiration of the Pope, King Philip, and sundry potentates of Italy: to employ all their forces for the subversion of the professors of the Gospel.

The Intention of the same formed to be extended against England, immediately after the subduing of the Prince of Conde and his associates.

The Spaniard daily avaunts in the Low Countries within short time to possess this realm without any battle.

The Opinion they have conceived of the weakness of this realm, by reason of the lack of experience of the subjects in feats of war . . .

Remedies

. . . That the Queene's Majesty unite all her faithful subjects that profess the Gospel sincerely . . .

The procuring of some aid secretly for the Prince of Conde if the French king will refuse to have the Queen a Moderator of Peace . . .

To view the Power of the Realm and to put it in order . . . by special commissioners.

To make the Navy ready.

To embrace such Leagues as the Princes of Almain do offer for Defence of Religion.[26]

While a few of the remedies answer specific perils, this document is best regarded as a combination of a list of problems with a list of actions to be undertaken. The main effect of the document is not to argue for a particular course of action, or even to weigh up the claims of competing

---

[23] Some of these memoranda were printed in eighteenth-century collections of documents: Samuel Haynes (ed.), *Collection of State Papers . . . left by Lord Burghley* (London, 1740), William Murdin (ed.), *Collection of State Papers relating . . . to the reign of Queen Elizabeth* (London, 1759) and John Strype (ed.), *Annals of the Reformation*, 4 vols. (London, 1725–7). Several of them are quoted or summarised in Read's two-volume biography (*Secretary Cecil* and *Lord Burghley*). Recently the memoranda up to 1570 have been subjected to thorough and thoughtful scrutiny in Alford, *Early Elizabethan Polity*, esp. pp. 18–19, 93–4, 133–8, 165–70, 183–6, 204–6.

[24] PRO SP 12.1.2, printed in Strype, *Annals*, I, pp. 6–7. Memo on defence, Strype, *Annals*, IV, p. 221.

[25] *CSP Foreign 1575–77*, pp. 431–2, 442–4, 583–5.   [26] Strype, *Annals*, I, pp. 580–1.

proposals but to show that the European situation facing England is menacing and to list the (largely domestic) measures that should be taken to improve security.

In 1559 Cecil composed a series of memoranda on the policy to be adopted towards Scotland. While Mary was both the Dauphin's wife and Queen of Scotland in her own right, Cecil was worried about the extent of French and Catholic influence in Scotland.[27] The one which I take to be the first of these papers, dated 31 August, sets out his general ideas about Scotland.

A Memorial of certain points for restoring the Realm of Scotland to the ancient weal.
 1. The best worldly felicity that Scotland can have is either to continue in perpetual peace with England or to be made one monarchy with it.
 If the first be sought, then Scotland must not be so subject to the appointments of France as it is; which, being an ancient enemy of England, seeks always to make Scotland an instrument to exercise their malice against her. Therefore when Scotland shall come to the hands of a mere Scotsman in blood, there may be hope of some such accord, but not as long as it is at the command of the French . . .[28]

From these initial premisses, Cecil elaborates proposals for actions the nobility and the estates of Scotland could take to minimise French influence and strengthen Protestantism in Scotland. The second paper, undated but evidently closely related propounds a question about the role England should play in bringing about its aims in Scotland.

A Short Discussion of the Weighty Matter of Scotland
 1. Question: whether it be meet that England should help the nobility and Protestants of Scotland to expel the French or no?
 2. That, No. 1. It is against God's law to aid any subjects against their natural Princes or their Ministers. 2. It is dangerous, for if the aid be secret, it cannot be great enough to suffice, and if open it will procure wars. 3. It may be doubted that when money be spent and aid given, the French may compound with the Scots and join both against England . . . 4. It may be doubted that to stay the progress of religion against the See of Rome, the Emperor, the King Catholic, the Pope and potentates of Italy, and the Duke of Savoy will rather conspire with the French King than suffer these two monarchies to be joined in one religion.
 3. That, Yea. 1. It is agreeable both to the law of God and nature that every Prince and public state should defend itself, not only from perils presently seen but from dangers that be probably seen to come shortly after. 2. Nature and

---

[27] Alford discusses these memoranda, *Early Elizabethan Polity*, pp. 18–19, 59–63.
[28] *CSP Foreign 1559*, pp. 518–19. There is a text of this memorandum in British Library MS Cotton Caligula B 10, fols. 22r–24v.

reason teach every person, politic or other, to use the same manner of defence that the adversary uses in offence.

4. Upon these two principles England both may and ought to aid Scotland to keep out the French.[29]

After stating the principal question, Cecil first outlines four arguments against intervention in Scotland. These arguments are derived from scripture, the difficulty of intervening effectively, the uncertainty of success and the contrary risk of a confrontation with the united Catholic powers. In terms of the topics of deliberative oratory, the first is derived from justice (*honestum*), the remaining three from practicality (*utile*). Cecil replies only to the first, arguing that the right of self-defence (also enshrined in scripture as well as in the law of nature and everyday experience) outweighs the objection to assisting rebellious subjects, particularly since in self-defence one is entitled to use the same tactics as the enemy. These arguments form the basis for Cecil's main conclusion, that England ought to intervene in Scotland. The paper goes on to elaborate two further arguments: that England has a feudal right to defend the liberties of Scotland from oppression and that England is in danger from foreign powers (and therefore can invoke the right to self-defence).[30] Then Cecil considers whether the dangers are so far off that they can be allowed to stand. Eventually he argues that present English weakness makes action obligatory.[31]

In this paper, Cecil is not in any doubt about the position he wishes to take, but he uses the form of arguing for and against to work out the key argument around which he needs to build his case. Up to this point he has used his dialectical skill to analyse the situation. Once he has found the key point he uses dialectical invention to discover further evidence and supporting arguments. The next paper begins with a list of recent French actions intended to prove their hostility to England and concludes with a set of questions to be proposed and preparations to be undertaken.[32] The questions are:

1. What is to be done to answer the French attempts?
2. Whether aid shall be given to Scotland or no?
3. What manner of aid? Secret or open?

[29] *CSP Foreign 1559*, pp. 519–20. There is a text of this memorandum in British Library MS Cotton Caligula B 10, fols. 86r–88v. A fuller draft of the same memorandum is in the same manuscript, fols. 33r–v.
[30] *CSP Foreign 1559*, pp. 520–2.
[31] 'The French have a great advantage, pretending outwardly to keep peace, and yet under pretence of this matter of Scotland do daily send soldiers into Scotland. And England, upon colour of peace, does not so much as talk about how to be defended.' *CSP Foreign 1559*, p. 523.
[32] Ibid., pp. 523–4.

Since the questions come at the end of the papers, the most likely conclusion is that these memoranda are Cecil's preparation of questions to propose and arguments to make to the Privy Council. Once he has decided what point he needs to establish (in this case, the malice of the French) he is remarkably skilful in assembling a list of appropriate facts or incidents. Even more importantly, knowing the key argument to make helps him decide how to frame the question for debate.

In 1562 Cecil wrote a series of memoranda on the question of a possible meeting between Elizabeth and Mary, Queen of Scots.[33]

Arguments against the Queen's Majesty meeting with the Queen of Scots
1. The resolution in Counsell in May last that if things wer compounded in France by the last of June, without prejudice to the state of this realm then hir Majesty might goo.
2. The affayres in France remayne not only uncompounded but by bloodshed on both partes lykely to increass in troubles, and to contynew in cyvill warr, which so doing wer convenient both to remayn and attend the event, and rather to comfort the protestants than the Guisans who shall receave comfort by the estimation that the Queen's Majesty is in these there troubles pleased to make a iornaye to mete with the Queen there neces. And what occasions may happen for the Queen's Majesty to take avantage is uncertan, and if any should be offred, the absence of his counsayle will lese the same.
Thirdly the desyre of the Queen of Scots to mete with the Queen's Majesty is to be intended cheffly for hir owne proffett. Which by this iornaye she may make many wayes. For seing she hath pretended title to the crowne, and hath done nothyng to renounce it, but rathe differeth to confess the Queen's Majesty right in the same by pretence made against some other part of the treaty. It may be thought that by her iornaye she wil insinuat hir self to some sorte of people of this realme, to furder hir clayme, and shall geve occasion to such people as love change, and specially the papists, to confirm them in there opinion, when they shall perceave that she reteyneth still notwithstanding hir conference with the Queene the Romayn relligion.[34]

Even without these other considerations it is too late in the year to make arrangements for food, houses, clothing for attendant Lords and Ladies, and carriages.[35] These arguments are followed by a list of arguments in favour, which may be summarised as follows:

Arguments to induce the journey
1. Desire of both Queens to meet, to express their mutual affection and to establish peace in their realms.

---

[33] British Library MS Cotton Caligula B 10, fols. 209r–12v, dated 30 June 1562. For the background see Alford, *Early Elizabethan Polity*, pp. 89–96, Read, *Secretary Cecil*, pp. 235–8.
[34] British Library MS Cotton Caligula B 10, fol. 209r.   [35] Ibid., fol. 209v.

2. If Mary feels grateful she may act according to our wishes in marriage.
3. Any opportunities that arise in France can be dealt with even if the Queen is a hundred miles from London. There is a danger of provoking an unaffordable war with France if the Queens do not meet.
4. There is time before winter.[36]

This last argument is backed up by a comparison with a journey which Henry VIII made late in the year to York and with detailed estimates of the food and wine required and the time needed to procure and transport them.[37] The next sheet provides a list of reasons in favour of a meeting, which I have summarised:

Reasons for the interview
1. Ernest desire of Mary to meet; her offer of friendship and peace
2. Elizabeth's desire for peace
3. Profit to England in breaking up the alliance between France and Scotland. Opportunity to solve long-term political problem. Now that France is stronger, the revival of the Franco-Scottish alliance would be dangerous. If we neglect Mary, she will turn to the French.
4. Chance of influencing Mary's marriage plans.[38]

The final sheet of the set briefly lists reasons against the meeting as a prompt for rebuttals of those reasons. This is the full text.

Reasons agains the view
1. The Scotts request is allwaise to be suspect that it is for there gaynes
2. Furtherance of hir title.
3. Avancement of the Guisians creditt in France
4. No profitt to England
5. Comfort to papists in the realm
6. Charges to England for so long a jornaye.
7. Tyme inconvenient because of the business in France.
8. and for difficultie of provisions (victuall, wardrobe)
Replycat
1. It can not be denyed but that the desyre comming from them it ought to be suspect but yet not to be furder suspected than reason may induce. For as they may think of there commodities, so wisdom here may thynk of ours, and provyde that they may be disappoynted of that they seke preiudiciall to us and specially may be provided that during the Queen's tyme and her issue quiet may be provided.
2. as to furtherance of hir title to molest the Quene, that pretence remayneth untill the treaty may be confirmed. Whereof ther is no hope to have it performed without presence of both the pryncess for so hath the Scottish Quene differed.

---

[36] Ibid., fol. 210r.   [37] Ibid., fol. 210r–v.   [38] Ibid., fol. 211r–v.

3. as for the Guises avancement, I see not but if the Scottish Queen like of the Queene the honour is our mistress's and if the matter end not well in France for our purpose within 20 dayes it is mete to forbeare for this yere except the Scottish Quene will com nearer to London, and if it fall out well shortly in France than is there no peril for the Guise's avantage.

4. the former reasons amyty contentation of the Quene, treaty confirmed, French leage kept unknitt, religion of the Scottish Quene to be amended.

5. Good order to looke to: suspected papists, execution of the lawes

6. Order to be taken for abridgement of charges in consideration that the tyme is farr past.

   Some progress is mete for the Quene and when so ever it shalbe, chargeable it will be.

   lett such be called as have not bene at charge and such favored as have been charged.

7. the perill in France is not so great indeed as may be made to appear to show di [sic][39]

It seems most sensible to regard these as a pair of papers working towards a prepared set of arguments rather than as a single memorandum. Cecil begins by stating a range of arguments against and for the meeting. At this stage some arguments are set aside and he produces a more compelling set of reasons for the interview: it is what the Queens want, it may promote peace and it may help in breaking apart the alliance between France and Scotland. Reflection on these arguments and reconsideration of the original set leads him to produce a list of objections to arguments in favour of the meeting ('Reasons agains the view'). He then replies to each of the objections in turn ('Replicat'). Viewed in this light, the memorandum comes to resemble the pattern of an academic disputation, in which a case is outlined, objections are made and responded to in turn. But Cecil uses the format of a disputation for internal purposes, as a means of refining his position and preparing arguments against objections which might be raised. Rudolph Agricola urged students of logic always to consider the arguments against their own views, because in many controversies the strongest arguments on one side are derived from refutation of the opponent's points.[40]

Cecil's refutations depend partly on maxims of conduct (one ought not to suspect further than reason allows), partly on showing that the objection relates to an effect which is independent of (and may even be

---

[39] Ibid., fol. 212r–v. Alford mentions this group of memoranda but fails to see the conclusiveness in favour of the meeting of the final 'Replicat'. Alford, *Early Elizabethan Polity*, pp. 18, 93–4.

[40] Agricola, *De inventione dialectica*, pp. 250–1; Mack, *Renaissance Argument*, pp. 188–9, 238–9.

ameliorated by) the action proposed (objections two and six), and partly on proposing additional countermeasures (objections one and five). Some of these arguments are in turn underpinned by the making of distinctions (in the degree of suspicion required; between effects and independent circumstances) which is one of the main tactics of academic disputation.

In that he gives a reply to each of the objections Cecil appears to argue in favour of the meeting, though it should be noted that the third response leaves open the possibility of delaying the meeting until a more favourable moment. The first paper was used to raise the apparent arguments on each side; the second to focus more clearly on a position, outlining reasons and taking account of objections. But even at the end of the paper, Cecil apparently envisages a lengthy presentation in several stages.[41]

Although the model of the academic disputation is probably the most important context for these memoranda, there may also be a connection with the rhetorical doctrine of status. Cicero's *De inventione* describes a process of statement and imagined reply by which a speaker can determine the main point at issue (the status of the question). This main point is then classified as conjectural, definitional, qualitative or translative.[42] The second book of the manual outlines a series of arguments for each type of status.[43] In *De inventione dialectica*, Rudolph Agricola treats the same process of questioning and reply less as a matter of classification than as a way of determining the proposition which will decide the case and to which all the resources of topical invention must be applied. Agricola defines the status of the question as 'that which as it is proved or refuted the case must be decided on one side or the other'.[44] He explores the means of finding the status of the question by considering the arguments underlying four of Cicero's orations: *Pro Plancio, Pro Milone, Pro Cluentio*

---

[41] The alternative view, which is persuasive in some other instances, is that Cecil used the memoranda to prepare effective counter-arguments to be used only if the objections he anticipated were made in council. But we know that Cecil sometimes made long speeches introducing important pieces of business.

[42] If the accuser says, 'you murdered Clytemnestra', Orestes might reply (a) 'no, I did not', in which case the dispute turns on the issue of fact (*conjectural*); (b) 'I killed her, but it was not murder', in which case the question of *definition* is crucial; (c) 'I murdered her, but it was in self-defence', where the case hinges on the quality of the action; or (d) 'this tribunal has no jurisdiction', in which case the arguments turn on legal and jurisdictional issues (*translative*). Cicero, *De inventione*, 1.8.10–12.16; Lucia Calboli Montefusco, *La dottrina degli status nella retorica greca e romana* (Hildesheim, 1986).

[43] Cicero, *De inventione*, 11.2.12–30.94.

[44] Agricola, *De inventione dialectica*, p. 241: 'Status enim quaestionis id est, quo vel probato, vel confutato, in hanc vel illam partem de quaestione pronunciari oportet.'

and *In Verrem*.[45] Like Agricola, Cecil uses the alternation of arguments to decide which propositions need to be furnished with arguments. Unlike the classical teachers of status theory Cecil devises arguments for a range of propositions rather than attempting to identify a single key issue to which to devote all the argumentative force at his disposal.

In 1578, at the age of forty-five, Queen Elizabeth received a proposal of marriage from the Duc d'Alençon which has left a considerable trail of memoranda in the archives. After Simier's embassy early in the year, on 27 March 1579 Lord Burghley wrote a two-part memorandum on the question of the marriage.[46] The form is rather similar to that of the second memorandum on the meeting of the Queens in that it consists of a brief statement of the reasons in favour of marriage, followed by a developed list of objections and (in the second part) a series of replies to those objections. The arrangement is more complex, though, in that the arguments are divided into objections from the person of the Queen and objections from the realm. The memorandum discusses a range of different problems: she might have no children, or die in childbirth, or have a son who was heir to England and France; Alençon might be unpleasing to the Queen, expensive, unpopular on grounds of race or religion, or he might agitate on behalf of the Catholics. The key problems that emerge are the question of the Queen's age, to which Burghley gives the answer that he believes her still fertile, and the difficulty of Alençon's religion. Burghley concludes that the Queen's judgment should be relied on. This paper probably assisted in the preparation of the long wide-ranging oration he made to the Privy Council on the topic in April.[47] This oration concentrated on the problems to be faced, and the remedies available, should the marriage not take place. Burghley forced his opponents to face the difficulties which rejection of the marriage would cause by putting them in the position of having to find other solutions to the problems confronting the country.

The Queen insisted on a preliminary visit from Alençon, which took place amid some secrecy in August. Early in October a small group of privy councillors who had been chosen as commissioners for the marriage held a series of meetings, for which Lord Burghley composed several memoranda. For the meeting on 2 October he prepared an agenda

---

[45] Ibid., pp. 241–2. Mack, *Renaissance Argument*, pp. 185–7.

[46] Read, *Lord Burghley*, pp. 208–11; Cecil Papers 148/23, listed at Historical Manuscripts Commission, *Calendar of Salisbury Manuscripts*, II (London, 1888), nos. 710, 711, p. 238. See also Susan Doran, *Monarchy and Matrimony: The Courtships of Elizabeth I* (London, 1996), pp. 156–76.

[47] *Calendar of Salisbury Manuscripts*, II, no. 723, pp. 249–52.

proposing five questions as part of a lengthy paper outlining arguments related to the first four. The questions clearly derive from the memoranda he composed in March.

An Order how to proceed to the Discussion of the Questions moved concerning the Quene's Mariadge with Monsieur d'Anjow, 2 October 1579.
1. To consider what Dangers are to be probably dowted that may follow to hir Majesty's Person, to hir Government, and to the State of the Realme in generall, if she shall not marry.
2. To consider how these Dangers may be removed, or withstode, though hir Majesty do not marry, and to consider how every Danger may have his proper Remedy.
3. To consider what Dangers may follow probably to her Majesty's Person, to her Government, and to the State of the Realme, if she shall marry.
4. To consider what Profitts or Benefitts may follow to hir Majesty and to the Realm by this hir Mariadg.
5. To compare together all the Dangers, as well those that may follow by hir not mariadg, and for lack of Provision of sufficient Remedyes, as also of those that shall follow probably by the Mariadg, and to see by Probabilities what are the grettar, that they may be most shuned, and the lesser admitted.
    Finally, if it shall appeare that the Mariadge shall seme to be accompannyed with the smallar Perrills, then to consider in what Order, and with what Cautions and Provisions the same is to be pursued.[48]

In his responses to the questions which he raises under 1, Burghley casts his net very wide, permitting himself, under 2, a complete review of foreign policy and suggestions for reforms of government finance. By putting the marriage within the context of the other problems facing the régime, he aims to make it more difficult for his opponents to reject the marriage as an unnecessary innovation. He puts the onus on them to provide better remedies to the dangerous international context. By reviewing foreign policy as a whole he can use his unrivalled command of all aspects of government policy to imply that his opponents lack plausible alternatives and to establish a position of authority from which to strengthen his support for the marriage proposal. His order of questions allows him to remind the commissioners that the Privy Council and parliament as a whole have often in the past urged the Queen to marry. He places the advantages of the marriage last, after all the problems have been disposed of, in order that they make the strongest impact.
    Once he reaches the dangers of the marriage he subdivides, with four arguments concerning the Queen's person (e.g. danger to her life in

---

[48] Murdin, *Collection of State Papers*, pp. 322–3.

childbirth, danger that she will be discontented with her husband) and three concerning the person of Alençon, now also Duke of Anjou (his religion, danger that he will outlive the Queen, danger that a son will be heir to both kingdoms). In the same way he divides the benefits into personal benefits for the Queen and public advantages for the country. He is also anxious to emphasise that all the arguments made concern probabilities, as if he wishes to avoid the response (the normal Elizabethan response, it has to be said) that since the matter is doubtful it is better to take no action. This memorandum serves as an agenda for the meeting but it also provides Burghley with the arguments to persuade his fellow commissioners to support the marriage. He makes considerable use of proverbs and historical reviews to support his arguments. But his conclusion is surprisingly moderate, as though he well understood the difficulty which he would have in securing support for marriage with a French Catholic.

And yet to conclude, ther is no Benefitt such by this Mariadg, but except ther be also Provisions accorded and wisely established to withstand certen apparent Perrills, no wise Man can make the Mariadg beneficiall; but being provyded for as far forth as comonly the Wisdom of Man can devise, the Event is to be left to God, according to the trew old Sentence, *Quod homo proponit, Deus disponit*; and therefor in such difficult matters, Intercession is to be made to God, the Director of Princes Harts, to direct hir to that, which shall be most for hir Honor, hir Comfort, and the Weale of hir Subjects.[49]

Burghley reassures his colleagues that provisions can be made to reduce the dangers and he appeals to their religious sensibilities by urging them to leave the final decision in such a complex matter to God. His fellow commissioners may have felt that the problem lay in allowing the Queen to declare the direction in which God moved her. Since the matter could not be resolved on 2 October, the commissioners met again on 4 October and the whole active Privy Council, in effect, considered it on 6 October.[50] For the meeting of 6 October we have Burghley's tabulation of the arguments for and against (presumably for his own use in the course of the meeting), his summaries of the speeches of the other councillors and his draft of an agreed final document prepared for the meeting with the Queen on 7 October. Burghley's summary follows a similar overall plan to his memorandum of 2 October but it goes further in acknowledging the shortage of political remedies for the problems inherent in the marriage (see Table 1).

---

[49] Ibid., p. 331.   [50] Read, *Lord Burghley*, pp. 217–18.

Table 1. *Concerning the Treaty with the Duke of Anjou, 6 October 1579*

Perils	*Remedies*
Comfort of Titlers and Favorers of the Quene of Scots.	Laws to be more sharp against Favourers of Titles.
Comfort of Obstinat Papists, Rebells.	Penalties increased upon Recusants.
Comfort to the Pope to follow.	To keep Papists under.
Revenge by Spayne and France.	To norish their Troubles.
King of Scots his Marriage.	To retayne him in Frendship by Ayde and to compass his Marriage.
Discomfort of her Majesty by Doubt of Mislyking.	None but Evil, if with Mislyke.
Ennimity of the Duke of Anjou.	The Mislyke of his Greatness, the Cause.
Marriage with the Spanish Daughter.	
Burden to the Realm to continuall Defences.	
Money, Men, Armor, Shipps	The Realm is welthy, and good People will ayd. In Parliament, if the Marriage be mislyked, Ayd will be given.
Dangers by the Marriage	*Remedies*
Doubtfullness of issue.	[both] In Gods Hands.
Danger in Childbearing.	
Contrariety of Religion.	To be by Articles help'd.
His Youth unequal to the Queen.	The Quenes good Constitution that may outlive hym.
The great misliking of Strangers.	So did they mislyke the King of Spayne.
His Nearness to the Crown of France.	That is in God's hand.
The Inconvenience of joining the two crowns.	This cannot be removed, but in Edward III's Days was born withall.[51]

Although Burghley's heading does not make this clear, the first half of the table lists dangers and remedies should the Queen not marry. Among them Burghley notes the Queen's anger and the enmity of Anjou, neither of which can be remedied without the marriage. It may be that he gives additional prominence to moves to counter Catholic influence in order to win favour with his audience. He would not wish to let his opponents imply that rejection of the marriage would remove all the dangers posed by Catholicism. The emphasis on objections and replies in this memorandum suggests that Burghley intends it to help him refute the arguments of his opponents. Within this structure Burghley finds no place for the advantages of the marriage (for example in relation to the succession), which he would undoubtedly have wished to assert at some point in the debate. His preparations reflect his awareness of the

---

[51] Murdin, *Collection of State Papers*, p. 331.

difficulty of persuading the council to support the marriage. Sir Walter Mildmay, Burghley's main adversary in the debate, had in August 1575 himself prepared a memorandum of arguments in favour of the marriage together with replies to each of them.[52]

Burghley's notes on the debate focus on Sir Walter Mildmay's speech, on which he took twenty-five lines of notes, most lines recording separate points. Burghley's notes, probably following Mildmay's partition of his speech, divide the arguments between 'marriage in general', which largely relates to the danger of pregnancy at the Queen's age and the likelihood of long life without it, and 'marriage in particular', which concern the problems raised by Alençon. These are divided into religion and family. Under religion Mildmay notes that Alençon is 'Adversary to the Quene's Religion', that he has twice taken part in battles against Protestants, and that if the Mass is tolerated at court it will be difficult to persecute it elsewhere. Under family he notes the risk that Alençon will inherit the French crown, reside in France and bring up his heirs as Frenchmen. Finally he argues that Burghley's confidence in articles of agreement is misplaced.

No Bonds, no Acts of Parliament will serve,
If Monsieur should draw the Queen into Wars for the Low Countries.
King Philip brought Queen Mary into Wars contrary to the Acts of Parliament.
Conscience will not bind. Non est Fides servanda Hereticis. No caution will serve.[53]

Six other contributions to the debate are recorded (with a majority against the marriage) but most of the subsequent speakers echo points which Burghley or Mildmay had previously made. Burghley's next memorandum, summarising from his notes the arguments made in the debate, analyses Mildmay's objections under five headings (hostility to the French, risk of inheriting French throne, risk of his heir uniting kingdoms, danger that the Queen will have no children or will die in childbed, dangers of Alençon's religion). Then he provides answers to each of these arguments in turn, very much in the manner of the university disputation.[54] Next he outlines five advantages of the marriage (parliament has urged it, prospect of an heir, foreign policy alliances, continuation of the royal line, removal of rival claimants). He claims that the dangers if the Queen dies without issue are certain, whereas those associated with her marriage are

---

[52] Northamptonshire Record Office, Fitzwilliam of Milton Papers, 111, fols. 8–18; S. E. Lehmberg, *Sir Walter Mildmay and Tudor Government* (Austin, 1964), pp. 157–64.
[53] Murdin, *Collection of State Papers*, p. 332.
[54] Ibid., pp. 333–4.

merely contingent 'and therfore may as probably follow as not follow'. Finally he claims that those who oppose the marriage underestimate the perils facing the country, while those who favour it hope to reduce the risks it entails by making agreements imposing conditions.[55] However much Burghley thought his arguments the stronger, the lukewarm support which the council gave the marriage, leaving it to the Queen's own decision, fell far short of what he had been expected to achieve.[56] He must have known that for many of his colleagues the risks attached to the Queen's marriage to a Catholic outweighed the (now reduced) possibility that an heir might resolve the problem of the succession. His task was to make the strongest possible arguments to diminish their conviction of the risk and to amplify the importance of the counterbalancing problems which the marriage might solve.

In form, Burghley's memoranda may be divided into three classes: lists of actions or conclusions, tables (or paired lists) in which perils are set against remedies, and three-part arguments, setting out reasons in favour of a course of action, objections to it and replies to objections. I have suggested that this last form, which is often the final form of a series of memoranda, is related to university practices of disputation.

If my interpretations are correct, Burghley sometimes uses memoranda to determine which arguments look most promising, where further evidence needs to be found and how to formulate questions for debate. Several of the memoranda appear to be preparations for meetings: listing responses to arguments he expects to encounter and setting out ways of presenting his own arguments most effectively and weakening the positions of his opponents. Characteristically the memoranda begin with large general issues.[57] Often they conclude with very detailed administrative arrangements (as when Cecil works out how many wagons would be needed to assemble provisions for a meeting of the Queens in Nottingham).[58]

Most of the supporting arguments and evidence which Cecil adduces arise from the political circumstances of each question, but he also employs proverbs and historical arguments. In a paper of September 1565 debating possible intervention in Scotland, he included the maxim that it is better to begin wars when the enemy is at a distance.[59]

---

[55] Ibid., pp. 334–5.   [56] Read, *Lord Burghley*, pp. 220–1.

[57] Some memoranda remain at a very general level, as in Cecil's list of moral arguments for and against Mary, Queen of Scots, 20 June 1568, British Library MS Cotton Caligula C 1, fols. 139r–40r. Alford, *Early Elizabethan Polity*, p. 165.

[58] British Library MS Cotton Caligula B 10, fol. 210v.

[59] Ibid., fol. 351r. Alford, *Early Elizabethan Polity*, p. 19.

He frequently uses arguments from expediency against moral reasons and on one occasion uses the distinction between certain and probable consequences to support his line. He is careful to distinguish between questions put and between perils and remedies. The memoranda tend to compare lists of arguments rather than attempting to focus on the key question in dispute. Indeed it may be a weakness of Cecil's method that it gives greater prominence to the number of arguments on each side than to their relative strength.

ARGUMENT WITHIN THE PRIVY COUNCIL

The Privy Council usually met at least every other day and transacted a wide range of business. The Queen did not take part in meetings but summaries of the council's views and recommendations on important issues were presented to her (usually by Cecil alone but occasionally accompanied by other councillors) for her approval.[60] Arguments in the Privy Council could determine policy provided they achieved a large measure of support and were not opposed to the Queen's private convictions. Cecil's memoranda show how carefully he prepared the order of debate of major issues and the arguments to be presented to the Privy Council. They also seem to indicate that, although in chairing the council he had considerable power to regulate debate and to respond to objections, everyone had the right to be heard and a majority view could be sustained against him.

Summaries of the arguments made in Privy Council meetings survive both in Cecil's hand and in that of his clerk Bernard Hampton.[61] Presumably these were intended either as aides-mémoire for Cecil or for direct presentation to the Queen. In June 1565 arguments made in a debate about the marriage of Mary, Queen of Scots to Lord Darnley, were collected under two broad headings:

1. First, what perills might ensue to the Queene's Majesty or this Realme of the mariadg betwixt the Queen of Scotts and the Lord Darnly.
2. Secondly, what were meet to be don to avoyde or remedy the same.[62]

Some councillors saw the perils as contributing to a general weakening of Elizabeth's government by raising the prospect of a rival succession

[60] Read, *Secretary Cecil*, pp. 119–22; Alford, *Early Elizabethan Polity*, pp. 9–14.
[61] E.g. Alford, *Early Elizabethan Polity*, p. 127, note 32.
[62] British Library MS Cotton Caligula B 10, fol. 301r.

and by encouraging Roman Catholics.[63] For others the threat was much more immediate: the aim of the marriage was to place Mary on the throne of England and to re-establish Roman Catholicism as the national religion.[64] Some supporting arguments for the second view are listed, based on the maxims 'that always the intention and will of any person is most manifest when their power is greatest' and 'foreyn powers never prevayled in this realme but with the help of some at home'.[65] In the course of discussion the dangers were 'made so apparent by many sure arguments as no one of the counsel could deny them to be but many and very dangerous'.[66]

Proposed remedies are digested under three headings: first, on which all were agreed, that the Queen should marry; second, that reformed religion should be established more firmly and Catholicism weakened; and third that Mary's marriage should be prevented or its disadvantages reduced.[67] Then follow many detailed proposals for improving religious uniformity, for penalties on Catholics at home and abroad, and for military preparations. Reservations of some members of the council about going beyond threats to actual military intervention are noted.[68] Finally the council urges the Queen to choose between these proposed measures

and to putt them in execucion *in deedes and not to passe them over in consultations and speeches* for it is to be assured that hir adversaries will use all meanes to putt their intention in execution, some by practise, some by force, whom time shall serve. And no tyme can serve so well the Queen's Majesty to interrupt these perills as now at the first before the Queen of Scots purposes be fully satled.[69]

This document records the main arguments and proposals put and the degree of support which they received, both as a summary of the deliberations of the council and in order to persuade the Queen to take action.

Records of speeches prepared for the Privy Council suggest that, at least on important issues, members of the council might expect to make lengthy and elaborate speeches. Bacon's speech to the council in 1559 takes up eighteen sides of one of his manuscript collections.[70] After a conventionally modest opening, a statement of the question being debated and a reminder of the opinions of previous speakers, Bacon states his own view on the question of whether military aid should be given to the Scottish Protestant nobles in order to expel French soldiers.

---

[63] Members of the council are listed as a group at the head of the document but are not named in connection with particular arguments.
[64] British Library MS Cotton Caligula B 10, fols. 301r–302r.   [65] Ibid., fols. 302r, 303r.
[66] Ibid., fol. 303v.   [67] Ibid., fols. 303v–304r.   [68] Ibid., fol. 307v.
[69] Ibid., fol. 308r, underlinings in manuscript.   [70] British Library MS Harley 398, fols. 12v–21r.

Now in my opinion neither is it necessary that assistaunce be openly and presently granted them nor yet utterly denyed to them, but raither that they be fedd and fooded with fourther answers and doings full of good hope, whereby both present wars and hostilities with France may be differred to be begun and inferred by us and also the succours and other commodities that may growe by the frendshippe of the Scotts to us may be conserved and contynued. The reasons that move me to refuse openly and presently to ayde them be these: first you ought not presently and openly unforced to assist them except they be able presently and openly to maintain warre with France which necessarily followeth of it. But you are not able presentlie and openlye so to doe.[71]

He develops the argument for caution mainly by elaborating the weakness of the English position and the desirability of postponing a confrontation with the French.[72] These practical considerations are supported with the moral objection to assisting subjects to resist their prince. But this does not prevent Bacon from suggesting that the Scottish nobles should be helped secretly so as to prolong their resistance until such a time as England is strong enough to enter into open hostilities. A letter which Bacon wrote to the Queen on 20 November 1579 in place of the speech about the perils facing the realm he intended to deliver to the council, provides an elaborate and balanced portrait of three great enemies (France, Spain and Rome), amplified with a personification of the topics of deliberative oratory, but his proposals for action are comparatively perfunctory (pay pensions to the Scots to pre-empt the French, vex the Spanish by supporting the Prince of Orange and increase penalties against Roman Catholics).[73] In general Bacon's Privy Council speeches appear to have been more elaborately structured and rhetorically ornamented but less substantial than Cecil's.

Sir Walter Mildmay's style of Privy Council oratory was more dialectical than Bacon's. His 1584 speech on the assistance to be given to the Dutch is dominated by his outline of the question being debated and the headings of his analysis.

The matter brought in deliberacion is
    Whether the Queen's Majesty should enter with forces into Holland and Zealand to give aid to those provinces agaynst the King of Spain or no.

---

[71] Ibid., fol. 12v.
[72] This speech forms part of the same sequence of conciliar debate as Cecil's 1559 memoranda quoted above. The debate is discussed in Read, *Secretary Cecil*, pp. 159–60 and Alford, *Early Elizabethan Polity*, pp. 66–9. Alford concludes that Bacon used the same basic assumptions as Cecil to reach different conclusions (p. 68). The difference lies in the commonplaces. Cecil selects commonplaces of resolution and pre-empting future risks; Bacon of financial and military weakness. British Library MS Harley 398, fols. 12v–21r.
[73] Strype, *Annals*, II, appendix, pp. 109–11.

Whereupon theis thinges are meete to be considered:
1. First, whether the enterprise be just
2. Next, for whom it shall be taken in hand
3. Thirdly, against whom
4. And last, what is like to follow.[74]

Mildmay's approach here resembles the grammar school mnemonic for commenting on a passage of text (for whom, against whom, what will follow) except that he opens with the moral issue. The justice of the enterprise will turn either on title to the country (which the Queen does not pretend to have) or cause of offence given. Mildmay argues that any resentment the English might have cause to feel against Spanish support of rebels in England and Ireland is at least equalled by Spanish anger at previous English interventions in the Low Countries.[75] Furthermore to support the Dutch would be to support subjects against their monarch.[76] Mildmay's apparently routine second heading on the people on whose behalf action would be taken leads to an attack on the inconstancy, ingratitude and unreliability of the Dutch.[77] This is contrasted with the power of the King of Spain and his ability to hurt English interests.

And therefore how hard yt shalbe for her Majesty to go through with this enterprise and to defend her owne if the King of Spayne invade her is meete to be thought on.

And thereunto the great exceeding charges that must needs grow by reason of this warr besides the perill of the success, for as it is said *Dubius belli eventus.*[78]

His financial responsibilities outweighing his Protestant commitments, Mildmay concludes that the war in the Netherlands would be too difficult, too dangerous and too expensive. Instead he urges the council to make a peace treaty with Scotland, in order to secure the northern border and the establishment of Protestantism in both countries. This last point enables him to give at least a veneer of religious principle to his advice to keep England's treasure for its own defence.[79]

The habit of restating and responding to earlier speeches, the clarity of structure and the deployment of supporting arguments reflect councillors' shared training in logic and experience of academic disputation. Competence in these skills was a requirement for effective participation and for being heard. But these shared skills could be employed to support

---

[74] British Library MS Sloane 326, fol. 88r. See Lehmberg, *Sir Walter Mildmay*, pp. 267–70.
[75] British Library MS Sloane 326, fol. 88v.   [76] Ibid., fol. 89r.   [77] Ibid., fol. 89r–v.
[78] Ibid., fol. 91v. Compare 'Belli exitus incertus... Dubius rerum eventus', Culmann, *Sententiae pueriles*, sig. A3r–v.
[79] British Library MS Sloane 326, fols. 93r–94r.

different positions in relation to a war or a royal marriage. Those who deployed them best and who had the best understanding of the political situation and their colleagues' values had the best chance of seeing their views represented in the council's submission to the Queen.

ESSEX'S *APOLOGY*

An Apology of the Earl of Essex, a long letter addressed to Anthony Bacon, is a public document which reflects an argument within the Privy Council. It may even be an expanded version of one of Essex's speeches. Between the summer of 1597 and June 1598, while Henry IV was negotiating the peace of Vervins with the Spanish, various attempts were made to draw England, formerly France's ally against Spain, into a comprehensive peace agreement. Neither Burghley nor the Queen relished being isolated by a peace between France and Spain, but both recognised that England could only make peace on terms which preserved the effective independence of the United Provinces of the Netherlands. The Queen was willing to exert force on the Dutch to make them take part, but Essex opposed negotiations with the Spanish and was branded a war-monger by Burghley.[80] Essex's *Apology* combines criticism of proposals of peace with Spain with a robust defence of his own conduct. Composed before Essex's public quarrel with the Queen in June 1598, it was made public by May 1599, probably to demonstrate his patriotism and political skill in the face of his weakening position. There was an edition in 1600 (STC 6787.7) which Essex tried to suppress. It was eventually printed and circulated in 1603 (STC 6788) after Elizabeth's death, with a rather sad letter from Essex's sister to the Queen, which must have been written shortly before her brother's execution in 1601.

The *Apology* is organised as a sequence of six argued propositions: that Essex prefers peace to war; that the particular charges against him which lead to the accusation that he generally favours war are unjustified; that Spanish offers of peace are to be suspected; that no peace can solve the problem of the Netherlands; that England is well placed to make war on Spain; and that the circumstances are wrong for making peace. All these arguments serve either to defend his reputation or to undermine the peace proposal but Essex provides transitions from one to the next (usually arguing that even if what he has just shown were impossible

---

[80] Read, *Lord Burghley*, pp. 537–45; Wallace MacCaffrey, *War and Politics 1588–1603* (Princeton, 1991), p. 214–16, 515–16; Penry Williams, *The Later Tudors* (Oxford, 1995), p. 364.

could be achieved, still it would fail for another reason) rather than attempting to build them into a single over-arching argument. Under each of these chief propositions, though, his arguments are carefully co-ordinated and subdivided. In defending his own conduct, for example, he lists six arguments made by his opponents.

> I have thought good to answer some objections of my detractors who will say mine entering into the action of the lowe countreyes, ere I was out of pupill age, my putting myself into the journey of Portugall without chardge or licence, my procuring my selfe the conducting of her Maiesties succours to the Frenche king in the year 91, my sea journeies these twoo last sommers, wherein booth my selfe and my friendes ventured deepely of our owne private meanes, my neare friendshippe with the chiefe menne of action and generall affection to the men of warre of our nation, and lastly my opposing myself against the treatie of peace at this time when others perswade unto it: that all these say are arguments that I wish not peace but delight in warre.[81]

For the next ten pages he explains his reasons for each of these actions, usually making several defensive arguments against his opponents' interpretations of each of them. This manner of opening also gives him the opportunity to display his personal involvement in military actions on behalf of his country. Within subdivisions some of his arguments are organised through the topics of invention. Thus in explaining his reasons for undertaking the campaign in Portugal he adduces the circumstances according to person, enemies, cause and time.[82] In his argument that the circumstances are wrong for peace, he considers the issue under the headings of time, persons, assurance and circumstances of breakdown.

> The materiall circumstances which any prince or state should weigh before they enter into treatie, I judge to be these: the time of treating, whether it yeald most advantage for peace or warre; the persons of the treators, whether or no the enemy with whom we treate may make advantage by pretence if nothing be concluded. The assurance of the treatie, or strength of the knotte which is tyed, and the state and condition wee are like to be in whensoever it breakes and dissolves.[83]

Essex debates these headings, which are so general that they might almost be taken from a lesson on the topics of deliberative oratory, for the last three pages of the *Apology*. Essex uses the established forms of argumentation. One of his principal propositions is established through

---

[81] Essex, *Apology* (London, 1603) STC 6788, fol. A2v. [82] Ibid., fols. A2v–3r.
[83] Ibid., fol. D4r. This may be connected with the emphasis in demonstrative oratory on persons, places and times, e.g. Melanchthon, *Institutiones rhetoricae*, sig. A4v.

induction. Peace can be sought for three purposes, utility (that is, to obtain advantage), convenience (to preserve what they have) and necessity.[84] Since peace with England is neither convenient nor necessary for Spain (for reasons which he adduces), and since his opponents will not allow that Spain could gain an advantage from peace, Essex argues that there will be no peace with Spain.[85] He seeks to establish the universal negative by showing that each of the subordinate propositions has a negative result. He constructs a dilemma to prove that even if peace were to be made, the issue of the Netherlands would make it untenable for England.

But if I allow our peacemakers their assurance of peace, let me see what is their purchase. If they can make any peace with Spaine good for us, it must be by including our confederates in the low countries or excluding them, but I suspect neyther of these can be good or safe for us, therefore I iudge they can make no good peace at all.[86]

The Low Countries can only be included in a peace if they acknowledge the King of Spain, whch they will never do because it will mean the end of their political and religious liberty. No conditions that can be made could guarantee them against such enslavement, 'so that I conclude it were both folly and impietie for them to make any such peace, or for us to drawe them to it'.[87]

Now let us consider how good it may be if we abandon them. I have ever thought that such a peace might bee good for us, if they that persuade unto it can prove three thinges. First that they of the lowe Countries will have both will and strength to maintaine the warre, though we make peace and forsake them. Secondly, so we leave them wee may have good conditions for ourselves. And thirdly, that as our affaires nowe stand a neutralitie can be possible kept by us, while the united provinces and the enemie are in warre.[88]

Essex then denies that any of these conditions can be met. Although the Dutch have the will to resist, without English support they will be conquered. Spanish conditions will be impossible for us, while conditions we devise will be easily broken. Since without help the Dutch would be conquered and since helping them would give the Spanish justification for war, English neutrality is impossible. Both sides of the dilemma lead to the impossibility of peace.

---

[84] These terms may be derived from the topics of deliberative oratory: advantage, necessity and safety. Melanchthon, *Institutiones rhetoricae*, sig. B2v; Wilson, *Rhetoric*, p. 71.
[85] Essex, *Apology*, fols. C1r–2r.   [86] Ibid., fol. C2r.
[87] Ibid., fols. C2r–3r.   [88] Ibid., fol. C3v.

Alongside the strong dialectical structuring of the speech, Essex from time to time uses the technical terminology of dialectic to underpin his argument. Near the beginning of the work he draws on the distinction between thesis, a general principle, and hypothesis, the application of that principle to particular circumstances.[89] He attacks his opponents' argument that Spain wants peace by criticising their syllogism. They have proved, not that Spain wants peace but that it wants to talk about peace.[90] Overt reference to and employment of dialectic helps Essex project himself as a prudent and educated counsellor, trading reasons in a form of disputation, rather than hotheadedly promoting religious war.[91]

Essex makes use of rhetorical techniques at key moments of his argument. In his opening protestation that he prefers peace to war he develops a commonplace of the ills of war and the benefits of peace, beginning with his personal experience.

And nowe if time, reason and experience have taught me to wish that to myself which is best for myself, what would I not wish rather than martial imploiements, in which I have impaired my estate, lost my dear and only brother, the halfe arch of mine house, buried many of my dearest and nearest friendes, and subiected myselfe to the rage of the seas, violence of tempestes, infections of generall plagues, famines and all kinde of wantes, discontentment of undisciplined and unruly multitudes and acceptations of events . . . So I have ever thought wars the diseases and sicknesses, and peace the true naturall and healthfull temper for all estates. I have thought excellent mindes should come to the wars as surgions do to their cures, when no easie or ordinary, yea no other remedie will serve.[92]

This passage also gives Essex the opportunity to contrast his own sufferings through war with the machinations of his enemies in council who make themselves into judges of his conduct. Late in the *Apology* while attacking the view that a bad peace is better than any form of war, he uses comparisons, anaphora and epithet to amplify the implied affront to the nation and its soldiers.

But iniurious are these to the men of warre that fight for them and defend them, in thinking our armes which have ever done honour to our countrey, stricken

[89] 'These principles having made me conclude this generall *thesis* common to all states, that *peace is to be preferred before warre*, I will come to an *hipothesis* proper to the state of England, wher most part of the wealth of the land and revenewes of the crowne growe by traffique and intercourse, and whereas almost all traffique is interrupted by the warres.' Ibid., fols. A1v–2r.
[90] 'Allow this for a good *syllogisme* and you may put to schoole all the *logicians* in Christendome' (original italics). Ibid., fol. B3v.
[91] Paul Hammer, *The Polarisation of Elizabethan Politics* (Cambridge, 1999) argues that Essex deserves to be regarded as a serious politician (pp. 5–8, 395–404).
[92] Essex, *Apology*, fol. A1v.

terrour to the heartes of our enemies, lesse able to defend our country then their treaties which have never beene free from scorne and disadvantage. Iniurious are they to the countrey which bredde them, which being one of the bravest strongest and happiest states of Christendome, is iudged by these men as weak as their owne weake hearts. Iniurious they are to her Maiestie who hath ruled them, who being so great, so glorious, so victorious a Queene, shall be iudged unable to maintaine warre, when she cannot have peace but at the pleasure of her enemie. Iniurious and most unthankfull to God himselfe are they that hitherto fought for them, in that for an unsafe peace with an Idolatrous and irreligious nation they would leave an honourable and iust warre: when they have done all that they can, if the enemie will not conclude peace, we must have warre.[93]

This leads directly into an enumeration of the reasons England is strong enough to fight a war. He makes a series of comparisons with ancient and biblical examples, concluding with the rhetorical question that if luxuries of various kinds can be afforded, can England not rather afford to defend its liberty?[94] Although amplification and stylistic elaboration is appropriate as the work draws to a close, it also runs the risk of abandoning the persona of the logical statesman which Essex has constructed throughout the work in favour of the enthusiastic and jingoistic proponent of war, which his enemies accuse him of being. Essex finds powerful arguments for Spanish strength, when he wishes to prove that they have no need of peace, and for their weakness, when he argues that this is the time to pursue the war.[95] This emotional passage is placed firmly within his penultimate argument and is not treated as a classical rhetorical peroration.

   Most of Essex's arguments are drawn from the contemporary political and strategic situation, for example Spanish intentions as revealed by secret intelligence, the importance of Flushing and Brill for attacks on England or the Netherlands, expectations of tax revenue and the Spanish financial position. He also makes an apparently detailed calculation of the resources available to continue the war.[96] Especially at the beginning of the *Apology* he makes several arguments through comparisons.[97] Like most of the writers I have discussed, Essex uses Latin maxims of statecraft to strengthen key passages of the speech.[98]

---

[93] Ibid., fol. D2v.   [94] Ibid., fol. D3r–v.   [95] Ibid., fols. C1v, D4r–v.   [96] Ibid., fols. D1v–4v.
[97] Ibid., fols. A1r (face in the mirror), A1v (surgeons), A2r (physician), C3r (effect of poison).
[98] Ibid., fols. A4r ('vana sine viribus ira', Livy, 1.10.4), E1v ('Iustissimum iis bellum, quibus necessarium, copia arma, quibus nulla nisi in armis spes est', compare Livy IX.1.10). Essex's use of maxims from Livy may be connected with the predelictions of his secretary Henry Cuffe. James, *Society, Politics and Culture*, p. 437.

DIALECTIC AND RHETORIC IN POLITICAL ARGUMENT

Diplomatic letters, political memoranda and Privy Council debates demonstrate the importance of logical argument in Elizabethan political discussion. Council decisions about diplomatic instructions or about proposals to be put to the Queen were reached through sifting of written evidence and through spoken argument among privy councillors. Envoys used dialectical skills to interpret events at foreign courts and to present policy options to the council. Cecil and Mildmay employed topical invention and criticism of stated arguments to determine the most effective way to conduct their cases in council. Essex and Cecil made long, logically organised speeches in order to present themselves as prudent and knowledgeable politicians whose views deserved to be heard.

Much of Elizabethan political decision-making was a matter of balancing conviction against expediency. Did, for example, the religious motive to assist the Protestants in the Netherlands justify the expense involved and the risk of provoking a European war? Did the constitutional need for a legitimate Protestant heir to the throne outweigh the disadvantages of a Catholic consort? Making arguments for one policy or the other in the light of conflicting principles is the task of practical reasoning, rhetoric and dialectic. Dialectical training provided the means for speakers to connect large principles with particular policies and actions. Rhetoric taught politicians how to enlarge the apparent threat or promise of one side of the argument and diminish the other.

The initial question addressed is of crucial importance in political argument. Cecil rehearsed his and his opponents' arguments in the light of his aims in order to arrive at a formulation and an ordering of questions for debate in the Privy Council. Diplomats used questions as a structure for presenting and understanding facts; in Winwood's letter to change the question was to change the significance of events. This emphasis on identifying and formulating the question to be debated may be connected to Agricola's instructions for generating and choosing between a range of possible questions before applying topical invention.[99] Agricola's discussion of dialectical reading insists that an understanding of the question being debated is an essential prerequisite for reconstructing the underlying argumentative structure of a text.[100]

---

[99] Agricola, *De inventione dialectica*, pp. 247–52; Mack, *Renaissance Argument*, p. 188.
[100] Agricola, *De inventione dialectica*, pp. 358–62; Mack, *Renaissance Argument*, pp. 227–33. See discussion in chapter two above pp. 73–4.

Once the proposition has been stated, events, statements and arguments can be brought to bear on it through topical invention. Wilson lists
indications on either side of the proposition that a peace will be made in
order to show that peace is possible but not certain, and in order to make
a distinction between talk of peace and the actions required to bring it
about. Propositions connecting supporting arguments to conclusions are
generally left implicit, though Essex on occasion uses the technical vocabulary of argumentation to attack his opponents' arguments. After stating
his questions Cecil sets out arguments for and against each proposition.
Then he adds replies to each argument on both sides. This process of
stating an argument and then replying to it is learned from experience of
academic disputation. Disputation encourages students to make distinctions, to find counter-examples which weaken assumptions and to point
out mistakes in the formulation of arguments. Essex uses these devices to
justify his hostility to peace with Spain and to project his image as a prudent advisor. Cecil uses the techniques and tactics of disputation to prepare himself for speeches and meetings and to work out where he needs
to discover further arguments. The exercise of arguing on both sides enables him to discover the strengths and weaknesses of his own position.

Logic helps organise political argument. Mildmay and Nicholas Bacon
state the main points they will argue at the beginning of their speeches.
Essex divided his *Apology* into six propositions, each of which he then argued through a sequence of supporting propositions. Essex and Winwood
use the topics of invention to classify supporting arguments they have discovered. Cecil subdivides arguments according to different persons and
different effects. His explorations of arguments on both sides of a case
helped him determine the most advantageous order for debating questions. Agricola had discussed the arrangement of questions in *De inventione
dialectica*.[101]

Among rhetorical techniques, letters and Privy Council speeches employ amplification, and commonplaces in praise of peace and in fear of
war. Cornwallis used comparisons to enable the Privy Council to reverse
their view of Spanish perceptions of British actions. Anecdotes from
ancient history are often retold to dignify a proposed course of action.
Authors use political and ethical axioms and proverbs to make actions
seem prudent or normal. Maxims strengthen Cecil's support of decisive actions; they reinforce Mildmay's and Bacon's timidity. Although

---

[101] Agricola, *De inventione dialectica*, pp. 428–39; Mack, *Renaissance Argument*, pp. 221–5.

councillors are expert at finding elements in the political situation related to their chosen proposition, in many cases they prefer to use ethical principles and arguments from history. Arguments which depend on the characters of the people involved are very frequent.

Politicians often employ arguments about usefulness, honour and necessity taken from the topics of deliberative oratory and from *De officiis*. Preferably arguments from honour and advantage should be made to support the same proposition (as when Winwood urges James that the threat to provide the Protestant pretenders to Cleves and Juliers with military support will deter their Catholic opponents and enhance James's honour), but politicians also argue about conflicts between the two and occasions on which deception may be justified. Mildmay finds that the doubtfulness and expense of war outweigh the obligation to support Protestantism in the Netherlands. Those who want action undertaken or who value the cause of religion above difficulties in execution emphasise topics of resolution whereas their opponents dwell on topics of danger and uncertainty.

The question of political deception is also related to the ethical topic of seeming and being, which is treated in different ways according to the person involved. Like Essex, Wilson assumes that the Catholic powers always dissemble their true intentions. More cautiously he sometimes argues that their deceptions justify his deceiving them. When Burghley suggests that his son consider dealing falsely with the Scots he supports the idea with the same proverb as Wilson. Wilson also employs the related topic of words and deeds in setting out the conditions under which peace will be achieved.

The foundational topics of Elizabethan political debate are religion, peace, war and money. No one doubts the importance of religion or the benefits of peace so in this élite policy-making forum neither needs to be developed as an explicit commonplace. The arguments focus on how much to risk war in order to achieve objectives or whether the possible political gains of marriage (the prospect of an heir, alliance with France) compensate for the religious risks. Dialectical training enables politicians to connect evidence and policy with these large principles and to find arguments to resolve the conflicts between them one way or the other. The topics of deliberative oratory (enhanced by the more philosophical exploration of Cicero's *De officiis*) offer politicians a framework for registering and comparing competing political arguments. By weighing up a range of arguments on both sides Cecil determined which questions to pose and which reasons to emphasise but this was not always enough to persuade men whose convictions had been strongly engaged on the opposite side. Argument is a crucial component of Elizabethan political persuasion but even in the Privy Council victory may go to those who have the skill and knowledge to direct their appeal to the fundamental feelings of their colleagues. The best orator combines logical skill with the ability to invoke emotion at the key moment; in the prudential ethos of the administrative élite dialectical argument about practicalities played the largest but not always the decisive role.

7

Elizabethan parliamentary oratory

Parliament was the highest public arena of debate in Elizabethan England. In parliament gentlemen from the shires could watch the greatest officials of state explain their policies and legislative projects, sometimes in the face of critical arguments and counter-proposals. Thanks to the enthusiasm of seventeenth-century antiquarians quite substantial records of Elizabethan parliamentary speeches and debates survive, now collected and edited in three handsome volumes by T. E. Hartley.[1] Parliamentary oratory enables us to examine the impact of humanist rhetorical training in practical life. At the same time rhetorical theory can help us understand the effect of individual speeches and the broader import of parliamentary discourse.

Many of the formal features of parliamentary speeches can be connected with rhetorical training. The format of long parliamentary speeches reflects a compromise between rhetorical teaching about introductions and structures derived from dialectic and the practice of disputation. Short debating speeches take their form entirely from dialectic and resemble interventions in university disputations. While the restrained style predominates in both kinds of speech, all the speakers employ amplification to mark important passages and to drive home arguments. Some speakers, especially later in the reign, cultivate a more elaborate style throughout. History plays a crucial role in longer speeches, with government speakers elaborating the contrast between Elizabeth's government and her inheritance from Mary, while other orators cite biblical and classical histories. Proverbs and moral sentences are very prominent in all types of speeches. Many arguments are elaborated with commonplaces and lively descriptions. Several speakers use rhetorical principles to create an individual ethos, or a persona, as a means of persuasion.

---

[1] T. E. Hartley (ed.), *Proceedings in the Parliaments of Elizabeth I*, 3 vols. (Leicester, 1981–95).

Rhetorical theory explains that speech may have other purposes besides persuasion. A speaker may retell narratives and outline arguments which the audience already accepts in order to celebrate shared history and interests.[2] Speakers may employ amplification and heightened style to demonstrate skill and maintain decorum rather than to move an audience to a course of action. Many of the parliamentary speeches which survive function in a way that is as much ceremonial as persuasive. By the same token ritualised exchanges of compliments at the opening or closing of parliament could be framed to convey real political messages. The distinction between display and persuasion is highly permeable in the discourse of the Elizabethan parliament.

Elizabethan parliamentary speeches also raise some more general political and ethical issues. Members argued about whether there were limitations on the freedom of speech allowed to them, whether this meant raising issues which the Queen regarded as outside their competence or questioning the obligation to listen to views repugnant to the majority. In view of the ethical lessons studied at school and the preoccupations of popular philosophy this raised questions for parliamentarians about the nature of good counsel and the role of exchanges of views.[3] Parliament often faced conflict between arguments based on religious or ethical principles and more pragmatic responses offered by those with responsibility for, and experience of, conducting government business.

The speeches survive in two kinds of record.[4] In the first place, men like Nicholas Bacon collected and polished the texts of their speeches as examples of eloquence. Secondly, members of parliament serving particular political interests wrote journals summarising daily proceedings. These two types of record indicate the existence of two types of parliamentary intervention: the long formal speech, usually delivered by a government speaker, often on a ceremonial occasion and the shorter argumentative intervention in reply to a proposal or to a previous speaker. Although this distinction is probably sharpened by the nature of the

[2] Where classical authorities regarded epideictic rhetoric mainly as a matter of writing speeches of praise or blame (Aristotle, *Rhetoric*, 1366a23–67a38; *Rhetorica ad Herennium*, III.6.10–8.15) twentieth-century theorists of rhetoric have emphasised its role in creating and unifying communities. Chaim Perelman and Lucie Olbrechts-Tyteca, *The New Rhetoric* (Notre Dame, 1969), pp. 47–59; Kenneth Burke, *A Rhetoric of Motives* (Berkeley, 1969), pp. 35–59.

[3] Good counsel and the need for frankness of speech is a major topic in Elyot's *The Book Named the Governor*, Lord Berners's translation of Guevara's *Golden Boke of Marcus Aurelius* and William Baldwin's *A Treatise of Morall Philosophie*, discussed in chapter five above. See also John Guy, 'The Rhetoric of Counsel in Early Modern England', in Dale Hoak (ed.), *Tudor Political Culture* (Cambridge, 1995), pp. 292–310.

[4] On the incompleteness of the record: T. E. Hartley, *Elizabeth's Parliaments: Queen, Lords and Commons 1559–1601* (Manchester, 1992), pp. 8–9.

sources, journal reports of the ceremonial speeches at the opening of parliament or of introductory speeches by representatives of the Privy Council tend to be more elaborate, while reports of the interventions of individual members are briefer and more strictly argumentative.[5] A third type of speech, the formal reply on a ceremonial occasion, may be considered as a hybrid of these two kinds.[6]

In this chapter I shall examine the rhetorical and dialectical form of both main kinds of parliamentary discourse, beginning by analysing examples of each. Then I shall discuss the related issues of free speech and honest counsel and opposition to the government line, which form a contested context for parliamentary oratory. Finally I shall discuss the special use Queen Elizabeth made of her own addresses to parliament.

SIR NICHOLAS BACON'S SPEECH FOR THE OPENING OF PARLIAMENT 1571

Sir Nicholas Bacon's speech as Lord Keeper at the opening of parliament on 2 April 1571 survives both in a full text in his collection of speeches and in the reports of two journals.[7] Bacon's commitment to the humanist programme of rhetorical education is well established by the part he played in the founding of Redgrave Grammar School and by his reforms of the curriculum at Bury St Edmunds and St Albans. In 1561 he submitted to Cecil a plan for providing a better education for the wards of court and in 1574 he donated seventy volumes from his library to Cambridge university.[8] In *The Arte of English Poesie*, Puttenham reports, 'I have come to the Lord Keeper Sir Nicholas Bacon, and found him sitting in his gallery alone with the works of Quintilian before him, in deede he was a most eloquent man.'[9]

---

[5] For example the anonymous journal for 14 and 15 May 1572, Hartley, *Proceedings*, I, pp. 319–26, gives the long introductory speech of Thomas Wilbraham in contrast to the shorter arguments and replies of the debate.

[6] At the opening of parliament the Lord Keeper replied on the Queen's behalf to the newly elected speaker's two speeches, the first denying his suitability for the post and the second requesting the customary privileges of parliament; at the closing of parliament he replied to the speaker's speech presenting the bills and subsidies for approval.

[7] The very full report in the anonymous journal provides a close and reliable record of all the main points made in Bacon's text but adds a section on the importance to the body politic of its head (placed at the start of section 3a in the analysis below) and places the reasons for the lack of money (3b2) before the benefits the realm has received (3b1). Hooker reports a passage about money as the sinews of the state which appears neither in Bacon's text nor in the anonymous journal. Perhaps Bacon spoke a passage comparing the state and the body which he dropped from his revised text. Hartley, *Proceedings*, I, pp. 182–7, 195–7, 243.

[8] R. Tittler, *Nicholas Bacon: The Making of a Tudor Statesman* (London, 1976), pp. 58–61.

[9] Puttenham, *Arte* (1936), p. 140. Compare Ben Jonson, *Discoveries* (1641), ed. G. B. Harrison (London, 1922, repr. Edinburgh, 1966), p. 37.

The Lord Keeper's speech was part of the ceremony of the state opening of parliament. It was delivered to both houses of parliament, in the
presence of the Queen. It aimed to explain why the Queen, on the advice
of her Privy Council had chosen to summon parliament.[10] In 1571, the
main reason for calling parliament was to raise revenue. Bacon begins
his speech with sentiments and phrases which had become expected on
such occasions.

The Queene's most excellent Majestie our most dread and gracious soveraigne
Lady haveinge comaunded me to declare unto yow the causes of your callinge
and assembly at this tyme, which I meane to doe as breifely as I can, leade
thereto as one very loath to be tedeous to her Majestie, and alsoe because to
wise men and well disposed (as I iudge yow be) a fewe wordes doe suffice. The
causes be cheifely two: th'one to establishe or dissolve lawes as best shall serve
for the good governance of the realme, th'other soe to consider for the Crowne
and state as it may be best preserved in the time of peace and best defended in
the time of warre, according to the honour due to it.[11]

The first sentence is a formula.[12] Bacon pauses only momentarily to
explain that he can be brief because his audience is wise and well-disposed
(almost in the words of *Rhetorica ad Herennium*)[13] before proceeding to his
division. The purpose of the parliament is two-fold: to establish laws and
to consider the measures to be taken for the preservation of the state.
Bacon's expression becomes a little more elaborate as he goes on to talk
about ecclesiastical laws:

And because in all counselles and conferences first and cheifely there should be
sought the advancement of God's honour and glory as the sure and infallible
foundacion whereupon the pollicy of every good publique weale is to be erected
and builte, and as the straight line whereby it is principally to be directed
and governed and as the cheife piller and buttres wherewith it is continually
to be sustained and maintained, therefore, for the well performeinge of the
former touchinge lawes yow are to consider first whether the ecclesiasticall
lawes concerninge the discipline of the Church be sufficient or noe, and yf any
wante shalbe founde to supply the same . . .

This paragraph is organised in the logical form of an enthymeme:
because God's honour and glory come first, therefore we should first

---

[10] Sir John Neale, *The Elizabethan House of Commons* (London, 1949), pp. 340–1, Elton, *Parliament*,
     pp. 29–32.
[11] Hartley, *Proceedings*, I, p. 183.
[12] Compare Bacon's opening sentence in 1563 (ibid., I, p. 80). The 1571 opening is briefer than
     others and omits the elaborate statement of his unworthiness found elsewhere. Ibid., I, pp. 33
     (1559), 80 (1563).
[13] *Rhetorica ad Herennium*, 1.4.6–5.8.

consider ecclesiastical law. This is elaborated with a persistent doubling of epithets and a series of architectural images. Then he sets out the very tight logical arrangement of the speech.

Structure of the Oration

lines		Laws
8	1. Introduction and Division	Supply
11	2. Laws (a) Ecclesiastical	
11	(b) Temporal	
	3. Provision	
10	(a) Remember extraordinary charges	
16	(b) Reasons for granting subsidy	Benefits
		Necessity
4	3b1. Benefits Realm has from Queen	
8	Restoration of God's word	
25	Peace	
27	Clemency and Mercy	
	3b2. Necessity	
16	Charges: North, Scotland, Ireland, Sea	
6	Decay in income from customs	
24	And note the Queen's economies	
4	3c. Therefore we must contribute	
6	4. Apology for length of speech	

The speech is organised as a series of divisions. Parliament is concerned with laws and supply. Laws are ecclesiastical or temporal. Supply must be granted because of benefits and necessity. Bacon discusses benefits in some detail, necessity in rather less. Before closing he anticipates an objection by insisting on the frugality of the Queen's expenses. He ends on a low key, with a brief conclusion and an apology. The emphasis on successive division makes the structure of this speech more like a medieval thematic sermon, a scholastic determination, or even a Ramist treatise, than the four-part classical oration which Bacon's interests might have led us to expect. There is no peroration to speak of, but both the techniques of the introduction and the use of a reply to objections indicate some influence of ideas about disposition from classical rhetoric.[14] While the plan sets out a series of divisions which provide a structure for all the activity of the parliament, the weight of the speech is placed on the

---

[14] The classical oration can be regarded as having four parts: introduction or exordium, narration, argument and peroration. The section on argument was divided into proof, of one's own case, and refutation, of what one's opponents had said. Aristotle, *Rhetoric*, III.1414a30–b18, Cicero, *Partitiones oratoriae*, I.4, *Rhetorica ad Herennium*, I.3.4 and Quintilian, *Institutio oratoria*, III.9.1–7. Some authorities recognise the same pattern but regard it as having more parts because they divide division from narration and/or proof from refutation.

benefits the realm has received, the charges the Queen has to bear and the removal of the objection of wastefulness. In form Bacon restates the general duties of parliament, as he must, but the content of the speech is mainly directed to the financial issue.

Bacon introduces the question of supply by reminding his audience of the number of extraordinary charges on the crown and of the principle that such charges have to be met by extraordinary revenue. Then he appears to hesitate, in order to draw on the goodwill of his audience.

> But here I rest greatly perplexed whether I ought to open and remember unto yow such reasons as may be iustly produced to move you thankefully and read-ily to grante this extraordinary reliefe or noe. I knowe the Queen's Majestie conceaveth soe great hope of your prudent foreseeing what is to be don, and of your good willes and readines to performe that which by prudency yee forsee, that fewe or noe perswasions at all are needefull for the bringinge this to passe.[15]

He begins by apparently artlessly setting out the dilemma he faces as a speaker. The hesitation gives him the opportunity to build up the audi-ence's sense of its own prudence and to draw out the Queen's favourite theme of her special relationship with her subjects. This is noticeably subtler and more courteous than the tone he adopted in 1559, when he instructed members of parliament about the manner in which they were to debate.[16] Once the Queen's expectation has been established he returns to his own person to make the arguments. Although the Queen thinks you are so wise and so well-disposed as to need no persuading, still to fulfil the duties of his office he will add a few arguments. From this rhetorical highlighting of his own persona and the response expected of his audience he moves very quickly back into the restrained, dialectical manner.

> True it is that there be two thinges that ought vehemently to move us franckly, bountifully and readily to deale in this matter; the former is the greate benefittes that we have received, the seconde is the necessity of the cause. Yf we should forgette the former we are to be chardged as most ungrate and unthankefull,

---

[15] Hartley, *Proceedings*, I, p. 184.
[16] Ibid., I, pp. 34–5: 'And therewith that you will also in this your assemblye and conference clearely forbeare and, as a greate enemye to good councell, flee from all manner of contentious reasoninges and disputacions and all sophisticall, captious and frivolous argumentes and quiddities, meeter for ostentation of witt then consultacion in weightie matters, comelyer for schollers then for counsellors, more beseeminge for schooles then for parliament howses; besides that commonly they be greate cause of much expence of tyme and breed few good resolucions.'

and the forgettefullnes of the seconde doth chardge us as uncarefull of our owne liveinges and libertyes, and of our lives: the former moveth by reason and the seconde urgeth by necessity.[17]

Bacon justifies his division in argumentative terms: if you neglect benefits you are ungrateful; if you ignore necessities you are taking risks with life and liberty. But the patterning makes the argument more effective as display than as persuasion. There is also an unmistakable allusion to rhetorical teachings about deliberative oratory, in which benefits and necessity are two of the topics through which one expects to persuade an audience in a political speech.[18] More obviously rhetorical techniques are at work in the following paragraph, in which Bacon elaborates a commonplace in praise of peace. He enriches the style of this passage with doubling, rhetorical question, metaphor, isocolon, ploce (repetition of individual words) and synoeciosis (linking of contraries).

The seconde is the inestimable benefitte of peace dureinge the time of tenn wholl yeares raigne togeither and more. And what is peace? Is it not the richest and most wished for ornamente that pertaines to any publique weale? Is not peace the marke and ende that all good govermentes directes their actions unto? Nay is there any benefitte, be it never soe greate, that a man may take the full commodytie of without the benefitte of peace, or is there any soe litle commodytie but thoroughe peace a man may have the whoall fruition of it? By this we generally and ioyfully possesse all, and without this generally and ioyfully possesse nothinge.[19]

Within the context of a restrained, logical speech, this section certainly achieves a certain stylistic flourish, but no one would call it a purple passage. It functions more as a demonstration of rhetorical skill than a forceful persuasion. Bacon is fulfilling the obligations of his assignment, elaborating a commonplace out of an argument his whole audience will be happy to agree with.

Rather than dwelling for too long on the inadequacy of the ordinary income available (to which he gives a mere six lines) Bacon prefers to answer an anticipated objection. Whereas ordinary princes create financial problems for themselves by extravagant spending, our Queen has cut down on expenses and contented herself with what is necessary. He

---

[17] Ibid., I, p. 184.

[18] Cicero, *De inventione*, II.56.168–58.175; Wilson, *Rhetoric*, pp. 71, 79, 144. The topics of the honourable and the necessary, with many sub-topics on the individual virtues are discussed at length in Cicero's *De officiis*, one of the standard grammar school texts.

[19] Hartley, *Proceedings*, I, pp. 184–5. Although Bacon does not quote it, the maxim from the grammar school Latin reader *Sententiae pueriles* 'omnia bona pace constant' (Culmann, sig. A8v) can certainly be thought of as underlying this passage.

amplifies this idea with a series of patterned phrases, in which the extravagant delights of unnamed other princes are contrasted with Elizabeth's restraint and practicality.

> To discend in some perticulers, what neede I to remember to yow howe the gorgeous, sumptuous, superfluous buildinges of times past be for the realme's good by her Majestie in this time turned into necessary buildinges and uphouldinges; the chardgeable, glitteringe glorious triumphes into delectable pastimes and shewes, the pompes and solempe ambassadores of chardge into such as be voide of excesse and yet honorable and comely. This and such like were draweinge draines able to dry upp the floweinge fountaines of any treasurye, these were quilles of such quantity as would soone make the many pipes to serve in tyme of necessity such an expendit [as] is hardly satisfied by any collector; and yet those imperfections have bin comonly princes' peculiers, especially younge. One free from these, *rara avis etc.* And yet (God be thanked) a phenixe, a blessed birde of this brood God hath blessed us with.[20]

The initial sentence is a rhetorical question, with a hint of occupatio (I have no need to tell you...). This is elaborated with parison, and alliteration when 'gorgeous, sumptuous, superfluous buildinges of times past' is set against 'in this time turned into necessary buildinges and uphouldinges'. The main idea here is of contrasting the vainglorious and excessive expenses of other princes with the useful and honourable spending of the Queen. In the second sentence the prodigality of other princes is amplified through metaphor and alliteration. The synonym of the phoenix is decorated with alliteration and polyptoton (in the repetition of 'blessed' with different emphasis and different grammatical functions). This passage contains far more verbal ornament than the rest of the speech, but the effect of the amplification is not the emotional persuasion which was the original purpose of amplification, according to the rhetoric manuals.[21] Rather it serves to compliment the Queen and perhaps also to gloss over the awkwardness involved in balancing considerations of money and honour, praising her parsimony while at the same time asking for money. By comparison the ending of the speech is plain in the extreme.

[20] Hartley, *Proceedings*, I, pp. 186–7, with one alternative reading from the collation (draines for dames) and one addition, in square brackets. Quille here means 'water-pipe', OED sense 2.
[21] *Rhetorica ad Herennium*, II.30.47–9; Cicero, *De inventione*, I.53.100; Quintilian, *Institutio oratoria*, VI.2.20–24, VIII.4. Erasmus acknowledges the connection between amplification and the manipulation of emotions but he insists that skill in amplification has other purposes too. Erasmus, *De copia* (1988), pp. 32–4, 218–20, 276–9 (trans. *Collected Works*, XXIV, pp. 301–2, 592–5, 654–7).

Here I would put yow in mynde of extraordinary chardges to come which in reason seemes evident, but soe I shalbe over tedeous unto yow and *frustra fit per plura quod fieri potest per pauciora.* And therefore here I make an ende doubtinge that I have tarried yow longer then I promised or meante or perchance needed (your wisedomes and good inclinacions considered), but yow knowe thinges are to be don both in forme and matter; and my trust is, yf I have stayd, I may be warranted by either or by both, and that yow will take it in good parte.[22]

The plainness of the ending partly serves to establish an attractive humility in relation to the wisdom and understanding on which he compliments his audience, but also responds to the occasion. There is no purpose here in amplification and emotional manipulation (which the classical manuals of rhetoric regarded as an essential part of the peroration)[23] because there is no immediate action or decision in prospect. The comment of the anonymous journal ('surely noe wordes might suffice or skill serve to containe the tennour of that speech, if it shoulde or could be toulde with due report, even as I thinke the hearers wholy in conscience did acknowledge right well')[24] suggests that the audience was satisfied by Bacon's display of eloquence. Throughout Bacon aims more at clear exposition than emotion, trusting his audience to draw the conclusion, yet he permits himself to compose a commonplace on peace and an amplification of the benefits the country has derived from its monarch. These elements, which could have formed part of an epideictic oration (for example a speech in praise of Queen Elizabeth), connect the logically organised speech with its celebratory occasion.

Sir Nicholas Bacon's speeches became the pattern for introductory orations in later parliaments. In 1597 Sir Thomas Egerton's speech opens with almost the same phrase, following it with an apology for his inadequacy.[25] Although Egerton omits Bacon's clear division, his speech has the same broad structure (Introduction; Reform of Laws; Request for Supply; brief Conclusion) and emphasises the same topics: Queen Elizabeth's establishment of true religion, peace and political stability; the external threats from the Catholic powers; the charges borne by the Queen. Egerton's praise of peace, like Bacon's, celebrates the success of Elizabeth's régime and makes a contrast with the misfortunes of other

---

[22] Hartley, *Proceedings*, I, p. 187.
[23] Quintilian, *Institutio oratoria*, VI.I.I and the references in note 21.
[24] Hartley, *Proceedings*, I, p. 197. Sir John Neale discusses this speech in *Queen Elizabeth I and her Parliaments*, 2 vols. (London, 1953–7), I, pp. 186–7.
[25] Hartley, *Proceedings*, III, p. 185.

countries.[26] Like Bacon, he supports his exhortations with Latin ethical maxims.[27] In explaining the need for more revenue Egerton praises the Queen's parsimony (as Bacon had) and contrasts the low level of taxation with the great need of money. Towards the end of his speech he amplifies the folly of avoiding public expenditure and the justification for the war being fought.

> He cannot be well-advised which in this case will not be forward to contribute and bestowe whatsoever he hath. For if with the common wealth it goeth not well, well it cannot be with anie private or particular person. That beeing in danger he that would seeke to laie upp treasure to inriche himselfe should be like unto him that would busie himselfe to beautifie his howse when the cittie where he dwelleth were on fire, or to decke up his cabbane when the shipp wherein he saileth were readie to bee drowned... To spare in that case is to spare for those which seeke to devoure all, and to give is to give to ourself... there is no cause at all to feare, for the warr is iuste. It is in the defence of the religion of God, of our most gratious soveraigne, of our naturall countrey, of our wives and children, our liberties, lands, lives and whatsoever we have.[28]

Egerton elaborates the need to contribute to paying for the war with anadiplosis and with similes illustrating the superficiality and futility of self adornment. The ploce on 'spare' and 'give' emphasises the contradiction between the actual and intended effects of these actions. The justice of the war is amplified by enumerating the valued people and things to be defended. Rather than building up an emotional effect, Egerton demonstrates his competence in rhetoric.

DEBATES FROM 1572 AND 1593

Debate in the Elizabethan parliament is usually summarised by the journal writers as a relatively calm conflict of opposing views. The journals generally record the main arguments of the speakers and indicate whether they supported or opposed a proposal. At times the grammar of the report, the detail of the vocabulary or the patterning of the expression suggest that the orator's actual words have been recorded. Since Elizabethan schoolboys were trained to record phrases from their reading and from sermons they heard for reuse in their own compositions,

---

[26] Unsurprisingly he omits the comparison with Mary's reign which had been obligatory in Elizabeth's early years.

[27] 'mora in peccat[i]s dat incrementum sceleri', 'quod iustum est, necessarium est'; Hartley, *Proceedings*, III, pp. 186, 187.

[28] Ibid., III, p. 187.

it should not surprise us that the journal writers might at times record parliamentary speech verbatim.

In the debate on the punishment of Mary, Queen of Scots, on 19 May 1572 when Francis Alford rose to speak he was opposing all those who had spoken before him and, if Graves and Elton are right, the party-line of the chief privy councillors.[29] His opening was appropriately conciliatory, wishing for the goodwill of the House, explaining that he may be speaking rashly, and expressing his preference for following the lead of those wiser than himself, especially the Queen:

> and therefore he is moved to like best the Queene's opinion. Her opinion also likest to take effect. We, treating of the other, may delay tyme and so endanger her Majestie. Not convenient to passe to the condemnation of a queene without calling her to answere. He unfit person to deale in the iudgement of a queene. The iudges by deliberacion did determine we not to proceede rashlie. He would have us consider the Queene's safetie with her honner. She remaineth a queene not withstanding her deposytion.[30]

The journal summarises Alford's main arguments, first opposing the view that the execution of Mary is the best protection for Elizabeth, then restating the need for legal procedure and concluding with the decisive argument of precedent. Alford's solution is based on distinguishing between terms. He proposes that Mary should forfeit her title, not her life and should be considered an enemy, not a traitor. Thomas Wilson, whom we have already met as a diplomat and as an author of textbooks, opposed each of Alford's arguments in turn.[31]

> Mr Wilson. Wisheth Mr Alford had beene a commyttee in the cause, for that then he doubteth not he should have beene satisfied. The Queene he declareth made noe determinacion, onely shewed her inclination to mercy. He trusteth she will iudge well of us, and though she desireth to proceede more mildely, not seeing the danger she standeth in, which we weepe to see and therfore desire to proceede more safely, it is else to be feared many monthes will not pass before we feele it. Kings' cases must needes be rare, becawse there is but fewe kings. It is not meant to be denied but she shall be hearde by her counsell, and since the Queene's mercy is such as is admirable, we ought importunatly to cry for iustice, iustice.

He begins with an appearance of courtesy, wishing that Alford had been a member of the committee of both Houses, which actually prepares

[29] Elton, *Parliament*, p. 376; M. A. R. Graves, 'The Management of the Elizabethan House of Commons: The Council's Men of Business', *Parliamentary History* 2 (1983), 11–38 (24–30); Hartley, *Elizabeth's Parliaments*, pp. 65–7.
[30] Hartley, *Proceedings*, I, p. 364.   [31] Ibid., I, p. 365.

the ground for his counter-argument: because Alford was not a member of the committee he cannot be so well informed either about Mary's misdeeds or about Elizabeth's reaction. Making effective use of disputation tactics, Wilson distinguishes between the Queen's inclination, which he hopes to change, and her decision, which, if it had been made, the House would have to accept. Unless the House can persuade the Queen of the reality of the danger she faces, within a few months it is likely to experience the calamity it now foresees. Wilson compares apprehension and experience: we weep to see the disaster which is as yet far away, but it will be worse when we feel it. To the argument that the Queen prefers delay he opposes the urgency of preventing the evil which may follow. To the arguments about the inappropriateness of a parliamentary decision about a Queen, Wilson replies that royalty are always special cases and that there was no intention to deprive Mary of the legal right of reply. Wilson turns the Queen's inclination to mercy into a reason for parliament to make an even stronger demand for justice. He opposes Alford's arguments from legal principles and precedents with counter-examples of the same type. He insists that Mary has been tried and found guilty and that the law has more weight than any historical examples.

Although the weight of opinion in the House was strongly in favour of the bill, Wilson still thought it important to reply to Alford's arguments. Alford's speech was opposed to the sentiment of the majority in the House, but it expressed the point of view which ultimately prevailed and the reasons it gives are at least a shrewd guess at the Queen's own reasons for forbidding further action against Mary.[32]

In parliamentary debate positions unwelcome to the Queen and her councillors could be expressed and maintained. Councillors needed to respond to the arguments made, in order to achieve their objectives. In 1593 there was a protracted and difficult debate about the size and timing of the subsidy, an especially sensitive area for the government. In view of the parlous state of the Queen's finances and the seriousness of the Spanish military threat, the Privy Council wanted the Commons to agree to the payment of three subsidies within a shorter timescale than was usual, three years or at most four.[33]

Then Mr Francis Bacon assented to three subsedies but not to the payments under six yeares, and to this propounded three questions which he desiered might be aunswered:

[32] Elton, *Parliament*, p. 125.
[33] Hartley, *Proceedings*, III, pp. 104–8; Neale, *Parliaments*, II, pp. 298–307; David Dean, *Law-making and Society in Late Elizabethan England* (Cambridge, 1996), pp. 43–7.

1. Impossibilitie or difficultie
2. Danger and discontentment
3. A better manner of supply then subsedye.

For impossibilitie the poore man's rent is such as they are not able to yeald yt, and the generall commonalty is not able to paie so much uppon the present. The gentlemen they must sell their plate and the farmers their brasse pottes before this wilbe payed. And for us we are here to search the wounds of the realme and not to skynne them over, wherfore wee are not to perswade our selves of their wealth more then it is.

The daunger is this. Wee breed discontentment in the people and in a cause of jopardie her Majestie's saftie must consist more in the love of her people then in their welth, and therfore not to geve them discontentment in paying theis subsedyes. Thus wee runne into perills; the first in putting twoe paymentes into one we make it a dubell subsedie, for it maketh 4*s* in the pound a payment; the second is that this being graunted in this sort other princes herafter will look for the like, so we shall putt an ill president uppon our selves and to our posteritie. And in histories yt is to be observed that of all nations the English care not to be subiect, base, and taxeable.

The manner of supplie may be levie or imposition when need shall most require, so when her Majestie's coffers and pursse shalbe emptie they may be embassed by this meanes.[34]

Francis Bacon, son of Sir Nicholas, states his position on the subsidy very clearly at the beginning of his speech. Like his father he makes a prominent division of his speech into three headings, or questions he wishes to raise. Within the issue of impossibility, Francis Bacon divides between the poor, who cannot pay at all, and the better off, who cannot pay so quickly. Rather than backing these points up with quantitative arguments, he illustrates them with the emotion-rousing vignette of the householders selling their possessions to pay their taxes.[35] He uses a metaphor, expressed almost as a proverb to drive home this point. Parliament must investigate the wounds of the commonwealth, not hide them. Under 'danger', he argues that the Queen would be threatened by the discontent that would arise from further taxation and that she needs the love of the people more than she needs their money. Trivial though this argument may seem, it responds to a position which the Queen often

---

[34] Hartley, *Proceedings*, III, pp. 109–10. I have adopted two variants from other sources recorded in Hartley's footnotes: 'questions' in line two and 'care not' in line twenty.

[35] For the argument about how heavily taxed the English were see David Harris Sacks, 'The Paradox of Taxation: Fiscal Crises, Parliament and Liberty in England, 1450–1640', in P. T. Hoffman and K. Norberg (eds.), *Fiscal Crises, Representative Institutions and Liberty in Early Modern Europe* (Stanford, 1994), pp. 7–66 (48, 65–6); M. J. Braddick, *Parliamentary Taxation in Seventeenth-Century England* (Woodbridge, 1994), pp. 2–14; Dean, *Law-making and Society*, pp. 41–2 (who lends some support to Bacon's view).

takes up in her speeches, that she is more pleased with the love of her subjects than with the sums of money they offer her.[36] Bacon divides the danger into two aspects: the excessive amount of the subsidy if two payments are put together and the precedent it offers to future princes. He supports his argument about the danger of excessive taxation by referring to the lessons of the chronicles.[37] Finally he suggests that means other than subsidy should be found for providing for the Queen's needs.[38] Bacon's announced structure is very clear but he supports his points with comparisons and historical instances rather than with strong logical arguments.

Francis Bacon's speech was answered by Sir Thomas Heneage and Sir Robert Cecil. Both began their speeches by enumerating Bacon's arguments and replying to each in turn. This summarising of the points to be answered seems to derive from the practice of academic disputation, the main form of intellectual exercise at Tudor universities. According to Robert Sanderson, the first duty of the respondent in a disputation was to repeat the argument of the opponent, before indicating whether he agreed or disagreed.[39] This pattern of speech-making helps keep debate focused and enables each speaker to locate his position in relation to others expressed.

Heneage pointed out that the proposed tax could not be regarded as impossible since the poor and the better off had frequently been taxed in the past. To Bacon's second point he argues that the people will not be discontented with the Queen since they share her religion and are loyal to her. Then he turns to the necessity of the time, arguing that the swift payment of additional taxation is essential to the survival of the state. Heneage elaborates this point by reiterating the issues of time, extraordinariness and necessity and concludes his argument with a maxim. Rather than being led by past examples, people should be moved by present danger. Cecil repeats the metaphor with which Bacon expressed parliament's obligation to respond to the state of the commonwealth. He opposes the topic of poverty with that of danger. On the basis of the ethical maxim that one must choose the lesser of two evils he argues

---

[36] David Harris Sacks, 'The Countervailing of Benefits', in Dale Hoak (ed.), *Tudor Political Culture* (Cambridge, 1995), pp. 272–91 (284–8) has an interesting passage on the exchange of love between monarch and subjects.

[37] *Mirror for Magistrates* for example identified excessive taxation as one of the reasons for the collapse of Richard II's support. Baldwin, *Mirror for Magistrates*, pp. 113–14.

[38] In this opinion too, Bacon has the support of modern historians. Guy, *Tudor England*, pp. 381–5, relying mainly on F. C. Dietz, *English Public Finance 1485–1641*, 2 vols. (Urbana, 1921).

[39] Sanderson, *Logicae*, sigs. T3v–4r.

that taxes will have to be raised in spite of the difficulties this will create. On the issue of setting a precedent, he argues that precedents always depend on causes. We should not risk losing the best monarch because we are worried about what a worse one might do.[40] Cecil is not eloquent but he is logical and forceful. He backs up his arguments with maxims and historical evidence. The committee accepted his arguments and the House agreed to the payment of three subsidies in four years.[41] Bacon paid for his intervention with a period of royal disfavour.[42]

Reports of speeches in debates show how much emphasis the parliamentary audience placed on outlining propositions and answering them. Although individual speakers sometimes made their points most effectively using rhetorical techniques (for example, comparisons or proverbs), the mainly dialectical mode of parliamentary speech recalled expectations of academic disputations. This shared educational background compelled members of the Privy Council to respond to arguments put to them by ordinary members of parliament.[43]

STRUCTURE OF INTERVENTIONS

Nicholas Bacon's introductory speeches appear to present a general pattern for formal speeches on the government side.[44] Such speeches usually begin with a formula expressing the Queen's command and an expression of the orator's unfitness for his task. After a short attempt to win the goodwill of the audience, in the manner suggested in *Rhetorica ad Herennium*,[45] the orator makes a series of divisions to make clear to the audience the shape of the oration. All the speakers dwell on the achievements of the government before attempting to justify the taxation they request. As Chancellor of the Exchequer, Sir Walter Mildmay[46] introduced

---

[40] Hartley, *Proceedings*, III, pp. 112–13.   [41] Ibid., III, pp. 113–14.

[42] Neale, *Parliaments*, II, p. 309; J. Spedding, *The Letters and the Life of Francis Bacon*, I (London, 1861), pp. 231–8.

[43] There may be some relation between the privilege of the university, which allows questions to be raised and disputed which would not be permissible elsewhere (as for example in the disputation, in the Queen's presence, as to whether monarchy was the best form of government) and the more restricted and more contested privilege of parliamentary free speech.

[44] They may even have been used as a structural model by later orators. The exordium of Sir Christopher Hatton's speech at the opening of parliament in 1589 is written in a far more elaborate style but it covers exactly the same ground as Bacon's. Hartley, *Proceedings*, II, p. 414.

[45] *Rhetorica ad Herennium*, 1.4.7–5.8.

[46] On Mildmay's educational interests and his foundation of Emmanuel College, Cambridge, see Lehmberg, *Sir Walter Mildmay*, pp. 222–31, 235. Among the books he gave to Christ's College and Emmanuel College were complete editions of Aristotle, Nizolius's dictionary of Ciceronian Latin and Rudolph Agricola's *De inventione dialectica* (Lehmberg, pp. 222, 230).

his speech for supply in 1576 even more briefly than Bacon had, elaborating his announced three-fold structure with a series of arguments about the Queen's financial difficulties and the mistakes of her predecessors.[47] Government speakers frequently forestall objections by pointing out the Queen's parsimony in comparison with other princes.[48] The refutation of objections is usually followed by a brief summary and an apology for the time the speech has taken.[49] That this was a parliamentary expectation is confirmed by Archbishop Heath's use of successive divisions and his apologetic conclusion in his speech against the Bill of Supremacy in 1559.[50] This suggests a basic pattern very like that which we discovered in Bacon's speech:

> Introduction and Division
> Three points (more or less)
> Refutation of Objections
> Summary and Apology

This pattern was capable of further adaptation but was rarely abandoned. For example, Sir Christopher Hatton's opening speech in 1589 begins by observing Bacon's pattern, but he soon adds to his model, arranging the argumentative section of the speech around two lengthy parallel accounts of the past misdemeanours and present plans of the Catholic powers.[51] When he replaces the summary and apology with an elaborate peroration, this results in an overall structure closer to (though certainly not identical with) the four-part oration recommended in the classical manuals of rhetoric.[52]

Hatton's speech:	Classical four-part oration:
Introduction and Division	Exordium
Past Dangers from Catholics	Narration
Present Dangers: Puritans and Catholics	Proof and Refutation
Conclusion: Remedies	Conclusion

---

[47] Hartley, *Proceedings*, I, p. 440. The financial arguments are on pp. 443–4. On the speech in general see Neale, *Parliaments*, I, pp. 346–8; Lehmberg, *Sir Walter Mildmay*, pp. 129–34.

[48] Hartley, *Proceedings*, I, pp. 186, 443, 506. In later parliaments there is more emphasis on the contributions which the Queen has made to the costs of war from her ordinary income than on the frugality of her court.

[49] Ibid., I, pp. 77, 187, 444. The apologies are less frequent in the later parliaments.

[50] Ibid., I, pp. 12–17.

[51] The accounts are parallel because they both have successive sections on the English seminary priests, Pope Sixtus V and Philip II of Spain.

[52] See note 14 above.

As the classical manuals suggest,[53] Hatton uses the peroration to summarise the argument, to turn to the audience and to propose the solution with the greatest possible emotional force.

If, then, my Lords, our enemies, so manie and so mightie, in so lewde a cause as theirs is, have combined themselves together against us, yf in the respects before mencioned thei are fullie resolved to set up their rests either nowe or never to subdue us, either nowe to conquere us or to lay themselves open to be conquered of others, yf accordinglie thei ioyne together and are in devisinge all the waies and meanes whereby thei maye be able to execute their furie upon us, to overthrowe our religion, to depose hir Majestie, to possesse our lande, and with all kinde of crueltie to murther everie one of us; what care then I say, my Lords, ought we to have in so holie, so iust, so honourable, so profitable and so necessarie a quarell to ioine together, to foresee these daungers, to provide for them and to set up our rests either nowe or never to be able to withstande them?[54]

The argument is a hypothetical syllogism, whose conclusion is delayed by a rhetorical question. Hatton uses the form to summarise the intentions of the state's enemies, with a series of if-clauses, amplifying the consequences of their intentions by going into detail. His lengthy question emphasises the topics of deliberative oratory (holy, just, honourable, necessary) and expands on the general themes of unity, foresight and determination. The summarising aspect of the argument corresponds with the expectations of the classical peroration, in which the speaker summarises his key arguments before arousing the emotions of his audience. But there is also a way in which the argumentative form here is decorative, setting up a balance between the threats and the response required, providing an elegant form for restating the main shape of the speech. Putting the conclusion in the form of a question turns the speech towards the audience, asking them to reflect on their role in relation to these events. Hatton's peroration clearly depends on rhetorical principles, most obviously on Quintilian and on a study of Cicero's perorations. For other speakers, though, an introduction which gestures towards conciliating the audience leads on to a dialectically organised speech. For their introductions the letter-writing manuals could have provided sufficient guidance.[55]

[53] *Rhetorica ad Herennium*, II.30.47–31.50; Cicero, *De inventione*, 1.52.98–56.109; Quintilian, *Institutio oratoria*, VI.1–2.
[54] Hartley, *Proceedings*, II, pp. 423–4.
[55] For example, Erasmus, *De conscribendis epistolis*, p. 316, (trans. *Collected Works*, XXV, p. 74).

Contributions to debate observed a purely dialectical structure. Speakers would summarise the points made by a previous speaker and would answer each point in turn, concluding with a statement of their position on the issue in question, sometimes backed up by an argument. The model for this form of debating speech and for the methods of refutation it employs (pointing out logical contradiction, distinguishing the ways words are understood) is provided by the university practice of disputation.

Some parliamentary ceremonies take the same form as debates. When the speaker petitions the Queen for parliamentary privilege at the opening of parliament, and when he thanks her and craves her pardon at the close, the Lord Keeper (or whoever is speaking for, and after consultation with, the Queen) lists each of the points that has been made and replies to each in turn. The topics of both speeches are largely fixed but may be varied to convey political messages. At the opening ceremony in 1559, Bacon glosses the agreement to freedom of speech 'so as they be neither unmindfull nor uncarefull of their dutyes, reverence and obedience to their soveraigne'.[56] In 1571, Bacon thanks the members of parliament for the subsidy, noting that some members have behaved in an arrogant way, ignoring the advice to avoid certain topics, which he gave at the beginning of the session.[57]

MEANS OF PERSUASION

Elizabethan parliamentary orators drew their arguments from a range of sources: from history, from personal experience, and from the topics of deliberative rhetoric. Sometimes these arguments functioned to decorate the speech or to win the audience's favour, while the persuasive weight of the speech rested on more rhetorical resources and techniques, for example proverbs, commonplaces and fictional narratives.

Historical arguments play a large role in the longer speeches. Nicholas Bacon, Hatton and Mildmay all give considerable space to accounts of the Queen's achievements in reforming religion, maintaining peace and security and promoting wealth. They all emphasise a temporal contrast between the remote past of the failures of Mary's reign, the immediate past of Elizabeth's successful reforms and the present in which the country is threatened by the Catholic powers. Where the Tudor myth, as we find it in chronicles, dwells on the anarchy of Richard III's reign

---

[56] Hartley, *Proceedings*, I, p. 43.   [57] Ibid., I, p. 188.

to justify a strong central government, Elizabeth's councillors bolster the legitimacy of her régime by continual reference to the weakness, poverty and false religion of Mary's reign. None of their audience can have needed to be convinced of what the Queen had done. The reiteration of this material, and the rehearsing of the threats facing the country from abroad, form part of the ritual of parliament, reminding the audience of what unites them and what they have to be grateful for, before moving on to requests or admonitions.

Parliamentary speakers often had recourse to examples, from ancient and foreign history, and authorities. Archbishop Heath assembled a range of examples from Christian history and quotations from the Creed, the Bible and the Church fathers to demonstrate that in passing the Act of Supremacy the church would be forsaking not only Paul IV but all general councils, all canonical laws, the judgment of all Christian princes and the unity of Christ's church.[58] When in 1572, parliament was attempting to persuade the Queen of the necessity of executing Mary, the bishops assembled sixteen pages of arguments supported from scripture, while the laymen produced fourteen pages of arguments from civil law backed up with historical examples and citations from Roman law.[59] They had no effect on what everyone knew was a political decision, and indeed the speed and ease with which such batteries of evidence could be assembled (on both sides) exposes the ornamental nature of this type of arguing. It was a fine way to dress up a case and to build confidence among those who supported a particular line but it carried little weight in persuasion.

Closely related to historical arguments are technical arguments based on personal experience. In his speech for supply in 1576, Mildmay sought to disable the objection that since a payment had been made four years previously, the Queen ought not to need more money now. In reply he listed six reasons for the weakness of the Queen's finances. These include difficulties in collecting taxes and the expense of repaying debts as well as extraordinary expenditure caused by the northern rebellion, the expedition to Edinburgh and campaigns in Ireland. Mildmay claimed that these expenses had only been met to date because of the Queen's use of her ordinary revenues.[60] He uses his inside knowledge to increase the authority of his arguments, presenting himself as a financial expert, favouring his audience with privileged information, for which they ought to show due respect and gratitude:

---

[58] Ibid., I, pp. 13–16.   [59] Ibid., I, pp. 274–90 (with manuscript foliation).   [60] Ibid., I, p. 443.

to that I answere that, albeit her Majestie is not to yield an accompt how she spendeth her treasure, yet for your satisfaccions I will lett you understand such thinges as are very trew, and which I dare affirme, having more knowledg thereof then some other in respect of the place that I hould in her Majestie's service.[61]

His additional information and enhanced authority are then incorporated into an essentially ethical argument. The country ought to reward the Queen's financial prudence, in establishing sound coinage and avoiding land sales, with a greater willingness to grant subsidies for extraordinary expenses.[62] Then he appeals to members' own experience of the rising costs of ordinary expenditure.

Many speakers, including Nicholas Bacon, use topics of deliberative oratory, such as necessity and power, to provide the overarching argumentative force of their speeches. These arguments are often combined with ethical principles, such as equality of treatment in similar cases or avoiding ingratitude. Bacon was particularly fond of Latin proverbs. Two Latin tags which he uses in the section of his 1571 opening speech dealing with law reform, *gladius gladium iuvaret* in relation to church law and *acriores enim sunt morsus remissae quam retentae libertatis* in relation to temporal law, are both repeated from his opening speech of 1563.[63] In his closing speeches he three times urged a speedy payment of the subsidy with the tag *bis dat qui cito dat*.[64] Arguments based on the necessity of the time were powerful in political debate. Heneage argued that Francis Bacon's hope of extending the timescale of the proposed taxation was impolitic because the money was needed quickly. Knollys tried to reject amendments to his bill about vagabonds by arguing that it was better to do some good now than to lose the chance of achieving anything in arguments about how to do better.[65]

Where many of Bacon's proverbs are used decoratively, other speakers used a pithy phrase or an epigram to express the main argumentative force of their speech. For example, in the debate quoted earlier, Francis Bacon explained the duty of parliament with a pseudo-proverb: 'we are here to search the wounds of the realme and not to skynne them over'. Heneage replied that 'the necessitie of the tyme is to be considered', and that 'it is strange to counte that impossible which hath beene proved, or that difficulte which hath been used'. Robert Cecil founded his response

---

[61] Ibid.   [62] Ibid., I, p. 444.   [63] Ibid., I, pp. 82–3, 183.

[64] Ibid., I, pp. 48, 189, 466. This proverb is discussed in Erasmus's *Adagia*, *Opera omnia*, II, col. 330. [Cato], *Libellus* approaches it with 'Inopi beneficium bis dat, qui dat celeriter' (D5r). On Bacon and proverbs, see Elizabeth McCutcheon, *Sir Nicholas Bacon's Great House Sententiae* (Amherst, 1977).

[65] Hartley, *Proceedings*, I, pp. 367, discussed at note 80 below.

on a maxim of practical conduct: 'of twoe mischeifs we must choose the lesser'.[66] Perhaps the apparently artless commonsense of proverbs made them seem more convincing than pages of evidently worked up authorities.

Some speakers made use of rhetorical commonplaces to add stylistic gloss and emotional force to parts of their speeches, as we have seen in Bacon's praise of peace and shall see in Hatton's vituperation of Cardinal Allen. Many speeches also employ lively description and dramatisation of a scene to elicit an emotional response from the audience. Mildmay attempts to drive home the message of his rather plain speech with the image of wise mariners in time of calm preparing their tackle to withstand a tempest.[67] Francis Bacon amplified his argument against the payment of three subsidies in six years with the vignette of the farmers selling their cooking pots to pay the tax.[68] In the peroration to his opening speech in 1589, Hatton linked together hypothetical syllogism, rhetorical question and vivid portrayal (with dialogue) of the shipwreck scenario to persuade his audience that they ought to start paying for the next war. He capped his point with comparison, exclamation, proverb, and lively depiction, with personification and dialogue, of the recrimination afterwards if they failed to agree.

In times past our noble predecessours have bene able to defende this realme, when they wanted such meanes as we maie have; and shall we nowe disable ourselves and through our negligence loose it? . . .

I am persuaded there is none here present whoe woulde not sweare it yf he were asked, that yf he had an hundreth lives he would spend them all rather then anie soch matter shoulde come to passe. Marie, our cares and indevours for good meanes of defence must be therunto agreable; or else where deedes are necessarie it is but vanitie to stande upon woords. Our ship is yet safe; and therefore, as one said once in the like case, 'Looke mastere, looke mariner, looke everie bodie, that it be not overthrowen by wilfullnes and negligence: for yf the sea get the masterie then it is too late.' God forbid that we shoulde ever come to these woords: Lord, whoe woulde have thought we shoulde have come to this? Alas, alas, yf we had done thus and thus all had bene well.[69]

STYLE

In most of the earlier formal parliamentary speeches by members of the Privy Council the generally sober style of Bacon predominates. His

[66] Ibid., III, pp. 109–12. Below there are examples of proverbs used by Francis Knollys and Queen Elizabeth at notes 80 and 110.
[67] Ibid., I, p. 442.   [68] Ibid., III, p. 109.   [69] Ibid., II, p. 424.

choice of style may have been dictated by the occasion. At the end of the opening of parliament, the Commons will return to their chamber to elect a speaker. The speech for supply will be followed by other speeches. In neither case is there any immediate action towards which an audience can usefully be driven by the arousal of emotion. In his speech for supply Mildmay's style is very plain with only the slightest doubling of adjectives or adverbs to suggest any ambition to impress his audience with his command of elegant expression.[70] Hatton's speech at the opening of parliament in 1589 shows that it was possible to speak in a very different way. In presenting the dangers facing the country he attacks the English Catholics, beginning with a list of individuals and their misdeeds (Cardinal Pole, Gardiner, Harding, Morton, Saunders, Campion), which he then abbreviates through occupatio.

I omit here to speake of Morgan, Charles Paget, Throckmorton, and diverse others whoe have bene longe practitioners; but yet of all the villanous traitors that I thinke this lande ever bred or brought up, that wicked preist, that shamelesse atheiste and bloodie Cardinall Allen, he in deede excelleth. Looke what late daungers have bene anie way towards us and you shall finde him a cheif dealer in them. He especiallie by his false libells hath sought to bringe this state with all the worlde into perpetuall hatred. He greatlie commendeth Stanlei's treasons and persuadeth others to followe his example. He was the procurer of this last bull, and, it is verie apparaunt, the penner of it. He like a proude and an impudent verlet dareth by his letters to sollicite the nobles and comminalitie of England to ioine with the enemie. He is not ashamed to confesse, and that in writinge that the memorie of his villanie maie never die, howe this Spanish hostilitie hath bene greatlie farthered by his and the reste of these ffugitives indevers. His woords are these. His Majestie (meaninge the King of Spaine) was not a little moved by my humble and continuall suite, together with the afflicted and banished Catholickes of our nation of all and everie degree, to take upon him this holie and glorious acte: that is, the destruccion of this land, the overthrowe of religion, the ruine of hir Majestie and the death of us all. O savage and barbarous preiste! It is much to have suche crueltie attempted by anie foraine enemie: it is more that preists shoulde so delight in bloode. But that English subiects, beinge preists, shoulde take upon them to be the woorkers of such an extremitie, and that against their owne native countrie: before this devilish broode was hatcht, I thinke it was never hearde of amongst the verie Scythians. It is said that the snakes in Siria will not bite nor stinge the people that are borne there; but these most venemous snakes you see doe not onelie labour to bite and stinge us, but, as a generation of cruell vipers, to teare us in peeces and to feede themselves with our bloode.[71]

---

[70] E.g. Ibid., I, p. 442.   [71] Ibid., II, pp. 417–18.

This is almost a textbook example of amplification, in the form of a sustained vituperation. Hatton prepares for it by passing over several names to concentrate on Allen. Then he builds a series of patterned phrases (anaphora, isocolon) setting out different aspects of Allen's encouragement of treason, making it seem greater by going into detail in the way *De copia* recommends.[72] Next he develops Allen's shamelessness, in leaving a permanent record of his urging of the invasion, and his hypocrisy, by pointing out the gap between Allen's emollient words and the barbarous deeds they refer to ('this holie and glorious acte: that is, the destruccion of this land'). Hatton works this up by three patterned phrases elaborating its implication ('the overthrowe of religion, the ruine of hir Majestie and the death of us all') before bursting out with his apostrophe ('O savage and barbarous preiste!'). This leads, after a pause no doubt, to a new amplification through an incremental series of comparisons (incrementum): this would be dreadful in a foreign enemy, worse in a priest, but unthinkable until now in an English priest.[73] Finally he turns to ancient barbarians and 'unnatural natural history' to expand on the unprecedented savagery he attributes to Allen.

It is a highly emotional passage, almost Marlovian in its stylistic intensity and excess. More an episode of vituperation than a deliberative argument, this is far more emotional than anything Bacon attempts. But why? There is no question of the members of parliament rushing to Rome and dismembering Allen at the end of this speech. Not even any question of an immediate subsidy vote. Rather they will return to the Commons to elect a Speaker, who has already been chosen for them. The motivation for this impressive speech is rather similar to Bacon's. Hatton is rehearsing a set of emotions that the whole House can subscribe to. Rather than inflaming them to action, he aims to unite them. The emotion he arouses is at the service of the ritual, or epideictic, function of identification. His style may also reflect the mood of the times, when his audience had every reason to feel threatened by the 'holy and glorious acts' undertaken by the King of Spain. But we should also notice the placing of this emotional episode within Hatton's speech. Once he has described the aggressive intentions of the Catholic powers and established that their main objective is to bring about a change in religion, he turns to the extreme Protestants in parliament.

And yet herewithall hir Majestie is not so much greived – because she ever accounted them hir enemies and never looked for anie better at their handes – as

[72] Erasmus, *De copia* (1988), book II, methods 1–4, pp. 197–202.   [73] Ibid., p. 218.

she is that ther are diverse of latter daies risen up, even amongst hir freinds, whoe beinge men of a verie intemperate humour doe greatlie deprave the present estate and reformacion of religion, so hardlie attained to and with such hir daunger continued and preserved, whereby hir lovinge subiectes are greatlie disquieted, hir enemies are incouraged, religion is slaundered, pietie is hindered, schismes are maintained, and the peace of the Church is altogether rente in sunder and violated.[74]

By emphasising the difficulty and danger with which the present settlement has been attained, Hatton is able to portray the puritans as intemperate people who risk what has already been won with difficulty for the sake of getting their own way in minor details. He employs amplification from effects, isocolon and doubling of epithet to emphasise the dangers caused by their actions.

The paragraph which follows is even firmer, emphasising the Queen's absolute commitment to the present state of the Church ('that both in forme and doctrine it is agreable with the scriptures, with the most auncient generall councells, with the practise of the primitive church and with the iudgementes of all the olde and learned fathers') and her rejection of its Protestant critics ('absurde ... intollerable innovacion ... unspeakable tyrannie ... most daungerous to all good Christian government'). She entreats parliament, and if that will not suffice she requires them, not to discuss such matters. It is noticeable that Hatton delivers this section of the speech very definitely in the Queen's name, before adding his own view that parliament should carry out her wishes.[75] Once the instruction has been delivered he returns to the plans of Cardinal Allen and the activities of the seminary priests.

The vituperation against a common enemy aims to unite parliament before his much more contentious criticism of Protestant innovation. It also aids his presentation of the Queen as an embattled but firm champion of protestantism, whose church settlement it would be foolish and ungrateful to attack. The, in this context, unprecedented emotional force of Hatton's opening oration may be a consequence of the occasion, the first assembly of parliament after the defeat of the first armada, when it was widely believed that another threat of invasion would soon follow, or of his personality, but the more elaborate style which he employs may also reflect a shift in literary taste. Speaker Yelverton's oration at the close of parliament in 1598 employs an almost euphuistic degree of stylistic elaboration.

---

[74] Hartley, *Proceedings*, II, p. 419.   [75] Ibid., II, pp. 419–20.

If that comon wealth (most sacred and most renowned Quene) was reputed in the world to be the best-framed, and the most likely to flourishe in felicitie, where the subjectes had there freedome of discourse, and there libertie of likeing, in establishing the lawes that should governe them; then must your Majestie's mighty and most famous realme of England (by this your most gratious benignitie) acknowledge it self the most happie of all the nations under heaven . . . Singuler was the commendation of Solon that sett lawes among the Athenians; passing was the praise of Licurgus that planted lawes among the Lacedemonians; and highly was Plato extolled that devised lawes for the Magnesians; but neither yet could the inconveniences of the state be so providently foreseene, nor the reason of the lawes be so deeply searched into . . . as when the people themselves be agents in the frameing of them.[76]

As well as being much freer in his use of classical allusion and alliteration combined with parison in Lyly's manner than earlier speakers, he also indulges in a series of parallels from natural history and cosmology.[77] The structure which underpins the decorative elaboration is based on argument from comparison and contrary. Yelverton's amplification usually serves to flatter the Queen but he uses the favourable atmosphere this creates to make serious points about the impact of court monopolies.[78]

OPPOSITION, FREE SPEECH AND HONEST COUNSEL

The practice of debate in the Elizabethan parliament enabled views opposed to the government line to be registered, to make an impact and to be managed. Members of parliament could make interventions which annoyed privy councillors and which altered the direction of legislation in ways that the council did not foresee. In the debate on the bill on vagabonds in 1572 several members suggested amendments and additions to Sir Francis Knollys's bill. Many of these men (Sampole, Lovelace and Norton, for example) are normally thought of as supporters of the Privy Council line.[79] These speakers made a series of detailed points, which may be divided into three categories: notices of defects in the bill and suggestions for their improvement (for example Norton's three drafting points, which restrict the definition of vagabond; Seckerston's comment on the lack of provision for the smaller boroughs, including Liverpool which he represented; and Sampole's comments about bail and division of costs of carriage of rogues), observations on the causes

---

[76] Ibid., III, pp. 197–210 (197).   [77] Ibid., III, p. 198, Hunter, *John Lyly*, pp. 264–8.
[78] Hartley, *Proceedings*, III, pp. 203–4.
[79] Ibid., I, pp. 366–7; Elton, *Parliament*, pp. 101, 352; M. A. R. Graves, *Thomas Norton: The Parliament Man* (Oxford, 1994), esp. pp. 71–6, 86–8, 187–96, 339–46.

of poverty (Seckerston's comment on the reluctance of wealthy men to employ servants, St John's remark on the folly of building cottages without adequate land to provide food), and suggestions for further measures (Lovelace's remarks on the suppression of poverty in Worcestershire and Slege's wish to extend the provisions of the bill to towns and to restrict the minstrels covered by it).

Set against these comments are the attempts by the Lord Treasurer, Sir Francis Knollys, presumably representing the Privy Council view, to push the bill through without extensive revision. He pointed out to the House that this was their own bill which was lost in the previous session and which has now been returned to them by the Lords. To attempts to add to the bill, he replied with a maxim that it was 'better to do some good than by trying to do all good to doe no good'.[80] Knollys was supported by Thomas Seckford, the Master of Requests,[81] who argued that Justices of the Peace already had the powers to carry out Lovelace's proposals and that if there were defects in the bill they could be reformed at the end of the seven-year trial period. Although the government supporters of the bill appeared to prevail at this stage,[82] when it returned to the House it ran into so much opposition that it had to be sent to committee. Some of the objections we have noted re-emerged. For example the issue of the inclusion of minstrels in the bill, which was much debated later,[83] and St John's proposal about land for cottages, which was eventually defeated in this parliament.[84]

Ordinary members could oppose councillors apparently on equal terms, could refuse to allow them the last word and could, on occasion have the satisfaction of seeing their views prevail even after the councillors had outgunned them, as Francis Alford did in 1572, when he argued against the execution of Mary, Queen of Scots. An individual member could offend all shades of opinion in the House and at the same time divide the government speakers on the best way of dealing with him, as Arthur Hall did (as we shall see) in proposing that the Duke of Norfolk should be pardoned.

[80] Hartley, *Proceedings*, I, pp. 367.
[81] This seems most probable, in view of Seckford's involvement with this bill at a later stage (ibid., I, pp. 313, 367) but Hartley treats the two Seckfords as different.
[82] The bill received a second reading on 22 May. Ibid., I, p. 372.
[83] Peter Roberts, 'Elizabethan Players and Minstrels and the Legislation of 1572 against Retainers and Vagabonds', in A. Fletcher and P. Roberts (eds.), *Religion, Culture and Society in Early Modern Britain: Essays in Honour of Patrick Collinson* (Cambridge, 1994), pp. 29–55, (34–41); Elton, *Parliament*, pp. 269–70.
[84] Hartley, *Proceedings*, I, pp. 311, 372, 384.

One particular member, Peter Wentworth, could say the unthinkable, without incurring disqualification or, apparently, affecting the conduct of parliamentary business. Here is the climax of his speech at the beginning of the session in 1576,[85] running through the point at which he was interrupted and sent to the Tower.

And shall I passe over this weighty matter so lightly or soe slightly? May I discharge my conscience and dutye to God, my prince and country soe? Certaine it is, Mr Speaker, that none is without fault, noe, not our noble Queen. Since then that her Majestie hath committed great faultes, yea dangerous faultes to her selfe and the state, love, even perfit love voyd of dissimulacion, will not suffer me to hide them to her Majestie's perill but to utter them to her Majestie's safetye. And these they are. It is a dangerous thing in a prince unkindly to intreat and abuse his or her nobility and people as her Majestie did in the last parliament; and it is a dangerous thing in a prince to oppose or bend her selfe against her nobility and people, yea, against most loving and faithfull nobility and people. And how could any prince more unkindly intreate, abuse and oppose her selfe against her nobility and people then her Majestie did the last parliament? Did shee not call it of purpose to prevent trayterous perills to her person and for noe other cause? Did not her Majestie send unto us two billes, [probably Wentworth was interrupted here] willing to make a choyce of that we liked best for her safety and therof to make a law, promising her Majestie's royall consent therto? And did we not first chuse the one and her Majestie refused it, yielding noe reason, nay, yielding great reasons why she ought to have yielded to it? Yet did not we never the lesse receive the other and agreeing to make a law thereof did not her Majestie in the end refuse all our travells?[86]

From the purely stylistic point of view this passage is perhaps excessively repetitive and too reliant on the figure of rhetorical question. But it is nevertheless impressively vehement and passionate as well as being extraordinarily daring in its open and forthright criticism of the Queen's conduct. The narratives in Wentworth's speech make it clear that, although the speech is nominally concerned with freedom of speech, his real concern is to resist the Queen's manipulation of parliamentary business and to impose parliament's views on her. There is reason to think that other parliamentarians felt as frustrated as he did at her refusal of both the bills against Mary,[87] but for the most part they recognised her

---

[85] Ibid., i, pp. 425–34. Elton, *Parliament*, p. 347. The opening of this speech is discussed in my Introduction, pp. 1–2.

[86] Hartley, *Proceedings*, i, pp. 430–1. The point of interruption is indicated in Cromwell's journal, ibid., i, p. 476.

[87] In Thomas Cromwell's account of the House's discussion of Elizabeth's rejection of the first of the two bills, on 23 May 1572, there is a strong sense of the frustration of the members of parliament. The Speaker sums up by saying, 'I have heard none shewe any liking thereof, so as

right to take the final decisions and certainly would not have chosen such provocative expressions. In his interrogation by the committee of the House, Wentworth confessed that as he walked on his land, preparing the speech, he half expected that it would take him to the Tower. He decided that his duty to the Queen outweighed the risk of imprisonment. When he began to deliver this section of the speech he paused and looked around him.

> Yet when I uttered these words in the House, that there was none without fault, noe, not our noble Queen, I pawsed and beheld all your countenances and sawe plainlye that those words did amaze yow all. Then I was afraid with yow for company and feare bad me to put out those wordes that followed, ffor your countenances did assure me that not one of you would stay me of my journey.[88] Yet the consideracion of a good conscience and of a faithfull subject did make me bould to utter that in such sorte as your honours heard; with this heart and mind I spake it and I prayse God for yt and, if it were to doe, I would with the same minde speake it againe.[89]

Wentworth's comment conveys vividly his sense of the shock and amazement with which the House received his words. As he spoke he knew that he had no prospect of persuading his audience and that his words would bring him into danger, yet his conscience and his listeners' fascinated astonishment enabled him to utter several more sentences. The speech illustrates what could be said in parliament, as well as the consequences of such speech.[90] Though far more passionate than Archbishop Heath's speech against the Bill of Supremacy in 1559, Wentworth's was equally peripheral to normal parliamentary politics: Wentworth did not expect to persuade anyone and no one was persuaded. No one attempted to prevent his arrest or, so far as we can tell, spoke publicly in the House in mitigation of his fault. It is possible that the Queen was pleasantly surprised by the House's unanimous agreement that his speech had overstepped acceptable bounds.[91] Certain kinds of opposition speech created unity more effectively than anything the government could say on its own behalf.

by silence they have all confirmed that which hath beene said by others. It remaineth yow grow to resolucion for the proceeding. Yowe knowe it must finally proceede from the prince.' Ibid., 1, pp. 373–8.

[88] Presumably this phrase means 'would prevent me being sent away' (to the Tower).

[89] Hartley, *Proceedings*, 1, p. 439.

[90] Wentworth was committed to the Tower by a committee of the House on 8 February and was forgiven by the Queen and returned to the House on 11 March. Ibid., 1, pp. 477, 491.

[91] She took the initiative in returning Wentworth to the House; she made no reference to the incident in her warm (though ultimately evasive) speech at the close of session and she once again prorogued the parliament rather than dissolving it. Ibid., 1, pp. 471–5, 491, 495.

Puritan initiatives in the parliaments of 1584/5 and 1586/7 illustrate the relationship between the freedom to propose measures of any kind and the calculation by a group within the Commons of what might command assent. Early in the 1584 parliamentary session Peter Turner proposed a bill to establish presbyterianism and to adopt the Geneva liturgy as the official church prayer book. No one supported this bill initially or defended it against the attacks of Hatton and Knollys when Turner reminded the House of it. At the same time there was widespread support for more moderate puritan petitions criticising the state of the clergy and Archbishop Whitgift's disciplinary measures. On 1 March the Queen forbade further discussion of these petitions, but when the Commons returned to the subject she allowed them to pass a bill which was sent to the Lords, debated there and forgotten.[92]

Presumably the group which presented and supported the petitions which focused on abuses in the church was embarrassed by Turner's proposal for root-and-branch reform of liturgy and church organisation. They correctly calculated that a petition with vague final aims which concentrated on present grievances had more chance of achieving widespread support. The Queen was strongly opposed to even the more moderate proposal but she allowed puritan members the satisfaction of speaking their minds and achieving a fruitless Commons victory rather than risk antagonising the whole House by curtailing their freedom of speech.

In 1586/7 the radical puritans who favoured a presbyterian church organisation prepared more thoroughly. On 27 February 1587 Anthony Cope presented a bill (whose lengthy preamble denounced the whole course of the English reformation) which proposed the repeal of all existing laws on church government and which required the use of the Genevan *Forme of common prayer* in all churches. When the Speaker and other members tried to prevent a reading of the bill its supporters made a succession of speeches in favour until the adjournment. Overnight the Queen sent for the bill and the book. Since the bill could not be read a number of members made speeches criticising the poor state of the church and demanding more godly preachers. On 1 March Peter Wentworth made a speech asserting the liberties of the House and was sent to the Tower, where several of the bill's other supporters joined him, charged with holding meetings outside parliament. On 4 March

---

[92] Collinson, *Elizabethan Puritan Movement*, pp. 282–8; Hartley, *Proceedings*, II, pp. 44–57; Neale, *Parliaments*, II, pp. 58–83, 97–101.

Mildmay, Egerton and Hatton delivered lengthy speeches denouncing the bill and the *Forme of common prayer*, and defending the Church settlement. Further attempts at discussion of religious grievances were effectively silenced by the Queen.[93]

Proponents of extreme Protestant reform enjoyed enough support in the House of Commons to get their views heard and to resist the Speaker's attempts to avoid contentious business. But by displaying their organisation they called down upon themselves the more effective resources of the Privy Council. Once her spokesmen had answered the assertions of the bill, the Queen felt justified in preventing all further discussion of religious topics. The right to make extreme criticisms of the Queen was rendered ineffective by the Privy Council's power of response and because moderate Protestants continued to support the council against extremists. But restrained use of parliamentary support could (as in 1585) secure symbolic victories and send messages. On religious issues the Queen ignored such messages (partly on grounds of prerogative and partly for reasons of foreign policy), arguably at the cost of the future unity of the church.

Free speech was a privilege of parliament, that is to say a temporary and institutionally specific suspension of the normal rules of public speech. The existence of limited freedom of speech was itself part of the political contest.[94] In May 1572 when Elizabeth instructed parliament not to consider bills on religion which had not been discussed by the bishops, the anonymous journal noted both the affront to the liberties of the House and the fact that no one spoke to object.[95] Wentworth and other less radical speakers could emphasise the importance of freedom of expression in order to enlarge the range of what could be discussed. But many of the same people could insist on the limitations on freedom of speech to attempt to silence views which offended them. In the debate on the punishment of Mary, Queen of Scots, Arthur Hall argued that both the Queen and the Duke of Norfolk should be pardoned on the grounds that their proposed marriage was essentially a private matter. He is also reported to have said to members of parliament, 'yow will

---

[93] Collinson, *Elizabethan Puritan Movement*, pp. 306–16; Hartley, *Proceedings*, II, pp. 311–54, 390–6.

[94] Elton, *Parliament*, pp. 341–9; David Colclough, '*Parrhesia*: The Rhetoric of Free Speech in Early Modern England', *Rhetorica* 17 (1999), 177–212; Alford, *Early Elizabethan Polity*, pp. 3, 7–8, 151; Guy, 'Rhetoric of Counsel', pp. 301–4.

[95] 'The messag that forbad the bringinge of billes of religion into the House seemed much to impugne the libertie of the House, but nothinge was saied unto it.' Hartley, *Proceedings*, I, p. 331. It is almost inconceivable that this comment could have been made by someone writing primarily for Burghley, as Elton assumes (*Parliament*, pp. 9–15).

hasten the execucion of such whose feet hereafter you would be glad to have againe to kisse'.[96] The following day, Nicholas St Leger argued that the views Hall had expressed could not be tolerated in parliament ('Speech ought to be contained in boundes, cankers not to be suffered') and that Hall should be sent to a more secure place.[97] Edward Fenner replied that while he liked the zeal of the previous speaker he preferred 'libertie of speech without restraint'.[98] Long-standing parliament men like Alford and Norton saw the need for evenhanded treatment of the is-sue of liberty and were prepared to speak up for the rights of those whose views they opposed.[99] Freedom of speech allowed parliament to define what it was prepared to be persuaded by and what it would unite to oppose (for example the very different views of Wentworth and Hall). In that sense freedom of speech allowed consensus to be defined. Cromwell reports Sir Francis Knollys's words on Hall's speech.

He sheweth that he wisheth speech in the Howse to be free, and that he had rather knowe men by their speech then not to knowe them by their scilence. He would have all blockes removed from the perverse, who otherwise would saie that they were denied speech, that they were able to answere but durst not. Therfore give them scope, let them speake their fill. We are not to be wonne from this course, nor to be abused by their sayinges.[100]

This is a stronger defence of free speech than the government side usually gave, but it emphasises a gap between what might be said and what might persuade.

THE QUEEN IN PARLIAMENT

Much has been written about the way privy councillors used parliament to put pressure on the Queen.[101] The Queen could, and did on occa-sion, respond to such pressure merely by refusing her consent to the bill parliament passed.[102] But she preferred not to do this. When the House raised topics which she considered to lie within her own prerogative, or to be more a matter for convocation than parliament, she sought to cut short discussion before it could reach a conclusion.[103] This tactic was not

[96] Hartley, *Proceedings*, I, pp. 273, 326, 354, 365–6; Graves, 'The Management', pp. 24–30.
[97] Hartley, *Proceedings*, I, p. 355. [98] Ibid.
[99] Ibid., I, pp. 360–1. Graves, *Thomas Norton*, pp. 353–8. [100] Hartley, *Proceedings*, I, p. 359.
[101] Graves, 'The Management', pp. 24–30; Elton, *Parliament*, pp. 358–77; Hartley, *Elizabeth's Parliaments*, pp. 165–6.
[102] Hartley, *Proceedings*, I, pp. 172, 418; Neale, *Elizabethan House of Commons*, pp. 409–11; Elton, *Parliament*, pp. 125–6.
[103] Hartley, *Proceedings*, I, pp. 160–2; Neale, *Parliaments*, I, pp. 157–8, 221, 273, 419–20; Elton, *Parliament*, p. 123.

always successful and the House quite frequently discussed matters of religion or succession which she regarded as outside their competence.[104] On other occasions she herself made carefully crafted speeches to the House or to its representatives.[105]

Queen Elizabeth was notoriously conscious of the effect she created. In her speech of 12 November 1586 to a delegation from both houses of parliament which was attempting to persuade her to order Mary's execution, Elizabeth speaks openly about her preoccupation with the persona she is projecting.

For wee princes I tell you are set on stages, in the sight and veiw of al the worlde duly observed. Th'eyes of many behold our actions, a spott is sone spied in our garments, a blemish quickly noted in our doinges. It behoveth us therefore to be carefull that our proceedings be just and honorable.[106]

This awareness of her position in the public gaze and the need to present herself and her actions as entirely blameless emerges also in her account of her response to Mary's alleged crimes

And now albeit I finde my life hath bin ful daungerouslie sought, and death contrived by suche as no desurt procured it, yet am I thereof so cleare frome malice, which hath the propertie to make menne gladde at the falls and faultes of theire foes and make them seeme to do for other cawses when rancor is the ground, yet I protest it is and hath bin my grevous thoght that one not different in sex, of like estate, and my neare kinne, shold be fallen into so great a crime. Yea I had so litle purpose to pursue her with any coloure of malice, that as it is not unknowne to some of my Lords here (for now I will play the blabb) I secretlie wrote her a lettre upon the discoverie of sondry treasons, that if she wold confesse them and privatlie acknowledge them by her lettres unto my self, shee never should nede be called for them into so publike question. Neither did I it of minde to circumvent her, for then I knew as much as she cold confesse, and so I did write.[107]

---

[104] The notion of what parliament could properly discuss was highly malleable. Tudor monarchs invited parliament to discuss religion and the succession when it suited their purposes but Elizabeth wanted such matters discussed only on her terms. Hartley, *Elizabeth's Parliaments*, p. 60.

[105] Harris Sacks, 'The Countervailing of Benefits', pp. 278–85 considers the 'golden speech', especially the gestures (289). Among the considerable literature on Elizabeth's orations see Alison Heisch, 'Queen Elizabeth I: Parliamentary Rhetoric and the Exercise of Power', *Signs* 1 (1975), 31–55; Mary T. Crane, 'Video et Taceo: Elizabeth I and the Rhetoric of Counsel', *Studies in English Literature 1500–1900* 28 (1988), 1–15; Steven W. May, 'Recent Studies in Elizabeth I', *English Literary Renaissance* 23 (1993), 345–54; Elizabeth I, *Collected Works*, ed. L. Marcus, J. Mueller and M. Rose (Chicago, 2000) is a modernised and translated edition.

[106] Hartley, *Proceedings*, II, p. 251.

[107] Ibid., II, p. 249. This is Hartley's edition of British Library Lansdowne 94 with deletions removed.

Although Mary has sought her death, Elizabeth claims that she bears her no malice, but rather is saddened by her crime and anxious to offer her another chance of mercy. Elizabeth is aware that her suggestion is double-edged, because it invites Mary to incriminate herself, but she protests her innocence, while letting her audience draw the implication that Mary is unrepentant and therefore dangerous. In putting herself in the right and Mary in the wrong in so many different ways, Elizabeth risks giving the impression of excessive artfulness. That she is willing to take this risk shows how concerned she is to give a public display of her mercy, before a group who would have preferred severity. On this occasion she was seeking to impress and conciliate not the immediate audience but, as her use of the stage image implies, the European princes of her time and the judgment of a future generation. The Privy Council may have used parliament to put pressure on the Queen, but the Queen could also use parliament as a platform for addressing other audiences and for showing them the pressure she was under.

At the closing of parliament in 1576, she interrrupted Bacon's speech on her behalf to reply to the Speaker's remarks on the succession. She decided (and the unusual adjournment of the previous day's proceedings had given her time to ponder her speech) to approach the issue obliquely.

Doo I see Gode's most sacred woorde and text of hollie writt drawen to so divers senses bee it never so presiselie taughte, and shall I hope that my speach can pas foorth thorowe so meanie eares withoute mistakinge, wheare so meanie ripe and divers wittes doo ofter bende to conster then attaine the true and perfect understandinge? If anie looke for eloquence, I shall deceave theire hope. If sum thinke I can mach theire guiftes that spake before, theie houlde an open heresie. I can not satisfie theire longinge thristes that wach for thease delightes unles I shoulde affoorde them what my self had never in possession. If I shoulde saie that the sweetest toonge or eloquentest speach that evar was in man weare able to expres that restles care which I have ever bent to governe for your greatest weales, I shoulde most wronge myne entent and greatelie bate the meritt of my owne endevoure.[108]

In her opening sentence Elizabeth carefully doubles her epithets and balances her phrases to give an impression of distinction and seriousness, but her subject is the impossibility of being understood. The second sentence is as brief as it is symmetrical. Its successors imitate the openings of each

[108] Ibid., I, p. 471. The Queen's satisfaction with this speech is confirmed by her note sending a copy of the speech to her godson, John Harington: 'Ponder [these words] in thy hours of leisure and play with them till they enter thy understanding. So shalt thou hereafter perchance, find some good fruits hereof when thy godmother is out of remembrance.' Neale, *Parliaments*, I, pp. 367–8.

half ('If anie looke/If sum thinke; I shall deceave theire hope/I cannot satisfie theire longinge thirstes') but she uses the formal resources of style to disclaim eloquence. This opening paragraph takes the inexpressibility topos to a new extreme. Anything that she might say is effectively disabled, since her audience is bound to mistake her meaning, since she is incapable of eloquence, or even of matching previous speakers, and since even the greatest eloquence would fall short of describing her care for the commonwealth. In the second section of the speech she denies any personal merit for her success, attributing all the benefits which the Speaker had listed to God. Her greatest boast is the loyalty of her subjects, which she contrasts with a commonplace description of the inconstancy of all human relationships. The commonplace of ordinary human inconstancy is then in turn contrasted with her own constancy, especially in religion.

If pollicie had beene preferred before truth, woulde I, tro you, even at the first beginninge of my rule have turned upsidowne so greate affaires, or entred into tossinge of the greatest waves and billowes of the worlde that might, if I had sought my ease, have harbored and cast ancor in most seeminge securitie? It can not bee denied but worldlie wisdoome rather bad me knitt and mach my self in leage and fast aliance with great princes to purchase ffrendes one everie side by worldlie meanes, and theare repose the trust of my strength wheare force coulde never wantt to geave assistance. Was I too seeke that by mane's outwarde iudgmentt this must needes be thought the safest coorse? No, I can never graunt my self so simple as not to see what all mene's eies discovered. But all thease meanes of leauges, aliances and foreine strengthes I quite forsooke, and gave myself to seeke for truth withoute respect, reposinge my cheefe staie in Gode's most mightie grace. Thus I began, thus I did proceede, and thus I hope to eande.[109]

The logic of her position here is that in defiance of every kind of political expediency she had from the beginning of her reign committed herself to the truth of the reformed religion. This strong underlying theme is elaborated through hypotheticals and contraries, as if the position she has taken can only be explained by describing the attractions of the paths she has refused. Even her description of her religious commitment is introduced through a distancing device. While the balances and meanderings of the earlier sentences are effectively answered by the contrasting direct assertions at the end ('Thus I began, thus I did proceede, and thus I hope to eande'), her approach enables her to evade the possibility of setting out her own position clearly and in detail. The vagueness helps her claim

---

[109] Hartley, *Proceedings*, I, p. 472 (with minor alterations).

credit from her audience for their approval of Protestantism without spelling out the difference between her version of the reformed religion and theirs. There is also an implied criticism of their attempts to force further reform: how can you doubt my commitment to protestantism when I have stood up for it although every consideration of prudent statesmanship suggested caution?

Then she reminds her audience of the peace and prosperity they have enjoyed under her rule, before (again) deflecting all merit for her success to God and emphasising her care for the safety of her people. This part of the speech resembles the party-line of her councillors' speeches, when they extol the benefits of the Queen's reign before asking for additional subsidies. In this manner two thirds of the speech is given over to preparation before she touches on the topic of marriage (again in very similar words to those used by the Lord Keeper on her behalf). Personally she would prefer not to marry, yet she is willing to set aside her private wishes for the benefit of the state. She knows she is mortal and for that reason she prepares herself for death, opening the way for more commonplace reflections.

> My experience teacheth me to bee no fonder of thease vaine delightes then reason woulde, nether further to delight in thinges uncertaine then maie seeme convenient. But lett good heade bee taken least that reachinge to far after future good you perrill not the presentt, or begine to quarrell or faule together by the eares by dispute before it maie bee well discided who shall weare my crowne.[110]

After all this preparation and self-presentation the main message of the speech is delivered glancingly, in the form of a proverb: you may endanger the present by taking too much care over the future. She regards the topic of the succession as so divisive that she has no wish to broach it. In conclusion she urges them again not to misunderstand her, by promising them that she will provide for their future security and by bestowing her thanks and blessings on them. The speech is a masterpiece of obliqueness, emphasising her firmness where she knows her audience is on her side, insisting on her willingness to overcome her own preferences for their advantage, covering the subject at issue, on which she intends to disappoint them, with a surface show of pliancy. She is evidently negotiating her wish to present herself favourably and to please her audience against her need to keep open her freedom of manoeuvre by evading the commitment they seek. But one can also wonder whether her expression is not too elaborate. Although most of her audience would

---

[110] Ibid., I, p. 473.

have been charmed by her manner, they may also have been left with the impression that they did not know what position she was actually taking.

The Queen did not aim to persuade her direct audience, nor was there any pressure on her to do so. She did, however, prefer to charm them so as to lessen any resentment of her deferral of action. Although in strict terms of power she had no need of their approval, yet the situation of expressing herself to representatives of parliament produced a moral pressure to seek their understanding. Whatever the limitations on parliament's freedom of action, when it was in session it generated situations in which reasons came to be given by the most powerful people in the country to those who were, in the ordinary course of affairs, their inferiors.

CONCLUSION

Grammar school rhetoric contributed to the content and the technique of Elizabethan parliamentary speeches. Moral axioms, narratives, histories and the topics of deliberative oratory were frequently employed to support arguments. The structures of longer parliamentary orations reflected a combination of classical rhetorical doctrine (in the exordium and the refutation of objections) and parliamentary precedents (in the restrictions on length and the self-deprecating conclusions). Privy councillors sought to present themselves as attentive to the concerns of their audience. While parliamentary speakers generally preferred a sober, almost dialectical style, they used amplification and figures of rhetoric to develop commonplaces, to emphasise important passages and to demonstrate their skill.

University training in dialectic affected the structure and technique of parliamentary debate. Members often began by summarising the arguments of a previous speaker and replying to each point in turn, in the manner of university disputations. They employed enthymemes and hypothetical syllogisms, distinguished different senses of words (as in disputations) and made prominent and clear divisions (as recommended by textbooks on method). Habits of note-taking and dialectical analysis made possible the parliamentary journals' recording of debates. Indeed two of the parliamentary journals appear to be collections of pithy sayings such as might be recorded in a commonplace book, rather than records of the proceedings.[111]

---

[111] For example ibid., II, pp. 105–127 (the anonymous journal of the fifth parliament, 1584–5); III, p. 176 (1593).

The theory of epideictic rhetoric enables us to appreciate that many parliamentary speeches function in a way that is almost ritualistic, reaffirming the unity and identity, the shared history and interests, of the moderate Protestant élite. The collection and dissemination of arguments, the repetition of versions of recent history to which all subscribe, even Hatton's arousal of violent emotions against the safely absent Cardinal Allen, serve to unite the political community in preparation for more contentious requests or admonitions.

This seems to me to expose a limitation in Elton's generally convincing revisionist account of the Elizabethan parliament. Because he sees political history as exclusively concerned with legislation and executive action, he regards parliament as a place for talking, ultimately powerless, largely a pretence.[112] But the words spoken in parliament were weighed seriously by speakers, auditors and journal writers. Uncomfortable and unwelcome things could be said in parliament. In most cases the answers given by privy councillors won the day, but ordinary members of parliament could maintain disagreement and on occasion might even see their views prevail. Parliamentarians were members of an élite whose culture was formed by oratory and debate.[113] The form of debate and the shared experience of disputation, together with the possibility that maintained disagreement would be resolved by majority vote, produced some obligation on government speakers to answer arguments, to give reasons and to respond to messages. The Queen's councillors in the House of Commons, who did not have the right of veto or the resource of an effectively whipped party to enable them to avoid argument, evidently found it an ordeal to be called even to this weak form of account.

Parliamentary speeches altered legislation and provided the basis for action, but they had other purposes as well, the establishment of individual positions, the satisfaction of local needs and notably the creation and celebration of political community. Vituperation and immoderate opposition, as much as royal progresses, country-houses and sessions in London, helped establish community between the privy councillors and the geographically scattered landed gentry.

---

[112] Elton, *Parliament*, pp. 377–9. Patrick Collinson argues that Elizabethan 'men of business' like Norton, Beale and Morrice could favour further religious reform and could be viewed as troublemakers when they expressed opinions about religion and the succession. See 'Puritans, Men of Business and Elizabethan Parliaments', in his *Elizabethan Essays* (London, 1994), pp. 59–86.

[113] Both Nicholas Bacon's disparagement of 'contentious reasoninges and disputacions' as more suitable to the schools than to parliament in 1559 (quoted in note 16 above) and his urging of parliament to speak *logice* rather than *rhetorice* in 1571 (Hartley, *Proceedings*, I, p. 244) assume and draw on the House's shared experience of rhetoric and disputation.

In theory parliament embodied a form of exchange: the Queen expected to obtain financial support and to pass her legislative programme, while the Lords and Commons expected to air their grievances and to pass local laws useful to their supporters. Evidently there was a degree of fiction about this. The Queen was always in practice assured of the vote for supply, while she could always reject any other legislation. But these were final powers which she preferred not to use. Even within parliament the Privy Council could organise pressure on an individual member or secure a re-run of a vote which it had lost. But this may have been balanced by other forms of fiction. The writ of central government did not run uniformly and effectively throughout the realm. Many interests and shades of opinion were unrepresented in parliament. Members could vote taxes which in practice they would neither collect nor pay.[114] The very existence of parliament seems to have constrained the Queen and her ministers into financial and religious concessions. Parliament was a place where things could be said, where messages could be given in both directions. Among the many factors determining the extent to which Justices of the Peace and returning members were able or willing to carry out at the local level the demands of the Queen and her ministers were the extent to which they felt incorporated in a political community and the way in which the government responded to the arguments and concerns expressed in the privileged space and time of parliament.

[114] The council's anxiety about the commitment of local office-holders to parliamentary decisions may be reflected in the exhortation to members of parliament to enforce the laws they have made in the Lord Keeper's professedly ceremonial speech at the closing of parliament. E.g. Hartley, *Proceedings*, I, pp. 49–51, 111–12, 171, 190–1, 417, 464–5, 495; III, p. 492.

8

Religious discourse

The chief official aim of university education in Elizabethan England was the production of a learned and godly ministry. The Church of England employed more university graduates than any other profession and many university scholarships and fellowships required their benefi-ciaries to enter the Church. Even though declamation and disputation were not explicitly designed to prepare for sermon-giving and theological controversy, the skills these university exercises fostered were obviously helpful in such clerical duties.

At the same time the classical learning of the university arts course in some ways conflicted with Christian ideals. Christian thinkers tradi-tionally distrust pagan culture even when they recognise the practical usefulness of rhetoric. Even Erasmus thought that good preaching de-pended more on belief and inspiration than on rhetorical invention.[1] The classical educational ideals of the orator and the philosopher car-ried implications of exceptionalness, leadership, wealth and leisure which were opposed to Christian notions of simple piety. Protestant emphasis on predestination gave this tension a new twist. Where education aimed at moral and intellectual improvement and was in principle available to anyone with leisure and aptitude, salvation was unearned and by free gift of God to the elect alone. In practice humanist education was far from universally available, but it did create the means for some mobility in society and employment, particularly within the visible church. Predes-tination defined a different, unworldly, but theoretically closed élite, who believed in the essential corruption of the fallen human mind and for whom education might therefore seem positively harmful. John Morgan has shown that individual puritans could both believe in the harmfulness of worldly learning and prove effective patrons of learning.[2]

---

[1] Erasmus, *Ecclesiastes*, II, ed. J. Chomarat, *Opera omnia*, V–4 (Amsterdam, 1994), pp. 247–8.
[2] J. Morgan, *Godly Learning: Puritan Attitudes towards Reason, Learning and Education, 1560–1640* (Cambridge, 1986), pp. 64–72, 99–105, 179, 247–55.

In this chapter I describe and illustrate the ways in which preachers and writers of religious controversy made use of their training in
rhetoric, dialectic and moral philosophy. First I examine a controversy
about preaching. Then I discuss the use of rhetoric and dialectic in the
interpretation of the Bible, the use of logical techniques and terminology in religious pamphlets and sermons, the contribution of dialectic
and rhetoric to the organisation of religious texts and religious writers'
approaches to style. Having established the importance of rhetorical
techniques in religious texts and explored the different ways in which
religious writers use their rhetorical training, I examine the connections
between Elizabethan religious and moral discourse by discussing three
topics of religious writing which articulate ethical, social and political
questions raised in rhetorical education: funeral oratory and consolation, poverty and poor relief, and authority in church and state. Just as
Elizabethan politicians founded arguments and decisions on principles
derived from religion, so preachers drew on pagan moral sentences and
exempla as well as on scripture in proposing religious approaches to
problems confronting their audiences.

From the great mass of Elizabethan publications on religious topics
I have taken my examples from a few texts organised crudely into two
categories: sermons and controversies.[3] Controversies generally involve
attacks on the position of the established Church, either from Catholics
or from more radical Protestants, and defences of the official Church
position. Controversies within the reformed Church had greater impact
in Elizabethan England than controversies against Catholics, probably
because the political nation was entirely Protestant (at least in public)
and because puritan writings (and therefore the replies to them) were
composed in English and circulated widely. I shall be drawing examples
from the Admonition controversy of the early 1570s and from Richard
Hooker's attempt to conclude the controversy with the puritans, the first
five books of the *Laws of Ecclesiastical Polity* (1594-7).[4]

---

[3] Systematic treatises on Christian doctrine would fall somewhere between my two categories, while
I have excluded catechisms from this chapter because they were used within the system of formal
schooling.

[4] Although I accept that books six to eight of the *Laws* are consistent with the first five books,
I make only occasional reference to them, because they were not printed until 1648 (books VI
and VIII) and 1662 (VII). W. Speed Hill, 'The Evolution of Hooker's *Laws of Ecclesiastical Polity*',
in Hill (ed.), *Studies in Richard Hooker* (Cleveland, 1972), pp. 117–58; W. D. J. Cargill Thompson,
'The Philosopher of the "Politic Society": Richard Hooker as Political Thinker', in Hill, *Studies in
Richard Hooker*, pp. 3–76, reprinted in Cargill Thompson, *Studies in the Reformation* (London, 1980),
pp. 131–91; Helgerson, *Forms of Nationhood*, pp. 269–83; M. E. C. Perrott, 'Richard Hooker and
the Problem of Authority in the Elizabethan Church', *Journal of Ecclesiastical History* 49 (1998),
29–60.

The Admonition controversy takes its name from the *Admonition to Parliament* published by John Field and Thomas Wilcox shortly before the end of the parliamentary session in June 1572. In 1571 the clergy had been compelled to subscribe to the *Book of Common Prayer*, vestments and the Thirty-nine articles. In 1572 parliament had put forward a bill to reform the *Book of Common Prayer* which had been read, amended and then left to languish. The *Admonition to Parliament* attacked the established Church as 'far from being a Christian Church', argued for a learned ministry, properly administered sacraments and presbyterian church organisation, and attacked the 'popish remnants' in the *Book of Common Prayer*.[5]

This book is an unperfect book, culled and picked out of that popish dunghill, the Mass book full of all abhominations. For some and many of the contents therein be such as are against the word of God.[6]

Field and Wilcox were imprisoned for a year for writing the *Admonition*, which was banned.[7] By the end of October, John Whitgift, later Archbishop of Canterbury, had composed his *Answer to the Admonition*, though it was not published until February 1573. Thomas Cartwright, Whitgift's old adversary at Trinity College, Cambridge and the leading spokesman for presbyterianism, published his *Reply to an Answer* in May 1573. A warrant was issued for Cartwright's arrest but he went into exile for eleven years to escape it.[8] Whitgift replied with his *Defence of the Answer* which prints the original admonition section by section with his criticisms, Cartwright's replies and his answers to the replies, in 1574. The imperative to reply to the arguments of Field, Wilcox and Cartwright was so pressing that Whitgift was prepared in effect to reprint a banned book in order to do so. Although the arguments are largely concerned with questions of worship and church organisation, underlying assumptions about the interpretation of scripture and the nature of salvation are often explored in the course of the debate.[9] In his response Hooker went even further, beginning his *Laws* with an attempt to establish fundamental principles about the nature of law and the relation between God's gift of reason and Christian revelation from which to derive his defence of the Elizabethan Church settlement.

In discussing sermons, I have tried to make a balanced selection of the most widely heard and read preachers, guided by J. W. Blench's

---

[5] John Field and Thomas Wilcox, *Admonition to Parliament*, reprinted in W. H. Frere and C. E. Douglas (eds.), *Puritan Manifestos* (1907, repr. New York, 1972), pp. ix–xxii, 8–9; Collinson, *Puritan Movement*, esp. pp. 101–21.

[6] Field and Wilcox, *Admonition*, p. 21.   [7] Collinson, *Puritan Movement*, pp. 119–21, 149.

[8] Ibid., pp. 151–3, 295.

[9] Lake, *Anglicans and Puritans?*, pp. 1–70 is an admirable guide to the controversy.

thorough and non-partisan survey.[10] The official *Homilies* (first book 1547, second book 1563) naturally take pride of place since they were so widely distributed and because the Church establishment promoted them as a standard of orthodoxy, while many puritans rejected them as an offence to a preaching ministry. Henry Smith (1550–91) serves as an example of popular preaching of the middle years of the reign, partly because his sermons were so well appreciated in his time and partly for his interest in social questions, such as marriage and poverty. The sermons of John Rainolds and Richard Hooker appear because of their interest as writers and because other works of theirs are discussed in this book. As the most famous preacher of his age, Lancelot Andrewes (1555–1626) is included to represent the learned form of preaching, even though many of his most famous sermons were preached before James I.

ARGUMENTS ABOUT PREACHING

The place of preaching in reformed religion was debated in the Admonition controversy. The *Admonition to Parliament* attacked the established Church for failing to produce an educated clergy and for suspending learned ministers who were unwilling to wear vestments or subscribe to the Thirty-nine articles. For Field and Wilcox preaching was the essence of protestantism and the chief office of the clergy. Services without preaching or ministers who could not preach were simply unchristian.

By the word of God, it is an office of preaching: they make it an office of reading. Christ said goe preach; they in mockery give them the Bible, and authority to preach, and yet suffer them not, except they have new licences . . . With these such are admitted and accepted as are only bare readers that are able to say service and minister a sacrament. And that this is not the feeding that Christ spake of the scriptures are plain. Reading is not feeding, but it is as evil as playing upon a stage and worse too. For players yet learn their part without book, and these, many of them can scarcely read within the book.[11]

In their anxiety to insist on the pre-eminence of preaching and the need for a learned clergy, the authors of the *Admonition* attack all forms of service which lack preaching and, particularly, the reading of printed homilies instead of a preacher preaching his own sermon.[12] The proof of the inadequacy of the ministry is the decay of English Christian life.

---

[10] Blench, *Preaching in England*; now see also P. McCullough, *Sermons at Court: Politics and Religion in Elizabethan and Jacobean Preaching* (Cambridge, 1998) and L. A. Ferrell and P. McCullough (eds.), *The English Sermon Revised* (Manchester, 2000).
[11] Field and Wilcox, *Admonition*, p. 22.   [12] Ibid., pp. 22–3.

We will say no more in this matter, but desire you to consider with us what small profit and edification this seely reading hath brought to us these 13 years passed . . . surely our sins are grown ripe, our ignorance is equal with the ignorance of our leaders; we are lost, they cannot find us, we are sick, they cannot heal us; we are hungry, they cannot feed us; except they lead us by other men's lights and heal us by saying a prescript form of service, or else feed us with homilies, that are too homely to be set in the place of God's scriptures.[13]

Their condemnation is made more biting with figures of rhetoric like ploce ('ignorance . . . ignorance'), contentio ('we are lost, they cannot find us'), isocolon ('we are lost . . . we are sick . . . we are hungry') and paronomasia ('homilies . . . homely'). In his *Answer* Whitgift takes exception to this sweeping attack on the ministry and its leadership, protesting that there is effective preaching and that frequent preaching of itself is not necessarily edifying.

I am fully persuaded that he cometh nearer to the fulfilling of the mind of the apostle, which, diligently studying and labouring continually for knowledge, doth orderly, learnedly and effectually preach once in the month, than such as, backbiting at other men's tables, running all the day long up and down the streets, seldom or never studying, do negligently, unorderly, verbally (if I may so term it) preach every day twice.[14]

Whitgift insists that reading scripture is as important as preaching,[15] rejects the *Admonition*'s attacks on the existing clergy,[16] and argues that God's word can be preached as well in writing as in extempore preaching.[17] He asserts the importance of reading scripture against the *Admonition*'s taunts on the subject, and rejects the argument that reading the homilies is against the true nature of preaching.[18] In his *Reply to an Answer*, Cartwright claims that the *Admonition* never meant to attack the reading of scripture,[19] and mocks Whitgift's minimalist notion of preaching.

Here Mr Doctor would fain (as it seemeth) if he durst, interpret diligent preaching . . . to be preaching once a month. But because he dare not say so directly he compasseth it about . . . Granting that those (which he calleth verbal sermons) have some goodness and edifying, it must be very slender meat which is not better being given every day than the best and daintiest meat once only in a month. For with the one a man may live, although he be not liking, with the other he, being once fed, is afterward famished.[20]

[13] Ibid., p. 23.
[14] *The Works of John Whitgift*, ed. by J. Ayre, 3 vols. (Cambridge, 1851–3), Parker Society vols. XLIV, XLVIII, L, III, pp. 1–2.
[15] Ibid., III, pp. 7, 28–30, 34.   [16] Ibid., III, pp. 8–9.   [17] Ibid., III, pp. 40–3.
[18] Ibid., III, pp. 46, 50–7.   [19] Ibid., III, p. 28.   [20] Ibid., III, p. 2.

Whitgift's *Defence* rejects what he claims is Cartwright's distortion of his words. He finds Cartwright's comparison between preaching and feeding (which Cartwright would have considered scriptural) inappropriate in a number of ways.

The similitude betwixt the external meat that feedeth the body and the word that feedeth the soul doth fail in many things, and especially in these: that the meat of the body remaineth not in the stomach, but passeth through; the word of God continueth and endureth in the mind forever. The meat of the body, the better it is digested, the lesser while it doth continue: the word of God, the better it is digested and remembered, the longer it remaineth. The meat of the body once taken serveth but for the present time, be it never so good and wholesome; the word of God once preached and faithfully received doth nourish and feed continually; therefore one learned, effectual, orderly sermon, preached once in a month, containeth more nourishment in it, feedeth longer, worketh more in the hearts of the hearers, edifieth more, than all the unorderly and verbal sermons.[21]

Whitgift's reply uses figures of repetition and contrast to elaborate a distinction between worldly and spiritual feeding. He concludes this disputation-like rejection of his opponent's comparison with an amplification of the value of 'orderly' preaching. In comparison with Cartwright's witty thrust, Whitgift's rebuttal seems heavy-handed. His use of repetition and doubling is sonorous rather than pointed. The whole argument rests too much on a contrast of qualitative adjectives ('orderly, learned, effectual' set against 'unorderly and verbal') repeated from his initial *Answer* without being elaborated or defended against Cartwright's attack.

Many of the replies (and responses to replies) are given over to point-scoring,[22] sometimes achieved through deliberate misrepresentation of the opponent's view, and to tenacious defences of sometimes casually chosen words. The agenda for the argument is always set by the *Admonition.* Field and Wilcox attack the Church for failing to produce a learned ministry and a fully reformed religion. Whitgift is obliged to defend actually existing half measures. Beneath the point-scoring and above the simmering quarrel about the removal of non-subscribing ministers, it is possible to discern two different approaches to preaching. For Cartwright and the puritans, preaching is the daily bread of the Church, providing

---

[21] Ibid., III, p. 3.
[22] Whitgift is delighted to reprint his long attack on the puritan approach to scripture with the comment 'All this you have left unanswered', though in fact Cartwright had earlier replied that no attack on Bible-reading had been intended. Ibid., III, pp. 53–7, 28.

interpretation of scripture and guidance to the congregation at every step. For Whitgift a well-researched, learned and orderly sermon is a special event, something to be contemplated and returned to for a long time after it has been heard. Within the broad and simple framework of obligatory belief, Whitgift allows more space for the individual Christian to read the Bible and ponder, while Cartwright puts more emphasis on the directing role of the minister.

Because of his general approach and because he was writing almost twenty years after the rapid exchange of publications around the *Admonition*, Hooker took a much longer view of the nature of preaching and its place in the life of the Church.

Because therefore want of the knowledge of God is the cause of all iniquity amongst men, as contrariwise the very ground of all our happiness and the seed of whatsoever perfect virtue groweth among us is a right opinion touching things divine, this kind of knowledge we may justly set down for the first and chiefest thing which God imparteth unto his people, and our duty of receiving this at his merciful hands for the first of those religious offices wherewith we publicly honour him on earth. For the instruction therefore of all sorts of men to eternal life, it is necessary that the sacred and saving truth of God be openly published unto them. Which open publication of heavenly mysteries is by an excellency termed Preaching.[23]

Hooker acknowledges the centrality of preaching, but his explanation of its function permits him a definition of preaching wide enough to include public reading of the scriptures, printed commentaries and reading of homilies.[24] In order to establish a basis from which to refute puritan arguments against reading homilies, he elaborates a definition of the good sermon which he hopes will be widely acceptable.

When once we are agreed what sermons shall currently pass for good, we may at the length understand from them what that is in a good sermon which doth make it the word of life unto such as hear. If substance of matter, evidence of things, strength and validity of arguments and proofs, or any other virtue else which words may contain; of all this what is there in the best sermons being uttered which they lose by being read?[25]

Hooker lays the emphasis plainly on strength of arguments and weight of evidence, though he allows his opponents to add other qualities of

---

[23] The best edition is Richard Hooker, *Of the Lawes of Ecclesiasticall Politie*, ed. G. Edelen, W. Speed Hill and P. G. Stanwood, *The Folger Library Edition of the Works of Richard Hooker*, vols. I–III (Cambridge MA, 1978–81). Until the commentary of the Folger edition is published notes are available in *Hooker's Works*, ed. J. Keble, 3 vols. (Oxford, 1865). It is customary to cite by book, chapter and section: Hooker, *Lawes*, v.18.1.

[24] Hooker, *Lawes*, v.18.3–5, 19.2, 21.2–5, 22.19.   [25] Ibid., v.22.19.

language to the list. Later he mockingly offers them the alternative of placing all the emphasis on eloquence or delivery. He maintains the position that the most effectual parts of a good sermon must survive being written down. His broad view of the scope of religious teaching enables him to praise both Bible reading and sermons as effective ways of publishing God's truth.

Sith God, who knoweth and discloseth best the rich treasures of his own wisdom, hath by delivering his word made choice of the Scriptures as the most effectual means whereby those treasures might be imparted unto the world, it followeth that to man's understanding the Scripture must needs be even of itself intended as a full and perfect discovery, sufficient to imprint in us the lively character of all things necessarily required for the attainment of eternal life.[26]

So worthy a part of divine service we should greatly wrong, if we did not esteem preaching as the blessed ordinance of God, sermons as keys to the kingdom of heaven, as wings to the soul, as spurs to the good affections of man, unto the sound and healthy as food, as physic unto diseased minds.[27]

Having provided definitions of religious teaching and of the good sermon which it would seem perverse to dispute, Hooker is able to draw conclusions intended to bolster the position of the established Church, while acknowledging the enthusiasm of the puritans for sermons. Since God presented the treasures of his word in the scriptures, scripture reading must be an adequate form of religious instruction. At the same time it would be self-defeating (and an insult to the liturgy) not to amplify the effectiveness of preaching. Although he strives to include both sides of the controversy, Hooker's tactics are drawn from disputation. By crafting an apparently broad and unexceptionable definition he establishes the logical basis for conclusions which his adversaries would prefer not to grant.

In controversy Hooker favours exhaustive sentences, logically organised and carefully formulated. In expressing an enthusiasm he shares with his opponents he turns to a series of metaphors (wings, spurs, food, medicine) set out in equal cola and with chiasmus ('unto the sound and healthy as food, as physic unto diseased minds'). Hooker will join with the puritans in any praise of sermons, provided that they do not deny the effectiveness of reading scripture or insist that only *viva voce* preaching provides a route to salvation.[28] Hooker's method is at least as effective as Whitgift's in providing answers to puritan arguments but his discussion of

[26] Ibid., v.21.3.   [27] Ibid., v.22.1.   [28] Ibid., v.21.1, 8, 13–14, 19–20.

the wider aims and effects of religious teaching enables him to acknowledge their preference for preaching alongside his own praise of scripture. Hooker elaborates the puritans' complaint and Whitgift's debating point into a celebration of two parallel means of arriving at religious truth.

Having established that Field, Whitgift and Cartwright used dialectical strategies and figures of rhetoric to argue their opposing views of preaching and that Hooker's understanding of logical method enabled him to incorporate some of the puritans' enthusiasms while rejecting their exclusiveness, I shall now examine in a more systematic way the contributions of dialectic and rhetoric to different aspects of religious discourse.

RHETORIC AND DIALECTIC IN ELIZABETHAN RELIGIOUS DISCOURSE

a) Interpretation of the Bible

The interpretation of the Bible is the cornerstone of Christian discourse, yet it resembles, and draws on the techniques of, humanist exegesis of classical texts. Elizabethan preachers rework humanist pedagogical commonplaces in urging the study of scripture and employ dialectic and rhetoric to interpret it. The first of the *Homilies* is an 'Exhortation to the Reading and Knowledge of Holy Scripture'. Scripture is said to be the food of the soul, 'for in Holy Scripture is fully contained what we ought to do, and what to eschew, what to believe, what to love, and what to look for at God's hands at length'.[29] Cranmer describes the effects of Bible-reading.[30]

And there is nothing that so much strengtheneth our faith and trust in God, that so much keepeth up innocency and pureness of the heart, and also of outward godly life and conversation, as continual reading and recording of God's word. For that thing, which by continual use of reading of Holy Scripture and diligent searching of the same is deeply printed and graven in the heart, at length turneth almost into nature.[31]

Through diligent reading and pondering, in what amounts to a form of imitation, the Christian in some sense becomes the book. The one who benefits most from the Bible is 'he that is most turned into it, that

---

[29] *Sermons or Homilies Appointed to be Read in Churches* (London, 1833), p. 1.
[30] The traditional attributions of the homilies are listed in Blench, *Preaching in England*, pp. 42, 101.
[31] *Homilies*, p. 3.

is most inspired with the Holy Ghost, most in his heart and life altered and changed into that thing which he readeth'.[32] Cranmer surpasses any humanist in his enthusiasm for the reading of his text and his confidence in its effectiveness. Henry Smith emphasised the importance of rhetorical education to correct understanding of the Bible.

> If you mark, you shall see throughout that all the testimonies which the papists allege for their heresies are either tropes, or figures, or allegories, or parables, or allusions, or dark speeches, which when they presume to expound allegorically, or literally, without conference of any other scriptures, then they wander and stray from the mark, or else it is impossible that the truth should maintain error, that is, that the Scriptures should speak for heresy, if it were not wrested and perverted; therefore we see that Eve never erred until she corrupted the text.[33]

Unless what is expressed figuratively is so understood, heresy is bound to follow. Smith holds that the doctrine of transubstantiation depends on a literal interpretation of a metaphor.[34]

Elizabethan sermons typically use scripture in two ways, one of which usually predominates in any particular sermon. Bible texts can be used to back up a religious argument not taken directly from scripture, as the texts in praise of scripture were above, or the text itself can be analysed, exploring its meaning by reference to other texts and applying its teaching to contemporary circumstances.

The former is the dominant mode in the *Homilies* as it is also in many of the sermons of Henry Smith, such as his 'Preparative to Marriage', in which observations about the nature of marriage and the duties of the two partners are confirmed by citations from scripture.[35] In these sermons, as in the controversial works, the Bible is used as a storehouse of necessarily true axioms which can be used to support, or prove, the writer's assertions.

---

[32] Ibid.

[33] Henry Smith, *The Works*, 2 vols. (Edinburgh, 1866–7), I, pp. 47–8. Less forcefully, Sherry had pointed to the difficulty of interpreting scripture without an understanding of figurative language (*Schemes and Tropes*, sig. A7r–v).

[34] Smith, *Works*, I, pp. 46–8. Peter Martyr becomes involved in an argument with a Catholic spokesman about which verses must be taken literally and which figuratively, *Disputatio*, sigs. b3r–4r. See chapter two above, pp. 60, 72.

[35] Smith, *Works*, I, pp. 5–42, structure summarised in Blench, *Preaching in England*, pp. 103–5. On the basis of a remark by Kathleen Davies (*Social History* 5 (1977) p. 580), Lorna Hutson claims (*Usurer's Daughter*, p. 19) that Smith's sermon is a republication of Coverdale's translation of Bullinger. In fact the two texts are quite different and Hutson has graciously acknowledged this (personal communication, 29 September 2000). H. Bullinger, *The Christen State of Matrimonye*, trans. M. Coverdale (Antwerp, 1541) STC 4045.

When a supporting text is analysed in more detail, this way of using the Bible comes to resemble the second way. This also happens in controversy, when a respondent disputes the meaning of a text. The second way of using the Bible is customary in more formal sermons and necessary in sermon commentaries. It is also more like the commentary on classical texts practised at grammar school and university.

The 'Homily on Repentance', from the second series, first published in 1563, after asserting the importance of repentance, focuses on a pair of verses from the second chapter of Joel.[36] The homily draws on the context of the text,[37] explains the logic of its argument and explores the implication of each phrase, both in itself and in its linkage with the overall argument.

In which words he comprehendeth all manner of things that can be spoken of repentance, which is a turning again of the whole man unto god, from whom we be fallen away by sin. But that the whole discourse thereof may the better be borne away, we shall first consider in order four principal points, that is: from what we must return, to whom we must return, by whom we may be able to convert, and the manner how to turn to God.[38]

The homilist analyses the text according to logical categories derived from a topical consideration of the notion of returning: initial situation from which to turn, aim or direction of turn, assisting cause and manner. These topics resemble Brinsley's instructions for schoolboys analysing a classical text. Each aspect is explored in sequence, the point being made is explained logically and confirmed with further quotations. The sermon does not make significant use of rhetorical terminology, though it takes account of the speaker's point of view and his immediate audience.

John Rainolds's Oxford sermon on Obadiah, verses 12–14, part of a series constituting a commentary on the whole book, is more obviously learned in its range of linguistic reference and in its dialectical approach. Whereas in the previous verses the prophet had explained the reason for the destruction of the Idumeans on the general grounds of their cruelty to the Israelites,

he doth now in these words particularly lay the same out, that the poisoned sore of their barbarousness being declared, the justice of God in cutting them off might be shewed unto them.

---

[36] Joel 2, verses 12–13: 'Therefore also now the Lord saith, return unto me with all your heart, with fasting, weeping, and mourning. Rend your hearts and not your clothes, and return unto the Lord your God; for he is gracious and merciful, slow to anger and of great compassion, and ready to pardon wickedness', *Homilies*, p. 366. This homily is largely a translation from R. Gualter.
[37] *Homilies*, p. 367.   [38] Ibid., pp. 367–8.

Which causes in particularitie are delivered by way of admonition, wherein is opened what they should have done, and they concern

	Either their	1. Affections
		2. Actions
1. Affections	hatred	testified by their gladness and
	envy	rejoicing at their harms and
		afflictions.
2. Their actions are either concerning	words	proud and spightful: *Thou shouldst not have spoken insolently*;
	deeds	spoiling them of: goods: *Entred into the gate. Laid hands on substance*;
		life: *Stood in the breach to cut off them that escaped. Betrayed the remnant.*

Wherefore in these points consisted the cruelty of Edom in wishing, speaking and doing evil against Israel.[39]

Rainolds explains that each of these actions is opposed to the behaviour of well-wishers. All these actions, though grievous in themselves, are increased by the circumstances, of persons, in that they were brothers, and of time, in the day of affliction, when Jerusalem was sacked.[40] Rainolds uses an approach rooted in dialectical reading to explain the process of amplification by which the cruelty of the Idumeans' actions is brought out. This in turn implies an obligation on Christians to be patient and to show brotherly love. Rainolds amplifies the difficulty of this charge with citations from the New Testament about the suffering involved in the Christian life, before making a comparison between the persecution of the Israelites and the St Bartholomew's Day Massacre, which he elaborates by applying each of the key words of his text to that event.[41] Rainolds then organises his charge to Christians around the words which Obadiah used to describe the cruelty of the Idumeans, by way of contraries.[42]

Thus while Rainolds uses logical techniques to analyse the structure of the text and to extract lessons from it, once he speaks of contemporary events and gives instructions to his own audience he bases the structure of his speech on the words of Obadiah. The words of the Bible are subjected to logical analysis but then provide the structure for Rainolds's application of Obadiah's teaching to the late sixteenth century. Unlike the homilist, Rainolds occasionally refers to the original

---

[39] John Rainolds, *The Prophecy of Obadiah opened* (Oxford, 1613) STC 20619, sig. N1r–v.
[40] Ibid., sig. N2r.　　[41] Ibid., sigs. N3r–O1r.　　[42] Ibid., sigs. O1v–2v.

Hebrew text.[43] While amplifying the injunction not to take away some-one's living, Rainolds finds contemporary and classical parallels.

> Do not they commit this wickedness which take money from that which was provided to maintain the poor, either in the University publicly or privately in any college ... But they will not say that they lay hands upon them, but that they take that which is offered. Alas, poor souls, do they offer it? Yea, even as men their purses on Salisbury plain. They yield their goods to save their lives. This was right Verres's answer, *he took nothing but what was offered him.*[44]

Both the biblical text which was his principal object and the classical allusion are used to reflect on and instruct about contemporary ills.

Like Rainolds, Andrewes combines logical overall structures (which we shall examine later) with close attention to the words of his text, repeating, amplifying, providing contexts and alternatives. T. S. Eliot describes this feature of Andrewes's court sermons:

> Andrewes takes a word and derives the world from it; squeezing and squeezing the word until it yields a full juice of meaning which we should never have supposed any word to possess.[45]

His public sermons make more restrained use of this technique of verbal meditation, which seems to be related to the techniques of producing *copia* by periphrasis and dwelling on the circumstances of a thing.[46] Even to a lay audience, of merchants in the courtyard of the Spittal, Andrewes begins from the Latin text of 1 Timothy 6, verse 17.

> *Praecipe divitibus*: Charge the rich of this world etc. Beloved here is a charge, a *praecipe*, a precept, or a writ, directed unto Timothy, and to those of his com-mission to the world's end, to convent and call before him; He, the rich men of Ephesus, and we, the rich men of this city, and others of other places of the earth, and to give them a charge.
>
> Charges (as you know) use to be given at Assises in Courts from the Bench. from thence is taken this judicial term παράστολλα, as it appeareth Acts 5.28. Did not we charge you streightly? saith the Bench in the Consistorie judicially assembled. Wherby we are given to understand, that in assemblies such as this the Lord of Heaven doth hold His court, whereunto all men and (they that of all men seem least) the rich and mighty of the world owe both suit and service ...

---

43 Ibid., sigs. L4v, N2r.
44 Ibid., sig. O2v. This phrase does not occur in Cicero's speeches against Verres, but Rainolds may allude to accusations of gifts made under duress, e.g. *In Verrem*, II.I.10.28, 31.78, 38.95, 52.137–53.140, II.7.20, 9.25–10.27, 19.47.
45 T. S. Eliot, *For Lancelot Andrewes* (London, 1928), pp. 24–5.
46 Erasmus, *De copia* (1988), pp. 61–2, 201–2 (trans. *Collected Works*, XXIV, pp. 331–2, 576–7).

It is a charge then, and consequently to be discharged. To be discharged? Where? Charge (saith he) the rich. He speaketh to the rich: you know your own names.[47]

Andrewes attends intently to the words employed, their synonyms, homonyms and contexts, in the manner of the fullest grammatical commentary on a classical text. He explores the implications of their connections and applies them to his audience like Brinsley drilling his class on a sentence from Cato.

Dialectical argument over the application of a text can be exemplified from the Admonition controversy. The *Admonition to Parliament* had claimed that sermons ought to be preached before the administration of the sacraments, on the basis of the citation of Matthew 3, verse 12. Whitgift in his *Answer* reconstructs the full argument and quotes the text. The *Admonition* aims to prove that the sacraments are not sincerely ministered in the Church of England, for three general reasons, of which the first is that, whereas in the early church the word was preached before the giving of the sacraments, now it is only read.

To prove that the word was preached before the sacraments were ministered, you allege the third of Matthew, verse 12: 'Which hath his fan in his hand, and will make clean his floor, and gather his wheat into his garner, but will burn up the chaff with unquenchable fire.' I understand not how you can of this place conclude that there must of necessity be preaching and not reading before the administration of the sacraments. If you say, John preached unto such as came unto his baptism and read not unto them, therefore of necessity there must be preaching and not reading, I deny the argument; for it is a common rule that we may not conclude a general doctrine of a singular and particular example; and I am sure it is against all logic.[48]

Whitgift makes two university counter-arguments, first showing the inapplicability of the words cited, and then arguing that the fact of John preaching (the verse cited is part of the address Matthew reports) does not constitute a general rule, for reasons of logic. Cartwright answers that because it was part of John's duty as a priest to preach first, the precedent is effective.[49] Whitgift replies by correcting the logical form of Cartwright's argument. He insists that, in the scriptures 'a general doctrine may not be concluded of particular examples, except the same examples be according to some general rule or commandment'. He supports his interpretation with arguments from comparison and changed

---

[47] Lancelot Andrewes, *XCVI Sermons* (London, 1629) STC 606, sigs. Aaaaa2v–3r.
[48] *Works of Whitgift*, III, p. 14.   [49] Ibid., III, p. 15.

circumstances.[50] Whitgift accepts that scripture is the source of maxims which can be applied more generally, as we saw the homilist arguing in his analysis of Joel, but he wants to limit such applications to general rules, commandments and universal examples. Both Whitgift and Cartwright apply principles drawn from the study of logic and the practice of reading classical texts in interpreting the Bible.

b) Logic

Logical techniques are very common in commentaries, controversial works and sermons. Indeed religious writing is more informed by dialectic and disputation than any other genre. Both Whitgift and Cartwright are proud of their accomplishments as trained logicians. As Lake points out, they accept that logical rules govern their disputation and they frequently accuse each other of errors in logic.[51] In one of his introductions, Whitgift singles out some of the *Admonition*'s forms of argumentation and topics of argument for particular critical comment.

> Their proofs consist especially of these arguments. The first is *ab eo quod est secundum quid, ad id quod simpliciter est*: as, Such and such things were not in the apostles' time; ergo, they ought not to be now. Which kind of argument is very deceitful ...
>
> Another kind of argument is much like unto this, and is taken *ab auctoritate negative*, which in matters of salvation and damnation holdeth when we reason *ab auctoritate scripturae*, 'from the authority of scripture', but not else. For this argument, It is not commanded in the scripture to be done, nor there expressed; ergo, it ought not to be done, is so far out of the way and so erroneous, that it is not tolerable, for it taketh away the most part of all due circumstances.[52]

In the first case he suggests that historical conditions are fallaciously suppressed; in the second that his opponents argue negatively from the silence of scripture. In both cases the authors of the *Admonition* hope to identify scriptural practices which need to be transferred directly to Anglican worship. Whitgift objects to the content of these arguments as much as to their forms or origins. A little later Cartwright picks up the point about negative arguments from authority, stating that arguments from *human* authority hold neither negatively nor affirmatively.[53] This draws a stinging response from Whitgift, referring to axioms from Aristotle's *Topica* and *Rhetoric*.[54] In the preface to the *Defence of the Answer*, he accuses Cartwright of paying too little attention to his logic textbooks.

---

[50] Ibid., III, pp. 15–16.   [51] Lake, *Anglicans and Puritans?*, pp. 14–15.
[52] *Works of Whitgift*, I, pp. 60–2.   [53] Ibid., I, p. 176.   [54] Ibid., I, p. 178.

I will not lay to your charge that you have not learned Aristotle's *Priorums . . .* But have you not learned that which Seton, or any other halfpenny logic, telleth you, that you cannot conclude affirmatively in the second figure?[55]

Whitgift amplifies his argument with comparison from the greater. With a kind of occupatio, he passes over Cartwright's ignorance of the primary text on the syllogism, Aristotle's *Prior Analytics*. But contemptuously he expects that even Cartwright would know his Seton. Later in the book he gives Cartwright lessons in argument from contraries,[56] and mocks the way he draws conclusions from evidence.

This is a strange collection that the book of common prayer 'maintaineth an unpreaching ministry', because 'it appointeth a number of psalms and other prayers and chapters to be read, which may occupy the time to be spent in preaching'. Would you have preaching only, and neither reading nor praying in the public congregation? Or do you think that the chapters and prayers that are read occupy too much time? Or are you persuaded that there cometh no profit by reading and praying?[57]

It is understandable that Whitgift and Cartwright, as Cambridge rivals, should use the technical vocabulary of logic to attack each other's methods of arguing. Thomas Nashe mocks the Cambridge puritans' methodical teamwork in their collection of quotations for Cartwright's attack on the Douai translation of the Bible in his *An Almond for a Parrat*.[58] Sermons offer only occasional opportunities for refutation but there too we find opposing arguments being measured according to norms of scriptural implication. The second part of 'The Homily concerning prayer' considers for whom and to whom one ought to pray.

Why then do we pray one for another in this life? Some man perchance will here demand. Forsooth we are willed to do so by the express command both of Christ and his disciples, to declare therein as well the faith that we have in Christ towards God, as also the mutual charity that we bear one towards another, in that we pity our brother's case, and make our humble petition to God for him. But that we should pray unto saints, neither have we any commandment in all the Scripture, nor yet example which we may safely follow. So that, being done without authority of God's word, it lacketh the ground of faith, and therefore

---

55 Ibid., I, p. 84.   56 Ibid., II, pp. 441–2.   57 Ibid., II, p. 455.

58 'Oh, so devoutly the [elect of Cambridge] met every Friday at Saint Laurence his monastery [i.e. Chaderton's college, Christ's], where the councils and fathers were distributed amongst their several companies, and every one of the reformed society sent their combined quotations week by week in a capcase to my brother Thomas, yet wandering beyond sea; such a chaos of commonplaces no apothegmatical Lycosthenes ever conceited.' T. Nashe, *Works*, ed. R. B. McKerrow (Oxford, 1958), III, p. 368, quoted in Collinson, *Puritan Movement*, p. 235.

cannot be acceptable before God. For whatsoever is not of faith is sin. And the Apostle saith that faith cometh by hearing, and hearing by the word of God.[59]

John Jewel differentiates two kinds of prayer. Texts are adduced to demonstrate that the first is commanded. It is also justified on grounds of charity. The second is not commanded or exemplified and therefore it must be sinful. Jewel backs up this argument with a series of inferences supported by scripture. He responds to the counter-argument that the saints pray for us out of charity, by objecting that no one has any knowledge of that. In this case the official Church line rests on the negative argument from silence which Whitgift rejected when the puritans used it.

Earlier on in the same homily, Jewel argued that Christians ought to pray only to God, first from four conditions of prayer (the person prayed to must be able to grant the prayer, must be willing to help, must hear the prayers and must understand what we need) which only God meets,[60] and from definition.

But that the truth hereof may the better appear, even to them that be most simple and unlearned, let us consider what prayer is. St Augustine calleth it a lifting up of the mind to God; that is to say an humble and lowly pouring out of the heart to God. Isidorus saith, that it is an affection of the heart, and not a labour of the lips. So that, by these places, true prayer doth consist not so much in the outward sound and voice of words, as in the inward groaning and crying of the heart to God.

Now then, is there any Angel, any Virgin, any Patriarch or Prophet among the dead, that can understand or know the meaning of the heart? The Scripture saith, It is God that searcheth the heart and the reins, and that he only knoweth the hearts of the children of men.[61]

The argument is derived from the topic of definition, but both the definition and the evidence that the saints cannot meet requirements of the definition are drawn from the topic of authority, from Isidore, and especially later from St Augustine.[62]

---

59 *Homilies*, p. 225. The second sentence of the paragraph has marginal references to Matthew 6, James 5, Colossians 4 and 1 Timothy 2. The last two sentences to Hebrews 6, Romans 14 and Romans 10.

60 Ibid., pp. 222–3. There is a resemblance between these conditions and those set out by Erasmus for the letter of petition.

61 Ibid., p. 223, referring to Augustine, *De spiritu et littera*, 50 (*Patrologia Latina*, XL, 816; later scholars follow Erasmus in doubting Augustine's authorship) and Isidore, *Liber sententiarum*, III.7.4 (*Patrologia Latina*, LXXXIV, 672A). The last sentence is referenced to Psalm 7, Revelation 2, Jeremiah 17 and 2 Chronicles 6.

62 *Homilies*, p. 223, citing Augustine, *Liber de cura pro mortuis agenda*, 16 (*Patrologia Latina*, XL, 604; that the saints in heaven have no knowledge of what goes on on earth), *De vera religione*, 108 (*Patrologia Latina*, XXXIV, 169; that they should not be prayed to), and *De civitate Dei*, XXII.10 (that they were not prayed to in the primitive church).

Hooker's speciality is long arguments from general principles, as we saw in his argument that the Church's primary duty of publishing knowledge of God justifies both preaching and other forms of religious teaching. At the start of book five of the *Laws*, he compares his procedure with the teachers of mathematics, who begin by establishing generally accepted axioms from which arguments can proceed.[63] He then seeks to establish, through reason, basic principles more satisfactory than those proposed by the puritans. His first concern is with the nature of the external forms appropriate to a religion.

In the powers and faculties of our souls God requireth the uttermost which our unfeigned affection towards him is able to yield. So that if we affect him not far above and before all things, our religion hath not that inward perfection which it should have, neither do we indeed worship him as our God.

That which inwardly each man should be, the Church outwardly ought to testify. And therefore the duties of our religion which are seen must be such as that affection which is unseen ought to be. Signs must resemble the things they signify. If religion bears the greatest sway in our hearts, our outward religious duties must shew it as far as the Church hath outward ability . . .

Let our first demand be therefore, that in the external form of religion such things as are apparently, or can be sufficiently proved, effectual and generally fit to set forward godliness, either as betokening the greatness of God, or as beseeming the dignity of religion, or as concurring with celestial impressions in the minds of men, may be reverently thought of, some few, rare, casual and tolerable or otherwise curable inconveniences notwithstanding.[64]

This whole argument derives from logical principles rather than from scripture. God's greatness requires that he be loved far above other things. Outward signs must reflect inner realities. Therefore external forms of religion should set out God's greatness, even at the cost of some inconveniences. It is the simplest and most secular of Hooker's maxims ('Signs must resemble the things they signify') which has the greatest force in authorising magnificence in religious display.

c) Organisation

Training in logic is the dominant factor in the organisation of religious texts. The texts of the Admonition controversy, adapting the form of academic disputations, are based on sentence by sentence refutation of the opponent's text. In his *Answer to the Admonition*, Whitgift attempted

---

[63] Hooker, *Lawes*, v.5.1. Debora Shuger compares Hooker's epistemology with Andrewes's (*Habits of Thought in the English Renaissance* (Berkeley, 1990), pp. 17–68).
[64] Hooker, *Lawes*, v.6.1–2.

to introduce some method into his response by dividing the objections of the Admonitioners into different subject-headings (for example,
'Whether Christ forbiddeth rule and superiority unto the Ministers', 'Of
the Authority of the Church in things indifferent').

Hooker's defence of the Church of England responded to the issues
raised by the *Admonition* and made use of many of Whitgift's arguments
but within the framework of an argument from first principles.[65] He
defends his approach by explaining that in order to show the force and
usefulness of just laws, it is necessary to examine their causes.

Is there anything which can either be thoroughly understood or soundly judged
of, till the very first causes from which originally it springeth be made manifest?
If all parts of knowledge have been thought by wise men to be then most orderly
delivered and proceeded in, when they are drawn to their first original, seeing
that our whole question concerneth the quality of ecclesiastical laws, let it not
seem a labour superfluous that in the entrance thereunto all these several kinds
of laws have been considered, inasmuch as they all concur as principles, they all
have forcible operation therein, although not all in like apparent and manifest
manner.[66]

Like Aristotle and Ramus, Hooker advocates a methodical approach,
beginning from the most general principles and explaining the causes of
phenomena. Before defending the religious practices of the Church of
England (in book v), he establishes the nature of law and its role in human
society (book I) and uses this foundation to attack the principles which
underlie the puritan criticism of the Church (books II–IV), for example
by showing that scripture alone cannot be the basis of church law.

The *Homilies* divide their arguments into a number of simple elements
which are stated at the beginning and end of each part of the homily and
proved and illustrated in various ways in the course of the part. Thus, for
example, the first part of the 'Sermon of the Salvation of Mankind' begins by stating that since no man can be justified before God by his own
actions, every man is constrained to seek justification from God. Thomas
Cranmer explains the effectiveness of Christ's sacrifice in obtaining justification, answers the objection that justification cannot be given freely
if a ransom has been paid, and distinguishes three elements required
for justification (God's mercy, Christ's satisfaction of God's justice, and
true faith). The second part of the same sermon collects quotations from
Paul's epistles on justification by faith and explains how justification by
faith alone is to be understood. The opening of the third part summarises

[65] Cargill Thompson, *Studies in the Reformation*, pp. 143–6.   [66] Hooker, *Lawes*, 1.16.1.

the argument of the first two parts and its connection with the message of the third, that in return for the gift of salvation, the Christian's duty to God is obedience and good works.[67]

It hath been manifestly declared unto you, that no man can fulfil the Law of God, and therefore by the law all men are condemned; whereupon it followeth necessarily that some other things should be required for our salvation than the Law; and that is, a true and lively faith in Christ bringing forth good works and a life according to God's commandments.[68]

In this transition Cranmer reminds his hearers of the overarching logical structure of the sermon. Since no human can fulfil the requirements of the law, there must be another way for people to be saved, which is faith. The sermon substantiates the negative part of this argument, clarifies the meaning of faith and explains its consequences. The teaching of the sermon, articulated in three parts depends upon, and is arranged around the elements of, this overall argument.

Henry Smith usually divides a sermon on a text into three considerations, a sermon on a theme sometimes into more. For example his sermon, 'Preparative to Marriage', has five main sections.

First I will show the excellency of marriage, then the institution of it, then the causes of it, then the duties of it, and lastly the divorcement from it.[69]

Within each section, he subdivides, for example providing thirteen subsections to the praise of marriage, beginning with author, time and place, and ending with the custom of nations and the fanciful derivation of marriage from merry age.[70] Most of the subsections are supported by quotations from scripture, sometimes with explanation and further subdivision.

Andrewes's sermons begin with a classical exordium, gaining the attention of the audience by explaining the importance of the text he is going to explain. There then follows a careful logical division, grounded in the divisions of his chosen text. In the main section of the sermon, each of the divisions is explained, amplified and applied, on the basis of close analysis of the words of the text. Finally, he reverts to the classical oration with a recapitulation and an emotional appeal to the audience to follow the instruction he has expounded. The role of logical analysis in the organisation of Andrewes's sermons can be shown in the division of the text into sections.

---

[67] *Homilies*, pp. 13–21.   [68] Ibid., p. 18.   [69] Smith, *Works*, I, p. 5.   [70] Ibid., I, pp. 6–8.

1. This whole Scripture hath his name given it even in the first word: *Charge* (saith he) *the rich etc.* It is a *Charge.*
2. It is directed to certain men; namely, to *the Rich of this world.*
3. It consisteth of four branches: whereof Two are *negative*, for the removing of abuses.
1. The first, *Charge them, that they be not high minded.*
2. The second, *Charge them, that they trust not in their riches*:
   The reason is added (which is a *Maxime* and a *Ground* in the *Law* of *Nature*, that we must trust to no uncertaine thing) *Trust not, in the uncertaintie of riches.*
   The other two are *affirmative*, concerning the use of riches.
1. The first: *Charge them that they trust in God.* The reason: Because, *He giveth them all things to enjoy plenteously.*
2. The second: *Charge them that they do good*; that is the *substance*; The *quantitie*, that *they be rich in good works*; the *qualitie*, That *they be ready to part with* (and a speciall kind of doing good) to *communicate*, to benefit the *publique*.
   And all these are one *Charge.* The *reason* of them all doth follow: Because by this means they shall *lay up in store*, and that, *for themselves, a good foundation, against the time to come.* The end: *that they may obtain eternal life.*[71]

Virtually the whole text of 1 Timothy 6, verses 17–19 is set out in italics within the sections of this division. Initially Andrewes divides into type of text, persons addressed and content, very much as a letter might be analysed in a commentary on Cicero. Then content is subdivided into negative and positive commands. The two negative commands are followed by a reason, derived from a maxim of conduct. Each positive command is provided with its own reason, the second being further subdivided, in accordance with Aristotle's *Categories*, into substance, quantity and quality. The text ends with the final cause: in order to obtain eternal life. On top of this intensely dialectical reading of the organisation of the text, Andrewes will lay a grammatical analysis and a rhetorical amplification of the words employed.

d) Style

Few of the sermons delivered outside the court make great use of the repertory of figures of speech, though many have short passages of amplified language at key points. The high style was certainly not the general mode of preaching and religious controversy, but elaborate and emotional language was part of the preacher's repertory, for use in especially important or awkward situations. The most commonly found tropes are similes and comparisons. The Bible encourages the use of similes and

---

[71] Andrewes, *XCVI Sermons*, sig. Aaaaa2v.

some of the most striking simple comparisons in the sermons are derived from scripture, as when the 'Sermon on Faith' borrows the comparison between the blessed man and the tree by the waterside from Jeremiah 17.[72] Cranmer's description of good works performed without faith is founded on a maxim from Romans 14, but develops the idea with a contrast between dead and living actions and a simile about art.

To the Romans he saith, Whatsoever work is done without faith, it is sin.[73] Faith giveth life to the soul; and they be as much dead to God that lack faith as they be to the world whose bodies lack souls. Without faith, all that is done of us is but dead before God, although the work seem never so gay and glorious before man. Even as the picture graven or painted is but a dead representation of the thing itself, and is without life or any manner of moving, so be the works of all unfaithful persons before God, They do appear to be lively works, and indeed they be but dead, not availing to the everlasting life; they be but shadows of lively and good things, and not good and lively things indeed.[74]

Cranmer's task in this passage is to explain and make palatable a particularly uncompromising passage from St Paul. In order to show that good works without faith are wrong, he first connects the lack of faith to death. Anything that seems lifelike in a dead object is false; at best a shadow of what is good, at worst a deception. The point depends on an absolute contrast between life and death and a complete devaluation of what is dead. The emphasis on seeming and the doubling of 'gay and glorious' in the second sentence prepare for the introduction of 'graven or painted' pictures in the third. Henry Smith's comparisons tend to be more homely and can be presented through other figures.

There is no salt but may lose his saltness, no wine but may lose his strength, no flower but may lose his scent, no light but may be eclipsed, no beauty but may be stained, no fruit but may be blasted, nor soul but may be corrupted. We stand all in a slippery place, where it is easy to slide, and hard to get up, like little children which overthrow themselves with their clothes, now up, now down at a straw, so soon we fall from God, and slide from his word and forget our resolutions, as though we had never resolved.[75]

Smith uses a series of comparisons expressed through zeugma with parison as a form of induction to demonstrate the fallibility of everything worldly, before capping the argument with a simile from everyday human life. The 'Homily against Rebellion' uses aposiopesis, rhetorical

[72] *Homilies*, p. 24, Jeremiah 17, verses 7–8.   [73] Romans 14, verse 23.   [74] *Homilies*, p. 31.
[75] H. Smith, *Sermons* (London, 1657), p. 500, quoted in Blench, *Preaching in England*, pp. 184–8.

question, correctio, traductio and elaboration of parts to amplify the evil of rebellion.[76]

What shall we say of those subjects – May we call them by the name of subjects? – who neither be thankful, nor make any prayer to God for so gracious a Sovereign? but also themselves take armour wickedly, assemble companies and bands of rebels to break the public peace so long continued, and to make, not war, but rebellion, to endanger the person of such a gracious Sovereign, to hazard the estate of their country – for whose defence they should be ready to spend their lives – and, being Englishmen, to rob, spoil, destroy and burn in England Englishmen, to kill and murder their own neighbours and kinsfolk, their own countrymen ... What may be spoken of them? So far doth their unkindness, unnaturalness, wickedness, mischievousness in their doings, pass and excel any thing, and all things that can be expressed and uttered in words.[77]

The overarching structure of the passage is provided by an inexpressibility topos: what rebels do is beyond description. The homilist lays stress on the excellence of the sovereign and the long-continued peace in contrast with the violence and chaos of civil war. Obligations are contrasted with actions throughout. The passage builds up to a series of violent verbs combined with a reiteration of words expressing national identity. The verbs then give way to a series of abstract nouns emphasising the wickedness and unnaturalness of what is proposed. As in parliamentary speeches, the intense amplification of this passage is intended to provoke an emotional and unifying response in the audience. In order to avoid civil war the people must reject opposition to the civil authority.

Later in the homily, the author establishes an imaginary dialogue (prosopopeia and sermocinatio) with King David, in which the speaker puts reasons for rebelling against an unjust ruler, which David rejects on the basis of his reluctance to attack Saul, no matter how great the provocation in 1 Samuel 18–26. Henry Smith turns to imaginary dialogue in his 'The Triall of Vanitie', imagining someone disputing against Ecclesiastes on behalf of vanity.

It may be that sin is vanity and pleasure is vanity, but shall we condemn all for sin and pleasure? What say you to beauty which is nature's dowry and cheereth the eye as sweetmeat doth the taste? Beauty is like a fair picture; take away the colour and there is nothing left. Beauty indeed is but a colour and a temptation; the colour fadeth and the temptation snareth ... But what say you to honour, which sets a man aloft, and makes the knee bow and the tongue forsooth, and the head stand bare as though they were other kind of creatures above men?

---

[76] Erasmus, *De copia* (1988), pp. 197–200 (trans. *Collected Works*, XXIV pp. 572–5).
[77] *Homilies*, p. 391.

Honour is like a King in a play: when his part is done, his ornaments are taken away from him, and he which held the bason to him is as good as he. Honour indeed may command all but life; he makes a fair show now, but when death comes all is one.[78]

Within the form of the imagined dialogue, delivered in carefully patterned sentences, Smith gives considerable weight to descriptions of circumstances, personification and comparisons. Beauty and honour are first praised through metaphor, simile and evidentia and then rejected, with comparisons providing much of the logical force to the rejection. Painting and acting are presented as alluring forms of deception. Beauty and honour are shown to be illusions which pass with time. It is possible to think of Smith's imaginary dialogue as a stepping stone between the treatment of honour and vanity of Berners's Guevara and Shakespeare's Falstaff.

The controversial works are primarily argumentative, setting up chains of inference or disputing the validity of arguments or the interpretations of particular passages. Rhetorical techniques are used either as ethos, to develop the self-presentation of the author, or as vituperation, to hit hard at the opponent's moral or religious values. The authors of the *Admonition* seek to explain their purpose in writing.

Now because many men see not all things, and the world in this respect is marvellously blinded, it hath been thought good to proffer to your godly considerations a true platform of a church reformed, to the end that, it being laid before your eyes to behold the great unlikeness betwixt it and this our english church, you may learn either with perfect hatred to detest the one and with singular love to embrace the other, or else to be without excuse before the majesty of our God, who (for the discharge of our conscience and manifestation of his truth) hath by us revealed unto you at this present the sincerity and simplicity of his Gospel.[79]

This long sentence is constructed around a logical argument (because, therefore, in order that) and a series of topics (cause, purpose, comparison, agent). It is decorated with doubling of key phrases and isocolon. To the well-disposed, the *Admonition* serves as information, assisting in formulating a critical attitude to the Church of England. To those who resist its message, it serves the harsher Calvinist purpose of making their obduracy inexcusable before God. From Whitgift's response there is no mistaking the anger aroused by its blanket dismissal of the Elizabethan

---

[78] Henry Smith, *Thirteen Sermons upon Several Texts of Scripture* (London, 1592) STC 22717, sigs. I2v–3r, *Works*, I, p. 380.
[79] Field and Wilcox, *Admonition*, p. 8.

Church settlement. Its publication history and Cartwright's *Reply to an Answer* imply that extreme puritans found it an invigorating rallying-cry.

Although religious controversy usually followed contemporary stylistic fashions at some distance, there was one important instance in which it was innovatory. John Field wrote the most biting and memorable phrases from the *Admonition*. His notes are also thought to form the basis for the racy ridiculing pamphlets of 'Martin Marprelate' which started to appear in 1588. When the bishops decided to commission replies in the same lively, scurrilous vein they fostered the extravagant, colloquial satire of Greene and Nashe, which was the dominant literary fashion of the early 1590s.[80]

Where Whitgift's tone is often as short with his opponents as their's was with him, Hooker attempts to present a persona which is reluctant, patient and moderate.

Though for no other cause, yet for this: that posterity may know we have not loosely through silence permitted things to pass away as in a dream, there shall be for men's information extant thus much concerning the present state of the Church of God amongst us, and their careful endeavour which would have upheld the same.[81]

Although Hooker is fully confident of the rightness of his argument, and although he does not shirk the controversialist's burden of pointing out the errors on the opposing side, he also seeks to emphasise what the establishment and puritan wings of the Protestant Church share, in the hope of reconciliation.

Far more comfort it were for us (so small is the joy we take in these strifes) to labour under the same yoke, as men that look for the same eternal reward of their labours, to be joined with you in bonds of indissoluble love and amity, to live as if our persons being many our souls were but one, rather than in such dismembered sort to spend our few and wretched days in a tedious prosecuting of wearisome contentions.[82]

While the tone remains restrained, Hooker manages to amplify both the joy of fellowship, through four equivalent membra, and the weariness of strife, by expolitio, piling on adjectives of similar meaning ('wretched, tedious, wearisome').

Andrewes amplifies relatively sparingly. His preaching achieves grandeur through the sustained application of verbal and logical analysis.

---

[80] Collinson, *Puritan Movement*, pp. 120, 391–6; C. S. Lewis, *English Literature in the Sixteenth Century* (Oxford, 1954), pp. 405–16.
[81] Hooker, *Lawes*, Preface. 1.1.   [82] Ibid., Preface. 9.3.

In his Lent sermon of 1593, delivered before the Queen, on Mark 14, verses 4–6, which he calls 'a disputation or plea about Mary Magdalene's act'[83] in pouring the box of perfume on Christ's feet, he first analyses (and praises) Judas's argument against the waste of a precious commodity which could have been sold to benefit the poor.

When I consider the sobriety, bounty, zeal of the speech, I think many wise heads could not in so few words have contrived a better or more pithy motion; that which was other wise lavished upon one may be employed to the benefit of many . . . rather on necessary relief, than upon needless delight; rather on continual good, than on a transitory smell.[84]

Andrewes uses epithet, comparison, zeugma and parison to praise Judas's words, but then, in good rhetorical fashion he turns to consider the speaker and the purpose of the speech, which he finds to be sacrilegious and hypocritical. Christ's response leads him to re-examine the use of the perfume.

Perhaps our particular will more move us. It is Christ that created for us nard and all other delights whatsoever, either for use or necessity we have, or for fruition and pleasure we enjoy. It is He that hath enriched us that we be able to bestow it, by this long prosperity, plenty and peace, as no other kingdom under heaven. Is there any good mind can think that this is an indignity? that He is not worthy, hath not deserved, and doubly deserved this, and ten times more, at our hands.[85]

Andrewes's argument from cause is amplified with circumstances (especially from England's prosperous peace) and decorated with parison, alliteration, rhetorical question and a bilingual wordplay on dignity and *dignum*, meaning worthy. Enjoyment is now treated as equal to necessity, rather than obviously inferior to it as was the case above. In her own house, Mary's action was condemned, but within the Christian church and in the judgment of eternity it is approved.

This is Mary Magdalene's part, as Christ telleth: that howsoever Mary Magdalene be, in Simon's house, or in a corner, found fault with, amends shall be made her; and as wide as the world is, and as far as the Gospel shall sound, 'she shall be well spoken of'. Yea, when the great and glorious acts of many monarchs shall be buried in silence, this poor box of *nardus* shall be matter of praise and never die.[86]

Through doubling of phrases ('as wide . . ., as far') or pairing of circumstances ('in Simon's house, or in a corner'), alliteration ('great and

---

[83] Andrewes, *XCVI Sermons*, sig. Bb5v.   [84] Ibid., sig. Bb6v.
[85] Ibid., sig. Cc4v.   [86] Ibid., sig. Cc5v.

glorious ... many monarchs') and opposition with a kind of chiasmus ('buried in silence' compared with 'matter of praise and never die'), Andrewes here achieves a striking hyperbole. The light use of mostly ordinary figures produces a strong effect.

Rhetorical techniques and stylistic effects are less common in religious writing than arguments or logical organisation. They are used to illuminate difficult ideas or to point up important passages. Sermon writers show knowledge of the harder ornaments (such as sermocinatio and parison) but their use of them is more effective because it is sparing. Passages of amplification are sometimes linked with secular moral commonplaces, such as the vanity of worldly success and the evil of war. Cranmer and Smith use comparisons with material objects (a painting, a slippery place) to bring out the meaning of religious ideas.

MORAL ARGUMENTS IN RELIGIOUS WRITING

Religious discourse treated many of the same subjects as ethical and political writing. Like historians and parliamentarians preachers drew on a range of commonplaces, classical and biblical. A knowledge of this shared heritage helps us understand the different emphases of particular religious writers. Through their rhetorical analysis of Christian sources and because of their understanding of their special duties, preachers were able to develop arguments about moral and social issues which went beyond the worldly prudence of politicians and secular moralists. Funeral sermons negotiated between philosophical and Christian topics of consolation. Poverty called for compassion and charity as well as policy. Debates about church government implied new approaches to arguments about secular authority.

a) Funeral sermons

Funeral oratory requires a public, sympathetic and often simplified presentation of Christian answers to universal human questions. Classical philosophy presented consolatory approaches to the problem of loss and grief which humanist education incorporated. Christian preachers, while not disdaining the support of the ancients, needed to show that the comforts they could offer were stronger and more persuasive.[87]

---

[87] On funeral oratory see Richard L. Greaves, *Society and Religion in Elizabethan England* (Minneapolis, 1981), pp. 704–6; Pigman, *Grief and Elegy*, pp. 1–39; R. Houlbrooke (ed.), *Death, Ritual and Bereavement* (London, 1989); David Cressy, *Birth, Marriage and Death* (Oxford, 1997), pp. 379–95; R. Houlbrooke, *Death, Religion and the Family in England 1480–1750* (Oxford, 1998), pp. 295–330.

Richard Hooker's *A Remedy Against Sorrow and Fear, delivered in a funeral Sermon* links grief and fear as the two major emotions which Christian consolation needs to address. Although grief is natural, it may be reproveable, 'sometime in the cause for which, sometime in regard of the measure whereunto it groweth'.[88] In the biblical text for the sermon,[89] Christ urged his disciples not to grieve because he was going before them and would provide them with a comforter.[90] Later, he urged his followers to weep not for him, but for themselves.[91] Hooker uses Psalm 73 to warn Christians not to grieve that the wicked enjoy happiness, because their happiness is temporary and incomplete.[92] He supports this traditional philosophical argument exclusively from biblical sources.

Erasmus had discussed arguments for moderating grief in his treatment of the letter of consolation in *De conscribendis epistolis*. If it cannot be argued that the misfortune will be short-lived, the letter-writer must show that it is not so serious as it appears, that some good will come of it or that it is part of the human condition.[93] Erasmus's second model letter consoles a father on the loss of his son. After showing his respect for the father's grief, Erasmus urges him that as a philosopher he ought at least to moderate it. Since bereavement and the death of the young is a common experience, reason and law urge that mourning should be kept within bounds.[94] Excessive grief will be harmful to the people grieving and their associates and will become an evil in itself, useless to the person mourned and harmful to the mourner. Erasmus concludes this section of the letter with a maxim: 'You must endure, not blame, what cannot be changed.'[95] After a series of examples from Greek and Roman history, common experience and Latin poetry, Erasmus warns that grief for the death of a child may be interpreted as ingratitude for the original gift.[96] He combines pagan and Christian arguments for the immortality of the soul before making specifically Christian arguments, for resignation, for death as a gateway to eternal life and for the happiness of the son living in heaven.

From these arguments, Hooker chooses two: the danger of excessive grief and the necessity of accepting what God sends.[97] Such acceptance is an imitation of Christ and an education in the virtue of patience.

---

[88] Richard Hooker, *Tractates and Sermons*, ed. L. Yeandle and E. Grislis, *The Folger Library Edition of the Works of Richard Hooker*, vol. v (Cambridge MA, 1990), p. 368.

[89] 'Let not your hearts be troubled, nor fear.' John 14, verse 27.   [90] Hooker, *Sermons*, p. 367.

[91] Ibid., pp. 368–9.   [92] Ibid., pp. 369–71.

[93] Erasmus, *De conscribendis epistolis*, p. 434 (trans. *Collected Works*, xxv, p. 150).

[94] Ibid., pp. 441–4 (trans. *Collected Works*, xxv, pp. 156–7).

[95] 'Feras, non culpes, quod mutari non potest', ibid., p. 444 (trans. *Collected Works*, xxv, pp. 157).

[96] Ibid., pp. 444–51 (trans. *Collected Works*, pp. 157–61).   [97] Hooker, *Sermons*, p. 371.

Seeing that as the Author of our Salvation was himself consecrated by affliction, so the way which we are to follow him by is not strewed with rushes but set with thorns, be it never so hard to learn, we must learn to suffer with patience even that which seemeth almost impossible to be suffered.[98]

In rejecting the sin of blaming God we learn the virtue of patience, which limits grief, strengthens endurance and enables us to prepare for a Christian death.[99]

'The Exhortation against the Fear of Death' from the *Homilies* examines three kinds of fear. Worldly men fear to be deprived of earthly happiness. All people naturally fear the dissolution of the body and the agony of death. Everyone ought to fear judgment and eternal damnation. None of these reasons should move the Christian to fear death. On the contrary, death will be a deliverance from pains, sorrows and cares.[100]

Thus is this bodily death a door or entering into life; and therefore not so much dreadful, if it be rightly considered, as it is comfortable: not a mischief, but a remedy for all mischief; no enemy, but a friend; not a cruel tyrant, but a gentle guide; leading us not to mortality but to immortality, not to sorrow and pain but to joy and pleasure, and that to endure for ever.[101]

Where Erasmus uses Christian arguments as the climax of a series of classical philosophical persuasions, Cranmer regards the Christian attitude to death as a reversal of the worldly and pagan view. Death is to be welcomed as the gateway to a new life of joy. Hooker is far less bold. He sees fear as natural, as subject to limitation through reason (we fear only what we can avoid but not resist), and as beneficial in that it enables us to avoid danger.[102] Hooker argues that all those who benefit from the endurance of their prince, the growing up of their children and the long life of their friends should thank God for his gift of fear.[103] As part of nature, fear cannot be a sin in itself. The sin to be avoided lies in the extremes of fearing too little or too much. Do not presume; do not despair.

For our direction, to avoid as much as may be both extremities, that we may know, as a shipmaster by his card, how far we are wide, either on one side or on the other, we must note that in a Christian man there is first nature, secondly corruption, perverting nature; thirdly grace, correcting and amending corruption. In fear all these have their several operations.[104]

---

[98] Ibid., p. 371.   [99] Ibid., pp. 372–3.   [100] *Homilies*, pp. 61–2.
[101] Ibid., p. 63.   [102] Hooker, *Sermons*, pp. 373–5.   [103] Ibid., p. 375.
[104] Ibid., p. 376. The allusion is to Scylla and Charybdis and to Aristotelian notions of virtue. Compare Spenser, *Faerie Queene*, II.2.24, 12.3–9.

Nature teaches the wise man to hide. But grace and faith teach him to repair to God, who provides comfort: the peace which passes all understanding.[105] The remedies against sorrow and fear are patience and peace.

Hooker's answers are firmly Christian and they offer strong comfort to his audience, but he acknowledges the role of nature in providing the human conditions for a Christian solution and, without Erasmus's panoply of names and quotations, he exploits the resources of philosophy, in examining the nature and direction of emotions, and plotting a moderate course to virtue.

b) Poverty and alms-giving

Pamphlets, legislation and parliamentary oratory bear witness to a widespread Elizabethan concern about the phenomenon of poverty, together with a fear of the revenge of the dispossessed upon the well-off.[106] Legislation enshrined a distinction between the deserving poor, primarily orphans, the old and the disabled, who should be cared for within the parish with the proceeds of local taxes, and sturdy beggars who were to be punished and forced back to their place of origin. The Christian tradition provided both sweeping commands to give to the poor and a philosophical calculus of charity, in which obligations were narrowed.

Since it is not possible for one individual to relieve the needs of all, we are not bound to relieve all who are in need, but only those who could not be succoured if we did not succour them.

Accordingly we are bound to give alms of our surplus, as also to give alms to one whose need is extreme; otherwise almsgiving, like any other greater good, is a matter of counsel.[107]

'The Homily of Alms-Deeds' develops three main points: documenting the strength of God's exhortations to giving of alms, setting out the spiritual benefits to the donor and reassuring potential donors that they will never themselves become impoverished through alms-giving.[108] Each of these points is backed up with several quotations and examples from the Bible. It is no advantage to anyone to heap up riches at the cost of their soul. Alms-giving, by contrast, offers a way to purge the soul of

---

[105] Hooker, *Sermons*, p. 377.

[106] Greaves, *Society and Religion*, pp. 547–94; Paul Slack, *Poverty and Policy in Tudor and Stuart England* (London, 1988), esp. pp. 17–36, 91–104, 124–31.

[107] Aquinas, *Summa Theologiae*, II.2.32.5, trans. English Dominican Fathers (Chicago, 1952), II, p. 544.

[108] *Homilies*, p. 263.

infection.[109] The chief example of God's special care for those who give alms is the story of the widow of Zarephthah, from 1 Kings 17, who gave the last of her flour to feed Elijah and was rewarded with a self-replenishing supply of flour and oil. The homilist amplifies the faith and generosity of the poor widow in giving her last food, as a reproach to the unbelieving wealthy who doubt whether they have anything to spare.

Hearken, therefore, ye merciless misers, what will be the end of this your unmerciful dealing. As certainly as God nourished this poor widow in the time of famine, and increased her little store, so that she had enough and felt no penury, when others pined away; so certainly shall God plague you with poverty in the midst of plenty. Then, when others have abundance and be fed at full, you shall utterly waste and consume away yourselves; your store shall be destroyed; your goods plucked from you; all your glory and wealth shall perish.[110]

Henry Smith's 'The Poor Man's Tears', on the text 'He that shall give to one of the least of these a cup of cold water in my name, he shall not lose his reward' (Matthew, 10, verse 42), saves the story of the widow of Zarephthah, very plainly told, for his concluding paragraph.[111] Like the homilist he reminds his audience of God's injunctions to give alms, and of the punishments promised to those who fail to give.[112] Augustus Caesar thought any day wasted on which he did not give relief to some poor person.[113] The weight of Smith's appeal rests on compassion rather than on threats.

The tears of men, women and children are grievous and pitiful, and tears give cause of great compassion, especially the tears of such as therewith are constrained to beg for their relief. But if the tears of the rich for the loss of their goods, or the tears of parents for the death of their children . . . ought generally to be regarded or pitied, then much more should the tears of those breed great compassion in the hearts of Christians, whom beggary, want and extremity of miserable hunger constraineth to shed tears in most miserable sort.

Tears are the last thing that man, woman or child can move by; and where tears move not, nothing will move. I therefore exhort you by the lamentable tears which the poor do daily shed through hunger and extreme misery, to be good unto them, to be charitable and merciful unto them, and to relieve those whom you see with misery distressed.[114]

---

[109] Ibid., pp. 267–8. The homilist is careful to remove the implication that salvation could be merited by explaining 'we doing these things according to God's will and our duty, have our sins indeed washed away . . . not for the worthiness of them, but by the grace of God, which worketh all in all'. Ibid., p. 270.

[110] Ibid., p. 273.   [111] Smith, *Works*, II, p. 53.

[112] Ibid., II, pp. 41–2. He also reminds them of God's promise to return the value of alms to the giver (ibid., II, p. 47).

[113] Ibid., II, p. 43.   [114] Ibid., II, pp. 45–6.

Smith's strongest appeal is humanitarian, based on the impulse of any human being to pity a person reduced to tears. His attitude is far from the calculated exploitation of tears and reduction of their impact prescribed by the rhetoric textbooks.[115] Calvin had insisted on the obligation of Christians to put themselves in the place of the poor so as to be impelled by common humanity to go to their aid.[116] Rather than citing biblical texts Smith aims at a lively evocation of the scenes at which, and the motives for which, tears are shed. The tone is exhortatory rather than threatening.

Although Smith acknowledges the problem of sturdy beggars, 'which ought to be suppressed by godly policy',[117] he exhorts his audience to provide relief to all who ask for it 'if we know them not for such persons, and let their bad deeds fall on their own necks; for if they perish for want, we are in danger of God's wrath for them'.[118] Furthermore, because life is short, alms-giving may be the best way to spend money, since it lays up rewards in heaven.

Short is man's life while we are within this world. David compareth it to a vapour, to a bubble, to wind, to grass, to a shadow, to smoke, and every fading thing that consumeth in a moment . . . So that our life is short; and after a few days, though you think them many, whatsoever you mercifully bestow upon the poor here on earth, you shall certainly find the same again, both in heaven and on earth.[119]

Smith uses the idea of the eternal afterlife to reduce the worth of earthly assets, to increase the value of good deeds, and thereby to encourage relief of the poor in this world. Furthermore he questions the notion of possession.

St Paul saith, No man giveth but he that hath received;[120] and an ancient father of the church doth charge the rich with waste, for which they shall surely answer. Art thou not, saith he, a robber, in keeping another man's substance, and to reckon it as thine own? It is the bread of the hungry which thou dost retain, the coat due to the naked thou lockest in they house, the shoes that appertain to the barefoot lie drying in thy house, and the gold which should relieve the poor lies cankering in thy coffers.[121]

[115] For example *Rhetorica ad Herennium*, II.31.50; Cicero, *De inventione*, 1.55.106–56.109; Quintilian, *Institutio oratoria*, VI.1.21–35.

[116] John Calvin, *Institutes of the Christian Religion*, trans. F. L. Battles, 2 vols. (Philadelphia, 1960), III.7.7.

[117] Smith, *Works*, II, p. 44.   [118] Ibid., II, p. 45.

[119] Ibid., II, p. 48.   [120] 1 Corinthians 15, verse 3.

[121] Smith, *Works*, II, p. 48. This quotation (from St Basil) is cited in Aquinas, *Summa Theologiae*, II.2.32.5.

Although he is careful to attribute the quotation, Smith uses the fundamental question of the contingent basis of all possession to urge the wealthy to be generous. One of Andrewes's earliest sermons was preached on 10 April 1588 at St Mary's Hospital to an audience of London merchants. Addressing the wealthy, Andrewes seeks mainly to encourage them. In return for giving up the uncertainty of earthly wealth, by a heavenly bill of exchange, they can lay up imperishable wealth in heaven.[122]

> Look you, how excellent a groundwork here is, (not for a cottage) whereon you may raise your frame to a notable height, as, standing on it, you may lay hand on and lay hold of, eternal life. O that you would mind once these high things, that you would in this sense be high-minded! St Paul's meaning is to take nothing from you, but give you a better to requite it by far. He would have you part with part of your wealth to do good; he will lay you up for it treasure in heaven for your own use. He would have you forsake the world's sand and uncertainty wherein you cannot trust; but therefore, he marks you out a plot out of the rock, whereto you may trust.[123]

Andrewes employs the vocabulary of building (groundwork, cottage, frame), paronomasia on 'high' and an allusion to Matthew 7, verses 24–6, to amplify the value of giving. He holds out the eternal life as a place where deeds of charity can hope to be rewarded, but, like Smith, he also invokes eternal life to diminish the worth of earthly riches and, briefly but tellingly, to warn of the consequences of damnation.

> If we heap not up the treasure of immortality, we heap up treasure of wrath against the day of wrath. If your wealth be not with us to life, *pecunia vestra vobiscum est in perditionem.*[124]

Eternity adds to the punishments as well as to the rewards. While he uses the language of bills of exchange, assurance and investment to decorate his theme for this particular audience, Andrewes also reveals himself as a practical reformer. He accepts the distinction between the poor who must be relieved (captives, orphans, widows, strangers and scholars) and the sturdy poor. But he demands that something should be done to employ the latter and he insists that, expensive as it would be, it is not beyond the means of the city to do so.

---

[122] Andrewes, *XCVI Sermons*, sig. Bbbbb1 r–v.   [123] Ibid., sig. Bbbbb2v.
[124] Ibid., sig. Bbbbb3r. 'Your money is damned with you', Acts 8, verse 20 (varied from singular to plural).

I mean beggars and vagabonds, able to work, to whom good must be done, by not suffering them to be as they are, but to employ them in such sort as they may do good . . .

Me thinketh it is strange that the exiled churches of strangers, which are harboured here with us, should be able in this kind to do such good, as not one of their poor is seen to ask about the streets, and this city, the harbourer and maintainer of them, should not be able to do the same good . . . I know the charges will be great, but it will quit the charges, the good done will be so great.[125]

Andrewes is gentler with the wealthy than were the *Homilies*. He never employs the argument of compassion in a way that can approach Smith's fervour. But he is far-sighted and practical in earthly relief as well as committed to the superiority of heavenly treasure. Rather than accusing the rich, he would prefer to befriend them and to find uses for their wealth.

c) Authority

For the Elizabethan Protestant élite preaching was an important medium of social control. The 'Homily on Obedience' declared that the power and authority of the ruler was an ordinance of God, part of his plan for the orderly running of the universe.[126] Subjects may not obey commands which are against God's instructions, but even in such cases they are forbidden to rebel against the magistrate.[127] The 'Homily against Rebellion' reiterates the command of obedience, forbids subjects to judge monarchs and amplifies the miseries of civil war.[128] Since God sends wicked rulers as a punishment to nations, people who are governed evilly should submit themselves to God, in order that he might provide a better ruler.[129] While Henry Smith, in his sermon 'The Magistrate's Scripture' accepts that magistrates are appointed by God, he urges them to remember their duty to rule justly on God's behalf. At their death they will be equal to other men.[130] In life, God makes examples of the errors of great men.[131] For Smith, the greatness of the magistrate's charge constitutes a warning and a responsibility for those who take it on. While reiterating the subject's duty of obedience, the main focus of the sermon is on what magistrates need to do in order to be better rulers.

[125] Andrewes, *XCVI Sermons*, sig. Bbbbb1r.   [126] *Homilies*, pp. 72–3.
[127] Ibid., pp. 75, 77.   [128] Ibid., pp. 384–5, 388, 391, 398–402.
[129] Ibid., pp. 388–90.   [130] Smith, *Works*, I, pp. 357, 361–2, 365–7.
[131] Ibid., I, p. 366. Shuger discusses the views of Hooker and Andrewes on monarchy, in *Habits of Thought*, pp. 120–58.

In late sixteenth-century England, while it would have been impossible in public outside an academic disputation to question monarchical authority, it was possible to maintain public controversy about the legitimacy of bishops. For the Admonitionists and Thomas Cartwright, although they publicly accepted 'the lawfulness, necessity and singular commodity' of secular authority,[132] scripture provided reasons for rejecting hierarchy among the clergy in general, and the institution of bishops in particular. Cartwright formulates the argument, derived from Matthew 20, verses 25–6, as a syllogism.

The distinction of the office he noteth in these words: 'The kings of the gentiles have dominion over them, and the princes exercise authority over them; but it shall not be so with you.' Whereupon the argument may be thus gathered, That wherein the civil magistrate is severed from the ecclesiastical officer doth not agree to one minister over another. But the civil magistrate is severed from the ecclesiastical officer by bearing dominion. Therefore bearing dominion doth not agree to one minister over another.[133]

Whitgift's initial response to this argument is to reject it on logical grounds, because the major premiss is a circular argument, since it assumes that the civil magistrate differs from the minister in bearing dominion, which is the matter in dispute. At the same time the minor premiss is equivocal, in that dominion might mean anything from 'rule with oppression' to any kind of superiority or jurisdiction. Some of these senses would be acceptable, some not.[134] Later Whitgift cites Musculus's arguments, first, that had Christ intended equality among his ministers he could have chosen a more definite form of expression, secondly that the analogy of the organisation of heaven supports hierarchy, and thirdly that the necessity of state requires that, in the Church as in the commonwealth, there should be superiors and inferiors.[135] This suits Whitgift's general view that the organisation of the Church should reflect the organisation of the state in which it resides.

I am persuaded that the external government of the church under a Christian magistrate must be according to the kind and form of government used in the commonwealth; else how can you make the prince supreme governor of all states and causes ecclesiastical? Will you so divide the government of the church from the government of the commonwealth, that, the one being a monarchy, the other must be a democracy or an aristocraty?[136]

---

[132] *Works of Whitgift*, I, p. 79.   [133] Ibid., I, p. 149.
[134] Ibid., I, p. 150.   [135] Ibid., I, p. 161.
[136] Ibid., II, pp. 263–4.

Whitgift's view was that scripture supported the institution of bishops, but he preferred to defend the Elizabethan episcopacy on the ground of its similarity with the state and to leave the question to be decided by the prince, rather than to treat episcopacy as divinely ordained. In 1587, when the bishops were feeling more confident in relation to the state, John Bridges argued that bishops were instituted by divine law, an argument noted by contemporaries as an innovation and, as such, resisted by some.[137]

Hooker acknowledged the possibility of a *de iure divino* defence of the episcopacy but preferred to ground his argument elsewhere.[138] He had devoted the first book of the *Laws* to arguing that not scripture alone, but scripture together with the law of reason, enabled human beings to determine God's instructions.[139] Laws of human institutions he regarded as subject to local variation in their organisation.[140] There were no fixed divine injunctions governing the organisation of churches or of states, and even if there had been it would not be possible to derive them from scripture without also taking into account the demands of reason. This meant that the institution of the episcopacy was alterable, dependent on the decisions of the legislative authority.[141] Hooker explicitly extended this argument to the monarchy, insisting that any form of human rule could only be legitimate through the will of God or the consent of the legislative authority.

Their power must needs be either usurped, and then unlawful; or if lawful, then either granted or consented unto by them over whom they exercise the same, or else given extraordinarily by God, unto whom all the world is subject.[142]

Hooker keeps the argument about the primacy of scripture firmly in view. In order to avoid the puritan claim that the Church must be reorganised in a way that reflects their understanding of scripture, he insists on the role of reason and natural law in establishing God's teaching.

---

[137] Lake, *Anglicans and Puritans?*, pp. 88–97; Cargill Thompson, *Studies in the Reformation*, pp. 101–8.

[138] Lake, *Anglicans and Puritans?*, pp. 220–4.

[139] Hooker, *Laws*, I.16.5. Cargill Thompson, *Studies in the Reformation*, pp. 151–3. Hooker's conception of laws of reason may owe something to Melanchthon's distinction between law and gospel as foundations of Christian ethics (Sachiko Kusukawa, *The Transformation of Natural Philosophy* (Cambridge, 1995), pp. 65–74), but Hooker does not cite Melanchthon, whose name would have been offensive to some Calvinists.

[140] Hooker, *Laws*, I.10.9–11.

[141] Ibid., VII.5.8. Cargill Thompson, *Studies in the Reformation*, pp. 181–3.

[142] Hooker, *Laws*, I.10.4.

He explains in the preface his fear that extrapolations from tendentious biblical interpretation could fuel tyranny and chaos.

That your discipline being (for such is your error) the absolute commandment of Almighty God, it must be received although the world by receiving it should be clean turned upside down; herein lieth the greatest danger of all. For whereas the name of divine authority is used to countenance these things, which are not the commandments of God, but your own erroneous collections; on him you must father whatsoever you shall afterwards be led, either to do in withstanding the adversaries of your cause, or to think in maintenance of your doings.[143]

Hooker thinks that once people are confident that God's will speaks through them, they will believe themselves entitled to use any means to counter opposition. The most extreme forms of action will seem justified. Knowing that interpretation can make free with the text of the Bible, he elevates reason (closely connected with custom and universal agreement)[144] as a counterweight to scripture. The participation of reason then necessarily qualifies other claims to absolute authority. Since he believed that parliament had in the past acknowledged the authority of the monarch, Hooker did not argue that the monarch could be controlled by parliament, though he did maintain that the monarch's power was limited by law.[145] But neither would he have accepted that the claim of parliament to represent the will of the people, together with the privileges which accrued thereto, belonged to it by monarchical permission. For Hooker, human laws, including the law which establishes the rule of the monarch, are made by politic societies which represent the consent of the governed.[146]

By the natural law, whereunto [God] hath made all subject, the lawful power of making laws to command whole politic societies of men belongeth so properly unto the same entire societies, that for any prince or potentate of what kind soever upon earth to exercise the same of himself, and not either by express commission immediately and personally received from God, or else by authority derived at the first from their consent upon whose persons they impose laws, it is no better than mere tyranny.[147]

---

[143] Ibid., Preface. 8.5.
[144] 'The general and perpetual voice of men is as the sentence of God himself. For that which all men have at all times learned, Nature herself must needs have taught; and God being the author of Nature, her voice is but his instrument.' Ibid., 1.8.3.
[145] Ibid., VIII.2.5, 12, 17. [146] Ibid., 1.10.11.
[147] Ibid., 1.10.8. Hooker thought that in England consent had been given in a form that was in practice irrevocable. Ibid., VIII.2.10. Cargill Thompson, *Studies in the Reformation*, pp. 166–7.

Hooker's attempts to subject inferences from scriptural interpretation to the disciplines of reason led him to address issues of parliamentary privilege which were contentious in Elizabeth's time and would prove explosive in the reigns of her successors.[148] The analogy between religion and politics, which the monarchy used to pre-empt certain types of religious questioning, forced Hooker to extend the implication of his argument against puritan scriptural absolutism. The culture of debate, which informed religious controversy, licensed objections and responses which developed the argument in unforeseen ways.

CONCLUSION

Rhetorical education both contributes to the achievement of Elizabethan religious writing and offers us ways to understand it. University training in dialectic had an even greater impact on religious writing than on political debate. Preachers used logic to divide up their texts, to explore the implications of each section and to debate the interpretation of a particular text. Religious controversialists employed their knowledge of forms of argumentation and tactics of disputation to criticise their opponents' arguments. Hooker used logical method to order arguments and to plan the overall structure of his *Laws of Ecclesiastical Polity*. Preachers used the figures of rhetoric to interpret the Bible and to embellish key passages of their sermons. They drew on commonplaces of humanist education to describe civil war, to mock worldly vanity and to console the bereaved.

The connections between humanist education and religion run much deeper than such techniques of composition. Humanist preoccupation with the primacy of the original text and humanist textual scholarship as applied to the Bible had been among the founding intellectual impulses of the reformation. The English reformation liturgy privileged Bible-reading and the priest's continual explanation of the meaning of Christian belief.[149] Teaching and the interpretation of the Bible became the main religious functions of the priest, thus placing an even greater value on humanist literary training. This in turn fuelled further religious controversy as puritans interpreted the Bible as requiring a further revolution in the Church, while Hooker used the tools of logic to make human reason and law a counterbalancing force to scriptural fundamentalism.

---

[148] J. P. Sommerville, *Politics and Ideology in England 1603–1640* (London, 1986), pp. 1–5, 29, 47, 61–8.
[149] Mack, 'Rhetoric and Liturgy', pp. 82–109 (86–7); G. J. Cuming, *A History of Anglican Liturgy*, 2nd edn (London, 1982), pp. 47–9, 75–81.

The argument about the religious legitimacy of reading *Homilies* was a struggle between those who hoped that by securing pulpits for learned Protestants they could hasten reform and those who hoped to maintain unity through central control.[150]

Religion provides some of the most important assumptions of Elizabethan political writing. For Protestants, as we have seen, religion was an important factor in defining and expressing national unity.[151] Elizabeth's ministers sought to unify the political élite by recounting the story of the struggle for the reformed religion. In a more political and adversarial sense, religion provided axioms which ethics and reason might have questioned, for example about the malevolence of the Pope, the inferiority of women and the unreliability of peace treaties with the Catholic powers. Religion licensed the harbouring of, and provided a language for expressing, certain forms of hatred, especially the hatred of other Christian sects.[152]

At the same time religious thought and writing helped to destabilise the Elizabethan political and religious settlement. Field, Wilcox and Cartwright reminded puritan sympathisers in parliament of the inadequacies and inconsistencies of the established Church. The puritans wanted a truly reformed church even though it would have required many excommunications to achieve it.[153] Protestant diplomats and councillors argued for whole-hearted military intervention on behalf of continental protestantism. On the other side Hatton and Cecil used the shared commitment to protestantism and the difficulty that the reformed nation had experienced in resisting the Catholic powers as arguments against extremist adventures. Both Cecil and Mildmay had to negotiate between their personal commitment to further religious reform and their secular political preference for prudence and restraint.

Religion provided principles from which both sides of such debates could draw arguments but it also offered perspectives which go beyond humanist prudence. Funeral sermons used the commonplaces of

[150] On the role of 'prophesyings' in pursuing further reformation, see Collinson, *Puritan Movement*, pp. 168–77.
[151] Helgerson, *Forms of Nationhood*, pp. 249–93; Patrick Collinson, 'Truth and Legend: The Veracity of John Foxe's Book of Martyrs', in his *Elizabethan Essays*, pp. 151–77 reviews the literature and the issues sanely and sceptically.
[152] In 1586 Richard Hooker was severely criticised by puritans and moderate Anglicans when he said that, prior to the reformation, members of the Catholic church had been saved. Even Archbishop Whitgift, who was responsible for appointing Hooker as master of the Temple, was reluctant to support this charitable opinion. Hooker, *Sermons*, pp. 200–2, 261–97.
[153] Collinson, *Puritan Movement*, pp. 291–2, 348–50.

humanist ethical consolation but joined them with Christian understandings of the importance of grief, the strength of divine comfort and the promise of the life beyond. Religious authors drew on Bible texts to think more compassionately and more creatively than politicians about poverty. Debate on church organisation opened up explosive questions about the relation between parliament and the monarch.

Conclusion

In 1605 Francis Bacon identified an excessive concern with words as one of the enemies of learning. In Bacon's reconstruction, Martin Luther, finding that no theologians in his own time would support his reforms, was forced to look to ancient authors for assistance.[1]

This by consequence did draw on a necessity of a more exquisite travail in the languages original, wherein those writers did write, for the better understanding of those authors and the better advantage of pressing and applying their words. And thereof grew again great delight in their manner of style and phrase and an admiration of that kind of writing.[2]

The need to consult original texts led to investigations of language and delight in ancient expression. This enthusiasm for pure Latin was increased by hatred of the scholastics and their technical neologisms, and by the need to preach effectively to ordinary people.

So that these four causes concurring, the admiration of ancient authors, the hate of the schoolmen, the exact study of languages, and the efficacy of preaching, did bring in an affectionate study of eloquence and copie of speech, which then began to flourish. This grew speedily to an excess; for men began to hunt more after words than matter; and more after the choiceness of the phrase, and the round and clean composition of the sentence, and the sweet falling of the clauses, and the varying and illustration of their works with tropes and figures than after the weight of matter, worth of subject, soundness of argument, life of invention or depth of judgement.[3]

---

[1] While Bacon is incorrect in making Luther the patron (rather than the beneficiary) of humanism, nevertheless his mistake reminds us both that in England promoters of Protestantism carried through the humanist reform of education and that for Lorenzo Valla and Erasmus improvement of the text of the Bible was the ultimate purpose of philological studies. Sir Francis Bacon, *The Advancement of Learning*, ed. Michael Kiernan, in *The Oxford Francis Bacon*, vol. IV (Oxford, 2000), p. 21.

[2] Ibid., pp. 21–2. Spelling modernised in all quotations.   [3] Ibid., p. 22.

Bacon constructs an argumentative and eloquent condemnation of the excesses which have arisen from humanist pleas, like Ascham's,[4] for the importance of words. Although Bacon understands why this preoccupation arose, and although he can see the advantages of dressing philosophy in 'sensible and plausible elocution',[5] nevertheless he condemns his contemporaries' obsession with style, which he regards as the consequence of the humanist reform of education.

It seems to me that Pygmalion's frenzy is a good emblem or portraiture of this vanity: for words are but the images of matter; and except they have the life of reason and invention, to fall in love with them is all one as to fall in love with a picture.[6]

At the same time Bacon's work is evidently the product of the system he criticises. His condemnation of eloquence, no less than his praise of King James,[7] is an instance of amplification based on copia of things. In his review of the present state of learning he speaks sympathetically of rhetoric, 'a science excellent and excellently well laboured'.[8] Bacon uses and praises the use of maxims and aphorisms.[9] He employs historical examples, quotations from authors (especially Virgil) and comparisons. He defends the use of commonplace books.[10] In introducing the work, just like a humanist disputer or a parliamentary orator, he first lists the objections to learning, then sets out the arguments for each objection and finally replies to each of them in turn.[11]

Thus, Bacon uses humanist argumentative skills to call for a more practical, more instrumental approach to learning. In so doing he demonstrates the effectiveness of the humanist legacy in enabling the presentation of new ideas. In this conclusion I shall revisit the skills outlined in chapters one and two, in order to draw together the different facets of the method of reading described in this book, and review the implications of some of the categories in the light of their use in the texts analysed in later chapters. Finally I shall discuss some general characteristics of Elizabethan writing which emerge from the approach taken in this study.

---

[4] 'Ye know not, what hurt ye do to learning, that care not for wordes, but for matter, and so make a devorse betwixt the tong and the hart...Whan apte and good wordes began to be neglected,...than also began ill deedes to spring.' Roger Ascham, *The Scholemaster*, in *English Works*, p. 265. Compare Erasmus, *De ratione studii*, p. 113.
[5] Bacon, *Advancement*, p. 23.   [6] Ibid.   [7] Ibid., p. 3–5.   [8] Ibid., p. 127.
[9] Ibid., p. 124.   [10] Ibid., p. 118.   [11] Ibid., pp. 5–33.

AN APPROACH TO READING FOUNDED ON
ELIZABETHAN RHETORIC

In chapter one I outlined eleven rhetorical skills which Elizabethan grammar school boys could be expected to have acquired as a result of their training in Latin language, literature and composition:

1. Moral sentences
2. Moral stories
3. Narratives
4. History
5. Structures for compositions
6. Rhetorical topics
7. Thinking about an audience
8. Amplification
9. Commonplaces
10. Note-taking and commonplace books
11. Figures of rhetoric

In chapter two, while recognising the wide range of studies pursued at Oxford and Cambridge I identified a group of skills associated with the core training in Latin literature, rhetoric and dialectic and with the exercises required of all students in disputation and declamation:

1. A complete syllabus of classical rhetoric
2. Declamations and sermons
3. Logical invention and the topics
4. Argumentation and the syllogism
5. Organisation and method
6. Distinctions and definitions
7. Tactics for disputation
8. Dialectical reading

The range of skills taught and their different places in categorisations of knowledge encourage students to prioritise and combine them in new ways. For the purposes of thinking about individual texts my categories can be crudely reorganised into three groups, based on three of the five skills of classical rhetoric.

Content (Invention)	Structure (Disposition)	Inflection (Style)
Moral sentences	Letters	Amplification
Stories	*Progymnasmata*	Approach to audience
Examples	Genre expectations	Figures of rhetoric
Analysis of text	Declamation	Logical forms
Arguments	Disputation tactics	
Rhetorical topics	Logical method	
Descriptions	Dialectical reading	
Commonplaces		
Definitions		
Distinctions		

All the components listed in the first column are found in texts analysed in this book. Many of the texts include several of these items. I think that anyone who had passed through an Elizabethan grammar school would notice the existence of such elements in a text and, as part of his process of reading, would consider how they were used. Some of the skills were reinforced at different stages of education. Examples were taken from histories and grammar school literary texts, and from private reading in chronicles and conduct manuals like Elyot's *Governor*. The method of collecting examples was learned at school and from reading *De copia*.

Compared with the single model of disposition proposed in classical manuals of rhetoric (the four-part oration), Elizabethan students were taught a wide range of different structural models and studied exemplary texts combining different principles of organisation. The *Progymnasmata* and the letter-writing manuals prescribed many different forms of writing (and the contents for each form) appropriate to different occasions. Some of the letters studied in chapter four and some segments of the texts analysed in chapter five followed these instructions closely. Many texts examined combined different principles of structure. After an introductory passage derived from the rhetorical exordium, the letter-writing manual or the expectations of a particular genre, many texts presented a prominent division of the main arguments. In several cases this division was an enumeration of points made by previous speakers or of accusations made against the writer. Such formats seem to derive from habits of disputation. Some texts were arranged on the basis of doctrines of logical method, while others derived mainly from generic structures associated with the sermon or particular types of parliamentary speech.

Notebooks and university practices of reading illustrate contemporary interest in analysing the structures of texts. The combination of structures derived from different sources was anticipated by the development of moderate-length declamations within the framework of the academic disputation. While parliamentary speeches or sermons provided particular generic expectations, individuals could vary them through the methods of rhetoric and the models of other kinds of writing. Because their training had provided so many resources for producing acceptable forms, writers had the opportunity to make new combinations and to play with their audience's expectations.

As well as classifying elements of the content and analysing the structure of a text, Elizabethan readers would have noted the particular flavour deriving from the words and rhetorical figures chosen, the relation between writer and audience constructed and the way amplification was employed. Although amplification and attitude to an audience can certainly lead a writer to introduce additional components (such as descriptions, examples and asides) and alter the order and the overall structure of a text, both imply decisions about how a particular audience is to be manipulated. Material derived from dialectic could be used for decorative purposes, while comparisons, carefully crafted sentences and proverbs were used to express the main argumentative force of a speech. Orators aroused strong emotion for different purposes: to oppose a proposal emanating from the Privy Council or to create a sense of community of belief between councillors and ordinary members of parliament. While content and structure are largely generated from the context of writing, inflection is the area of composition in which the writer is most self-conscious and most aware of adapting the material to achieve a particular outcome. The choice of how fully and formally to set out one's reasoning affects the implied relationship to the audience in the same way as asides, changes of tone or the choice of particular figures of rhetoric.

Given that I have chosen the categories and the texts for analysis, it is to be expected that the examples of Elizabethan writing should seem to me to reflect all the nineteen skills promoted by Tudor education. The more important test will be whether other readers find these categories derived from Elizabethan educational practice helpful in guiding their own understanding of other early modern texts.

HOW PRACTICE CHANGES THE CATEGORIES

The skills identified in the first two chapters derive from formal education but the analysis of texts demonstrating their use in practice results in a continuing refinement of our ideas about those skills and their implications. Analysis of examples also shows us how skills taught in different parts or at different stages of the syllabus could be combined.

Moral sentences, proverbs and quotations from authors are ubiquitous in Elizabethan discourse. Pupils learned them by heart as examples of Latin grammar. They identified and excerpted them during their reading of classical texts. They were recycled in English in conduct manuals like Elyot's *Governor* and in popular collections of philosophy like Baldwin's *Treatise of Morall Philosophie*. In letters of consolation moral sentences were used to establish emotional identification between writer and recipient, as though the repetition of appropriate moral sentiments guaranteed the understanding of a particular person's share in the common human burden of sorrow. Queen Elizabeth used them to evade the commitments her subjects sought from her.

In histories and diplomatic letters moral sentences were used to interpret actions as instances which illustrate continuing norms of ethical, military or political behaviour. Understood in this way occurrences in the world call forth expected responses and become in turn exemplifications of the fund of political wisdom. Moral sentences served to familiarise and classify events. Projected forward they could become starting points for arguments about policy or legislation. Parliamentary speakers often supported their arguments with moral sentences which appeared to draw on a tested fund of agreed wisdom in preference to more detailed arguments drawn from the particular circumstances of the issue in question. The proverb or moral axiom was easier for an audience to understand and harder for an opponent to argue against.

Because there were so many different moral sentences they could be applied in a wide range of situations. The fact that equally authoritative axioms were sometimes contradictory meant that they helped secure consideration for both sides of contentious issues. For example, Elizabethan politicians sometimes cited classical axioms of political behaviour because they knew they contradicted (and gave authority for breaking) Christian moral rules. Diplomats urging intervention cited maxims of resolution, while councillors resisting them called on axioms of prudence and commonplaces of the suffering caused by war.

Elizabethan writers drew arguments partly from the topics of invention taught by humanist dialectic and partly from the topics of deliberative oratory presented through the letter-writing manuals and discussed in Cicero's *De officiis*. Memoranda by Nathaniel Bacon and William Cecil illustrate the process of assembling arguments and devising responses to anticipated points on the other side (as Agricola recommended).[12] Forms of argumentation were rarely set out in full,[13] though in some political and (especially) religious pamphlets authors used the technical terminology of dialectic to point out the deceptiveness of their opponents' logic. In writing for an educated audience authors could assume recognition of logical terminology but they were generally wary of letting their own positive arguments appear too artful.

Narratives were often retold to exemplify moral teaching or to amplify suffering or glory. Humanists composed histories and history was taught in humanist schools to provide moral and political lessons. Politicians returned the compliment by using historical examples to support their political arguments. In trying to persuade the Privy Council to support armed intervention in the Netherlands Wilson cited the success of the English in foreign wars and the preference of Scipio and Demosthenes for fighting abroad rather than at home.[14] In Hall's *Chronicle* Exeter cites Cato to support an invasion of France.[15] Hall's presentation of the early fifteenth-century argument between Westmoreland and Exeter about whether to invade France or Scotland shares the basic assumptions of Burghley's memoranda on pacifying Scotland and the measures to be taken in preparation for invasion. Under the influence of epideictic rhetoric, parliamentary orators related histories known to their audience to create and celebrate a community of political interests. Persecution narratives provided co-religionists with identity, hope, and hatred of their oppressors. Plausible and detailed narration was a means of creating trust in court testimony.

History endorsed its moral teaching with its claim of true exemplification but Elyot argued that fiction could be equally instructive.[16] Fiction played a large part in teaching as boys acted out imagined dialogues or wrote letters and speeches on behalf of fictional characters. Real letters could become models and model letters could be used for real-life purposes. Or model letters could be written as fictional exchanges or as

---

[12] Agricola, *De inventione dialectica*, pp. 250–1.   [13] Compare ibid., pp. 279–82.
[14] PRO SP 70.145.1237.   [15] Hall, *Chronicle*, pp. 50–6.   [16] Elyot, *Governor*, p. 231.

components of fictions. At the same time fiction's imperative to enter-
tain and surprise resulted in inversions and (temporary) questionings of
conventional moral teaching.

The habit of compiling commonplace books encouraged readers to
ask whether any particular sentence was worth recording and, if so, under
which heading. Mentally filing statements under appropriate headings
promoted sensitivity to dialogues on particular issues within and between
texts. Commonplace collections provided a means for the recycling of
sentences, arguments and narratives. The studies of conduct manuals,
romances and parliamentary speeches in chapters five and seven have
provided abundant evidence of the reuse of materials from earlier texts.
Training in composing commonplaces from the *Progymnasmata* (and reading of commonplaces in Cicero and Elyot) produced decorative and
emotional passages for sermons, narratives and speeches. Against the
fragmenting tendency exemplified by the commonplace books may be
set the emphasis on the structure of a text promoted by letter-writing
manuals, commentaries on classical texts and the practice of dialectical
analysis of sermons.

The most commonly used figures of rhetoric were alliteration,
anaphora, parison, isocolon, colon, comparison, metaphor, simile, vivid
description, antithesis, sententia, apostrophe and rhetorical question.
The first five of these figures are connected with repetition and patterned language; the next five with descriptions, comparisons and copia;
and the last three with placing the material in a particular relation to the
audience. Some of the most characteristic and effective uses of rhetoric
resulted from combinations of doctrines.

Amplification was taught through *De copia* and commentary on classical texts. Recognition of figures helped pupils learn the use of particular
figures from their reading. Elizabethan readers distinguished between
a normal mode of writing (which might in euphuistic and related texts
itself be quite strongly ornamented) and specially worked up passages,
dense in figures or marked by comparisons, proverbs, examples and descriptions. In some of Nicholas Bacon's speeches amplification serves
more to indicate his skill than for emotional effect but Hatton's speech at
the opening of parliament worked much harder for emotional identification. Hall's Henry V and Francis Bacon used images to dramatise the
concrete impact of proposed actions, where Cornwallis's series of images
aimed to stimulate a change in the English court's understanding of the
Spanish view of events.

Self-presentation and manipulation of the audience was an issue in all the diplomatic letters and political speeches. Wilson and Winwood knew whom their dispatches had to convince and they crafted their letters accordingly, but they also knew that they had to give the impression of being detached observers passing on facts and interpreting events, ready to do the bidding of the Privy Council rather than seeking to persuade its members. Mildmay favoured members of parliament with a glimpse of the government's financial position. Burghley often prefaced a speech to the Privy Council with a review of the international situation designed to bolster his authority and justify the course of action he proposed. Schoolboys learned about self-presentation through the letter-writing manual, writing on behalf of historical and fictional people, and ethopoeia. Grammar school education helped writers to understand audiences by making them learn and use moral axioms, principles of conduct which pupils (they themselves and their future audience) were taught to think of as true. Training in interpreting classical literature and analysing sermons taught writers how their works would be read.

ETHICS AND POLITICS

Rhetorical education provided Elizabethan writers, statesmen and priests with content as well as techniques. Reflections on humanist moral topics are found across a wide range of texts and genres. Moral themes and axioms at times constituted the subject-matter of a chapter or sermon, or they were used in a letter, speech or treatise to provide grounding principles to support an argument. Some speakers employed them as commonplaces to make themselves appear prudent or sympathetic. Sometimes different texts answered each other's discussion of such themes, as when Sidney questioned the effectiveness of textbook moral philosophy in mitigating the irrational effects of love, and histories pointed out the political dangers of ill-advised friendship.

The most important political arguments of the reign concerned war. Those who advocated interventions on behalf of Protestants on the continent always spoke of the need for resolution, often claiming that resolution on its own would deter England's enemies. Privy councillors seeking to raise funds for defensive wars would emphasise the suffering which war and defeat would bring. The *Homilies* urged obedience to the crown with vivid descriptions of the devastation of civil war. When Nicholas Bacon wanted to make the Commons grateful for the benefits of Elizabeth's rule he composed a commonplace on the rewards of peace. Peace was invoked when gratitude was expected; the threat of war to justify additional expense. As well as being the event most likely to confound the hopes of the landed classes (since their sons would be required as officers), war was also the occasion on which the Queen most needed parliament to agree extraordinary revenue. Consequently it was her best opportunity for raising additional taxation. Her reluctance to wage war was financially and politically prudent, in spite of the support her councillors and ambassadors expressed for fighting to protect continental Protestants, but equally the need to raise money encouraged talk of the threat of war. Instead of being left to admirals and the aristocracy these debates were increasingly conducted by university graduates of 'middling' origin and slender military experience.

Although the Elizabethan régime was repressive in Ireland and towards Catholic missions from the continent, the widespread use of rhetorical methods reflected and reinforced a distinctive kind of civil society among the élite. Some of the characteristics of this society can be connected with the skills which were required for entry and promoted through education. It was a society whose intellectual life was founded on the interpretation of texts. While the foundational texts (for example the Bible, *Sententiae pueriles*, the *Chronicles*, Ovid and Virgil) were fixed, individual readings of these texts, however constrained by custom, inevitably resulted in differences of understanding. These differences of interpretation could be debated. Criteria could be suggested for preferring one or other of them, but disagreement could be maintained. English rhetoric manuals commented on the usefulness of knowledge of the figures of rhetoric in biblical interpretation. Religious controversies turned on the difference between literal and figurative understandings of particular verses. Preachers employed rhetorical terminology in analysing scripture. Queen Elizabeth used the example of biblical exegesis as a point of comparison in her amplification of the difficulty of being understood. She implied that interpretation generates extra ways of making meaning (and therefore extra ways of being misunderstood).

The Elizabethan Church hierarchy tried to enforce outward conformity. Though publication and sedition were punished, there was no attempt to establish an inquisition to root heresy out of people's souls.[17]

---

[17] Strong government measures against puritans were usually prompted by publication of inflammatory opinions (Field, Wilcox, Waldegrave, Udall), by attempts to establish secret and separate church organisation (Barrow, Greenwood, Penry) or by episodes of violence (Birchet, Hacket). In 1584 Burghley protested to Whitgift about the inquisitorial nature of the Twenty-four articles and

Whitgift in effect reprinted banned puritan polemics in order to answer their arguments. The expectations of debate also shaped (and restricted) the organised puritan movement. In principle higher conferences were supposed to dictate policy, but in practice local committees of preachers found reasons to take independent positions. When the movement needed to agree the text of the *Book of Discipline* it found itself embroiled in lengthy formal disputations in many localities.[18]

Late Elizabethan England was a society in which positions were taken up and decisions made in the awareness of competing principles of action. People knew that ethical and religious maxims could be cited on different sides of the debate. Cecil weighed the need to protect the state against the obligation not to encourage rebellion against a foreign prince. Cecil and Wilson negotiated the Christian obligation to truthful and just dealing against classical maxims allowing prudential deceit of enemies. The need of money for the defence of the kingdom had to be argued against parliamentary sensitivities as to people's ability and willingness to pay. Prejudices against Catholics could provide arguments to counterweigh the political advantages claimed for a French alliance. Rhetorical categories and rhetorical training made possible argument and negotiation between opposing principles (and between reasoned principles and prejudices).

Thanks to the limited privilege of free speech and the elevation of the duty of good counsel, privy councillors and members of parliament thought themselves not just entitled but actually obliged to state opinions about subjects on which they knew they disagreed with the monarch. In practice the Queen and her ministers could always ensure the defeat of proposals to which they were opposed and the right of free speech was hedged around with privileges and limitations. Nevertheless Elizabethan ethical, political and religious discourse was founded on the expectation that reasons would be given and objections answered. This expectation, which I attribute in part to the university practice of disputation, formed a deep cultural bulwark against absolutism in England.

Humanist education aimed to develop wise and pious men who could serve the state. By claiming a connection between true friendship and good counsel and by their cult of friendship, humanist pedagogical

got their use restricted. The ministers arraigned in the Star Chamber in the 1590s were released because the accusation that they intended to establish a separate discipline in the Church could not be proved. Collinson, *Puritan Movement*, pp. 120, 148, 150–1, 164, 263–72, 274, 295, 336, 391, 407, 417–31.

[18] Ibid., pp. 296, 318–20, 402.

theorists encouraged the replacement of the landed aristocracy in the Privy Council by classically educated civil servants 'of the middling type'. Their education provided them with religious and prudential principles of conduct which were sometimes in conflict. Rhetorical and dialectical training enabled both sides of such conflicts to be heard. Against the absolute claims of Essex's honour and Cartwright's biblical fundamentalism, Egerton and Hooker could argue the duties of prudent government and the role of human reason. In confronting the problem of poverty and poor relief, religious arguments at first conflicted with, and later made use of, considerations of worldly prudence. That participants in such debates were equipped with the means of weighing and making arguments does not mean that conflicts were resolved or that the losers were satisfied. But it did mean that the complexity of divided situations could be recognised and that principle and pragmatism could both contribute to a process of decision-making. The forms of argument together with the maxims and moral stories provided by rhetorical education defined the culture of debate and shaped the Elizabethan élite.

Bibliography

This bibliography does not include reference works, calendars of manuscripts and editions of classical texts. It does include renaissance editions of classical authors, of which in some English instances connected with Bynneman's patent I have thought it worthwhile to add the printer's name.

MANUSCRIPTS

Bodleian Library MS Autogr.e.2
Bodleian Library MS Bodl. 899
Bodleian Library MS Lat misc e. 114
Bodleian Library MS Rawl. D 47
Bodleian Library MS Rawl. D 273
Bodleian Library MS Rawl. D. 985
British Library MS Add. 4379
British Library MS Add. 4724
British Library MS Arundel 510
British Library MS Cotton Caligula B 10
British Library MS Cotton Caligula C 1
British Library MS Harley 398
British Library MS Harley 3230
British Library MS Sloane 326
Public Record Office SP 12.1
Public Record Office SP 46.15
Public Record Office SP 70.143
Public Record Office SP 70.145
Public Record Office SP 84.66
Public Record Office SP 94.16

PRINTED PRIMARY SOURCES

Abelard, Peter, *Dialectica*, ed. L. M. de Rijk, Assen, 1970.
Agricola, Rudolph, *De inventione dialectica*, Cologne, 1539, repr. Nieuwkoop, 1967.
 Lucubrationes, Cologne, 1539, repr. Nieuwkoop, 1967.

Allen, P. S. (ed.), *Opus Epistolarum Erasmi*, 12 vols., Oxford, 1906–58.
Andrewes, Lancelot, *Sermons*, ed. G. M. Story, Oxford, 1967.
  XCVI Sermons, London, 1629, STC 606.
Aphthonius, *Progymnasmata*, with the commentary of Lorichius, London: Thomas Marsh, 1575, STC 700.3.
Aquinas, Thomas, *Summa Theologiae*, trans. English Dominican Fathers, Chicago, 1952.
Ascham, Roger, *English Works*, ed. W. A. Wright, Cambridge, 1904.
Ault, Norman (ed.), *Elizabethan Lyrics*, London, 1925.
Bacon, Sir Francis, *The Advancement of Learning*, ed. Michael Kiernan, in *The Oxford Francis Bacon*, vol. IV, Oxford, 2000.
Baldwin, William, *A Treatise of Morall Philosophie (1547)*, facsimile repr. of the 1620 edition, ed. R. H. Bowers, Gainesville, 1967.
Baldwin, William, et al., *Mirror for Magistrates*, ed. L. B. Campbell, Cambridge, 1938.
Blundeville, Thomas, *The Art of Logike*, London, 1599, STC 3142, repr. Menston, 1967.
  The True Order and Methode of Wryting and Reading Hystories, London, 1574, STC 3161.
Boccaccio, G., *Decameron*, ed. V. Branca, in *Opere*, vol. IV, Milan, 1976.
Boethius, *De definitione*, in *Patrologia Latina*, vol. LXIV, cols. 875D–891A.
  De differentiis topicis, in *Patrologia Latina*, vol. LXIV, cols. 1173B–1216D.
  De divisione, in *Patrologia Latina*, vol. LXIV, cols. 891B–910B.
Braunmuller, A. R. (ed.), *A Seventeenth-Century Letter-Book*, Newark NJ, 1983.
Brennan, J. X., 'The *Epitome troporum ac schematum* of Joannes Susenbrotus: Text, Translation and Commentary', unpublished PhD thesis, University of Illinois, 1953.
Breton, Nicholas, *A Poste with a Madde Packet of Letters*, London, 1602, STC 3684.
  A Post with a Madde Packet of Letters, in *The Works in Verse and Prose of Nicholas Breton*, ed. Rev. A. B. Grosart, 2 vols. 1879, repr. New York, 1966, II, pp. 1–27 (separately paginated).
Brinsley, John, *Ludus Literarius*, London, 1612, ed. E. T. Campagnac, Liverpool, 1917.
Brinsley, John, *Ovid's Metamorphosis Grammatically Translated*, London, 1618, STC 18963.
Browne, John, *The Marchants Avizo*, London, 1589, STC 3908.4.
Bullinger, H., *The Christen State of Matrimonye*, trans. M. Coverdale, Antwerp, 1541, STC 4045.
Calvin, John, *Institutes of the Christian Religion*, trans. F. L. Battles, 2 vols., Philadelphia, 1960.
Case, John, *Summa veterum interpretum in universam dialecticam Aristotelis*, London, 1584, STC 4762.
Case, John, *Sphaera Civitatis*, Oxford, 1588, STC 4761.
[Cato], *Libellus elegantissimus qui inscribitur Cato*, London, 1572, STC 4846.
Cicero, *Ad familiares*, with the commentary of Hegendorff, London: Thomas Marsh, 1574, STC 5296.

Ad familiares, London: Vautrollier, 1575, STC 5297.
De officiis, with Erasmus's commentary, London: Orwin, 1590, STC 5266.6.
Orationum volumen primum, London, 1585, STC 5309.
Thre Bokes of Duties, translated by Nicholas Grimalde (1566), ed. Gerald O'Gorman, Washington, 1990.
Clark, A. C., *Register of the University of Oxford II*, 4 vols., Oxford, 1887–9.
Colet, J., *Rudimenta grammatices et docendi methodus... per Thomam cardinalem*, London: P. Treveris, 1529, STC 5542.3 (=25944).
Conybeare, F. C. (ed.), *Letters and Exercises of the Elizabethan Schoolmaster John Conybeare*, London, 1905.
Cordier, M., *Colloquiorum scholasticorum libri quatuor*, London, 1608, STC 5759.4.
Cox, Leonard, *Arte or Crafte of Rethoryke*, London, 1532, STC 5947.
Culmann, Leonhard, *Sententiae pueriles*, London, 1639, STC 6107.
Cusack, Bridget (ed.), *Everyday English 1500–1700: A Reader*, Edinburgh, 1998.
Day, Angel, *The English Secretary*, London, 1599, STC 6404, facsimile repr. ed. Robert O. Evans, Gainesville, 1967.
Devereux, Robert, Earl of Essex, *An Apology*, London, 1603, STC 6788.
Documents Relating to the University and Colleges of Cambridge, 3 vols., London, 1852.
Donno, E. S. (ed.), *An Elizabethan in 1582: The Diary of Richard Madox*, London, 1976, Hakluyt Society, series 2, vol. CXLVII.
Elizabeth I, *Collected Works*, ed. L. Marcus, J. Mueller and M. Rose, Chicago, 2000.
Elyot, Sir Thomas, *The Bankette of Sapience*, London, 1534, STC 7630.
The Boke Named the Governour, ed. Henry Croft, 2 vols., London, 1880.
The Book Named the Governor, ed. S. E. Lehmberg, London, 1962.
The Education or Bringing Up of Children, London, 1533, repr. in R. D. Pepper (ed.), *Four Tudor Books on Education*, Gainesville, 1966.
Erasmus, D., *Collected Works of Erasmus*, Toronto, 1974–.
Opera omnia, 10 vols., Leiden, 1703.
De conscribendis epistolis, ed. J. C. Margolin, in *Opera omnia*, I–2, Amsterdam, 1971.
De copia, ed. B. Knott, in *Opera omnia*, I–6, Amsterdam, 1988.
De copia, with commentary of Weltkirchius, London, 1569, STC 10472.
De ratione studii, ed. J. C. Margolin, in *Opera omnia*, I–2, Amsterdam, 1971.
Ecclesiastes, ed. J. Chomarat, in *Opera omnia* V–4, 5, Amsterdam, 1991–4.
Fehrenbach, R. J. and Leedham-Green E. S. (eds.), *Private Libraries in Renaissance England*, 5 vols., Binghamton, Tempe, 1992–8.
Fenner, Dudley, *The Artes of Logike and Rethorike*, Middleburg, 1584, STC 10766.
Field, John and Wilcox, Thomas, 'Admonition to Parliament', reprinted in Frere, W. H. and Douglas, C. E. (eds.), *Puritan Manifestos*, 1907, repr. New York, 1972, pp. 1–55.
Fleming, Abraham, *A Panoplie of Epistles*, London, 1576, STC 11049.
Fraunce, Abraham, *The Arcadian Rhetorike*, London, 1588, STC 11338.
Lawier's Logike, London, 1588, STC 11343.
Fulwood, William, *The Enemie of Idleness*, London, 1582, STC 11479.
Gardiner, S., *A Machiavellian Treatise*, ed. P. Donaldson, Cambridge, 1975.

Gibson, Strickland (ed.), *Statuta antiqua universitatis oxoniensis*, Oxford, 1931.

Gosse, Edmund, *The Life and Letters of John Donne*, 2 vols., London, 1899.

Green, Lawrence D., *John Rainolds's Oxford Lectures on Aristotle's Rhetoric*, Newark NJ, 1986.

Guarini, Battista, 'De ordine docendi et discendi', in E. Garin (ed.), *Il pensiero pedagogico dell'Umanesimo*, Florence, 1958, pp. 434–71.

Guevara, A. de, *The Diall of Princes*, trans. Sir Thomas North, selections ed. K. N. Colvile, London, 1919.

   The Golden Boke of Marcus Aurelius, trans. Lord Berners, London, 1535, STC 12436.

Haddon, W., *Lucubrationes*, London, 1567, STC 12596.

Hall, Edward, *The Union of the Two Noble and Illustre Families of Lancaster and York* [*Chronicle*], London, 1809.

Harrison, G. B. (ed.), *The Letters of Queen Elizabeth I*, New York, 1935, repr. Westport, 1968.

Hartley, T. E. (ed.), *Proceedings in the Parliaments of Elizabeth I*, 3 vols., Leicester, 1981–95.

Harvey, Gabriel, *Ciceronianus*, ed. H. S. Wilson, Lincoln NE, 1945.

Hassell Smith, A., et al. (eds.), *The Papers of Nathaniel Bacon of Stiffkey*, 4 vols., Norwich, 1979–2000, Norfolk Record Society vols. XLVI, XLIX, LIII, LXIV.

Haynes, Samuel (ed.), *Collection of State Papers . . . left by Lord Burghley*, London, 1740.

Hayward, John, *An Answere to the First Part of a Certaine Conference concerning Succession . . . [by] R. Dolman*, London, 1603, STC 12988.

Hegendorff, Christopher, *Dialogi pueriles*, London, 1532, STC 21810.

   Methodus conscribendi epistolis, Cologne, 1537.

Hemmingsen, Niels, *The Preacher*, London, 1574, STC 13065.

Hoby, Margaret, *The Private Life of an Elizabethan Lady: the Diary of Lady Margaret Hoby*, Stroud, 1998.

Hooker, Richard, *Hooker's Works*, ed. J. Keble, 3 vols., Oxford, 1865.

   Of the Lawes of Ecclesiasticall Politie, ed. G. Edelen, W. Speed Hill and P. G. Stanwood, *The Folger Library Edition of the Works of Richard Hooker*, vols. I–III, Cambridge MA, 1978–81.

   Tractates and Sermons, ed. L. Yeandle and E. Grislis, *The Folger Library Edition of the Works of Richard Hooker*, vol. V, Cambridge MA, 1990.

Horace, *Poemata omnia doctissimis scholiis illustrata*, London: Norton, 1574, STC 13784.

Hoskins, John, *Directions for Speech and Style*, ed. H. H. Hudson, Princeton, 1935.

Howson, J., *Uxore dimissa*, Oxford, 1602, STC 13886.

Huygens, R. B. C. (ed.), *Accessus ad auctores*, Leiden, 1970.

Hyperius, Andreas Gerardus, *The Practice of Preaching*, London, 1577, STC 11758.

Johnson, Ralph, *The Scholar's Guide*, London, 1665; repr. Menston, 1971.

Jonson, Ben, *Discoveries* (1641), ed. G. B. Harrison, London, 1922, repr. Edinburgh, 1966.

Kempe, William, *The Education of Children in Learning*, London, 1588, facsimile repr. in R. D. Pepper, *Four Tudor Books On Education*, Gainesville, 1966.

Klene, Jean, C.S.C. (ed.), *The Southwell-Sibthorpe Commonplace Book*, Tempe, 1997, RETS 7th series, vol. xx.

Koll, B. M., *Henry Peachams The Garden of Eloquence*, Frankfurt, 1996.

Leedham-Green, Elisabeth, *Books in Cambridge Inventories*, 2 vols., Cambridge, 1986.

Lever, Ralph, *The Arte of Reason, rightly termed, Witcraft*, London, 1573, STC 11541.

Lily, William, *Brevissima institutio*, London, 1573, STC 15616.

Lily, William and Colet, John, *A Shorte Introduction of Grammar*, London, 1572, STC 15616.

Lyly, John, *Works*, ed. R. W. Bond, 3 vols., Oxford, 1902.

Martyr Vermigli, Peter, *Disputatio de Eucharistia*, in *Tractatio de sacramento eucharistiae*, London: R. Wolfe, 1549, STC 24673.

McClure, N. E. (ed.), *The Letters of John Chamberlain*, 2 vols., Philadelphia, 1939.

Melanchthon, Philipp., *Opera omnia*, ed. C. Bretschneider, *Corpus Reformatorum*, 28 vols., Brunswick, 1834–60.

De Rhetorica libri tres, Basel, 1519.

Institutiones rhetoricae, Hagenau, 1521.

Minnis, A. J. and Scott, A. B. (eds. and trs.), *Medieval Literary Theory and Criticism*, Revised Edition, Oxford, 1991.

Mosellanus, P., *Paedologia*, London, 1532, STC 21810.

Tabulae de schematibus et tropibus, London, 1573, STC 21810.3.

Murdin, William (ed.), *Collection of State Papers relating . . . to the reign of Queen Elizabeth*, London, 1759.

Nichols, J. G. (ed.), *Literary Remains of King Edward VI*, 2 vols., London, 1857, repr. New York, 1964.

Narratives of the Days of Reformation, London, 1859, Camden Society original series, vol. LXXVII.

The Progresses of Queen Elizabeth, 3 vols., London, 1823.

North, T., *Plutarch's Lives of the Noble Grecians and Romans*, 8 vols., Oxford, 1928.

Ovid, *Metamorphoses*, with the commentary of Sabinus, Cambridge, 1584, STC 18951.

Metamorphoses, London: Vautrollier, 1582, STC 18951.5.

Peacham, Henry (the elder), *The Garden of Eloquence*, London, 1577, STC 19497 repr. Menston, 1971.

The Garden of Eloquence, London, 1593, STC 19498, facsimile repr. ed. W. G. Crane, Gainesville, 1954.

Pepper, R. D. (ed.), *Four Tudor Books on Education*, Gainesville, 1966.

Peter of Spain, *Tractatus*, ed. L. M. de Rijk, Assen, 1972.

Plummer, C. (ed.), *Elizabethan Oxford*, Oxford, 1887.

Poel, Marc van der, 'The "Scholia in orationem pro lege Manilia" of Rudolph Agricola', *Lias* 24 (1997), 1–35.

Puttenham, George, *The Arte of English Poesie*, London, 1589, STC 20519.
    The Arte of English Poesie, ed. G. D. Willcock and A. Walker, Cambridge, 1936.
Quinn, D. B. (ed.), *The Roanoke Voyages*, 2 vols., London, 1955, Hakluyt Society, series 2, vols. CIV–CV.
Rainolde, Richard, *Foundacion of Rhetorike*, London, 1563, STC 20604, repr. Menston, 1972.
Rainolds, John, *A Defence of the Iudgment of the Reformed Churches. That a man may lawfullie not onelie put awaie his wife for her adulterie, but also marrie another*, [Dort, 1609], STC 20607.
    Orationes duodecim, Oxford, 1614, STC 20613.
    The Prophecy of Obadiah opened, Oxford, 1613, STC 20619.
Ramus, Petrus, *Dialecticae libri duo*, Paris, 1574.
    Scholae in Liberales Artes, Basel, 1569, repr. Hildesheim, 1970.
    The Logike, trans. R. McIlmain, London, 1574, STC 15246.
Rojas, Fernando de, et al., *Las Celestinas*, ed. J. M. Valveda, et al., Barcelona, 1976.
Sallust, *De Catilinae coniuratione*, London: Thomas Marsh, 1569, STC 21622.2.
    Jugurthine War, trans. Barclay [?1520], STC 21626.
Sanderson, Robert, *Logicae artis compendium*, ed. E. J. Ashworth, Bologna, 1985.
Sawyer, Edmund (ed.), *Memorials of Affairs of State collected from the Winwood Papers*, 3 vols., London, 1725.
Schofield, B. (ed.), *The Knyvett Letters 1620–1644*, Norwich, 1949, Norfolk Record Society vol. XX.
Sermons or Homilies Appointed to be Read in Churches, London, 1833.
Seton, John, *Dialectica*, with the notes of P. Carter, London, 1563, STC 22250.5.
    Dialectica, with the notes of P. Carter, London, 1572, STC 22251.
Sherry, Richard, *A Treatise of Schemes and Tropes*, London, 1550, STC 22428, facsimile repr. ed. H. W. Hildebrandt, Gainesville, 1961.
Sidney, Sir Philip, *An Apology for Poetry*, ed. G. Shepherd, Manchester, 1973.
    The Countess of Pembroke's Arcadia (Old Arcadia), ed. J. M. Robertson, Oxford, 1973.
    The Countess of Pembroke's Arcadia (New Arcadia), ed. V. Skretkowicz, Oxford, 1987.
    The Poems of Sir Philip Sidney, ed. W. Ringler jr, Oxford, 1962.
Silvayn, A., *The Orator*, London, 1596, STC 4182.
Smith, Henry, *Thirteen Sermons upon Several Texts of Scripture*, London, 1592, STC 22717.
    The Works, 2 vols., Edinburgh, 1866–7.
Sorlien, R. P. (ed.), *The Diary of John Manningham of the Middle Temple 1602–1603*, Hanover NH, 1976.
Spenser, John, *A Learned and Gracious Sermon: God's Love to his Vineyard*, London, 1615, STC 23096.
Spitz, L. W. and Sher Tinsley, B., *Johann Sturm on Education*, St Louis, 1995.

Stockwood, John, *A Plaine and Easie Laying Open of the Meaning and Understanding of the Rules of Construction*, London, 1590, STC 23280.

Strype, John (ed.), *Annals of the Reformation*, 4 vols., London, 1725–7.

Sturm, Johann, *De litterarum ludis recte aperiendis*, Strasburg, 1539.

Le style et manière de composer . . . toute sorte d'epistres, Lyons, 1566.

Susenbrotus, *Epitome troporum ac schematum*, Zurich, undated, facsimile in J. X. Brennan 'The *Epitome troporum ac Schematum* of Joannes Susenbrotus: Text, Translation and Commentary', unpublished PhD thesis, University of Illinois, 1953.

Szegedinus, Stephanus, *Tabulae Analytical*, London: Richard Field, 1593, STC 15015.3.

Terence, *Comoediae*, London: Thomas Marsh, 1583, STC 23886.

Trevelyan, W. C. (ed.), *Trevelyan Papers, Part III*, London, 1872, Camden Society, first series vol. CV.

Valerius, Cornelius, *In universam bene dicendi rationem tabula*, London, 1580, STC 24584.

Virgil, *Opera*, with commentary of Melanchthon, Lyons, 1533.

Opera, London, 1572, STC 24788.

Opera, London: H. Middleton, 1580, STC 24789.

Opera, London: Felix Kingston, 1597, STC 224791.

Webster, John, *The Duchess of Malfi*, ed. J. Russell Brown, Manchester, 1976.

Whitgift, John, *The Works of John Whitgift*, ed. J. Ayre, 3 vols., Cambridge, 1851–3, Parker Society, vols. XLIV, XLVIII, L.

Wilson, Thomas, *The Art of Rhetoric*, ed. Peter E. Medine, University Park PA, 1994.

The Rule of Reason, ed. R. S. Sprague, Northridge, 1972.

Wright, L. B. (ed.), *Advice to a Son*, Ithaca, 1962.

Wright, Thomas (ed.), *Queen Elizabeth and her Times: A Series of Original Letters*, 2 vols., London, 1838.

SECONDARY SOURCES

Alford, Stephen, *The Early Elizabethan Polity*, Cambridge, 1998.

Altman, Joel, *The Tudor Play of Mind*, Berkeley, 1978.

Bald, R. C., *John Donne: A Life*, Oxford, 1970.

Baldwin, T. W., *Shakspere's Five-Act Structure*, Urbana, 1947.

Shakspere's Small Latine and Lesse Greeke, 2 vols., Urbana, 1944.

Barthes, Roland, 'L'ancienne rhétorique: aide-mémoire', *Communications* 16 (1970), 172–229.

The Semiotic Challenge, Oxford, 1988.

Bates, Catherine, *The Rhetoric of Courtship in Elizabethan Language and Literature*, Cambridge, 1992.

Bernstein, B., *Class, Codes and Control*, 3 vols., London, 1971–5.

Binns, J. W., *Intellectual Culture in Elizabethan and Jacobean England*, Leeds, 1990.

Blench, J. W., *Preaching in England in the late Fifteenth and Sixteenth Centuries*, Oxford, 1964.

Bourdieu, P. and Passeron, J. C., *La réproduction: éléments pour une théorie du système d'enseignement*, Paris, 1970.

Braddick, M. J., *Parliamentary Taxation in Seventeenth-Century England*, Woodbridge, 1994.

Burke, Kenneth, *A Rhetoric of Motives*, Berkeley, 1969.

Bushnell, Rebecca, *A Culture of Teaching*, Ithaca, 1996.

Calboli Montefusco, Lucia, *La dottrina degli status nella retorica greca e romana*, Hildesheim, 1986.

Cargill Thompson, W. D. J., *Studies in the Reformation*, London, 1980.

Cave, Terence, *The Cornucopian Text*, Oxford, 1979.

Chomarat, J., *Grammaire et Rhétorique chez Erasme*, 2 vols., Paris, 1981.

Clark, D. L., 'The Rise and Fall of *Progymnasmata* in Sixteenth Century Grammar Schools', *Speech Monographs* 19 (1952), 259–63.

Cobban, A. B., *The Medieval English Universities: Oxford and Cambridge to c. 1500*, Aldershot, 1988.

Colclough, David, '*Parrhesia*: The Rhetoric of Free Speech in Early Modern England', *Rhetorica* 17 (1999), 177–212.

Collinson, Patrick, *Elizabethan Essays*, London, 1994.

The Elizabethan Puritan Movement, London, 1967.

Conley, Thomas M., *Rhetoric in the European Tradition*, New York, 1990.

Copeland, Rita, *Rhetoric, Hermeneutics and Translation in the Middle Ages*, Cambridge, 1991.

Costello, W. T., *The Scholastic Curriculum in Early 17th Century Cambridge*, Cambridge, 1958.

Crane, Mary T., *Framing Authority: Sayings, Self and Society in Sixteenth-century England*, Princeton, 1993.

'Video et Taceo: Elizabeth I and the Rhetoric of Counsel', *Studies in English Literature 1500–1900* 28 (1988), 1–15.

Crane, W. G., *Wit and Rhetoric in the Renaissance*, New York, 1937, repr. Gloucester MA, 1964.

Cressy, David, *Birth, Marriage and Death*, Oxford, 1997.

Cuming, G. J., *A History of Anglican Liturgy*, 2nd edn, London, 1982.

Dean, David, *Law-making and Society in Late Elizabethan England*, Cambridge, 1996.

Dean, David and Jones, Norman (eds.), *The Parliaments of Elizabethan England*, Oxford, 1990.

Dietz, F. C., *English Public Finance 1485–1641*, 2 vols., Urbana, 1921.

Doran, Susan, *Monarchy and Matrimony: The Courtships of Elizabeth I*, London, 1996.

Ebbesen, Sten, *Commentators and Commentaries on Aristotle's Sophistici Elenchi*, 3 vols., Leiden, 1981.

Eliot, T. S., *For Lancelot Andrewes*, London, 1928.

Elton, G. R., *The Parliament of England, 1559–1581*, Cambridge, 1986.

Fahnestock, Jeanne, *Rhetorical Figures in Science*, New York, 1999.
Feingold, M., 'The Humanities' and 'The Mathematical sciences and New Philosophies', in N. Tyacke (ed.), *The History of the University of Oxford*, vol. IV, *Seventeenth-Century Oxford*, Oxford, 1997, pp. 211–448.
The Mathematicians' Apprenticeship: Science, Universities and Society in England 1560–1640, Cambridge, 1984.
Ferrell, L. A. and McCullough, P. (eds.), *The English Sermon Revised*, Manchester, 2000.
Fletcher, J. M., 'The Faculty of Arts', in J. K. McConica (ed.), *The History of the University of Oxford*, vol. III, *The Collegiate University*, Oxford, 1986, pp. 157–200.
Fumaroli, Marc, *L'âge de l'éloquence*, Geneva, 1980.
Gálvez, J. M., *Guevara in England*, Berlin, 1916.
Goldberg, Jonathan, *Writing Matter*, Stanford, 1996.
Goyet, Francis, *Le sublime du 'lieu commun'*, Paris, 1996.
Grafton, Anthony and Jardine, Lisa, *From Humanism to the Humanities*, London, 1986.
'Studied for Action: How Gabriel Harvey read his Livy', *Past and Present* 129 (1990), 30–78.
Graves, M. A. R., 'The Management of the Elizabethan House of Commons: The Council's Men of Business', *Parliamentary History* 2 (1983), 11–38.
Thomas Norton: The Parliament Man, Oxford, 1994.
Greaves, Richard L., *Society and Religion in Elizabethan England*, Minneapolis, 1981.
Green, Lawrence D., *'Grammatica movet'*, in P. L. Oesterreich and T. O. Sloane (eds.), *Rhetorica Movet: Essays in Honour of Heinrich Plett*, Leiden, 1999, pp. 73–115.
'Modes of Perception in the *Mirror for Magistrates*', *Huntington Library Quarterly* 44 (1980–1), 117–33.
Green-Pedersen, N. J., *The Tradition of the Topics in the Middle Ages*, Munich, 1984.
Grendler, Paul, *Schooling in Renaissance Italy*, Baltimore, 1989.
Guy, John, 'The Rhetoric of Counsel in Early Modern England', in Dale Hoak (ed.), *Tudor Political Culture*, Cambridge, 1995, pp. 292–310.
Tudor England, Oxford, 1988.
Hadfield, Andrew, *Literature, Politics and National Identity*, Cambridge, 1994.
Halpern, R., *The Poetics of Primitive Accumulation: English Renaissance Culture and the Genealogy of Capital*, Ithaca, 1991.
Hammer, Paul, *The Polarisation of Elizabethan Politics*, Cambridge, 1999.
Harris Sacks, David, 'The Countervailing of Benefits', in Dale Hoak (ed.), *Tudor Political Culture*, Cambridge, 1995, pp. 272–91.
'The Paradox of Taxation: Fiscal Crises, Parliament and Liberty in England, 1450–1640', in P. T. Hoffman and K. Norberg (eds.), *Fiscal Crises, Representative Institutions and Liberty in Early Modern Europe*, Stanford, 1994, pp. 7–66.
Hartley, T. E., *Elizabeth's Parliaments: Queen, Lords and Commons 1559–1601*, Manchester, 1992.

Heisch, Alison, 'Queen Elizabeth I: Parliamentary Rhetoric and the Exercise of Power', *Signs* I (1975), 31–55.

Helgerson, R., *The Elizabethan Prodigals*, Berkeley, 1976.

Forms of Nationhood, Chicago, 1992.

Hogrefe, P., *The Life and Times of Sir Thomas Elyot, Englishman*, Iowa City, 1967.

Hornbeak, K. G., 'The Complete Letter-Writer in English', *Smith College Studies in Modern Languages* 15 (1934), 1–150.

Houlbrooke, R., *Death, Religion and the Family in England 1480–1750*, Oxford, 1998.

Houlbrooke, R. (ed.), *Death, Ritual and Bereavement*, London, 1989.

Howell, W. S., *Logic and Rhetoric in England 1500–1700*, Princeton, 1956.

Hunt, R. W., *The History of Grammar in the Middle Ages*, Amsterdam, 1980.

Hunter, G. K., 'Isocrates's Precepts and Polonius's Character', *Shakespeare Quarterly* 8 (1957), 501–6.

John Lyly: The Humanist as Courtier, London, 1962.

Hutson, Lorna, *The Usurer's Daughter*, London, 1994.

Hutter, H., *Politics as Friendship*, Waterloo, 1978.

James, Mervyn, *Society, Politics and Culture: Studies in Early Modern England*, Cambridge, 1986.

Jardine, Lisa, 'The Place of Dialectic Teaching in Sixteenth-Century Cambridge', *Studies in the Renaissance* 21 (1974), 31–62.

Jones, R. F., *The Triumph of the English Language*, Stanford, 1953.

Kahn, Victoria, *Machiavellian Rhetoric*, Princeton, 1994.

Rhetoric, Prudence and Skepticism in the Renaissance, Ithaca, 1985.

Kallendorf, Craig, *In Praise of Aeneas*, Hanover NH, 1989.

Kearney, Hugh, *Scholars and Gentlemen*, London, 1970.

Kelley, D. R. and Harris Sacks, D. (eds.), *The Historical Imagination in Early Modern Britain*, Cambridge, 1997.

Kelso, Ruth, *Doctrine of the English Gentleman in the Sixteenth Century*, Urbana, 1929.

Kennedy, George, *The Art of Persuasion in Greece*, Princeton, 1963.

The Art of Rhetoric in the Roman World, Princeton, 1972.

King, John N., *English Reformation Literature*, Princeton, 1982.

Kinney, Arthur, *Humanist Poetics*, Amherst, 1986.

Kintgen, E. R., *Reading in Tudor England*, Pittsburgh, 1996.

Knafla, Louis A., *Law and Politics in Jacobean England: The Tracts of Lord Chancellor Ellesmere*, Cambridge, 1977.

'The Law Studies of an Elizabethan Student', *Huntington Library Quarterly* 32 (1969), 221–40.

Kneale, W. and Kneale, M., *The Development of Logic*, Oxford, 1962.

Kretzmann, N., et al. (eds.), *The Cambridge History of Later Medieval Philosophy*, Cambridge, 1982.

Kusukawa, Sachiko, *The Transformation of Natural Philosophy*, Cambridge, 1995.

Lane Ford, Margaret, 'Importation of Printed Books into England and Scotland', in L. Hellinga and J. B. Trapp (eds.), *The Cambridge History of the Book in Britain*, vol. III, *1400–1557*, Cambridge, 1999, pp. 179–201.

Lanham, Richard A., *A Handlist of Rhetorical Terms*, 2nd edn, Berkeley, 1991.

Lake, Peter, *Anglicans and Puritans? Presbyterianism and English Conformist Thought from Whitgift to Hooker*, London, 1988.

Lausberg, Heinrich, *Handbuch der literarischen Rhetorik*, 3rd edn, Stuttgart, 1990.

Leader, D., *A History of the University of Cambridge*, vol. I, *The University to 1546*, Cambridge, 1988.

Lehmberg, S. E., *Sir Thomas Elyot: Tudor Humanist*, Austin, 1960.

Sir Walter Mildmay and Tudor Government, Austin, 1964.

Levy, F. J., *Tudor Historical Thought*, San Marino, 1967.

Lewis, C. S., *English Literature in the Sixteenth Century*, Oxford, 1954.

Logan, G. M. and Teskey, G. (eds.), *Unfolded Tales*, Ithaca, 1989.

MacCaffrey, Wallace, *War and Politics 1588–1603*, Princeton, 1991.

Mack, Peter, 'Ramus Reading: The Commentaries on Cicero's *Consular Orations* and Vergil's Eclogues and Georgics', *Journal of the Warburg and Courtauld Institutes* 61 (1998), 111–41.

Renaissance Argument: Valla and Agricola in the Traditions of Rhetoric and Dialectic, Leiden, 1993.

'Renaissance Habits of Reading', in S. Chaudhuri (ed.), *Renaissance Essays for Kitty Scoular Datta*, Calcutta, 1995, pp. 1–25.

'Rhetoric and Liturgy', in D. Jasper and R. C. D. Jasper (eds.), *Language and the Worship of the Church*, Basingstoke, 1990, pp. 82–109.

'Rhetoric and the Essay', *Rhetoric Society Quarterly* 23:2 (1993), 41–9.

'Rhetoric in Use: Three Romances by Greene and Lodge', in P. Mack (ed.), *Renaissance Rhetoric*, Basingstoke, 1994, pp. 119–39.

'Rudolph Agricola's Reading of Literature', *Journal of the Warburg and Courtauld Institutes* 48 (1985), 23–41.

Magnusson, Lynne, *Shakespeare and Social Dialogue: Dramatic Language and Elizabethan Letters*, Cambridge, 1999.

Major, John M., *Sir Thomas Elyot and Renaissance Humanism*, Lincoln NE, 1964.

Mason, John E., *Gentlefolk in the Making*, Philadelphia, 1935.

May, Steven W., 'Recent Studies in Elizabeth I', *English Literary Renaissance* 23 (1993), 345–54.

McConica, J. K., *English Humanists and Reformation Politics*, Oxford, 1965.

McConica, J. K. (ed.), *The History of the University of Oxford*, vol. III, *The Collegiate University*, Oxford, 1986.

McCullough, P., *Sermons at Court: Politics and Religion in Elizabethan and Jacobean Preaching*, Cambridge, 1998.

McCutcheon, Elizabeth, *Sir Nicholas Bacon's Great House Sententiae*, Amherst, 1977.

McLelland, J. C., *The Visible Words of God: An Exposition of the Sacramental Theology of Peter Martyr Vermigli*, Edinburgh, 1957.

Medine, Peter E., *Thomas Wilson*, Boston, 1986.

Meerhoff, Kees, 'Logique et éloquence: une révolution Ramusienne?', in K. Meerhoff and J. C. Moisan (eds.), *Autour de Ramus*, Montreal, 1997, pp. 87–132.

Rhétorique et poétique au XVIe siècle en France, Leiden, 1986.

Michael, Ian, *The Teaching of English: From the Sixteenth Century to 1870*, Cambridge, 1987.

Mills, J. L., 'Recent Studies in *A Mirror for Magistrates*', *English Literary Renaisance* 9 (1979), 343–54.

Monfasani, John, 'Humanism and Rhetoric', in A. Rabil jr (ed.), *Renaissance Humanism: Foundations, Forms and Legacy*, 3 vols., Philadelphia, 1988, vol. III, pp. 171–235.

Morgan, J., *Godly Learning: Puritan Attitudes towards Reason, Learning and Education, 1560–1640*, Cambridge, 1986.

Moss, Ann, *Ovid in Renaissance France*, Warburg Institute Surveys VII, London, 1982.

Printed Commonplace Books and the Structuring of Renaissance Thought, Oxford, 1996.

Mullinger, J. G., *The History of the University of Cambridge*, 2 vols., Cambridge, 1873–4.

Neale, Sir John, *The Elizabethan House of Commons*, London, 1949.

Queen Elizabeth I and her Parliaments, 2 vols., London, 1953–7.

Nelson, W., *Fact or Fiction: The Dilemma of the Renaissance Storyteller*, Cambridge MA, 1973.

O'Day, Rosemary, *Education and Society 1500–1800*, London, 1982.

Ong, W. J., 'Commonplace Rhapsody: Ravisius Textor, Zwinger and Shakespeare', in R. R. Bolgar (ed.), *Classical Influences on European Culture AD 1500–1700*, Cambridge, 1976, pp. 91–126.

Ramus and Talon Inventory, Cambridge MA, 1958.

Parker, Geoffrey, *The Dutch Revolt*, Harmondsworth, 1985.

Europe in Crisis 1598–1648, London, 1979.

Parker, Patricia, *Literary Fat Ladies: Rhetoric, Gender, Property*, London, 1987.

Patterson, A., *Reading Holinshed's Chronicles*, Chicago, 1994.

Pellegrini, Angelo M., 'Renaissance and Medieval Antecedents of Debate', *Quarterly Journal of Speech* 28 (1942), 14–19.

Perelman, Chaim and Olbrechts-Tyteca, Lucie, *The New Rhetoric*, Notre Dame, 1969.

Perrott, M. E. C., 'Richard Hooker and the Problem of Authority in the Elizabethan Church', *Journal of Ecclesiastical History* 49 (1998), 29–60.

Pigman, G. W., III, *Grief and English Renaissance Elegy*, Cambridge, 1985.

Plett, Heinrich, *Rhetorik der Affekte*, Tübingen, 1975.

Raab, F., *The English Face of Machiavelli*, London, 1964.

Read, Conyers, *Mr Secretary Cecil and Queen Elizabeth*, London, 1955.

Lord Burghley and Queen Elizabeth, London, 1960.

Rebhorn, W., *The Emperor of Men's Minds*, Ithaca, 1995.

Rhodes, Neil, *The Power of Eloquence in English Renaissance Literature*, London, 1992.

Rix, H. D., 'The Editions of Erasmus's *De copia*', *Studies in Philology* 43 (1946), 595–618.

Roberts, Peter, 'Elizabethan Players and Minstrels and the Legislation of 1572 against Retainers and Vagabonds', in A. Fletcher and P. Roberts (eds.),

Religion, Culture and Society in Early Modern Britain: Essays in Honour of Patrick Collinson, Cambridge, 1994, pp. 29–55.

Robertson, Jean, *The Art of Letter Writing*, London, 1942.

Salzman, P., *English Prose Fiction 1558–1700*, Oxford, 1985.

Scott Pearson, A. F., *Thomas Cartwright and Elizabethan Puritanism 1535–1603*, Cambridge, 1925, repr. Gloucester MA, 1966.

Shuger, Debora, *Habits of Thought in the English Renaissance*, Berkeley, 1990.

Sacred Rhetoric, Princeton, 1988.

Slack, Paul, *Poverty and Policy in Tudor and Stuart England*, London, 1988.

Sommerville, J. P., *Politics and Ideology in England 1603–1640*, London, 1986.

Skinner, Q., *The Foundations of Modern Political Thought*, 2 vols., Cambridge, 1978.

Reason and Rhetoric in the Philosophy of Hobbes, Cambridge, 1996.

Spedding, J., *The Letters and the Life of Francis Bacon*, vol. I, London, 1861.

Speed Hill, W. (ed.), *Studies in Richard Hooker*, Cleveland, 1972.

Stone, L (ed.), *The University in Society*, Princeton, 1974.

Struever, Nancy S., *The Language of History in the Renaissance*, Princeton, 1970.

Tittler, R., *Nicholas Bacon: The Making of a Tudor Statesman*, London, 1976.

Vasoli, C., *La dialettica e la retorica dell' umanesimo*, Milan, 1968.

Verhoeven, L. (ed.), *Functional Literacy: Theoretical Issues and Educational Implications*, Amsterdam, 1994.

Vickers, B., *Classical Rhetoric in English Poetry*, London, 1968.

In Defence of Rhetoric, Oxford, 1988.

Wagner, R. H., 'Thomas Wilson's *Arte of Rhetorique*', *Speech Monographs* 27 (1960), 1–32.

'Wilson and his Sources', *Quarterly Journal of Speech* 15 (1929), 525–36.

Whigham, Frank, *Ambition and Privilege: The Social Tropes of Elizabethan Courtesy Theory*, Berkeley, 1984.

'The Rhetoric of Elizabethan Suitors' Letters', *PMLA* 96 (1981), 864–82.

Williams, Penry, 'State, Church and University 1558–1603', in J. K. McConica (ed.), *The History of the University of Oxford*, vol. III, *The Collegiate University*, Oxford, 1986, pp. 397–440.

The Later Tudors, Oxford, 1995.

Worden, Blair, *The Sound of Virtue: Philip Sidney's Arcadia and Elizabethan Politics*, New Haven, 1996.

Woudhuysen, Henry, *Sir Philip Sidney and the Circulation of Manuscripts 1558–1640*, Oxford, 1996.

Wright, Louis B., *Middle-Class Culture in Elizabethan England*, Chapel Hill, 1935.

Index of rhetorical and dialectical terms

Entries in bold type designate definitions or explanations of terms, or particularly instructive examples. For further information see the *Note on the systems of rhetoric and dialectic*, pp. 9–10 above.

General index

active and contemplative life, 29–30, 162–3, 181
Addyter, Henry, 108
Admiralty Court, 129–30
advantage, 52–3, 117, 160, 180–2, 188, 191–4, 198, 205, 208, 216, 299, 303
advice to a son, 145–6, 157
Aesop, 13, 23, 35–6, 145
affability, 170, 178–9
Agricola, Rudolph, 7, 27, 44, 50–1, 53, 55–7, 67–74, 78, 83, 194–6, 211–12, 299
Alençon, Duke of, later Duke of Anjou, 196–201
Alford, Francis, 225–6, 240, 245
Allen, William, Cardinal, 236–8, 251
alms-giving, 282–6
Amyot, Jacques, 135, 139
Andrewes, Lancelot, 106–8, 256, 265–6, 272–3, 277–9, 285–6
Aphthonius, *Progymnasmata*, 13–14, 24, 27–8, 34–43, 54, 57, 65, 77, 100, 145, 147, 300
Aquinas, St Thomas, 282, 284
argumentation as decorative, 162, 216, 218–19, 221, 231–2
Aristotle, 271
  Ethics, 51, 165
  Organon, 10, 50, 55–7, 68–9, 83, 267–8, 273
  Rhetoric, 51–3, 66, 71, 267
Ascham, Roger, 11–12, 24, 79, 94, 294
audience, 19, 41–2, 47, 65, 80–2, 114–16, 151, 218, 220, 231, 234, 242, 246–7, 297, 301
Augustine, St, 87, 97, 104, 269
Augustus, 139, 152, 283
Austria, 183–7

Bacon, Lady Anne, 115
Bacon, Anthony, 206
Bacon, Sir Francis, 104, 172
  Advancement of Learning, 293–4
  speeches, 226–9, 234–5, 300

Bacon, Nathaniel, 117–18
  letters, 115, 118–19, 126–8
  memoranda, 110–11, 299
Bacon, Sir Nicholas, 119, 176, 216
  letters, 117–18, 126–8, 204
  speeches, 203–4, 212, 217–24, 229–37, 247, 251, 300–2
Badger, William, 29
Baldwin, William, 137, 141
  Treatise of Morall Philosophie, 137, 145, 165–7, 169–70, 173–4, 298
  see also *Mirror for Magistrates*
Barclay, Alexander, 139
Barlowe, Arthur, 130–1
Batt, Robert, 61–2
Berners, see Bourchier, John
Bible interpretation, 60–1, 87–8, 91, 247–8, 254, 261–7, 288–90, 302
bilingual context, 79–80, 101–2
Blundeville, Thomas, 78, 139
Boccaccio, Giovanni, 165
Boethius, 57, 78, 83
Bourchier, John (Lord Berners), 137, 152–3, 155, 276
Breton, Nicholas, 76, 110, 114–15, 138
Bridges, John, 288
Brinsley, John, 11–13, 18–19, 23–4, 26, 37–8, 45, 100, 145, 263, 266
Browne, John, 76
Buchanan, George, 13
Bynneman, Henry, 16, 21

Caesar, Julius, 13–14, 16, 18, 37–8, 51
Caesarius, John, 51, 55–6
Calthorpe, James, 110–11
Calthorpe, John, 110–11
Calvin, Jean, 276, 284
Cambridge University, 5, 48–9, 51–2, 55–6, 58–9, 66–75, 217, 295
Carew, Roger, 127–8

321

IDEAS IN CONTEXT

Edited by QUENTIN SKINNER (*General Editor*),
LORRAINE DASTON, DOROTHY ROSS and JAMES TULLY

Recent titles in the series include:

Titles marked with an asterisk are also available in paperback